THE HOLY WAY

Sunday
and Weekday
Meditations on
the Masses for
Ordinary Time

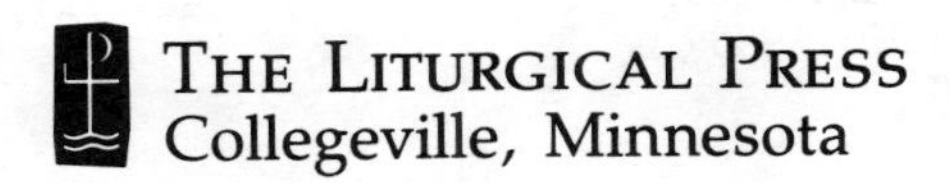

Cover design by Don Bruno and Janice St. Marie.

Printed in the United States of America.

1 2 3 4 5 6 7 8 9

Library of Congress Cataloging-in-Publication Data

Lawrence, Emeric Anthony, 1908–
The holy way : meditations on the Sunday and weekday masses for Ordinary Time / Emeric Lawrence.
p. cm.
ISBN 0-8146-1821-9
1. Church year meditations. I. Title.
BX2170.C55L29 1990
242′.3—dc20

90-36707
CIP

PREFACE

A highway will be there,
called the holy way (Isa 35:8).

The Holy Way, the title of this book, is adapted from the above phrase from the Prophet Isaiah. *The Jerome Biblical Commentary* (p. 280) says that the way is holy because it leads to Zion, the holy city, after one of the many periods of exile God's chosen people had to endure in the course of its history.

In the summer of 1989, I heard the Isaian phrase again in a public reading. Then it struck me that it would be hard to find a better description of the Church year, or any one of its seasons, especially its longest season, Ordinary Time. It is the Holy Way because it leads to God; it is the way to our everlasting home. It is holy, too, because of the divine nourishment that the Lord provides for us, namely, the Eucharist, with its inspired Word and, above all, with the Bread of Life, the Body and Blood of Christ, "Viaticum," "Food for the Way." It is the holy way because it invites us to live Jesus' life with him, as he makes that life present to us week after week, year after year.

I would be gratified if this book provides readers with insights that will enrich their yearly journey along the Holy Way.

Emeric A. Lawrence, O.S.B.

The Church Year is made up of the seasons of Advent and Christmas, Lent, Easter, and Ordinary Time. The Liturgical Press has already published my three books of meditations on the Sunday and weekday Masses of each of these seasons: *Jesus, Present and Coming* (Advent and Christmas); *Believe the Good News* (Lent and Holy Week); *Risen and with You Always* (Easter season).

This book, *The Holy Way: Reflections on the Sunday and Daily Masses in Ordinary Time,* (also the main feast days) completes the project. The book is the result of twenty years of study and reflection on the Sunday and weekday Masses with a view to preparing homilies for several parish communities, for an air base, and above all, for the community of Sisters at St. Scholastica's Priory in Duluth, Minnesota, where I spent about twelve and a half years as chaplain.

My purposes were to speak to the particular needs and hopes of each congregation, to see those needs in light of the readings and prayers, and to present the message of Jesus as the answer to those needs. I hoped always to make Christ loved more and more by my hearers and to inspire them to make their own responses to him and his holy message. I confess that my intentions were not always carried out successfully.

It is my hope, then, that this book might provide practical help not only to pastors and chaplains but also to Sisters and the laity. Because the Mass texts and prayers are inexhaustible in meaning, readers' reflections will probably differ from my own. No author would claim that his or her book is the final word. That word, I believe, belongs to and comes from those who hear the homilist and/or the reader. If the hearers are stimulated to utter that word either to themselves, to others, or—best of all—to the Lord, these reflections will be worthwhile.

I want to express deep gratitude to all my congregations, but especially to the Sisters of St. Scholastica's Priory for their kind encouragement of and appreciation for my efforts over the years. I hope that by God's grace I have enriched their lives. I know they have enriched mine.

ACKNOWLEDGEMENTS

Very special thanks to Sr. Timothy Kirby, St. Scholastica's Priory, Duluth, Minnesota, for having read and edited the text of this book. I am indebted to the following publications, which have provided considerable help and inspiration over the years: *Sunday Missal Service,* ed. Fr. William M. Carr, (Quincy, Ill.); *Homiletic Service,* Ottawa: Novalis; *Sunday Sermons,* Pleasantville, N.J.: Voicings Publications; and Fr. Robert Beck's Sunday commentaries in *The Dubuque Witness.*

Thanks also to our Sunday homily discussion group in Duluth: Frs. Bernard Brennan, James Crossman, John Doyle, John Golobich, Richard Partika, and Angelo Zankl, O.S.B.

Emeric A. Lawrence, O.S.B.
St. John's Abbey
Collegeville

ORDINARY TIME

Ordinary time is like life—everyday life. In life there are high points and low points, peak days and ordinary days. During the year, we look forward with hope and special anticipation to the big feasts, and we remember them with gratitude and even some nostalgia. But most of the year, like most of our life, is very "ordinary."

Nevertheless, the Sundays and weekdays in Ordinary Time are not all that "ordinary." Before any feasts were celebrated—in the early days of Christian history—every Sunday was a celebration of the Lord's resurrection. And that is still the case, for no single day is wide enough and large enough to contain a celebration of that great event.

What *is* common to every day's Eucharist is the word of God, which the Church offers as spiritual nourishment for her children. Jesus is with us and he speaks to us every day, and that's pretty special.

> A lamp to my feet is your word,
> a light to my path (Ps 119:105).

I like what Fr. Donald Burt says about this season of the year:

> [God] loves ordinary days as much as he loves ordinary people. He *loves* those days because he knows that it is on such days that we, the ordinary folks that he loves, carry him to our world. It is on these days that we have most of our opportunities for acting like decent people, people of faith, people who truly believe that God is in this world and indeed is *in us* as we make our way through the days of our lives. . . . Jesus is with us all the time, but he is with us especially on our ordinary days (*Emmanuel,* Collegeville: The Liturgical Press, 1988, 100–101).

Those words make me especially grateful for the inspiration for the title of this book, which came to me one day in Advent while listening to Chapter 35:8 of the prophecy of Isaiah: *The Holy Way: Reflections on the Sunday and Daily Masses in Ordinary Time.*

Ordinary Time does not run consecutively. It begins on the Monday after the Feast of the Epiphany (or the Baptism of the Lord) and continues until Ash Wednesday, the date of which varies from year to year, and resumes after the Easter season. The missalettes in use in most parishes keep the reader informed about the varying dates and weeks of the year or season.

If Lent and Easter are late, the number of pre-Lenten Sundays and weeks in Ordinary Time mounts to eight or nine. If these seasons are early, the number is reduced.

On weekdays in Ordinary Time, Reading I differs in the first and second year of a two-year cycle. Each day's gospel, however, remains the same for both years.

EPIPHANY

Where Epiphany is not a holy day of obligation, it is transferred to the Sunday after the octave of Christmas (between January 2 and 8). The Feast of the Baptism of the Lord is observed on the Sunday after January 6. When it coincides with the solemnity of the Epiphany, transferred to this Sunday, the Feast of the Baptism of the Lord is transferred to the Monday immediately following.

READING I **Isa 60:1-6** **READING II** **Eph 3:2-3, 5-6**
GOSPEL **Matt 2:1-12**

Reading I: Isaiah foresees the glorious return of the exiles to Jersualem, but his vision really foresees the coming together of Jesus and the Gentiles, who are represented by the three astrologers.

Reading II: Paul tells us that God has sent him to proclaim the good news of salvation to the Gentiles, whom God has chosen to be coheirs of the kingdom with the Jews.

Gospel: The astrologers arrive in Bethlehem, prostrate themselves before Jesus, and offer him gifts.

Christmas and Epiphany belong together and complement one another. It may be an oversimplification to say that Christmas is a feast for children and Epiphany a feast for adults. Children and adults alike need both, but Epiphany surely manifests the real meaning of incarnation more graphically. The very word "epiphany" means "manifestation." Our celebration today gives us a special insight into the identity of Jesus and God's purpose in sending him. It tells us how God feels about *all peoples* everywhere and what God expects of us all.

The gospel tells of the coming of astrologers from the East to Jerusalem. They ask, "Where is the newborn king of the Jews? We observed his star at its rising and have come to pay him homage." It is obvious that they are not looking for an earthly king, as Herod feared. They go to Bethlehem, find the child and his mother, offer gifts, then go home. But having seen Jesus, their lives will never again be the same.

What does it all mean? Why did they ever start on their long journey? It was the Lord who was responsible. It was God, creator of the human heart, who planted in their hearts the immense desire for the divine that no human acquisition can satisfy. They hungered for God because God first hungered for them. As Maria Boulding says, "God's longing for us is the spring of our longing for God" (*The Coming of God,* Collegeville: The Liturgical Press, 1986, 1).

In the case of the astrologers, God had not only given them the longing desire, he guided them to its fulfillment in that little child in Bethlehem. What was special about the astrologers is that they cooperated with divine grace, they read the signs, they followed the star. "They are symbols of hope, representing the unexpected, the gratuitous character, the wonder of God's glory breaking through the darkness of the nations" (Monika Hellwig, *America,* December 29, 1984).

Our life is like that of the astrologers: it is also a journey, a quest. We experience innumerable encounters with God in his Word in these yearly feasts, in the sacraments, and above all, in the Eucharist. We experience God in our Lady and in the saints as we celebrate their feasts year after year. But still we hunger for God. The greatest saints experienced God constantly, and their desire for God increased as they grew to old age. They possess God now in heaven, but they continue to desire God. That's the way we are; that's the way God is. Our desire for God is gratified in feasts like Epiphany, but it still remains.

Ours is a hunger for ever-deeper wisdom and understanding of our faith: of the meaning of the incarnation and of the Lord God who so dramatically and daringly reveals himself in yearly feasts like Christmas, Epiphany, and Easter.

What God reveals most of all is God's love for us and for all peoples everywhere—that deep, personal, divine love. But without a response from us, God's love is wasted. I once wrote: "Jesus is a child, he loves to receive gifts. He is God, he loves to receive love."

So we celebrate Epiphany today. Then we will go on in life. We will continue on to other celebrations, above all that of the death and resurrection of this child. We will celebrate the coming of the Holy Spirit upon us. And so it will go, year after year. But our final Epiphany will inevitably come. Then our prayer in this Mass will be answered:

> Your light is strong,
> your love is near;
> draw us beyond the limits which this world imposes,
> to the life where your Spirit makes all life complete.
> We ask this through Christ our Lord. Amen (Alternative Opening Prayer).

21 BAPTISM OF THE LORD

The readings for the Sundays in Ordinary Time begin on the Sunday following the Feast of the Baptism of the Lord. The prayers, antiphons, and readings of this feast are the same for all three cycles. Only the gospels are different, but each describes the essential features of the baptism of Jesus by John in the Jordan.

READING I Isa 42:1-4, 6-7 **READING II** Acts 10:34-38
GOSPEL Matt 3:13-17
Mark 1:7-11
Luke 3:15-16, 21-22

Reading I: This first of Isaiah's "Servant Songs" foretells the relationship between God and the Messiah and the kind of work the Messiah will do.

Reading II: Peter presents a short review of the public life of Jesus, beginning with his baptism by John.

Gospel: The synoptics each tell of the baptism of Jesus by John.

The first thought that might occur to us is that today's feast is rather sudden. We've been concentrating on Jesus' birth in Bethlehem and then on his manifestation to the Magi; today we see him as a grown man presenting himself to John for baptism. But then we realize that the entire Christmas season is a progressive revelation of God's plan of salvation for *all* peoples. Today's event dramatically describes the beginning of Jesus' messianic life of service to all peoples.

> Here is my servant whom I uphold,
> my chosen one with whom I am pleased,
> Upon whom I have put my spirit;
> he shall bring forth justice to the nations (Reading I).

Jesus came to John to be baptized in obedience to his Father's will. His baptism is a preview of Gethesmani and Calvary.

Jesus identifies himself with sinners when he presents himself to John for baptism. He is not just acting as *if* he were a sinner; everything about Jesus is authentic. He anticipates the words of St. Paul: "For our sake God made him who did not know sin, to be sin" (2 Cor 5:21).

Not only did Jesus take upon himself the sinfulness of all humankind but he also took upon himself the suffering and dying of all. When Jesus died on the cross, he endured not only physical pain but the pain and agony of all people who have lived and will live in this world until the end of time. "When you love someone, you suffer with the suffering of the ones you love" (Michel Quoist, *Christ is Alive,* Garden City, N.Y.: Doubleday, 1971, 100).

We might add that when Jesus loves someone, no suffering is too difficult to endure.

It is all this that Christ's baptism previews. And then there is the voice of the Father telling all the world who this Jesus really is: "You are my beloved Son. On you my favor rests." If he never knew it before, Jesus now knows who he is, he knows his identity. The Preface of today's feast has a fascinating comment on this aspect of the baptism: "Your [the Father's] voice was heard from heaven to awaken faith in the presence among us of the Word made man." Why fascinating? Because when we advert to that divine presence in the midst of our hearts, we are praying one of the best prayers of which we are capable.

If Jesus receives his identity today, so, too, do we. At the Last Supper Jesus tells us: "Live on in me, as I do in you. . . . I am the vine, you are the branches" (John 15:4-5). We are one with Christ; we share the same divine life that is in him. And to each of us the Father says: You are my beloved child. On you my favor rests.

If we are other Christs, then our lives must be lives of service like his. We can and *must* try to take upon ourselves the pain and suffering of others, try to share the compassion of Jesus for those who are in pain of any kind. Now we know that our life in this world is redemptive, like the life of Jesus our brother. May we all make our own the Alternative Opening Prayer of today's Mass:

> Father in heaven,
> you revealed Christ as your Son
> in the voice that spoke over the waters of the Jordan.
> May all who share in the sonship of Christ
> follow in his path of service to man,
> and reflect the glory of his kingdom
> even to the ends of the earth.

305 MONDAY OF THE FIRST WEEK IN ORDINARY TIME

(When the Feast of the Baptism of the Lord occurs on Monday of the First Week in Ordinary Time, the readings assigned to Monday may be joined to those of Tuesday so that the opening of each book will be read.)

YEAR I

READING I Heb 1:1-6
GOSPEL Mark 1:14-20

We know Jesus mostly from the Gospels. We know him as a man with human emotions, feelings, desires, and a deep sense of his vocation as Messiah-Savior. The author of Hebrews tells us that this Jesus is also the eternal Son of God, the reflection of the Father's being, the "blueprint" of all creation, the greatest proof of the Father's love for us.

Today we are present at the opening of Jesus' public life, and we hear him proclaiming the good news of God: "This is the time of fulfillmment. The reign of God is at hand! Reform your lives and believe in the good news!" So there we are again. We may have thought that we would be finished with the call to repentance in Advent. Now we have it again, and we will get more in Lent. It could very well be that repentance and faith are what the gospel is all about.

YEAR II

READING I 1 Sam 1:1-8
GOSPEL Mark 1:14-20

Today we begin the season in Ordinary Time—the longest season of the year. It will be interrupted by the Lenten and Easter seasons and will resume in the summer. Our first reading for the next few weeks will be from the First Book of Samuel and will center on Samuel, the last of the Judges, one of the Old Testament's noblest figures. You may be surprised by the similarity between his life and that of John the Baptist.

Our gospel will be that of Mark, the shortest and oldest of the gospels, written about A.D. 70. It begins with Jesus' public life and his first startling statement: "The time is fulfilled, and the kingdom of God is at hand; repent, and believe in the gospel." There is no better way of summing up Jesus and his message to us and to our hearts than this. Repentance and faith are what the gospel of Jesus is all about.

306 TUESDAY OF THE FIRST WEEK IN ORDINARY TIME

YEAR I

READING I **Heb 2:5-12**
GOSPEL **Mark 1:21-28**

Today's reading from Hebrews tells of our dignity: we are made only a little lower than the angels, we are crowned with glory and splendor, we are placed over all creation. Jesus is first among humans, but even though he is number one, he reaches his glory through suffering and death, that "through God's gracious will he might taste death for the sake of all men."

The gospel shows us this Jesus in action against Satan. It is extraordinary that the finest tributes to Jesus came from this enemy: "I know who you are—the holy One of God!" It may seem strange that the people call Christ's driving out of Satan a teaching. But that is God's own way. All through sacred history God teaches mainly through his deeds. He still does.

O Lord, our Lord,
how glorious is your name over all the earth! (Responsorial Psalm)

YEAR II

READING I **1 Sam 1:9-20**
GOSPEL **Mark 1:21-28**

Note and admire the parallel betwen the mother of Samuel and the mother of John the Baptist. These two barren women prayed with faith and perseverance, and the Lord heard their prayers.

I cannot emphasize too much the importance of having the right conception of Christ, because we become what our conception of Christ is. The Christ of the Gospels—especially the Gospel of

Mark—is vastly different from the sentimental, sweet, dreamy, pretty Jesus-image so many Catholics love. The gospel shows us a Jesus with a strong personality who speaks sharply and with such authority that the people are amazed: "What does this mean? A completely new teaching in a spirit of authority! He gives orders to unclean spirits and they obey!" May we listen to these Gospels with such openness and faith that Jesus himself will form in us the true image of himself. For remember, we become what our conception of Christ is.

307 WEDNESDAY OF THE FIRST WEEK IN ORDINARY TIME

YEAR I

READING I **Heb 2:14-18**
GOSPEL **Mark 1:29-39**

"Everybody is looking for you," said the apostles to Jesus. It was a statement true of the situation then, but it applies to every person in every age. We all need Christ, we all seek him, for he is the fulfillment of every heart's desire. Today he shows himself to us as a "merciful and faithful high priest. . . . Since he was himself tested through what he suffered, he is able to help those who are tempted."

Above all, Jesus shows himself to us as a man who shares his caring by healing all who were variously afflicted. Best of all, he shows himself to us as a man of prayer who goes off to a lonely place where he can commune with his Father in quiet and so restore his spirit. If we are really looking for Christ, the best place to find him is in the lonely places in our own lives. Seek and you shall find.

YEAR II

READING I **1 Sam 3:1-10, 19-20**
GOSPEL **Mark 1:29-39**

Today's Reading I teaches us what vocation is. God calls and Samuel answers, "Speak, for your servant is listening." The psalmist echoes Samuel's wonderful response to the divine call: "Here am I. You called me." Jesus will use practically the same words in the Garden of Gethsemani.

We know that there is a great variety of vocations to which God can call us. There is the vocation of marriage, the religious life, the priesthood, the single life in the world. What is common and essential to all is that God calls us to do his work and to become holy by living our vocation to the best of our ability. Here am I, Lord, I come to do your will is not only the ideal attitude if we are not yet sure of our vocation; it also gives us the best possible way of living out our vocation. By the way, can you think of a better attitude with which to hear the gospel than Samuel's "Speak, for your servant is listening."

308 THURSDAY OF THE FIRST WEEK IN ORDINARY TIME

YEAR I

READING I **Heb 3:7-14**
GOSPEL **Mark 1:40-45**

"Today, if you should hear his voice, harden not your hearts" (Reading I). God through Christ has been trying to enter our consciousness and capture our hearts and allegiance, even as he tried with the chosen people. But, incredibly we harden our hearts, we resist not only the divine Word but the living example of Christ's love. Why we harden our hearts is part of the mystery of human freedom. We can use our freedom to love or to resist love. But without freedom love is impossible.

Jesus too is free. Today he freely chooses to heal the leper. Some texts tell us that Jesus was "angry" as he healed the man. Evil angers him, for it hurts those he loves. This accounts for his many cures. We can be sure that he continues to cure now through the sacraments, for evil is still repugnant to him. Would that the evil of sin were as repugnant to us!

YEAR II

READING I 1 Sam 4:1-11
GOSPEL Mark 1:40-45

Superstition means attributing magical or divine powers to things. Statues, medals, pictures, relics, are valuable if we use them as reminders of God and the saints. It is too easy to forget the purpose and to use holy things in the wrong way. That is what the Israelites did in today's reading. They used the holiest of Jewish possessions, the ark of the covenant, as a charm to guarantee victory in battle. They learned the hard way that the holiest of *things* is no substitute for obedience to God's will.

This is a good lesson for us. Our statues, medals, pictures, rosaries, *can* remind us of Jesus and our Lady and can bring us closer to God. But a St. Christopher medal is no guarantee against careless driving. As substitutes for true love and obedience to God's will, these things are as useless to us as the ark was to the Israelites. "Save us, Lord, in your mercy" (Responsorial Psalm).

309 FRIDAY OF THE FIRST WEEK IN ORDINARY TIME

YEAR I

READING I Heb 4:1-5, 11
GOSPEL Mark 2:1-12

The Jews rightly believed that only God could forgive sin. Jesus tells the paralytic that his sins are forgiven and proves, by healing him miraculously, that "the Son of Man has authority on earth to forgive sins." The conclusion is obvious: he must be God. If he can forgive sins, can he not share that power with his Church? Do we not all need forgiveness of our sins?

The author of Hebrews discusses eternal rest. But what kind of rest *is* eternal rest? Surely, it is not lying in bed or on the beach all day; it is not a never-ending vacation. I think it is rather the highest kind of activity; it is the joy and satisfaction of exciting exploration and discovery; it is forever filling our hungry hearts with him who is in himself limitless truth, life, and love. May our hearts always be restless until they rest in thee, O God, and keep on being restless forever and ever.

YEAR II

READING I **1 Sam 8:4-7, 10-22**
GOSPEL **Mark 2:1-12**

Today we come to one of the turning points in Israel's history: the people demand a king. Samuel resists, for he realizes that their demand is an admission of national lack of faith in Yahweh. They want to be like other nations, and Yahweh grants their request, but not without warning them of the price they will have to pay. The rest of Israel's history relates the sad results of their choice.

Why does God grant their request when he knows what will happen? A nation, like a person, has to have a chance to make mistakes if it is to grow in responsibility. Freedom is a risk that God wanted to take, for he knew that if we were not free to sin, we would not be free to love. And that freely given love was what God wanted above all else. However, if one should sin, the gospel indicates how anxious Jesus is to forgive.

For ever I will sing the goodness of the Lord (Responsorial Psalm).

310 SATURDAY OF THE FIRST WEEK IN ORDINARY TIME

YEAR I

READING I **Heb 4:12-16**
GOSPEL **Mark 2:13-17**

Today, Hebrews sees God's word as God himself. The word exposes, lays bare our hearts so that nothing is concealed from God or from our own conscience. We may at times disobey our conscience and sin, but Jesus understands. He can sympathize with our weakness, since he himself was tempted in every way that we are, even though he never sinned himself.

His weakness for sinners and his deep love for them becomes evident in the gospel. Jesus invites Levi to follow him not only as a disciple but so he can forgive his sins and eat with him. Christ's weakness for sinners continues now. For what is the Eucharist if not a love feast, with the host Jesus continually indulging his glorious weakness for dining with the likes of us who are sinners all? This is the good news of the Lord.

YEAR II

READING I **1 Sam 9:1-4, 17-19; 10:1**
GOSPEL **Mark 2:13-17**

The Israelites now have their king, Saul. He is God's own choice, but he is also his own man, that is, he is free. We will see how he exercises his freedom badly and loses God's favor.

The gospel places Jesus where he belongs—at dinner with tax collectors and other unsavory characters. He has just invited Levi, a despised tax collector, to become his follower. Not only is the fascinated Levi willing to follow Jesus, he throws a party for him, which Jesus happily attends. I like to see this dinner at Levi's house as a kind of preview of the Mass. Except at the Mass Jesus is now the host and we are the sinful guests. "People who are healthy do not need a doctor; sick people do." The Mass is a marvelous experience of healing because the physician who heals and is himself our healing food is Jesus Christ himself.

SECOND SUNDAY IN ORDINARY TIME

READING I **Isa 49:3, 5-6** **READING II** **1 Cor 1:1-3**
GOSPEL **John 1:29-34**

Reading I: The prophet Isaiah foresees a servant whom the Lord will raise up to rescue the chosen people.

Reading II: Paul begins his letter to the community at Corinth, whom God has called to be a holy people.

Gospel: John calls Jesus "the Lamb of God who takes away the sin of the world" and recalls how he first came to know Jesus' identity.

The emphasis in today's readings is on God's calling a people and individual members of a people to do a special work for him. A vocation, any vocation, always begins with God's call. The call helps the person called to establish his or her self-identity. This is also the case with a people. Beginning with their liberation from slavery at the time of the Exodus, God worked long to give the people an identity, a sense of their having been loved and chosen, an awareness of their destiny.

Today's Reading I is a high point in God's formation of his people: "You are my servant, Israel, . . . through whom I show my glory. . . . I will make you a light to the nations, that my salvation may reach to the ends of the earth." This reading is one of the "Suffering Servant" songs that can be understood either of Israel or of Jesus, who will call himself the "light of the world" (John 8:12). The mission and vocation of the Suffering Servant will be to heal others by suffering and dying for them.

The theme of self-identity, of knowing who one is and what one's vocation will be, is also evident in Reading II: "Paul, called by God's will to be an apostle . . . send[s] greetings to the church of God which is in Corinth; to you who have been consecrated in Christ Jesus and called to be a holy people."

In the gospel, John the Baptizer sees Jesus coming toward him and he calls out: "Look there! The Lamb of God who takes away the sin of the world!" John admits that he did not at first recognize Jesus. But the one who sent him to baptize with water told him:

" 'When you see the Spirit descend and rest on someone, it is he who is to baptize with the Holy Spirit.' Now I have seen for myself and have testified. 'This is God's chosen One.' "

Jesus' baptism outlines his vocation. He knows what he is to do and how he is to accomplish what the Father wants. And he knows who he is: "beloved Son." The Responsorial Psalm reveals his response to his call: "Here am I, Lord; I come to do your will."

During his public life, Jesus will encounter rejection, scorn, pain, agony, death. He will accept it and transform it into an act of love, of salvation for the world. The cross on which he will hang will be a sign proclaiming to all peoples that love is stronger than death, that no evil, no violence, can triumph over love.

Like the Jews and Corinthians, like Jesus, we too have been called to work for God—to carry on what Jesus did by living, dying, and rising from the dead. God has called each of us to be "suffering servants" with Jesus, although not in exactly the same manner of life. There is a variety of vocations to which God calls his children: vocations to married life, religious life, priesthood, and to single life "in the world."

The role of every Christian is to reflect Christ. Jesus entered into his glory through suffering. Our task in the Church is the same. As individuals and as a community, we are called to show God's love and mercy to the world.

Jesus responded to God's call and so must we. And our response is the same: "Here am I, Lord, I come to do your will." We add our prayer:

> Father, . . .
> Help us to embrace your will,
> give us the strength to follow your call,
> so that your truth may live in our hearts
> and reflect peace to those who believe in your love (Alternative Opening Prayer).

SECOND SUNDAY IN ORDINARY TIME

READING I **1 Sam 3:3-10, 19** **READING II** **1 Cor 6:13-15, 17-20**
GOSPEL **John 1:35-42**

Reading I: Twice God calls Samuel while the boy is sleeping, and only on the third call does Samuel realize who it is who calls him.

Reading II: Paul tells us that our bodies are members of Christ and temples of the Holy Spirit. Therefore, we must act according to our dignity.

Gospel: Jesus calls his first disciples and changes Peter's name from Simon to Cephas, which is rendered "Peter" (rock).

Today's readings are again about vocations, but there are other themes as well, particularly that of prayer. The Lord calls Samuel, who at first thinks it is Eli who is calling. "Here I am," he says, "You called me." Finally a third call comes, and Samuel, following Eli's instruction, responds, "Speak, Lord, for your servant is listening." Samuel's response is echoed in the Responsorial Psalm: "Here am I, Lord; I come to do your will."

The truth is that vocations and prayer always begin with God, but both require a human response. It would be hard to improve on the one Samuel gives us: "Speak, Lord, for your servant is listening."

There is a lot of anxiety and worry in life. No one is without personal concerns. What do we do about anxiety? Some try to pretend it isn't there. Others become desolate. They give in to gloom and even despair, and unfortunately, they spread gloom around them.

What can we do about anxiety? As always, Jesus has the best answer to that question. "What are you looking for?" he asks John's two disciples. They respond, "Rabbi . . ., where do you stay?" "Come and see," he answers. They spend the rest of the day with him, and their lives are forever changed.

"Rabbi, where do you stay?" That's more than a question about Jesus' domicile. I suspect it is really a question about the meaning of life, and they believe he can tell them what that meaning is. His answer, "Come and see," is an invitation to faith, to trust, to the kind of trust that Jesus exemplifies in his own life. They accept his invitation, they become his disciples, and in that vocation they find the best possible insight into the meaning of life.

The dialogue between Jesus and the two disciples also gives us an excellent lesson on the meaning of prayer. As we have said, prayer begins with God's word to us, and that word can come to us not only in Holy Scripture but in numberless other ways: the beauty of nature in all her moods, the smile of a child, a beautiful piece of music, the embrace of a loved one.

But God's word requires a human response, and that response is prayer. Our response arises out of the special needs of our lives or from the mood the very word inspires in us. Thanksgiving is always in order. Notice the official responses with which we answer God's word at Mass: "Thanks be to God!" after Readings I and II. "Praise to you, Lord Jesus Christ!" at the end of the gospel. Those responses are our prayer, our reaction to God's word to us. And the Responsorial Psalm is one of our best prayers, because it expresses in the divinely inspired words of the psalms, our reply to God's message.

The special vocation to which God has called us also stirs up deeply personal prayers. Think, for example, of the anguished prayer of a parent who loses a loved one or the joy and gratitude of a newly professed Sister or a newly ordained priest.

God speaks, we reply. Prayer is dialogue. So, too, is vocation. Praise to you, Lord Jesus Christ!

> I have waited, waited for the Lord,
> 	and he stooped toward me and heard my cry.
> And he put a new song into my mouth,
> 	a hymn to our God (Responsorial Psalm).

67 SECOND SUNDAY IN ORDINARY TIME Cycle C

READING I **Isa 62:1-5** **READING II** **1 Cor 12:4-11**
GOSPEL **John 2:1-12**

Reading I: The prophet compares God's love for the Israelites to the love of a bridegroom for his bride.

Reading II: Within the Church, the body of Christ, there are different gifts but the same Spirit.

Gospel: At a wedding feast at Cana, Jesus works his first miracle by changing water into wine.

In today's readings, there is a wealth of ideas and doctrine that the Lord presents to us as nourishment for our minds and hearts. Reading I is like a divine love letter from Yahweh to the Israelites:

> You shall be a glorious crown in the hand of the Lord,
> a royal diadem held by your God. . . .
> You shall be called "My Delight,"
> and your land "Espoused."
> For the Lord delights in you,
> and makes your land his spouse.
> As a young man marries a virgin,
> your Builder shall marry you.

The nuptial theme surfaces again in the gospel. It is significant that one of the first places to which Jesus goes at the beginning of his public life is a wedding and that it is at this wedding feast that he works his first miracle, his first "sign" (John's favorite name for Jesus' miracles. A sign points to certain effects, but most of all, Jesus' signs point to his compassion and love). He changes water into wine—150 gallons of the very best vintage, a dramatic enough miracle in any circumstance. This is a sign that manifests divine power but also points to an even more dramatic change—that of the old covenant of Judaism to the new covenant of Christianity, the new wedding between God and his people. The change is effected through Mary and her command to the servants: "Do whatever he tells you."

A detailed description of the new people of God is given in Reading II, in which Paul depicts the inner composition of the new people of God, the Church. In his letter, Paul compares the Church to a human body with many members, each with its own function, each necessary for the well being of the whole, and all deriving power from the one life principle, the Holy Spirit.

Today's gospel provides us with insights into the dignity and holiness of the vocation of matrimony. Marriage is an image of God's love for the people of God and for each of us individually. "As a young man marries a virgin, your Builder shall marry you" (Reading I). The Alternative Communion Antiphon wonderfully expresses our reaction to that statement:

> We know and believe in God's love for us.

The wedding feast at Cana points to the Eucharist, which is really a celebration of love—divine and human: the love between each and all of us with our God; the love between wives and husbands; the love between members of families, communities, and parish families.

Love is never easy for anyone. It is tested and tried by family tragedies, by indifference, by selfishness, by hurts of all kinds. Human love has to grow, and it can grow only by mutual effort and sacrifice. Love has to be made, to be created, to grow and ripen. Above all, love has to be forgiving.

All that we have said of human love is true of divine love—the love between God and each of us. God does more than God's share, but our contribution is essential. God is helpless without it.

We know how much we need help, and that help is always available to us in the Eucharist, the wedding feast again made present. Here God again expresses his love for us, here we renew our wedding vows with God, here we plunge our commitment to the divine Bridegroom back into its roots. Here, above all, we come to know and believe in the Lord's love for us all.

311 MONDAY OF THE SECOND WEEK IN ORDINARY TIME

YEAR I

READING I **Heb 5:1-10**
GOSPEL **Mark 2:18-22**

Reading I gives an insight into Jesus' mentality that the gospels hardly touch. In today's gospel he claims to be the Bridegroom-Savior whose presence encourages celebration rather than fasting. In Hebrews he is the high priest whose main offering was "prayer and supplications with loud cries and tears to God."

Jesus identifies himself with us, his people; he is able to deal patiently with erring sinners, for he himself was beset by weakness. He is God's own Son, but because he is high priest and Savior, he chooses to learn obedience, as his people have to do, and to suffer. Why? Because he loves us, and because he wanted to show us that only by suffering ourselves in obedience to the Father's will can we become one with him in love, so that the Father can also say to us, You are my child; today I have begotten you. Praise the Lord!

YEAR II

READING I **1 Sam 15:16-23**
GOSPEL **Mark 2:18-22**

Saul begins his reign badly by disobeying God. The Jerusalem Bible explains that Saul acts in good faith and therein lies his tragedy; his sin consists in choosing his individual way of honoring God with a view to his own popularity. And God rejects him as king. We might conclude that our worship and service of God has to be totally unselfish—given to God out of love, not for any kind of self-promotion.

In the gospel, Jesus claims to be the Bridegroom whose presence encourages celebration rather than fasting. He is obviously referring to a time when he will be taken away from his followers and then they can fast. In his imagery about mending clothing and preserving wine, he is referring to the newness and power of the gospel, which will be in conflict with the practices of the Pharisees and will require a new outlook on God and religion. If fasting enhances your desire and love for Jesus, go to it.

312 TUESDAY OF THE SECOND WEEK IN ORDINARY TIME

YEAR I

READING I **Heb 6:10-20**
GOSPEL **Mark 2:23-28**

The Lord will remember his covenant for ever (Responsorial Psalm).

God will never forget the work we have done and the love we have shown him by our service. Our task as Christians is to give thanks to the Lord with all our heart, for "Great are the works of the Lord, exquisite in all their delights."

Those works began with the creation that God gave us to enjoy, to use (but not to abuse), and to bring to perfection. God could not keep the secret of his immense love, so he told the secret in creation and in human beings who could respond gratefully to that love. On the seventh day of creation God rested. God does not need rest. We humans need rest, we need the Sabbath in order to become more human. The Sabbath is made for us. Don't you think we need it?

YEAR II

READING I **1 Sam 16:1-13**
GOSPEL **Mark 2:23-28**

"I have found David, my servant," says the Lord in today's Responsorial Psalm. "A man after the heart of God," David is a complex figure: architect of the Jewish state, ancestor of the Messiah, a great poet and musician. He is also weak and human and capable of great sin. But perhaps he was greatest in his ability to repent. We will come to know him better in days to come.

The Sabbath was originally intended as a reminder of the right order of creation—that Yahweh is creator and we are his creatures. God wanted us to rest and acknowledge God's lordship, not because God needed our homage, but because God knew we needed it. We need it in order to become more human. We cannot reach our full stature as persons without it. This should help us understand Jesus' words, "The sabbath was made for man, not man for the sabbath."

313 WEDNESDAY OF THE SECOND WEEK IN ORDINARY TIME

YEAR I

READING I Heb 7:1-3, 15-17
GOSPEL Mark 3:1-6

Today Jesus asks, "Is it permitted to do a good deed on the sabbath—or an evil one? To preserve life—or to destroy it?" Actually, to preserve life, to enrich life, is the main purpose of the Sabbath. The Pharisees had erected a system of external observances around the Sabbath that obscured its inner purpose and goodness. The great Rabbi Abraham Heschel says that the Sabbath is eternity in time—it is a cathedral made not with stones and glass but with hours and minutes. It comes every week, inviting us not to strive and succeed but to taste and know that God is good, that the earth and the flesh are there to be shared and enjoyed.

The Sabbath was made for us, not we for the Sabbath. Without its spirit and meaning we can never be truly human, we can never be on our way to the divine.

YEAR II

READING I 1 Sam 17:32-33, 37, 40-51
GOSPEL Mark 3:1-6

David's encounter with Goliath is one of the great moments of history. Everybody knows about it, but few reflect on the secret of David's victory—his faith in the Lord. "I come against you in the name of the Lord of hosts," David tells Goliath. "Today the Lord shall deliver you into my hand." You cannot find a better principle for Christian living than that.

The gospel continues to instruct us on the true nature of the Sabbath. Jesus' enemies had perverted the meaning of the Sabbath with a network of picky rules. Jesus asks if it is lawful on the Sabbath to do good or to do harm—to save life or to kill. He is rightly angry at their silence, but mostly he is grieved at their hardness of heart. "Stretch out your hand," he commands. The man obeys, and his hand is restored. God's idea in giving us the Sabbath was to restore and to re-create our tired hearts and bodies. That's an ideal that needs constant emphasis.

314 THURSDAY OF THE SECOND WEEK IN ORDINARY TIME

YEAR I

READING I Heb 7:25–8:6
GOSPEL Mark 3:7-12

The unclean spirits in the gospel were right: Jesus is indeed the Son of God! He is also our Savior, our high priest, our mediator with the Father. He no longer needs to offer sacrifice day after day for the sins of his people, for "he did that once for all when he offered himself" on the altar of the cross. "Now every high priest is appointed to offer gifts and sacrifices; hence the necessity for this one to have something to offer."

The offering of Jesus could not have been greater; it was his very self. It was great because of the total obedience to and love for the Father with which he offered himself.

> In the written scroll it is prescribed for me,
> to do your will, O my God, is my delight,
> And your law is within my heart! (Responsorial Psalm)

The wonderful thing about this is that in his love Jesus has given us the Mass in which we can make his offering our own.

YEAR II

READING I 1 Sam 18:6-9; 19:1-7
GOSPEL Mark 3:7-12

The relationship between Saul and David is heading for a showdown, and the loser, Saul, is going to allow his personal jealousy to destroy him. He considers the praise given to David for his victory over Goliath as though it were stolen from him, and soon envy turns him into a potential murderer.

Envy is one of the commonest of human failings. It is also one of the deadliest and most destructive vices. Henry Fairlie says it is the nastiest, the most grim, the meanest of sins. It is sneering, sly, and vicious ("The Seven Deadly Sins," *The New Republic,* September 17, 1977). The face of envy is never lovely, never even faintly pleasant. If we are afflicted only God's grace can heal us, but only if we want to be healed. The gospel gives us the secret of all healing: "All who had afflictions kept pushing toward him to touch him." May we make our own the cry, "You are the Son of God!"

315 FRIDAY OF THE SECOND WEEK IN ORDINARY TIME

YEAR I

READING I **Heb 8:6-13**
GOSPEL **Mark 3:13-19**

Every time we take part in the Mass, we hear the priest say, "This is the cup of my blood, the blood of the new and everlasting covenant. . . ." Reading I gives the background of these words, spoken first by Jesus at the Last Supper when he instituted the Mass. A covenant is an agreement, a wedding alliance between God and his people that entails rights and duties for both parties.

The people of the first covenant were not too successful in upholding their part, so God, through Jeremiah, predicted that it would be replaced. We are now the people of God, we are the "other party" in God's contract-covenant. God has written the law of love in our hearts. Every time we celebrate the Mass we renew our covenant, our marriage vows with the Lord. At Mass the kindness and truth of God become ours more and more. Let us proclaim the mystery of our faith.

YEAR II

READING I **1 Sam 24:3-21**
GOSPEL **Mark 3:13-19**

Today we see Saul back in his misery, the sad victim of envy, trying to kill David. The contrast between envious Saul and forgiving David is striking. It is good for us to know the nature of envy. Confronted with the truth about David's goodness, Saul momentarily comes to his senses. But his contrition does not last. Whether or not we are more successful than Saul in overcoming whatever degree of envy consumes us depends on our willingness to face up to the truth about ourselves and the truth about the desire of Christ to heal us, above all, on our own desire to be healed.

> Have pity on me, O God; have pity on me,
> for in you I take refuge (Responsorial Psalm).

316 SATURDAY OF THE SECOND WEEK IN ORDINARY TIME

YEAR I

READING I **Heb 9:2-3, 11-14**
GOSPEL **Mark 3:20-21**

The holy of holies in the Jewish Temple, the dwelling place of the Lord, could be entered but once a year by the high priest and by him alone. Reading I describes the place nearest to this holy of holies. The real holy of holies is heaven, which Jesus entered with the offering of his own blood, thus opening heaven and making it accessible to all his followers.

We, too, have a sanctuary and a holy of holies. On this altar at every Mass, we recall and celebrate Christ's sacrifice, we make it our own. Because of Christ's sacrifice of himself, we have access to the holy of holies which is heaven. What we have is far greater than any temple, with all its holy places. Our Mass is the Last Supper and Calvary, made present in our midst. This is our holy place.

Sing praise to God, sing praise;
sing praise to our king, sing praise (Responsorial Psalm).

YEAR II

READING I **2 Sam 1:1-4, 11-12, 19, 23-27**
GOSPEL **Mark 3:20-21**

The day of Saul's tragic end finally arrives. David's reaction to the deaths of Saul and his dear friend, Jonathan, may seem exaggerated to us, especially in the light of Saul's treatment of him. But we have to remind ourselves of David's faith in God's choice of Saul. David's grief at this double death is easier to understand if we recall that belief in immortality was not as common than as it is now. Death for them was terribly final.

In the gospel, Jesus' friends are disturbed about him and the way he is attracting crowds. Maybe he is an embarrassment to them. they charge him with being out of his mind, of being a fanatic. We can imagine how he must feel about that. Of course, we would never do anything like that! But then, it may be just as serious to be indifferent to Jesus as to reject him. We should not try to take charge of him as his relatives did, but rather we should let him take charge of us.

READING I **Isa 8:23–9:3** **READING II** **1 Cor 1:10-13, 17**
GOSPEL **Matt 4:12-23**

Reading I: A people in darkness will see a great light which will shine on those in a land of gloom.

Reading II: Paul pleads with the Corinthian Christians to be united in mind and judgment and to heal their factions.

Gospel: Matthew recalls Isaiah's prophecy that the people in darkness will see a great light; he announces the theme of Jesus' ministry.

Isaiah's prophecy that the people who walk in darkness have seen a great light will be fulfilled in Jesus who, when he comes, announces: "I am the light of the world" (John 8:12). We might try to imagine life without him, to imagine living in spiritual darkness of mind and heart without his loving presence and guidance.

It is significant that Matthew quotes Isaiah's prophecy and has Jesus beginning his ministry in a heathen land. This is an indication that Matthew wants to depict Jesus as Savior of the whole world—not just of the chosen people.

It is equally significant that the chief theme of Jesus' preaching is: "Reform your lives! The kingdom of heaven is at hand." Reform your lives. Be converted. Turn from self to God. Open your hearts to God. Give up that most precious attachment that prevents your belonging totally to God. In a word, acknowledge God as the only Lord of your life.

This command of Jesus is intended for us as much as for the people of his time. In Reading II, St. Paul specifies one area of life in need of reform: our relationships with other members of our families, parishes, communities, any group we belong to: "Let there be no factions. . . . I have been informed . . . that you are quarreling among yourselves."

Disagreements and quarreling seem to be one of fallen human nature's chief weaknesses. But can we settle for that condition, take it for granted, not try to do anything about it, and still be true to Christ? If that is our attitude, we cannot have Christ as the light of our lives. Hearts closed to others who do not think as we do cannot be open to the Light who is Christ. In Reading II Paul says (and he is simply echoing Jesus): "I beg you, . . . in the name of our Lord Jesus Christ, to agree on what you say. . . . Be united in mind and judgment."

Notice that the problem of the Corinthians is one of authority, of support for a particular point of view. One says he belongs to Paul, one to Apollos, one to Cephas, another to Christ. Then comes Paul's devastating question: "Has Christ, then, been divided into parts? Was it Paul who was crucified for you? Was it in Paul's name that you were baptized?" Using the particular loyalty of each, they have been trying to score points against one another.

We all know of modern situations that duplicate the factions among the Corinthian Christians. Perhaps we have been involved ourselves. The chief enemy of Christianity is not persecution, it is divisiveness among Christians. This is the commonest way of rendering the cross of Christ void of its meaning.

Why do we have so much difficulty avoiding factions? It's hard to answer that question. The fact is that Christ does not yet possess our minds and hearts. We all need a favorable answer to today's Opening Prayer:

> All-powerful and ever-living God,
> direct your love that is within us,
> that our efforts in the name of your Son
> may bring humankind to unity and peace.

69 THIRD SUNDAY IN ORDINARY TIME Cycle B

READING I **Jonah 3:1-5, 10** **READING II** **1 Cor 7:29-31**
GOSPEL **Mark 1:14-20**

Reading I: Responding to Jonah's call to reform, the sinful Ninevites believe God and repent.

Reading II: Paul mistakenly believes that the second coming of Christ will happen in his own lifetime.

Gospel: Jesus begins his public life in Galilee, calls for reform, and invites his disciples to follow him.

All-powerful and ever-living God,
direct your love that is within us,
that our efforts in the name of your Son
may bring mankind to unity and peace.

This Opening Prayer is most appropriate as we begin the Week of Prayer for Christian Unity (January 18–25).

Back in the sixties and seventies, many Catholics were much concerned about the ecumenical movement. We do not hear much about it today. What has happened? Have we given up on it? Surely not Pope John Paul II. A few years ago he said that the divisions in Christianity were "an intolerable scandal." And when he visited the headquarters of the World Council of Churches in Geneva, he made this statement: "From the beginning of my ministry as Bishop of Rome I have insisted that the engagement of the Catholic Church in the ecumenical movement is irreversible and that the search for unity is one of its pastoral priorities" (*America*, January 19, 1983).

The figure of Jonah is interesting in connection with the ecumenical movement. God commanded Jonah to go and preach repentance to the Ninevites. Jonah did everything he could to escape the task. Finally, after three days in the fish's belly, he decided to go and preach. His message was negative: "Forty days more and Nineveh shall be destroyed." The Ninevites were converted. They were not members of God's chosen people, but God loved them and wanted them to return to him.

The lesson for us today is that there is much good in people who are not members of the Roman Church. It is time for us to overcome our attitudes of superiority over other denominations, pretending that we have all the truth, a monopoly on all goodness.

What do we want in the ecumenical movement? We should want what Christ wants. He surely cannot be happy about the divisions among his followers. At the Last Supper he said: "I pray . . . that all may be one as you, Father, are in me, and I in you; I pray that they may be one in us" (John 17:21). Human frailty and sinfulness have made that prayer of Jesus almost a mockery. How delighted Satan must be at the divisions among those who call themselves Christians!

What does Christ want of us? He wants us to respect one another's sincerity and honest convictions. He wants us to think of members of other denominations not as Lutherans, Baptists,

Methodists, but as *persons* whom God respects and loves, even as he loved the Ninevites, persons for whom Christ died.

Today, as when he began his ministry, Jesus says to all of us: "This is the time of fulfillment. The reign of God is at hand! Reform your lives and believe in the good news!" Those words mean that we are to change our thinking, our attitudes.

The goal of Christian unity among all denominations is so enormous it almost seems beyond achievement. Well, maybe for people, for theologians, but not for God, whom we should invoke daily. A favorable answer to Jesus' prayer for unity may be in our hands. Please God we will not fail him!

All-powerful and ever-living God,
direct your love that is within us,
that our efforts in the name of your Son
may bring mankind to unity and peace. Amen (Opening Prayer).

70 THIRD SUNDAY IN ORDINARY TIME Cycle C

READING I Neh 8:2-4, 5-6, 8-10 **READING II** 1 Cor 12:12-30
GOSPEL Luke 1:1-4; 4:14-21

Reading I: The priest Ezra reads and explains the Book of the Law to the people returned from exile in Babylon. They receive the word with great joy.

Reading II: Paul compares the Church to a human body. As the body is one but has many members each with its own function to perform, so it is with Christ's body, the Church.

Gospel: Returning to his hometown, Nazareth, Jesus goes to the synagogue, reads a passage from Isaiah, and claims that the prophecy is fulfilled this day in their midst.

As usual, there is a link between Reading I and the gospel. The exiles, back from Babylon, hear Ezra read the Book of the Law, and they respond with rejoicing: "Amen, amen!" In the synagogue in Nazareth, his hometown, Jesus reads one of Isaiah's messianic prophecies and claims to be its fulfillment. Further in Luke's gospel we are told how the people reject him. Reading II seems to have little connection to the other readings, but today it is so important, we will concentrate on it.

This reading has to do with the nature of the Church. Just what is this Church of which we are members? Paul uses the analogy of the human body to help the Corinthians (and us) understand how we are related to Christ and to one another: "The body is one and has many members, but all the members, many though they are, are one body; and so it is with Christ. . . . You, then, are the body of Christ. Every one of you is a member of it."

As the human body has a life principle, the soul, so too does the body of Christ. The same Holy Spirit who is in Christ the head is in us; we are all one in Christ. We can speculate on how aware most Christians are of our relationship with Jesus and with one another. In this Church of which we are members, each of us has an indispensable personal function to perform; without it the whole body suffers.

Since we are all one with one another and with Christ, if one member suffers, the whole body suffers, but because that suffering is joined to the suffering of Jesus, it is redemptive. So, too, our good deeds affect and build up the entire body. But the opposite is also true. Whatever evil we do diminishes the effectiveness and spiritual health of the whole body. There is no such thing as a sin that hurts only the one who commits it. If I discriminate against another person for any reason whatsoever, I hurt the entire body. Discrimination against another person is discrimination against Christ. There is no such thing as an isolated act or deed for a member of the Church, the body of Christ.

In his Letter to the Ephesians, St. Paul tells us how membership in the body of Christ should affect our actions: "Never let evil talk pass your lips. . . . Do nothing to sadden the Holy Spirit with whom you were sealed. . . . Get rid of all bitterness, all passion and anger, harsh words, slander, and malice of every kind. In place of these, be kind to one another, compassionate, and mutually forgiving, just as God has forgiven you in Christ" (4:29-32).

The positive and negative deductions from the doctrine of the Church as the body of Christ are inexhaustible. But what the body does most of all is to burst into song and celebrate, to be a community of praise, of gratitude, of loving worship of the Lord.

The Jews who heard the Book of the Law read by Ezra celebrated. We hear God's inspired word in every Mass; it is perfectly natural for us to celebrate as well. Celebration is our duty, it is our privilege, it is our joy. And celebration, better than anything else, can build us more and more into the body of Christ that we are. So, let us

> Sing a new song to the Lord! Sing to the Lord, all the earth. Truth and beauty surround him, he lives in holiness and glory (Entrance Antiphon).

317 MONDAY OF THE THIRD WEEK IN ORDINARY TIME

YEAR I

READING I Heb 9:15, 24-28
GOSPEL Mark 3:22-30

The hostility of Christ's enemies is growing and with it the absurdity of their accusations against him. Human perversity can reach terrible intensity when propelled by jealous hatred. And lack of logic, too, as when they accuse Jesus of being possessed by Beelzebul and driving out devils with his cooperation.

Has it ever occurred to us that even now we can replace the hatred of Christ's enemies by our own love? It helps us to grow in grateful love when we realize what Jesus has done for us. Reading I tells us: Jesus by his sacrifice on Calvary has taken away our sins once and for all. At the end of time he will appear a second time not to take away sin but to bring salvation to those who eagerly await him.

> Sing to the Lord a new song,
> for he has done marvelous deeds;
> All the ends of the earth have seen
> the salvation by our God (Responsorial Psalm).

YEAR II

READING I 2 Sam 5:1-7, 10
GOSPEL Mark 3:22-30

David is anointed king now by the elders of Israel. He will exercise his kingship by being a shepherd who will rule by love. He rules as representative of the Lord who promises, "My faithfulness and kindness shall be with him" (Responsorial Psalm). This happy condition persists as long as David recognizes his total dependence on the Lord. But he is human, and as we shall see, he will eventually succumb to vainglory and sin. But the Lord will never give up on him because David knows how to repent.

The gospel is hardly calculated to warm our hearts. It offends us to hear Jesus accused of being possessed by a devil. But he defends himself well. What is "blasphemy against the Holy Spirit"—the unforgivable sin? It is said to be a kind of total rebellion against God that would assign satanic power to God. Or it may be understood as an attempt to put limits on God's mercy and forgiveness. All of sacred history repudiates such thinking.

318 TUESDAY OF THE THIRD WEEK IN ORDINARY TIME

YEAR I

READING I **Heb 10:1-10**
GOSPEL **Mark 3:31-35**

A common theme unites all of today's readings:

> Here am I, Lord;
> I come to do your will (Responsorial Psalm).

Jesus accepts the body and the life God has prepared for him, and so he fulfills the Father's will, as has been predicted by the psalmist. Again and again in his lifetime Jesus will return to this total dedication and commitment, the last time being in Gethsemani the night before his death.

Jesus makes this desire to do the will of the Father the chief characteristic of discipleship, as the gospel indicates: "Whoever does the will of God is brother and sister and mother to me." How often have we heard this! Perhaps so often that it fails to impress us properly. Then come occasions when we are abruptly, even brutally, recalled to the heart of our profession as Christians, and we have to make our own the words of Christ, "Here am I, Lord; I come to do your will." May we always be ready.

YEAR II

READING I **2 Sam 6:12-15, 17-19**
GOSPEL **Mark 3:31-35**

Yesterday's reading saw David establishing Jerusalem as a political center; today he makes it the religious center. It is interesting that David acts here as a Jewish priest: he offers sacrifice, blesses his people, and distributes a kind of "communion" to them. It is fascinating that David manifests his enthusiastic worship of God in a violent dance, and he is clothed only in a loincloth. It is good that this feature of the Hebrew priesthood did not come down to us Christian priests. Most of us are terrible dancers.

Would you like to be related to Jesus? The gospel tells you how: "Whoever does the will of God is brother and sister and mother to me." In other words, we who strive to do God's will are closer to Jesus than we would be by any blood relationship. Mary's relationship to Jesus by obedience to the Father's will is closer than by her physical motherhood. Father, may your will be done in us.

319 WEDNESDAY OF THE THIRD WEEK IN ORDINARY TIME

YEAR I

READING I **Heb 10:11-18**
GOSPEL **Mark 4:1-20**

The seed is the word of God. God has been sowing his sacred word in human hearts all through history. God's word has a mysterious power, and it has never lost that power, but the word, the seed without rich soil in which to take root, is sterile. So today's parable is more about soil than about seed. It is about us, about the kind of soil that we are, about our receptivity to the seed. It is also about fertilizer, without which even good soil becomes fruitless. The traditional fertilizer is prayer and self-denial.

None of our Lord's parables so challenges us as this one. Sincerity demands that we ask ourselves about hardness of heart, about superficiality, about cares and pleasures and unlawful desires. In a word, how receptive are we as individuals and as a family to God's word?

YEAR II

READING I 2 Sam 7:4-17
GOSPEL Mark 4:1-20

It is a human trait to want to build a building that will perpetuate the builder's name. David would like to build a temple for the Lord, but he runs into opposition from the Lord himself. Instead, Yahweh is the one who will do the building for David. The house he will build will be David's dynasty. He tells David: "Your house and your kingdom shall endure forever before me. . . ." It is a prophecy that Jesus alone could fulfill.

Maybe we have heard the parable of the sower so often that its meaning for us is dimmed. We need to recall that, powerful though the seed may be, its expansion depends on the kind of soil that receives it. God wishes to enter and grow in our hearts through his word. God grant that our hearts are not stoney, superficial, thorny ground, but good, black, loam—ready for the adventure of God being harvested from us.

320 THURSDAY OF THE THIRD WEEK IN ORDINARY TIME

YEAR I

READING I Heb 10:19-25
GOSPEL Mark 4:21-25

What is our Lord talking about today? Of course we do not light a lamp and then conceal it under a basket! Jesus is talking about his teaching, which may not always be as clear as we would like. It is the task of the teacher, the disciple of Christ, to seek out his meaning in all its depths; and it is the task of the hearer to do some searching, too. Truth is to be meditated on, prayed over, explored, always in the hope of finding deeper insights.

We can never exhaust the meaning of the gospel of Christ, but to neglect to seek out that meaning is to risk losing everything, our faith included. "Lord, this is the people that longs to see your face" (Responsorial Psalm). It is in this spirit that we must approach the Scriptures, the Word of God. The hungrier we are for God, for his truth and his love, the more he will open himself to us. So, listen carefully to what you hear!

YEAR II

READING I **2 Sam 7:18-19, 24-29**
GOSPEL **Mark 4:21-25**

David's reaction to the Lord's promise to him is prayer. He probably does not foresee the Messiah coming from his line, but he is properly grateful as he begs God to bless his lineage. His final words are indeed prophetic: "By your blessing the house of your servant shall be blessed forever." Without knowing it, he is speaking of Jesus, Messiah, Savior, true head of the house of David, the Church.

In the gospel Jesus uses the purpose of a lamp to illustrate the nature of truth and how he hopes his truth will affect us. Truth is to be meditated on, prayed over, explored—always in the hope of finding new insights. Truth shares the nature of God—it is inexhaustible. If we neglect the thinking and the probing, we run the risk of losing what we thought we had. And the more we possess truth, the more of it God will impart. May our light shine forth.

321 FRIDAY OF THE THIRD WEEK IN ORDINARY TIME

YEAR I

READING I **Heb 10:32-39**
GOSPEL **Mark 4:26-34**

Is there any need to point out that the reign, or kingdom, of God is not political? It refers to God's supreme dominion over all things and all persons, and on our part the kingdom is our recognition that

God is indeed the Lord of our lives; God is supreme over all. We acknowledge that all we have—our very life, our faith, our salvation, our worth—come from the Lord of life and love.

In the gospel Jesus indicates that the growth of such an idea is gradual. But once it spreads universally, Christ's redemption is finally and marvelously fulfilled. We can help in that spread and growth by admitting in our own minds and hearts that Jesus is Lord of our lives. After all that we know about him and what he has done for us, is it all that difficult for us to make that admission?

YEAR II

READING I 2 Sam 11:1-4, 5-10, 13-17
GOSPEL Mark 4:26-34

It could be that David's great successes went to his head. He forgot that God, not he, was Lord of his life. He was overcome by lustful desire and two heinous crimes—adultery and murder. But who are we to be shocked, either by David's weakness or by Bathsheba's apparently willing cooperation? We can find ourselves in them both, especially when we allow success of any kind to go to our heads, and we begin to believe that it is we, not God, who are responsible for our success. "Be merciful, O Lord, for we have sinned!" (Responsorial Psalm) This is a necessary and beautiful prayer not only for David and Bathsheba but for us all.

In the gospel Jesus describes the kingdom of God. It is not an earthly realm but rather a state of mind, in which we recognize God as Lord of our life—an idea that spreads only gradually. May we not forget it as David did.

322 SATURDAY OF THE THIRD WEEK IN ORDINARY TIME

YEAR I

READING I **Heb 11:1-2, 8-19**
GOSPEL **Mark 4:35-41**

Both our readings are about faith, but they define it differently. For Abraham, faith is total trust and obedience to God's call and command. It involves action and decision—leaving a secure life and possessions for the great unknown, and with all the odds against him.

In the gospel we have an example of lack of faith, lack of trust. The apostles have Jesus in the boat with them, but the storm obscures his presence. Half believing, they cry out for help, and *only* half believing, they are afraid. They need reassurance and receive it. Apparently, they do not yet know Jesus. But they have promise, and they will do better. Filled with awe at Jesus' power, they cry out, "Who can this be that the wind and the sea obey him?" We can make that question our own. But we can also answer Christ's question about our own occasional lack of faith: "Why are you so terrified? Why are you lacking in faith?"

YEAR II

READING I **2 Sam 12:1-7, 10-17**
GOSPEL **Mark 4:35-41**

"You are the man!" How easy it is to recognize evil in our neighbors—in their motivation, their vicious intent—to get angry at them and cry out for punishment! Unfortunately, our consciences aren't as dramatic in accusing us as was Nathan, David's conscience in person. David is each of us. But if he is great in sinning, he is also great in repenting. As soon as he recognizes his sin, he brings forth the most universal, most heartfelt act of contrition the world has ever known. His sorrow is great because he recognizes not only his sin and guilt but also the cause of his fall—his wicked heart. So he cries out, "A clean heart create for me, O God, and a steadfast spirit renew within me" (Responsorial Psalm). It is only when we come to know ourselves as fragile, vulnerable, evil-inclined human creatures that true healing can come to us and we can cry out with David, "I have sinned against the Lord. . . . Create a clean heart in *me*, O God."

71 FOURTH SUNDAY IN ORDINARY TIME Cycle A

READING I **Zeph 2:3; 3:12-13** **READING II** **1 Cor 1:26-31**
GOSPEL **Matt 5:1-12**

Reading I: The prophet foresees a remnant of Israelites who will be faithful to the Lord and to their covenant.

Reading II: Paul here writes to the lower-class citizens of Corinth and points out their dignity as members of Christ.

Gospel: Jesus, the new Moses, begins his Sermon on the Mount with the Beatitudes.

Today's readings may seem to be strange doctrine for most Americans, especially for young people planning their future. Our culture emphasizes achievement and success, especially financial and social. And here is Zephaniah saying: "Seek the Lord, all you humble of the earth, . . . Seek justice, seek humility." And here is Jesus presenting his ideal: "How blest are the poor in spirit . . . . Blest are the lowly . . . . Blest too the peacemakers." With a philosophy like that, how can one make one's way in the world?

Ours is a culture that rewards high achievers. You are a success in life if you gain a high position in the financial, political, and business world. You know who you are, and everyone else does, too. But do you really know? Who am I? What is the meaning of life? These are basic questions that everyone faces and has to try to answer at some time or other. Our world replies: You are what you achieve; life means the satisfaction, the fulfillment, of all your hopes and ambitions.

Somehow or other, those answers do not seem to satisfy for long. Some of the world's unhappiest, most dissatisfied people are those who were the most successful according to accepted standards. Trying to find the meaning of life in what we accomplish is a useless effort. Years ago in *The Dubuque Witness* Father Carr wrote that the only way to find the meaning of life as well as one's own identity is in trying always to do the will of the Lord. It is only in emptying the self of self-will that we really find out who we are. We are *someone,* we are persons, we are God's daughters and sons, and we are precious in God's eyes. Not because of what we accomplish, but because of who and what we *are,* beloved by the Lord to such a degree that he sent his Son Jesus to live and die for us.

All this may require a different outlook on life for many Catholics. The gospel provides us with a blueprint for that outlook. It gives us a set of values from the mouth of Jesus himself. The Beatitudes describe the process of conversion to that new outlook. *A New Catechism* tells us that the Beatitudes do not represent eight classes of people, but that they all apply to one and the same group. They are not a summary of virtues. They have in view people who have nothing to hope for from this world but who look to God for everything, who are wholly open to God, full of expectation. "In a word, they are men and women whose lives resemble the way of submissiveness and loving service which Jesus himself adopted at his baptism" (New York: Herder and Herder, 1966, 99).

The Beatitudes may seem like an impossible dream to many people. Well, they are a dream, but not an impossible one, for they represent Jesus' dream for his followers, and he invites us all to help him make the dream come true—if not in our world, at least in our lives. We begin by striving and praying for the spirit of submissiveness and expectancy that characterized his and his mother's life, placing more emphasis on being human than on having great possessions. This spirit means being gentle, merciful, understanding, forgiving. It means serving others.

We can't be truly human, we have a hard time being Christian, if we do not try to make Jesus' dream our own, to share it with others. In today's Reading II, Paul tells us, "God it is who has given you life in Christ Jesus." God has also given us Jesus' dream. May all Christians work together to make it come true!

72 FOURTH SUNDAY IN ORDINARY TIME Cycle B

READING I Deut 18:15-20 **READING II** 1 Cor 7:32-35
GOSPEL Mark 1:21-28

Reading I: Moses promises that God will some day raise up a prophet like him. It is a prophecy that the first Christians saw fulfilled in Christ Jesus.

Reading II: Paul, while not downgrading marriage, says that the celibate life gives a person more time to devote his or her life entirely to Jesus.

Gospel: Teaching in the synagogue at Capernaum, Jesus astounds the people by delivering a man from an unclean spirit.

We begin today's Mass with an extraordinary prayer:

> Lord our God,
> help us to love you with all our hearts
> and to love all men as you love them (Opening Prayer).

We might well wonder if it is possible for us to love others as deeply as God does. The word "as" is the key to understanding the prayer. We can hardly love people with the same intensity and to the same degree that God loves them; but we can, with God's help, love *in the same way*, that is, by the gift of ourselves to them, by caring for them.

Reading II may sound strange to many, and it may even disturb married couples. Monika Hellwig, in the January 26, 1985, issue of *America,* writes that Paul is defending the goodness of marriage, not downgrading it; but Paul also teaches that celibacy, if motivated by love (I would add, *only* if it is motivated by love) is also good or better. Reluctant, loveless celibacy defeats its own purpose, which is to help us love God with all our hearts and our neighbors as God loves them.

As usual, there is a close relationship between Reading I and the gospel. In Reading I God promises to raise up a prophet from the midst of his people, one who will be a voice proclaiming God's will for all the people:

> If today you hear his voice,
> harden not your hearts (Responsorial Psalm).

In the gospel we see and hear this promised prophet in action; it is Jesus, the Lord. He begins to teach in the Capernaum synagogue, and the people are spellbound because he teaches with authority, "not like the scribes." We can surmise that he also teaches with deepest love and concern for the people and with the desire to answer their anxieties and worries. In his teaching, he is exercising his authority as the prophet that the Lord had promised to the people through Moses.

In the gospel Jesus confronts his enemy for the first time in his public life. A man with an unclean spirit recognizes Jesus and cries out: "What do you want of us, Jesus of Nazareth? Have you come to destroy us? I know who you are—the Holy One of God!" Jesus rebukes him sharply: "Be quiet! Come out of the man!" The unclean spirit convulses the man violently and, with a loud shriek, comes out of him.

The reaction of the people is most interesting: "What does this mean? A completely new teaching in a spirit of authority! He gives orders to unclean spirits and they obey him!" The people are wise. They hear Jesus' command, they see the results, and they call the whole process "a new teaching." In other words, healing and teaching go together. Healing *is* teaching. It is a vivid sign that discloses God's great love for his people. Jesus reveals the Father; above all he reveals himself and his mission, the prophetic mission as "the Holy One of God."

We are "other Christs." We too can teach, if not by word of mouth and with the authority of Jesus then surely by our bearing, our disposition, by the kind of joyous lives we lead. All teaching reveals not only one's mind but also one's heart. If our minds and hearts are filled with Christ, we become his voice to all we meet. What Jesus did in today's gospel he wants to continue to do in his Church, and we are the Church. Now we can see how essential that Opening Prayer is:

> Lord our God,
> help us to love you with all our hearts
> and to love all men as you love them.

73 **FOURTH SUNDAY IN ORDINARY TIME** Cycle C

73 FOURTH SUNDAY IN ORDINARY TIME — Cycle C

READING I Jer 1:4-5, 17-19 **READING II** 1 Cor 12:31–13:13
GOSPEL Luke 4:21-30

Reading I: Jeremiah relates how God called him to be a prophet before God had formed him in his mother's womb.

Reading II: Paul's renowned hymn speaks of the nature and beauty of love.

Gospel: The initial admiring reaction of Jesus' old neighbors to his first sermon in the Nazareth synagogue soon turns to anger and a death threat.

The praise of love in Reading II is a favorite reading that many young people choose for their wedding ceremony. It presents a magnificent ideal of married life. Unfortunately, many of them forget it. A growing number of those marriages end in divorce.

God calls us all to greatness—to the greatness of loving as God loves. Love is the greatest of the gifts that Paul writes about today. He calls this gift "a way." Love is a way of life to which we are all called.

We all have certain talents or gifts. But talents have to be developed, oftentimes by very hard work and practice. Talents can be buried, and that is tragic, for then the entire family or parish suffers, to say nothing of the one who buries them.

Flannery O'Connor was one of America's finest modern writers. She learned from the French philosopher Jacques Maritain how to develop what he called "the habit of art," habit not being a mechanical routine, but an attitude or quality of mind that is as essential as talent. Her habit of art drove her to exploit the potential of language and characterization, which eventually helped her to become a very talented writer.

She also acquired and developed *the habit of being,* an attitude or quality of interior disposition. What came out of her habit of being is a self-portrait of a deeply religious, very intelligent, humorous, humane, and genuine person. She lived and acted out of the fullness of her Christian being.

We can't all be writers as she was. But God has called each of us to be a lover. God has given us the talent, the power to love. If we bury that talent, fail to develop it by hard work and sacrifice in our daily contacts with others, we doom ourselves to a life of bitterness, frustration, and joylessness for ourselves and for our families, parishes, and communities. Nazareth failed to take its son Jesus to its heart. Nazareth rejected love, and so Jesus left his hometown to itself.

Today St. Paul spells out the characteristics of a way of life formed by love. We can consider the list as a personal examination of conscience, one that examines our relationships with God and with our neighbors. Paul says that true love is kind, patient, not jealous, does not put on airs, is not snobbish, is never rude, is not prone to anger, does not brood over injuries, is never self-seeking, always trusts, always hopes, always endures whatever comes.

An author wrote a book which he entitled *Looking Out For Number One.* His wife read it and divorced him. Looking out for number one is what love is *not.* There is only one Christian habit of being—the way of love. To follow that way, we always come back to the love that Jesus has for us. The conviction of our having been known and called and chosen because God has loved us from all eternity is the foundation of the habit of being we call "Christian."

God doesn't just love humanity as a whole. God loves each one of us personally. God loves us as we are, even with all our faults, our weaknesses. All God asks of us is that we believe in his love, open ourselves to it, and allow God to love in and through us. Here is a prayer God really wants to answer:

> Lord our God,
> help us to love you with all our hearts
> and to love all people as you love them (Opening Prayer).

323 MONDAY OF THE FOURTH WEEK IN ORDINARY TIME

YEAR I

READING I Heb 11:32-40
GOSPEL Mark 5:1-20

It is profitable for us to compare our sufferings with those of the Jewish martyrs listed in Reading I. These pre-Christian martyrs suffered for a faith in One still to come. Many of them did better than many of us, who now possess Christ, his word, his example, his redeeming act, his sacraments.

The gospel incident is not easy to figure out. What is clear is Christ's never-dying compassion for anyone in need; what is also clear is that we experience that same compassion now in the Eucharist and the sacrament of reconciliation. Why do you think the townspeople wanted to get rid of Jesus? If we had been there, what would have been our reaction? Well, we are here, and what we can do to prove our gratitude to Jesus for his mercy is to show by our words and our lives that Jesus is our beloved Lord.

YEAR II

READING I 2 Sam 15:13-14, 30; 16:5-13
GOSPEL Mark 5:1-20

David was great in his glory, his sin was great, and today we see him great in forgiveness. His son Absalom has revolted against him, and David grieves. He is cursed by some of his subjects, who throw stones at him. But he refuses to punish his unjust accusers. He may well have been the author of today's Responsorial Psalm:

> Many rise up against me! . . .
> But you, O Lord, are my shield;
> my glory, you lift up my head! . . .
> Rise up, O Lord!
> Save me, my God!

The gospel story is mysterious. One commentator says that the story teaches that evil is self-destructive; it cannot exist by itself, but only insofar as it can gain a foothold in the good. The one fact that stands out here—as in all Jesus' healings—is his compassion, his eagerness to heal, with everything motivated by love. And that compassion and love endure to our time in the sacraments.

324 TUESDAY OF THE FOURTH WEEK IN ORDINARY TIME

YEAR I

READING I **Heb 12:1-4**
GOSPEL **Mark 5:21-43**

No theology book could give us a better idea of the nature of the sacraments than today's gospel. The sick woman says to herself, "If I just touch his clothing, . . . I shall get well." She touches his coat and is healed. Jesus is conscious that healing power has gone out from him, and he says to the woman, "It is your faith that has cured you." When, conscious of our sinfulness and sorrow, we hold out our hand to touch Jesus, our faith unleashes his healing power now in the sacraments, even as it did then.

The advice in Reading I fits the gospel and us perfectly: "Let us keep our eyes fixed on Jesus, who inspires and perfects our faith." Eyes fixed on Jesus stirs longing for him in our hearts—and then praise.

> They who seek the Lord shall praise him:
> "May your hearts be ever merry!" (Responsorial Psalm)

A merry heart—may we always be grateful to God for such a great gift!

YEAR II

READING I **2 Sam 18:9-10, 14, 24-25, 30–19:3**
GOSPEL **Mark 5:21-43**

David's grief at his son's death is terrible to behold: "If only I had died instead of you!" he cries, as though Absalom were still alive.

But let's talk about the gospel. It provides a perfect demonstration of how the sacraments work. A stricken woman touches only Jesus' garments, and he feels that power go out from him to heal her. That's what happens in the sacraments: power goes out from Jesus to all of us who hold out our hands to him with faith.

Jesus' life-giving, "sacramental" action continues when he holds out *his* hand to the dead girl, lifts her up and commands, "Little girl, get up." And she obeys. Jesus does the same things to us every time we confess our sins with faith and sorrow. May we always remember that Jesus himself is a sacrament. He is the living sign of the compassion, mercy, and love of God to us.

325 WEDNESDAY OF THE FOURTH WEEK IN ORDINARY TIME

YEAR I

READING I **Heb 12:4-7, 11-15**
GOSPEL **Mark 6:1-6**

The counsel about suffering in Reading I is not always easy to accept: "Whom the Lord loves, he disciplines." Modern Christians might be tempted to say, if suffering means that God loves me, let God love me just a little less! But the author of Hebrews insists: "Endure your trials as the discipline of God, who deals with you as sons. For what son is there whom his father does not discipline?" What son, indeed? Even the Son of God himself. And he did not need it, as we do.

Suffering is a mystery into which the example of Jesus and the saints provides insight. We know from experience that all discipline and suffering is cause for grief and pain when it comes upon us, "but later it brings forth the fruit of peace and justice to those who are trained in its school."

> Bless the Lord, O my soul,
> and forget not all his benefits (Responsorial Psalm).

YEAR II

READING I **2 Sam 24:2, 9-17**
GOSPEL **Mark 6:1-6**

Sin is in the heart, the intent, before it is in the act. We can conclude from Reading I that David's motive for requiring a census was evil. Perhaps it was pride. In any case, he recognizes that he has sinned and asks God's forgiveness. The Responsorial Psalm perfectly expresses both David's sentiments and our own: "Lord, forgive the wrong I have done."

The gospel is familiar. Jesus returns to his hometown and is met first with admiration at his teaching, then rejection. The people could not believe in Jesus because they could not believe in themselves. How sad Jesus must be as he reflects, "No prophet is without honor, except in his native place, among his own kindred." The incident is instructive for us, too. Only when we can accept ourselves and believe in ourselves will we see our way clear to a greater faith in, and love for, Jesus.

326 THURSDAY OF THE FOURTH WEEK IN ORDINARY TIME

YEAR I

READING I **Heb 12:18-19, 21-24**
GOSPEL **Mark 6:7-13**

How do people react to God's holy presence? Reading I suggests that the human response of terror and trembling as illustrated by Moses gives way in the New Testament to an attitude of fascinated attraction. It is Jesus, the mediator of the new covenant, who makes the difference. His sprinkled blood speaks more eloquently to the Father and to us than the blood of Abel. Christ's blood tells us how much he has loved us. "God, in your temple, we ponder your love" (Responsorial Psalm).

It is above all in the Eucharist that we can personally renew our covenant with Jesus and there, too, that we can ponder his love. The gospel depicts the first missionary journey of the apostles, quite a contrast with what takes place today in the Church. But the basic elements remain: Christ's sending forth the apostles, his respect for human freedom, the call to repentance, and through it all, the love of Jesus for us to ponder, ponder, ponder.

YEAR II

READING I 1 Kgs 2:1-4, 10-12
GOSPEL Mark 6:7-13

David's life in this world is over, and all will agree that his greatness and goodness far outweighed his sinfulness. His final instruction to Solomon is good advice to us all: "Take courage and be a man." In other words, be a responsible person. David spells out the ideal he hopes Solomon will strive for. David belongs to all humankind; we can be grateful to God for him.

In the gospel, Jesus gives the apostles a preview of their future life as heralds of the good news. They are to trust in the generosity of those who receive the good news. Following the example of Jesus, they preach that all should repent—good advice in any age. They cast out demons, anoint the sick with oil, and heal them. What they did is continued now in and by the Church—a Church of sinners, for sinners, a healing Church, and thanks be to God, our home.

327 FRIDAY OF THE FOURTH WEEK IN ORDINARY TIME

YEAR I

READING I Heb 13:1-8
GOSPEL Mark 6:14-29

There is more drama in today's gospel than in almost any other New Testament incident. The chief characters demonstrate a full range of human weaknesses and strengths. There is Herod's vanity and his pathetic lust; there is violent, pitiless hatred and a spirit of revenge in Herodias; there is absolute steadfastness and dedication to God and God's law on the part of John. God knows what motivated Salome, the young girl, who may well be the really tragic figure in the whole drama. It is all part of the history of salvation that we take so much for granted, part of the mystery of redemption.

Our admiration and love for John can never be exaggerated. Jesus himself leads the way for us in praise and esteem. The evangelist says nothing about how Jesus feels about this tragedy. I think it is already part of Jesus' own passion.

YEAR II

READING I Sir 47:2-11
GOSPEL Mark 6:14-29

Hundreds of years after David, the author of Sirach gives us an admirable summary of David's triumphs and his insight into the nature of true religion: in all David did, he gave thanks to God and sang praise to him and loved him; he gave beauty to feasts and made the sanctuary resound daily with praise of God's holy name. Today's Responsorial Psalm, "Blessed be God my salvation," sums up David's response to God. Can we find anything better?

Even the starkness of Mark's style cannot conceal the fascinating power of the drama, the tragedy, of our gospel. The vengeful pitiless hatred of Herodias exploits the erotic talent of her daughter and Herod's despicable weakness and causes the death of John, the precursor. But John lives on. He continues to exhort us to prepare the way for Christ to come into our hearts and lives by removing the obstacles of sin.

328 SATURDAY OF THE FOURTH WEEK IN ORDINARY TIME

YEAR I

READING I Heb 13:15-17, 20-21
GOSPEL Mark 6:30-34

Can we ever exhaust the satisfying meaning of today's Responsorial Psalm?

> The Lord is my shepherd; I shall not want.
> In verdant pastures he gives me repose;
> Beside restful waters he leads me;
> he refreshes my soul.

All of the Father's loving solicitude toward his people is here described. Above all, the psalm depicts Jesus, the Good Shepherd, who, observing fatigue in the faces of his apostles, invites them to "come by yourselves to an out-of-the-way place and rest a little."

Human effort, exhausting activity for Christ, and the spread of the gospel are a solid duty for Christians. But Jesus himself knows by experience that all labor and no rest—even in a divine cause—can destroy an apostle. It is only in moments of solitude that we can recognize personal limitations and our absolute need for the power of Christ. To him be glory forever.

YEAR II

READING I 1 Kgs 3:4-13
GOSPEL Mark 6:30-34

Reading I gives a glimpse into the life and character of David's son, Solomon. His beginnings are most promising: he asks for an understanding heart, and God grants his prayer. How are we to understand the word "heart"—used so often in Scripture? It is the inner core of one's being that enables us to receive, ponder, and respond to God's word with grateful love and compassionate understanding of the needs of others.

This understanding heart is the goal of all education and of all prayer. We can learn all about science, literature, music, art, even theology; but if this knowledge does not reach the heart, if it is not treasured, pondered in the heart, it will never fully belong to us. For that, we need these moments of solitude in lonely places that Jesus speaks about in the gospel. May we seek our God with our whole heart.

FIFTH SUNDAY IN ORDINARY TIME Cycle A

READING I Isa 58:7-10 **READING II** 1 Cor 2:1-5
GOSPEL Matt 5:13-16

Reading I: Works of charity to those in need of any kind bring favors to those who practice them.

Reading II: Paul recalls his preaching of the gospel to the Corinthians and tells them that their faith rests not on human wisdom but on the power of God.

Gospel: Jesus tells us that, like his disciples, we are to be salt of the earth and light of the world.

Today's readings are about practical Christianity. Jesus uses vivid and familiar images to bring home to us, his followers, what it means to be a Christian. He tells us that unless people can see our faith reflected in our lives, influencing the way we think and live, it is a sham. In Reading I Isaiah speaks plainly about what is expected of us: "Share your bread . . . shelter the oppressed and the homeless . . . clothe the naked. . . . Then your light shall break forth like the dawn."

Christianity is not just for personal peace of mind or self-comfort. Jesus tells us today how important we are in God's plan to give himself to all the world, especially to those who most need God's caring love. In a word, Christianity is sharing. If it is not sharing, it is "salt free," and there is no such thing as a salt-free diet for Christ. Nor is there any kind of "salt substitute."

As always with our Lord's imagery, it is important to dig into the meaning of the words. What did he really mean when he said: "You are the salt of the earth. . . . You are the light of the world"? As we know, salt preserves food. It also seasons it, gives it taste and relish. Without salt, food is flat and uninteresting, just nourishment for the body. It doesn't make us want to praise God *or* the cook. Light is a signal: it enables us to see where we are going, points the way to a goal.

So Jesus is telling us today that what salt does for food and what light is in darkness, we, as Christians, must be for all with whom we come into contact. Our taking on the responsibility of being followers of Christ means that others, by observing us and our way of life, may find meaning, zest, and a goal for their own lives. Most of all, it means that they will be attracted to Christianity and so become salt and light themselves. And God knows how much everyone needs the salt and light of Christianity. For details, just read the daily paper, listen to the news, take a walk through the slum areas of our cities. Look at pictures of starving children in any of the Third World countries.

Today, Jesus speaks to *us.* Through you, he says, I want to open eyes to new possibilities, I want the world to be alerted to the transforming power of my love. The tragedy of so many Christian lives is that the salt they are supposed to be has become flat, no longer taste producing. And the light they are supposed to be has dimmed or has gone out. For them, Christianity has simply become a routine of spiritless religious practices. One often hears that some prominent public person is "a practicing Catholic," meaning that he or she goes to Mass regularly. But is that person's Catholicism salt and light for others?

All this does not imply that we should be demonstrative in our religious bearing and practice. That kind of Christianity is as harmful to true religion as being "unlit." Our main concern must be our *being,* our being possessed by Christ, allowing him to shine through us. If we allow him to be the light of our lives, we will light up the lives of others without our even knowing it. I doubt that Mother Teresa is concerned about being good salt and a shining light. She just *is.* She has allowed Christ to take over in her life; she is therefore possessed by his love and concern. And also by his joy. Is there anything more essential to the Christian life? If joy is absent from our lives and faces, it is a sure sign that we have allowed Christ to depart from us.

> "The just man is a light in darkness to the upright" (Responsorial Psalm). May our light shine forth!

FIFTH SUNDAY IN ORDINARY TIME Cycle B

READING I **Job 7:1-4, 6-7** **READING II** **1 Cor 9:16-19, 22-23**
GOSPEL **Mark 1:29-39**

Reading I: At a low moment in his suffering Job seems to have lost hope of seeing happiness again.

Reading II: Paul writes of his compulsion to preach the gospel and of his identification with all who suffer.

Gospel: After healing Peter's mother-in-law and many others, Jesus goes off to a lonely place to pray.

> Is not man's life on earth a drudgery?
> Are not his days those of a hireling? . . .
> My days are swifter than a weaver's shuttle;
> they come to an end without hope. . . .
> I shall not see happiness again (Reading I).

The book of Job was written between the seventh and eighth centuries B.C., but actually it might have been written yesterday or last year. We all know people who suffer without apparent hope, and perhaps we ourselves have felt that way from time to time. We have experienced moments when life seems more like an absurdity than a priceless gift from God. Often there seems to be no light at the end of the tunnel. And where is God? We pray, and even prayer seems to mock us.

Some years ago a TV station showed the soap opera *Life Can Be Beautiful. Can* life be beautiful? Yes, but not in the sense depicted by the soap opera. Fr. Ernest Larson writes:

> God does not offer a bed of roses. He offers a world with ups and downs, but a world in progress. He will set us in a thousand disparate places, places where we are needed, and asks us to be true. He will not baby us, shield us from pain. He will lead us through pain, loneliness, frustration, searching, to the strong, gentle wisdom he alone can create in us.

We Christians are often accused of being so preoccupied with the *after*life that we seem not to know how to live *this* life. And we do not know how to tell others how to live it either. But Christianity is not, must not be, a life-negating religion. Jesus did not come to take the joy out of life. He brought good news. Life is a gift of God, who loves and cares for each of us. It makes little sense to worry about the life to come in another world if we are not serious about learning how to live in this world.

But how can we find meaning and self-fulfillment? Certainly not without some positive human relationships with others in our families, communities, parishes. Not without friendship, compassion, and concern for others, especially for the needy and lonely. No person's life is a failure if he or she has learned how to love and sacrifice for others.

In today's gospel, Jesus is our model, overflowing with pity and compassion, healing the sick, dispelling demons, proclaiming the good news of God's love for all. Then rising early and going off to a lonely place to pray, to commune with his Father. He shows us how to live and find meaning in life. Apart from him and his example and never-ceasing grace, life can indeed be absurd and meaningless. "Everybody is looking for you," the apostles tell him. Instinctively they know that he had the answers to their needs. He still does.

Not that he will take away the pain and make life beautiful in the soap opera sense. Suffering is part of life. Someone has said that suffering is not a problem to be solved, but a mystery to be lived. Jesus alone can give insight into that mystery. But he wants us to come seeking, he wants us to want to be helped and healed. More than anything else, he wants trust, faith, and confidence in him—and all the love we can gather up.

When we need him most, Jesus is most present to us and with us. Our praying is best when we don't feel like praying, don't experience any apparent results. As a matter of fact, this experience of darkness might well be the sign that we are moving from childhood to adulthood in our lives as true followers of Christ.

Let us

> Praise the Lord who heals the brokenhearted . . .
> and binds up their wounds (Responsorial Psalm).

Being a follower of Christ is risky, because Christianity makes some frightening demands upon us. But then, is it possible to find any kind of meaning for life without risk and pain? The alternative is to be like Job: sitting on his manure pile, feeling sorry for himself, wallowing in self-pity.

Job came through in the end, because he learned how to trust in God. We can do the same—even more effectively—because, unlike Job, we have Jesus who is our life, our hope, our love. "Everybody is looking for you," the apostles said. Please God, we have looked too, and have found him!

76 FIFTH SUNDAY IN ORDINARY TIME Cycle C

READING I **Isa 6:1-2, 3-8** **READING II** **1 Cor 15:1-11**
GOSPEL **Luke 5:1-11**

Reading I: The prophet Isaiah has a vision of the glory of God and reacts with a deep awareness of his unworthiness, but he accepts God's call to do God's work.

Reading II: Paul, the last of the apostles to be called, gives the Corinthians a summary of the content of his preaching.

Gospel: Luke gives a short account of Jesus preaching from Peter's boat, a miraculous catch of fish, and the apostles accepting Christ's call to follow him.

The Old Testament is a history of God's calling the chosen people, their response, and also God's call to individual persons to work with God for God's purposes. It is a theme that Jesus continues in his own time and in all stages of the history of his Church. The theme of today's readings is vocation, the Lord's special call to us all. At the end of Reading I the voice of the Lord is heard: "Whom shall I send? Who will go for us?" The prophet Isaiah responds: "Here am I, . . . send me!" Noble words, the ideal response and prayer of every Christian.

God called Mary, the mother of Jesus, and her response is familiar to all: "I am the servant of the Lord. Let it be done to me as you say" (Luke 1:38). Doing the will of the Father motivated all of Jesus' life. Jesus invited his apostles to follow him and carry on his work, and today's gospel tells us that "they left everything, and became his followers."

This is vocation: a divine summons to leave the past behind and to launch out into the great unknown, into a life of adventure, the details of which are known to the Lord alone. Every vocation is a call to leave selfish ways and ambitions and to enter upon a new life—a life of service to God, by means of service to God's people.

Most Catholics, when they hear the word "vocation," immediately think of the vocation to the priesthood or the religious life. That conception is too limited. The great majority of men and women have a vocation to marriage or to the single life "in the world" rather than to membership in a religious community. And within these so-called "lay vocations," there are vocations to various professions.

Every vocation, whether it is to priesthood, religious life, marriage, or the single life, requires responsible, courageous persons capable of deep trust in the Lord who calls them, persons who are unafraid of risk.

To be sure, religious and priests do have a call from God to a particular way of life, a way of life that involves ministering to others in a very special way. And God knows how desperately the Church needs men and women to meet that call. Many, perhaps most, people need help in discerning whether or not God is calling them to a priestly or religious vocation, and such help is usually available from pastors, teachers, parents, or friends.

Many Catholics do not realize that the Church herself has a call from God, a special vocation to carry out the Lord's work in every age. The Church is an assembly of those who have been called to all the great variety of vocations. But the Church as such also has a call. Jesus is always calling his Church forward, onward, to meet the challenges and needs of the emerging, evolving world and its peoples *everywhere.* Every age has its own call, its own challenge, to invite people to respond to the lordship of God. Every age is a call to a new adventure for the Church as a whole, as well as for each individual member, a call always to go forward, never to be self-satisfied.

The Church is a living organism, not just an organization. Christ is the head, we are the members. Like every organism this body must grow, and if it does not grow and meet its challenges, it will die. It may be comfortable for the members of the Church to want to live in the past and to bask in the security of her glorious history (at some periods not so glorious).

Cardinal Suhard of Paris experienced this call at the end of World War II when he wrote his famous pastoral letter, *Growth or Decline,* in which he saw a new world taking shape. A contemporary writes: "He saw it [the new world] not as a sign of impending disaster, but as an extraordinary opportunity for the Church." The Church is constantly being called by God to give meaning and shape to the world that is forever in the making.

History is constantly being made by men and women who have responded to the call of Jesus: "Put out into deep water and lower your nets for a catch." The tragic figures of history are those who refused the call or, once having heard and heeded it, regret their choice and turn back.

Much could be written about these readings. I think especially about how God calls us from one stage of life to another, ultimately to the very special vocations of old age and finally death. These two are calls from God to serve the people of God, perhaps most of all by prayer, suffering, and mature joy. Each stage of life presents a challenge, each stage is a moment of grace for us and for our world. And Jesus is with us always, we are always with him in Peter's boat, the Church. Jesus says to us now and always: "Do not be afraid. From now on you will be catching men." In our hearts and on our lips we cry: Here am I, Lord. Send me!

329 MONDAY OF THE FIFTH WEEK IN ORDINARY TIME

YEAR I

READING I **Gen 1:1-19**
GOSPEL **Mark 6:53-56**

Today we begin the Book of Genesis and the story of creation. What is important in the account of creation and the fall of man is the theology behind the story and its deep meaning. We contemplate above all the theology of God as creator, as Lord and king over all creation, and the obligations on our part that follow from the fact of God's lordship over all. We will be following those obligations as the story in the first eleven chapters of Genesis unfolds.

Today I would only like to point out one interesting and important truth: God saw that everything he made was good. This is very instructive because there are some Christians who seem to dispute that truth. The fulfillment of the psalmist's prayer depends on us: "May the Lord be glad in his works." He will be glad if *we* are.

YEAR II

READING I **1 Kgs 8:1-7, 9-13**
GOSPEL **Mark 6:53-56**

The ark of the covenant was the most prized possession of the Jews. It contained the two tables of the Law Moses had received from God on Mount Sinai. Solomon enshrines the ark in the holy of holies—so sacred a place that only the high priest could enter, and only once a year.

For the Jews, the ark was the sign of God's abiding presence in their midst. The fact that the Temple—with its holy of holies containing the ark and the cloud indicating God's presence—exists no longer does not mean that God is no longer present in the people's midst. God is in the tabernacles of our churches, in the word we hear day after day, in each of us who lives the life of grace. Lord, grant us faith to believe St. Paul when he says: "Are you not aware that you are the temple of God. . . ? For the temple of God is holy, and you are that temple" (1 Cor 3:16).

330 TUESDAY OF THE FIFTH WEEK IN ORDINARY TIME

YEAR I

READING I **Gen 1:20–2:4**
GOSPEL **Mark 7:1-13**

Secrets are hard to keep. God could not keep the secret of his own goodness, so he told that secret in creation. He created the world and all that is in it, and he saw that it was good. He created human beings who resembled him in their ability to choose, to think, and to love—men and women capable of listening to God's secret and responding to it with love.

The Responsorial Psalm is one of humankind's most beautiful responses to God's beauty:

O Lord, our God,
  how wonderful your name in all the earth! . . .
What is man that you should be mindful of him, . . .
You have made him little less than the angels,
  and crowned him with glory and honor.

The essential point about the account of creation is that it is God who creates, that what God creates is good, and that when we forget how we are related to God and to the world, all hell breaks loose.

YEAR II

READING I 1 Kgs 8:22-23, 27-30
GOSPEL Mark 7:1-13

The Temple, completed by Solomon in 955 B.C., was destroyed by the Babylonians in 589. Solomon's prayer of dedication is magnificent. He recognizes that God cannot be confined in any earthly dwelling—heaven and earth cannot contain God. Temples made by men can be splendid, they can even provide a foretaste of heaven, as the Responsorial Psalm indicates:

How lovely is your dwelling-place,
Lord, mighty God!

But when the purpose of a temple or church as an expression of our love and reverence for God is forgotten and the building becomes a monument to human builders, when in the temple we honor God with our lips and not with our hearts, then our worship is in vain and the temple is in danger of destruction. Temples are not ends in themselves. They are means to bring us closer to God, to stir up our hunger for him.

331 WEDNESDAY OF THE FIFTH WEEK IN ORDINARY TIME

YEAR I

READING I Gen 2:5-9, 15-17
GOSPEL Mark 7:14-23

Today's account of creation is slightly different from yesterday's. Here God is depicted as creating humankind before the rest of creatures—the first object of God's activity, related to the earth that is destined for his use. He has a special kind of life, for the Lord God blew into his nostrils "the breath of life." So we have Adam settled in the garden to cultivate and care for it.

The stage is set for the trial of our freedom, and we know what will happen. There may be some who would question God's decision to make us free. Obviously, God thought the risk was worth taking, for he knew that without freedom there can be no love, and a world without love was definitely not the kind of world God was interested in—or wanted. Neither do we. Because we are free, we can say,

> Bless the Lord, O my soul! (Responsorial Psalm)

YEAR II

READING I 1 Kgs 10:1-10
GOSPEL Mark 7:14-23

Solomon's reputation for wisdom has spread far. When the queen of Sheba hears of it, she comes to see for herself. She is more than satisfied with his answers to her questions and her observations on how he conducts his life. "Blessed be the Lord your God, whom it has pleased to place you on the throne of Israel," she tells him.

In the Gospel Jesus corrects a false interpretation of the Law by the Pharisees: "What emerges from within a man, that and nothing else is what makes him impure," not any kind of food they eat. What comes out of a man are evil thoughts and every other kind of corruption. Jesus has nothing against sanitation. What he objects to is the notion that pious practices apart from sincerity can make a person religious. We can be as bad as the Pharisees when we exalt a literal fulfillment of Church regulations over love for neighbor and sincerity of heart.

332 THURSDAY OF THE FIFTH WEEK IN ORDINARY TIME

YEAR I

READING I Gen 2:18-25
GOSPEL Mark 7:24-30

We are told in today's account of the creation of woman that man and woman share the same human nature, the same rights and privileges, the same almost divine dignity. It is difficult to figure out how the position and dignity of women became lowered in mid-Eastern culture after these beautiful beginnings.

There is one exception to the general low opinion of women that developed—that of Jesus, whose respect for women was unbounded, who could never refuse any woman any favor. Today's gospel is typical. The woman would not take no for an answer. Jesus argues with her, but she wins because she knows how to attack him at his weakest point—his compassion. I am sure he smiled as he granted her plea: "Be off now! The demon has already left your daughter." Why not try the same argument the next time you need something?

YEAR II

READING I 1 Kgs 11:4-13
GOSPEL Mark 7:24-30

So Solomon is human like the rest of us! The author of Reading I blames his wives for turning him from the one true God, but his guilt is his own because his heart was no longer true to the Lord his God. God had made Solomon in God's own image and made him great; Solomon turned the tables; he tried to create a god after his own image and likeness. That has never worked in any age.

The pagan woman in the gospel is one of the most intriguing of all the gospel women. She beats Jesus in an argument and makes him like it! He actually seems to be playing with her. I prefer to think that he enjoys and admires her and her refusal to give up, especially her cleverness at repartee. Matthew has him say: "Woman, you have great faith! Your wish will come to pass." And so it was done. I can't believe that Jesus worked this miracle without a smile.

333 FRIDAY OF THE FIFTH WEEK IN ORDINARY TIME

YEAR I

READING I Gen 3:1-8
GOSPEL Mark 7:31-37

Only God knows the full extent of the tragedy contained in today's account of the fall of Adam and Eve. God had risked giving them freedom, trusted them, but they failed the test. They forgot that God was God and they were creatures; they wanted to be like God. They fell, and we still experience the sad results of their fall.

This is the entrance of evil into the world—the source of the wide river of evil into which we pour the evil flowing from our own wounded hearts. There is nothing very original about original sin. All humankind in some mysterious way fell in Adam, who disobeyed God. In an equally mysterious way, all humankind will be restored to God's friendship through the obedience of Jesus, the second Adam. God's love for us will not take no for an answer.

YEAR II

READING I 1 Kgs 11:29-32; 12:19
GOSPEL Mark 7:31-37

Reading I describes one of the tragic moments in Jewish history—the division of the kingdom between those faithful to the house and tradition of David and those in rebellion.

In the gospel, Jesus heals a man who is deaf and has an impediment of speech. It is a truism that we who are physically whole take our senses for granted, but taking anything (or anyone) for granted diminishes us. Too often we see without seeing and hear without hearing: we miss the full meaning of the value that seeks entrance into our heart. This, sadly, is what often happens to God's word. So today Jesus says to us, be opened, open the ear of your heart, for it is only when we *hear* with our hearts that we will be able to *know* in our hearts that Jesus has truly done all things well.

334 SATURDAY OF THE FIFTH WEEK IN ORDINARY TIME

YEAR I

READING I Gen 3:9-24
GOSPEL Mark 8:1-10

Reading I tells how sin shattered the correct relationships between us and our God, between us and our inner being, between us and the created universe. Adam no longer sees himself as a child of God but as a slave who hides from God. He is ashamed of his nakedness. The loving relationship with his wife gives way to accusation. And the earth will rebel against Adam, who must henceforth eat his bread in the sweat of his brow.

From this first sin flow all the wounded relationships of our lives. So Genesis helps us to understand ourselves, our world, our family and community life—yes, even the fact that water has to be filtered before it is drunk. It could be a dismal, hopeless picture, except for the promise God gives even here of hope and redemption. In every age the Lord has been our refuge, and so he will always be.

YEAR II

READING I 1 Kgs 12:26-32; 13:33-34
GOSPEL Mark 8:1-10

Reading I depicts the depths to which the kingdom of Israel, the northern kingdom, fell. The worship of idols is substituted for the worship of the one true God. How appropriate is the sentiment of the Responsorial Psalm:

> We have sinned, . . .
> we have committed crimes; we have done wrong.

The sin of the king and his people can happen to anyone, us included, when we refuse to remember all that God has done for us. We too can be in danger of worshiping false gods, we too can exchange the glory of God for "the image of a grass-eating bullock."

The gospel relates one of Christ's several miraculous multiplications of loaves and fishes for the hungry people on whom he has compassion. Here the people hardly seem to realize what he has done. Do we do any better at Mass, a much greater miracle? At Mass, where he does indeed remember us for the love he bears his people.

77 SIXTH SUNDAY IN ORDINARY TIME Cycle A

READING I Sir 15:15-20 **READING II** I Cor 2:6-10
GOSPEL Matt 5:17-37

Reading I: Keeping God's commandments depends on free human choice; God sees and knows all that we do.

Reading II: God grants the spiritually mature a share in divine wisdom, which enables us to make decisions in obedience to God's will.

Gospel: Jesus clarifies our ideas about true morality, which is obedience to God's law out of a motive of love.

The theme of today's readings is Christian morality—what it is and what it is not. Jesus says in the gospel, "Unless your holiness surpasses that of the scribes and Pharisees you shall not enter the kingdom of God." Today's readings make us ask ourselves: How much love is there in our observance of the commandments? Does Jesus' having lived, suffered, and died out of love for us make any difference in the way we live?

What is morality for us? If it is just a rigid, slavish, fear-inspired, loveless, mechanical obeying of rules and laws, it's plain ethics. And one doesn't have to be a Christian to be merely ethical. With ethics alone, we will hardly satisfy God's desire for our holiness. Jesus wants morality—Christian morality. And Christian morality is a free, personal, loving responsiveness to him who is divine love and goodness in person.

What is characteristic about genuine Christians is their wholeheartedness in their responsiveness to what Jesus is to them and what he has done for them. Saints become saints not because they are more ethical than ordinary people but because they are more in love. Christian morality tells us not so much what we are to do. Christian morality tells us that we are to live and act from a motive of deepest love for our God.

Fr. William Shannon writes:

> Jesus did not come simply to make us better persons [though he certainly did that]; primarily he came to make us *new persons.* The sequence is not that we improve our conduct and thereby become better persons; rather the sequence is that we become new persons in Christ, and because we have become new persons, our conduct is different. Jesus came not just to change what we do but to change who we are.

God does not want our literal obedience so much as he wants our personal, freely given love. The trouble with the morality of so many Christians is that it is devoid of love—a morality practiced either out of fear of eternal punishment or to win God's favor. We can fulfill the ideal of the Sermon on the Mount, the ideal of morality after the mind of Christ, only if we act out of the fullness of the newness he has given us in baptism.

Morality after the mind of Christ also involves relationships with our neighbor. "If you bring your gift to the altar and there recall that your brother has anything against you, leave your gift there at the altar, go first and be reconciled with your brother, and then come and offer your gift" (Gospel). Strong words: reconciliation with one's neighbor even takes precedence over worship of God. Theologian Frank Sheed used to say, "We cannot be rightly related to God unless we are rightly related to our neighbor."

Can we really love God in our hearts and lust after someone else or something that belongs to another? Does our newness in Christ, our identity with him, allow that kind of mentality? Conversely, the best remedy against sexual immorality is a deep reverence and respect for persons *as persons*—a respect based on their newness, their identity with Christ.

> Happy are they who follow the law of the Lord! (Responsorial Psalm)

Why happy? Because they have discovered what true love is. They have learned how to love and how to allow God to love them by giving them a new being in Christ, a new being with which they can fulfill the law of God as God wishes it to be fulfilled.

READING I Lev 13:1-2, 44-46 **READING II** 1 Cor 10:31–11:1
GOSPEL Mark 1:40-45

Reading I: We have Old Testament regulations for anyone with an infectious disease—especially, total separation from the community.

Reading II: Paul presents a very concise view of his philosophy of life: living for others and so glorifying God.

Gospel: Mark recounts how Jesus healed a leper by a word and a touch.

Reading I and the gospel speak of leprosy, and the thought that is likely to come to mind is that leprosy symbolizes sin. This is true, but there is something deeper here: it is what leprosy did to its victim in terms of the rest of the community. In that ancient Hebrew society a leper was ostracized, completely cut off from any kind of communication with other people. The leper had to shout, "Unclean, unclean!" when anyone approached, and he himself could never come near to anyone.

One wonders what was harder to bear—the disease itself or the dread feeling of rejection and scorn. In our own country and in South Africa black people can understand that better than the rest of us. The segregation from the community was mutual. No one could approach and certainly not touch a leper, even if he or she would want to.

That was the custom and the Law, as derived from Leviticus. So we can see that something completely out of the ordinary and even illegal takes place in today's gospel. Instead of standing far off, the leper comes to Jesus, kneels before him, and cries out, "If you will to do so, you can cure me." And Jesus, feeling pity for him, stretches out his hand, *touches* him, and says: "I do will it. Be cured."

Something extraordinary happens. The man is instantly cured and restored to happy membership in his community, but Jesus becomes, as it were, an outcast, unable to enter a town openly. In a way, this may be a preview of the passion.

This gospel has at least two applications for our lives. If leprosy is a symbol of sin, we need healing and we cry out to Christ, "If you will to do so, you can cure me." And the same Jesus who healed the leper says to us: "I do will it. Be cured." This incident is a perfect portrayal of what the sacrament of reconciliation is and does—and also what Lent can mean to us.

But there is another application. The gospel makes us ask ourselves: who are the lepers in our lives? Whom do we ostracize or try to segregate? How do we feel about people of different races, different religions? How does this attitude of ours—if it includes any desire for segregation—compare with that of Jesus? Remember, he *touched* the leper. Are we willing to reach out to those we have segregated and extend a hand of reconciliation and friendship? Is there anything in our attitude that would make them want to come to us for help?

If not, we might ask ourselves other questions: Do we really know ourselves as we are? Do we wear masks that conceal us from our true selves? The point is, if we are completely satisfied with ourselves as we are, we don't really need Jesus. And we may be worse off than the leper in the gospel. Then, surely, we need Christ's healing touch.

Finally, do we ourselves feel alienated and unwanted because of personal sins or physical appearance or a low opinion of ourselves? The answer to all these questions is Jesus Christ. All we have to do is to go to him and cry out, "If you will to do so, you can cure me." It might be a good idea to make our next confession with that thought in mind.

Jesus is aware of all our problems, our worries, our weaknesses, our inability or unwillingness to love and forgive, our bitterness, our lack of hope, our waning faith. No matter. He is still moved with pity and compassion. He is ready to effect a cure in us, to give us grace to change our lives and restore us to full, happy membership in the people of God. All we have to do is to make our own the sentiments of today's Responsorial Psalm:

> I turn to you, Lord, in time of trouble,
>   and you fill me with the joy of salvation.
> Then I acknowledge my sin to you,
>   my guilt I covered not.
> I said, "I confess my faults to the Lord,"
>   and you took away the guilt of my sin.

If you will to do so, you can cure me. "I do will it," Jesus says. "Be cured."

79 SIXTH SUNDAY IN ORDINARY TIME Cycle C

READING I Jer 17:5-8 **READING II** 1 Cor 15:12, 16-20
GOSPEL Luke 6:17, 20-26

Reading I: Desolate and desperate is the person who tries to find happiness in material possessions instead of in God.

Reading II: Paul presents a strong argument for the resurrection of Jesus as the basis of our hope in our own resurrection.

Gospel: Luke's version of the Sermon on the Mount contrasts the blessedness of the poor in spirit with the ultimate distress of those who put their trust in riches.

It is easy to narrow down today's readings and make them mean what *we* want them to mean. That is always a temptation when we study or hear God's word. Today both Reading I and the gospel present two ways of life—the one positive, the other negative: we are to trust in the Lord who alone can satisfy our hungers, not in wealth, superior knowledge, or any kind of human achievement.

First of all, Jesus does not idealize or romanticize poverty. Poverty is an evil about which the popes of recent years have been deeply concerned. Neither the Church nor the government can be indifferent to the destitution and homelessness in our own country or in the Third World, where people of all ages are dying of starvation.

Nor did Jesus ever condemn riches as such. Some of his best friends were wealthy. But he seriously warned against the dangers of riches—the possibility of allowing riches to possess the possessor, thus closing his or her heart to the plight of the poor and unfortunate and above all to God. The real danger of possessions is that we try to find security in them, that we place our trust and hope in things rather than in God.

Fr. John Jay Hughes points out that finding security in riches is a kind of "practical atheism." "To be an atheist you need not deny that God exists. You need only live *as if* God did not exist. . . . To be a practical atheist it is sufficient to put your trust anywhere but in God" (*The Priest,* January 1983).

The word "anywhere" has several potential meanings. Father Hughes describes one meaning that may surprise some Catholics: "It is even possible to have *spiritual* riches which prevent our trusting in God. Many Catholics trust more in the prayers they say and the good works they perform than they do in God's mercy. That, too, is practical atheism."

The armed forces used to give, perhaps still does, good conduct medals to members who never got into trouble and were faithful to their duties. There may be danger of Christians trying to earn "good conduct medals," too. The good works we do or have done are important, as is our fidelity to the demands of our way of life, especially our prayer life; but these are not to be looked upon as guarantees of heavenly dividends. They are not a spiritual "life insurance policy." At our judgment, if we appeal to our good works and good conduct, we are placing our trust not in an all-merciful God but in ourselves, our own personal achievements. We cannot buy salvation, we cannot put God in debt to us.

Remember our Lord's words in Matthew's gospel:

> "None of those who cry out, 'Lord, Lord,' will enter the kingdom of God but only the one who does the will of my Father in heaven. When that day comes, many will plead with me, 'Lord, Lord, have we not prophesied in your name? . . . Did we not do many miracles in your name as well?' Then I will declare to them solemnly, 'I never knew you. Out of my sight, you evildoers!' " (7:21-23)

This is not to downgrade good works—especially service and sensitivity to the poor. But works are our *response* of grateful love for all that God has done for us (and continues to do), not an eternal fire insurance policy. To quote Father Hughes again: "To be spiritually poor is to know that our greatest and best efforts for God are still inadequate as a response for all that God has done for us. To be spiritually poor is to know that before God we stand empty-handed."

Lent is about to begin. Lent is a time of spiritual renewal and conversion for us all, for the entire Church. The best way to experience Lent is to stand empty-handed, overflowing with hope and desire before our God, hoping in God, trusting, pleading that during this holy season the Lord will fill us to overflowing with faith and trust in Jesus.

> Blessed is the man who trusts in the Lord,
> whose hope is in the Lord (Reading I).

335 MONDAY OF THE SIXTH WEEK IN ORDINARY TIME

YEAR I

READING I Gen 4:1-15, 25
GOSPEL Mark 8:11-13

Cain forgets how he is related to God and to his brother. He assumes the creator's mastery over life and kills his brother. It is a replay of original sin. But why did the Lord look with favor on Abel's sacrifice and not on Cain's? Actually, both performed a religious act, both offered worthy gifts, so the problem had to be in the givers. It is not what we offer to God that matters but how it is offered.

This is our concern, too. Do we worship out of fear, wanting to put God in debt to us, or do we worship and acknowledge God's lordship over our lives because he is God and we are his children who love him? Offer to God a sacrifice of praise with no hope of reward: that is religion, pure and undefiled. As with Adam and Eve, God forgives Cain and promises him protection. And so he always does with us. If God forgives, should we not forgive ourselves?

YEAR II

READING I Jas 1:1-11
GOSPEL Mark 8:11-13

Today we begin readings from the Letter of James the apostle. The letter is said to be more a sermon stressing morality than an exposition of doctrine. It touches very practical concerns of Christians. Thus, James sees good in the trials a person encounters because trials produce steadfastness. When we ask God for a favor, we are to ask "in faith, never doubting."

The gospel shows Jesus in conflict with the Pharisees. They say they want a sign from heaven, presumably providing a proof that he is the Messiah. We can almost hear the sigh rising from the depths of Christ's being when he says, "Why does this age seek a sign?" What has he been doing in his miracles if not providing signs? No power on earth can make a person believe if that person doesn't want to. How willing are we to believe?

336 TUESDAY OF THE SIXTH WEEK IN ORDINARY TIME

YEAR I

READING I **Gen 6:5-8; 7:1-5, 10**
GOSPEL **Mark 8:14-21**

There is a never-ending fascination connected with the great Flood, and every once in a while there are reports of the remains of Noah's ark having been discovered on Mount Ararat. The real meaning of the story of the Flood is that people again refused to admit that they were creatures and that God was God. This is still another version of the fall of man and woman. People do not seem to be able to learn from history. As was said before, we all contribute by our sins to the river of evil that had its source in the fall of our first parents.

But the story of Noah and his family is also a story of forgiveness and, above all, of redemption. God shows mercy to those who remember that God is their God and they are God's creatures. Our hearts tell us:

> Give to the Lord glory and praise,
> Give to the Lord the glory due his name (Responsorial Psalm).

If we give that glory, then we too can be sure that "the Lord will bless his people with peace."

YEAR II

READING I **Jas 1:12-18**
GOSPEL **Mark 8:14-21**

James tells us that we cannot say that God tempts us. God tempts no one. It is our own evil desires that lure and entice us, not God. We can't blame sin and temptation on God, nor can we blame natural catastrophes like earthquakes on him. God is responsible only for the good endowments and perfect gifts we receive, the best gift being our very existence and God's grace in us. "He wills to bring us to birth with a word spoken in truth so that we may be a kind of first fruits of his creatures."

The gospel shows us Jesus almost losing patience with his apostles because of their lack of faith in him. Concern about empty stomachs makes them forget who it is who has called and cared for them up to now. What Jesus probably wants here is not a blind faith that will work a miracle for them, but that they at least begin to glimpse the spiritual nature of his mission, to which the miracles point. Do we see it?

337 WEDNESDAY OF THE SIXTH WEEK IN ORDINARY TIME

YEAR I

READING I Gen 8:6-13, 20-22
GOSPEL Mark 8:22-26

The emphasis in today's Reading I is on salvation. The saving vessel that carries Noah and his family is the ark, built according to the directives of Yahweh. To show his gratitude to his saving God, the first thing Noah does when he touches dry land is to offer sacrifice to the Lord. Compared to Adam and Eve and to all sinners who refuse to admit God's sovereignty, Noah has his relationships straight.

It does not take much imagination to see the ark as a symbol of the Church—also built according to God's directives—in which we ride the waves of the world, and to see Noah's sacrifice as a type of our sacrifice of the Mass. The Mass is essentially a sacrifice of praise and gratitude. With and in Christ we can cry out:

> To you, Lord, I will offer a sacrifice of praise.
> My vows to the Lord I will pay
> in the presence of all his people (Responsorial Psalm).

YEAR II

READING I Jas 1:19-27
GOSPEL Mark 8:22-26

As individuals and as a community, we could save ourselves a lot of pain and problems if we could follow through on all of James' practical suggestions for Christian living. His whole philosophy can be summed up in these words: "Humbly welcome the word that has taken root in you, with its power to save you. Act on this word." If the word does not shape our lives, what use is it? I believe that there is a deeper meaning to the word "word" than we usually attribute to it. We may see it as the Word, as Christ himself, who takes root in us in our baptism, who is constantly speaking to us in the gospel. He is the heart of our lives. If he is one with us and we with him, then we will not only avoid negative behavior unworthy of him, we will allow him to think, judge, and act in us. The gospel shows us Jesus restoring sight to a blind man. Fr. Carroll Stuhlmueller has a beautiful insight into this incident. Jesus heals the blind man in stages. First he takes him by the hand and leads him outside the town; then he touches his eyes with his spittle and lays hands on him twice. Why? Because he wants the man to *feel* his compassion. He bonds himself to him. And we, by reading or hearing this passage with faith, can also experience the compassion and caring of Jesus.

338 THURSDAY OF THE SIXTH WEEK IN ORDINARY TIME

YEAR I

READING I **Gen 9:1-13**
GOSPEL **Mark 8:27-33**

The rainbow, joining heaven and earth is the Lord's own sacrament, the beautiful sign of God's forgiving love for all God's children (see Reading I). Mark, Matthew, and Luke all have Jesus asking, "Who do you say that I am?" The question is addressed to the apostles, but also to us. We have to make up our minds about him. Peter's answer, "You are the Messiah," is perfect. The trouble is that Peter's idea of the Messiah differs from that of Jesus, who immediately speaks of his coming passion and death, and he strongly rebukes Peter when the latter tries to change his mind. Then in the first verse of tomorrow's gospel he tells the apostles and *us*, "If a man wishes to come after me, he must deny his very self, take up his cross and follow in my steps." Is it hard for us to accept that condition? Do we try to avoid it? It can't be done. But if the going gets hard, it will help a lot to remember the rainbow of God's love joining our suffering to that of Christ, and to take heart.

YEAR II

READING I Jas 2:1-9
GOSPEL Mark 8:27-33

The gospel tells us that Jesus wants all of his followers to make up their minds about him. Who is Jesus to you? "Who do you say that I am?" You alone can answer that question. No one can do it for you. Have you ever tried it? The Christ you have to decide about is he who will save you by suffering and dying.

In Reading I, James gives us some idea of what it means to try to live according to Christ's standards. We are to judge and esteem people not according to social or financial status but simply as persons. James undoubtedly remembers that Jesus identified himself with the poor, the deprived, the wretched ones of the earth. As James did, we might well wonder why it is that we pay so much honor to the rich and privileged and ignore or take for granted those who have nothing to give us in return but Jesus. "What you do to the least of these you do to me." Remember?

339 FRIDAY OF THE SIXTH WEEK IN ORDINARY TIME

YEAR I

READING I Gen 11:1-9
GOSPEL Mark 8:34–9:1

One way of defining sin is to see it as a refusal to recognize the relationship of total dependence humans ought to have upon God. This was the case with Adam and Eve. It is the case with the people in today's Reading I. They want to make a name for themselves by building a tower reaching to heaven. They want to be like God himself. But "the Lord brought the counsel of the nations to naught, he frustrated the plans of his people." And as the psalmist says, they suffered the consequences of their pride and ambition. So it always has been, so it always will be.

How different is the way of Jesus! "If a man wishes to come after me, he must deny his very self, take up his cross, and follow in my steps." Which way do we choose, the way of the people of Babel or the way of Christ?

YEAR II

READING I Jas 2:14-24, 26
GOSPEL Mark 8:34–9:1

Today James claims that "faith without works is as dead as a body without breath." But he would certainly reject the mentality that a person can buy God's favor by works—great or small. That was the way of the Pharisees that Jesus condemned. Salvation is a sheer gift from God that we can in no way merit by works. We can simply accept it with joyous gratitude and respond to it with works of charity. Faith and works belong together. True faith, that relationship of loving trust in Jesus, will necessarily manifest itself in works of charity toward others.

It is in this way that we are to understand Jesus' words to us in the gospel. Because he has died and risen to save us, should we not be willing to deny ourselves, take up the cross of daily suffering, illness, worry, and pain, and follow him?

340 SATURDAY OF THE SIXTH WEEK IN ORDINARY TIME

YEAR I

READING I Heb 11:1-7
GOSPEL Mark 9:2-13

Reading I, from Hebrews, defines faith and then illustrates the definition by the lives of illustrious Old Testament characters. These people were pleasing to God because by faith they obeyed God and accepted God's lordship, even though they did not understand what God asked of them. They did not understand. They loved. They trusted.

The gospel shows us Jesus as he really is—the God-man. The apostles had known him only as man, one they had come to love passionately. To prepare them for his coming passion and death, he now shows himself to them as more than man. They loved being there. It was a foretaste of heaven. They wanted to stay. Then they heard, "This is my Son, my beloved. Listen to him." The people of old mentioned in Hebrews lived by faith in a Messiah to come. We have him: beloved Son, beloved Jesus, Savior. Let us listen to him and follow him.

YEAR II

READING I Jas 3:1-10
GOSPEL Mark 9:2-13

The gospel illustrates the fundamental human attitudes in the presence of the divine. Peter is fascinated by the divine presence and wants to stay forever. But another attitude soon presses the apostles to the ground in fearful awareness of their sinfulness. Hopefully, we experience those same attitudes of fascination and peace along with a sense of awe whenever we are present at Mass. For what takes place here is every bit as splendid as the transfiguration.

It is hard to imagine a more cutting, harsh, but true analysis of how we sometimes think and speak than the one given by James today. With our tongues we can bless God, but we can—and do—curse, wound, and destroy people made in God's likeness by our words. The evil we speak comes from diseased hearts. That is why we pray: A clean heart create in us, O Lord. Deliver us from evil.

80 SEVENTH SUNDAY IN ORDINARY TIME — Cycle A

READING I Lev 19:1-2, 17-18 **READING II** 1 Cor 3:16-23
GOSPEL Matt 5:38-48

Reading I: God commands his people: "Be holy, for I, the Lord, your God, am holy." It is a command that can only be fulfilled by love.

Reading II: Paul tells us that we are temples of God, and therefore, we are to live up to our dignity.

Gospel: Mark gives Jesus' version of the Leviticus command: love of neighbor must even include love for enemies.

I heard of a Broadway play in which a character said: "God never made a better woman than I am, but somehow I just can't seem to live up to it." We could probably all make the same statement (except for the first part). We just don't seem to be able to live up to our dignity as children of God, indwelled by the Holy Spirit (see Reading II).

In Reading I the Lord tells the people: "Be holy, for I, the Lord, your God, am holy." And the Lord proceeds immediately to relate a person's holiness to his or her relationships with others. "You shall not bear hatred . . . in your heart . . . take no revenge . . . cherish no grudge. . . . You shall love your neighbor as yourself."

We probably all have to admit that we haven't quite been able to live up to this divine ideal. In no area of life is fallen human nature more evident. In practice, we seem to do everything possible to explain away the Lord's command.

Life involves human relationships through which we either grow in holiness or deteriorate as human beings and, even worse, as followers of Jesus. We all are aware of our common, day-to-day failings:

—So-and-so offends us in some way, even unintentionally. Do we forgive as Jesus commands us to forgive?
—We cherish grudges against persons, we seek occasions to be scandalized by what they say, do, or write. We develop the odious habit of judging others.
—There are the occasions when we deliberately trot out our grievances and antagonisms and share them with others—we indulge in the ugly, demeaning habit of gossiping, without realizing that gossiping harms us as much as it harms its victims.

Jesus insists so strongly on loving one another and on forgiveness because he knows that Christianity can attract others only if non-Christians can see love in the lives of Christians. "This is how all will know you for my disciples: your love for one another" (John 13:35).

Another reason why Jesus insists so strongly on this commandment is that there is no way of our being made whole, being made into his perfect disciple, without it. We cannot be fully redeemed without love. Lack of love frustrates and diminishes Christ's redeeming life and death. He came to make us whole and holy, and we reject his love.

If all this positive argument does not convince us of our need to grow in holiness by and through love, maybe Paul's threat can help bring us to our senses. He is writing to us as well as to the Corinthians:

> Are you not aware that you are the temple of God, and that the Spirit of God dwells in you? If anyone destroys God's temple, God will destroy him" (Reading II).

One commentator writes: "The implication is that anyone who causes division in a community is destroying what belongs to God. Such a person is inviting destruction."

But fulfilling this great commandment is not only avoiding destructive deeds, words, or attitudes, it is also essentially positive. God, the all-holy One is totally self-giving. The divine call to holiness means not only avoiding hatred, refusal to forgive and forget, and the like. It also includes compassion and being solicitous about others, especially the troubled, the unloved, the unlovable. It means sensitivity, gentleness, caring.

We cannot will ourselves to become holy. Holiness, even the desire for it, is God's gift. But God is more than willing to grant it to us. All we need to do is to open our hearts and lives to the love of God, who became flesh in Christ Jesus, and beg him to give us his heart. All that God wants of us is that we allow Christ to love us.

> "The Lord is kind and merciful" (Responsorial Psalm).

May the Lord's kindness, mercy, holiness, and above all, the Lord's love find themselves at home in our hearts so that we too can be kind, merciful, and loving.

> Father,
> keep before us the wisdom and love
> you have revealed in your Son.
> Help us to be like him
> in word and deed (Opening Prayer).

81 SEVENTH SUNDAY IN ORDINARY TIME Cycle B

READING I Isa 43:18-19, 21-22, 24-25 **READING II** 2 Cor 1:18-22
GOSPEL Mark 2:1-12

Reading I: God has Isaiah tell the people, who are about to leave Babylon, that their sins have been forgiven and that they are to begin a new life.

Reading II: Paul claims consistency in his preaching Christ, through whom we address our worship to the Lord.

Gospel: Jesus proves he can forgive sins by healing a paralytic.

Today's Reading I and gospel are about forgiveness and healing. My first thought was that this liturgy was an excellent introduction to Lent, which is so much concerned with repentance and conversion. Then I read a commentator who suggested that the liturgy is more a prolongation of the Epiphany theme, namely, the manifestation of the glory, love, and mercy of God. I think there is truth in both views.

I have often used this gospel to prove that if Jesus could forgive sins, he was God (and he proved his divinity by this miracle), and he could also pass on his power to his Church; and so, we have the sacrament of reconciliation.

Now I believe Jesus had a deeper purpose in mind: he wanted to reveal at the very beginning of his ministry the ultimate goal of his mission, namely, that God is Lord, that God will ultimately triumph over the forces of darkness. This is why the very first thing Jesus said to the paralytic was, "Your sins are forgiven," and why he said to the scribes, "that you may know that the Son of Man has authority on earth to forgive sins," and to the paralyzed man, "I command you: Stand up! Pick up your mat and go home."

We have all come to know the mercy and compassion of Jesus. Any kind of physical affliction is offensive to him, makes him angry. But he knows better than we do that there is a worse affliction than paralysis or blindness: it is paralysis of the heart, it is slavery to any sin, it is spiritual blindness.

It was this kind of affliction that he was and is primarily concerned with. That is why today's Responsorial Psalm is so true to life, especially our own lives. It is a universal cry from the depths of human misery, and it belongs to us all:

Lord, heal my soul,
for I have sinned against you.

Notice that we pray "Heal my soul," not "heal my body."

To get some idea of the universal extent of the spiritual paralysis that afflicts our world, all we have to do is read the papers or listen to the TV news. Consider, for example, the hatred between nations that threatens to destroy humankind. Think of the refusal to forgive in the lives of so many of us Catholics. Many of us suffer alienation from God because we are alienated from one another and refuse to forgive.

We pray in The Lord's Prayer: "Forgive us our trespasses as we forgive those who trespass against us. . . ." Which really means: We don't forgive, so, Lord, do not forgive us. We need reminding, too, that forgetting is essential to forgiving. We can't have one without the other. If we are unable to forgive and to forget, we can hardly call ourselves disciples of Christ. Achieving this ability is the work of a lifetime. Only God is well practiced in it. Here is what God says in today's Reading I:

It is I, I, who wipe out,
for my own sake, your offenses;
your sins I remember no more.

The entire Bible insists again and again on God's eagerness to forgive and forget. God wants to share that gift with us. But we have to want it and open our entire being to it.

I said at the beginning that this liturgy reflects the Epiphany theme and forms a transition to Lent. "The Lord sent me to bring Good News to the poor, and freedom to sinners" (Alleluia Verse). That's the Epiphany theme; it points to Christ's entire life of healing, forgiving, taking us back.

Remember not the events of the past,
the things of long ago consider not;
See, I am doing something new! (Reading I)

The "something new" he will do during Lent is reshape us, reform us, convert us; but only on condition that we come to him with the desire to be made new, a desire that is given excellent wording in today's Responsorial Psalm:

Lord, heal my soul,
for I have sinned against you.

SEVENTH SUNDAY IN ORDINARY TIME

READING I 1 Sam 26:1, 7-9, 12-13, 22-23 **READING II** 1 Cor 15:45-49
GOSPEL Luke 6:27-38

Reading I: David's enemy, King Saul, is delivered into his hands, but David refuses to kill "the Lord's anointed."

Reading II: Paul contrasts the first Adam, origin of our natural life, with Christ, the new Adam, the life-giving spirit of all who are reborn in him.

Gospel: Jesus preaches love of enemies, compassion, abstaining from judging and condemning others.

The Belle of Amherst depicts the life of the poet Emily Dickinson, who lived in the last century. She lived in a rigid, puritanical home in which the father was lord and master. Despite her questioning of some of his teaching and customs, her poetry revealed a keen awareness of the presence of God in the world and a deep consciousness of the mystery of life and death. She wrestled with doubts about God, religion, and life. But there comes a point in the play when she says, "I am sure that no person will ever be truly happy until that person can say 'I love Christ.' "

How wonderful! She makes us ask: Do I love Christ? And what does love of Christ entail? Does it not mean embracing his values in our own lives? "Love your enemies, . . . When someone slaps you on one cheek, turn and give him the other; . . . Give to all who beg from you . . . lend without expecting repayment. . . . Be compassionate, . . . Do not judge." Long before Christ, King David refused to kill Saul, who was determined to kill him (see Reading I).

One wonders if the most glaring failure of Christians down through history has been an unwillingness to follow the ideal that Jesus proposes in today's gospel. There may be several causes of this condition, but my opinion is that the chief cause is our failure to grow as mature human beings, mature Christians. Churches of all denominations are full of people whose growth into maturity was stunted, perhaps even stifled, by parents or teachers who never allowed children to make a single decision on their own, with the consequence that the children had few personal convictions when they became adults.

Normally persons pass from childhood—the stage of total dependence on others—to adolescence, when they begin to feel the first stirrings of independence and doubt and the need to know reasons for decisions made for them. Then they pass to adulthood, when they have to stand on their own convictions and make their own decisions. This generally is the stage when Christ confronts them and they have to make a personal response to his question: "Who do you say that I am?" What do you think of my teaching? Are you willing to follow me on your own, without being told what to do? If they have never been allowed to make a decision, what kind of response can one expect?

Christianity is an eminently personal as well as a community religion. It makes frightening appeals to minds, hearts, and consciences. We simply have to make personal decisions about Christ, and we can hardly call ourselves Christian until we do.

Numbers of Christians go through the motions of religious observance, but something is lacking. Most likely, what is lacking is that personal conversion of the heart, the core of the human personality, which Jesus and his forerunner, John the Baptist, demanded. What is required is the total commitment to the values and judgments that Christ proposes in the gospels, especially those he proposes to us today.

Such a commitment is difficult to make; it may be the task of a lifetime. That is why year after year, Lent after Lent, the Church summons us to conversion. It is this conversion that today's gospel is all about. It is a call to heroic living. With the help of divine grace, heroism is possible for us all.

What is most necessary is that we throw ourselves on the mercy of Christ and give our hearts over to him so that he can love in and through us. And if we have special difficulty loving and forgiving some particular person, we might give that person over to Christ and ask him to do the loving and forgiving for and through us.

Back to Emily Dickinson: "I am sure that no person will ever be truly happy until that person can say: 'I love Christ!' " Jesus would add: No person can ever be truly happy, no person can ever be truly Christian, until that person can say in his or her heart: "I love Christ, and the proof of my love is that I love my enemy as well."

341 MONDAY OF THE SEVENTH WEEK IN ORDINARY TIME

YEAR I

READING I **Sir 1:1-10**
GOSPEL **Mark 9:14-29**

Sirach knows how to observe life and to see meaning in it. Wisdom is defined as "God's external revelation of himself." Sirach says, "All wisdom comes from the Lord," and we can be sure the Lord is willing to share his wise understanding of life with those who seek it diligently, especially through the study of the Holy Bible. But he who would be wise must also study life, for God "has poured [wisdom] forth upon all his works, he has lavished her upon his friends." So love is the key to wisdom, as it is to everything that is good. How wonderful!

But there are times when life is difficult to understand, as was the case with the father of the deaf and dumb child in the gospel. Then all we can do is go to Jesus and cry out of the depths of our grief and pain, "I do believe! Help my lack of trust!"

YEAR II

READING I **Jas 3:13-18**
GOSPEL **Mark 9:14-29**

James continues to probe and dissect this human heart of ours. Today he points out the diabolical consequences of jealousy and selfish ambition, namely, "inconstancy and all kinds of vile behavior." The antidote he proposes is "wisdom from above . . . [which is] innocent, . . . peaceable, lenient, docile, rich in sympathy and the kindly deeds that are its fruits." Wisdom helps us define ourselves against ourselves. It shows us the truth about ourselves in relation to those who make us jealous, and it helps us accept ourselves for what we are. Who does not need this wisdom? We can find it in Jesus, who daily seeks to share his wisdom with us through word and sacrament, curing us of the inhumanity that is the constant temptation of the unwise. But we must realize our need, our helplessness without wisdom and cry out, Lord, help my lack of trust!

342 TUESDAY OF THE SEVENTH WEEK IN ORDINARY TIME

YEAR I

READING I **Sir 2:1-11**
GOSPEL **Mark 9:30-37**

Good common sense characterizes today's Reading I, as indeed it does all of Sirach. If, as vulnerable human beings, we expect temptations, we are not as likely to forsake the Lord and give in to them. When the author extols the fear of the Lord, he sees fear as loving trust and hope rather than as slavish self-abasement. "Compassionate and merciful is the Lord." Could anything in the New Testament characterize Jesus more exactly?

Even though Jesus chose the apostles and taught them, they retained all their human failings, including unhealthy ambition. With all their faults, they resemble the Church herself. Jesus tells them—and us—at least one of the secrets for turning sinners into saints: "If anyone wishes to rank first [and be a saint], he must remain the last one of all and the servant of all." Jesus—loving, compassionate, merciful, forgiving, servant of all—invites us to follow him. Shall we accept?

YEAR II

READING I **Jas 4:1-10**
GOSPEL **Mark 9:30-37**

James' evaluation of our human condition is not very pleasant to hear, but we have to admit that it is often verified in our own lives. What about the apostles? How terribly human they were! Jesus has just announced his forthcoming passion and death, but, says Mark, they did not understand his words and were afraid to ask him. Instead, they argued childishly about which of them was the most important. It seems unbelievable that these chosen pillars of the Church could be so vain, till it dawns on us: are we not often as childishly ambitious in our dealings with others? The remedy Jesus proposes is as valid today as it was then: "If anyone wishes to rank first, he must remain the last one of all and the servant of all." We may be fallen, weak, and fragile, but service to others lifts us up and makes us like Jesus himself.

343 WEDNESDAY OF THE SEVENTH WEEK IN ORDINARY TIME

YEAR I

READING I Sir 4:11-19
GOSPEL Mark 9:38-40

Today Sirach actually sees wisdom as a person whom we are to seek and love without ceasing if we expect to be fulfilled as human persons and be happy. "He who loves her loves life; those who seek her out win her favor." But wisdom also disciplines her children and tests them until she trusts them. We gather from Sirach that wisdom comes only as a result of necessary search and diligent study of its deepest source, Holy Scripture.

Wisdom also comes from observing life around us and learning from our own mistakes. Above all, it comes from observing and seeking to understand Jesus, who in his life, his words, and his works is wisdom in person. Today's gospel is a good example of his wisdom. Jesus tells us that it is not necessary to be a member of the inner circle of his followers to be able to work wonders in his name. He who is not against us is for us, says Christ. That is wisdom!

YEAR II

READING I Jas 4:13-17
GOSPEL Mark 9:38-40

Reading I insists on the transitoriness of our life in this world. We all live on borrowed time; this is one of the most difficult aspects of life for us to understand. We think we are going to live forever. James tells us to shape up and try to understand that only "if the Lord wills it, [we] shall live."

The gospel brings up an age-old problem in the Church: how are we to look upon those who do not belong to the official Church but who obviously do much good in the name of Jesus? The apostle John's answer did not suit Jesus, who said simply, "Anyone who is not against us is with us." It might well be that this principle of tolerance is one that has been most ignored by Catholics. We are terribly exclusive. What good does a person do? is a much better criterion of following Christ than what denomination does he or she belong to?

344 THURSDAY OF THE SEVENTH WEEK IN ORDINARY TIME

YEAR I

READING I Sir 5:1-8
GOSPEL Mark 9:41-50

Even though Sirach's recommendations today are all negative, they contain useful and timely kernels of wisdom for daily living. For example, the principle about not following the inclinations and desires of our own hearts is very necessary in these days when people like to form their consciences according to what appeals to them. We need negative admonitions, but they need to be complemented with positive ones like "Happy are they who hope in the Lord, . . . [who] delight in the law of the Lord. . . ." (Responsorial Psalm).

In the gospel Jesus comes down hard on those people who lead others into sin. His condemnation may seem extremist, and he surely does not intend that anybody should cut off his foot or pluck out his eye. But he is God, so he knows the enormity of the evil of sin, how destructive it is to the human person. He is man; he will die to rescue humankind from the effects of sin. The danger of peer pressure leading others to evil habits is more pervasive today than ever.

YEAR II

READING I Jas 5:1-6
GOSPEL Mark 9:41-50

It's hard to imagine a more outspoken condemnation of riches than this one by James. But the example and words of Jesus seem to indicate that being rich is not wrong in itself. The evil comes from undue attachment to *whatever* possessions one has. As one New Testament commentator puts it: "A man who has an abundance of the world's goods is in great danger, not merely of becoming avaricious, grasping and oppressive, but also of becoming insulated from life and the meaning of life."

The Christian life involves relationships to things, to persons, and to God; they are all interdependent. To cut oneself off from others, worse still, to make it difficult or impossible for them to be rightly related to God, is to expose oneself to the terrifying doom that Jesus puts in such vivid words in today's gospel. Here is Christ's ideal:

> Happy the poor in spirit (Responsorial Psalm).

345 FRIDAY OF THE SEVENTH WEEK IN ORDINARY TIME

YEAR I

READING I **Sir 6:5-17**
GOSPEL **Mark 10:1-12**

Sirach seems to agree with the opinion that friendship is one of God's best gifts to humans:

> A faithful friend is beyond price,
> no sum can balance his worth (Reading I).

But friendship, though a gift, also has to be made. You make friends, and it takes hard work and no little sacrifice to maintain and to grow in friendship. A friend is a person with whom you feel comfortable and in whom you can confide, a person in whose presence you can be silent.

The gospel is about divorce, the failure of friendship. Friendship has failed because one or both parties have lost the ideal of self-giving, the heart of marriage or friendship. Everything beautiful that Sirach says about friendship can and must be true of marriage. If both husband and wife work hard at making their union a true friendship, this tragic question need never be asked: Is it lawful for a man to divorce his wife?

YEAR II

READING I **Jas 5:9-12**
GOSPEL **Mark 10:1-12**

Is it lawful for a man to divorce his wife? What tragedy there is behind the very need to ask such a question! It means that one of the partners of the most beautiful of friendships, marriage, has failed the other, and failed himself or herself. Marriage is a holy vocation that demands very hard work and tremendous sacrifice, not just from one but from both parties, and it is a lifelong work that is never finished. It demands mutual self-giving. Husband and wife have to be good, not only *to* one another, but *for* one another, and that's the hardest part.

If husband and wife are always friends, if they learn to communicate (and commune) with one another, if they are responsible persons, they can make any union work. Sirach has good advice for married couples—they have to be steadfast, and like the Lord himself, they have to be compassionate and merciful to each other. Is that asking too much?

346 SATURDAY OF THE SEVENTH WEEK IN ORDINARY TIME

YEAR I

READING I Sir 17:1-15
GOSPEL Mark 10:13-16

"The Lord's kindness is everlasting to those who fear him." This verse of the Responsorial Psalm perfectly sums up the content and meaning of Reading I. The very fact of a person's relationship to the earth, the fact of being made in the image and likeness of God, of being able to understand and to love—all this results from the everlasting goodness and kindness of the Lord. If we only realized who and what we are and all that God has done for us, our hearts would burst with praise of God's holy name and undying appreciation of the Lord's creative majesty. This reading gives us some idea of the enormity of the crime of exploitation and pollution of nature in all its forms.

In the gospel, Jesus uses the openness and joyful receptivity to gifts that children possess to illustrate the ideal attitude to God's goodness and salvation that we all ought to have.

YEAR II

READING I Jas 5:13-20
GOSPEL Mark 10:13-16

Reading I is the basis of the Roman Catholic Church's belief in the scriptural foundation of the practice of the anointing of the sick—the sacrament that manifests Jesus' mercy, compassion, and will to heal the sick and infirm. The reading also insists that the sacrament is not only for the dying but for those who are sick.

In the gospel, Jesus proposes little children as an example of the kind of attitude all Christians should have toward God. Children have many faults. But they can be very loving, and they are always willing to receive love. They seem to know how to give in to love, how to allow themselves to be loved, protected, nourished. They are totally dependent on parents and they know it. Today Jesus tells us that's the way we all have to want to be with God.

83 EIGHTH SUNDAY IN ORDINARY TIME Cycle A

READING I **Isa 49:14-15** **READING II** **1 Cor 4:1-5**
GOSPEL **Matt 6:24-34**

Reading I: Even though Zion (symbol of Israel) thinks that God has forgotten her, God strongly corrects that conjecture.

Reading II: Paul seeks to justify his preaching and asks the Corinthians not to judge him. That is the Lord's prerogative.

Gospel: Jesus tells us that we cannot serve God and wealth simultaneously and then pleads with us to place all our trust in God's loving care.

There are two different lessons in today's gospel:
—service and loyalty to two masters simultaneously is impossible;
—a warning against excessive concern about one's future welfare.
The Responsorial Psalm seems to draw both concerns together:

Only in God is my soul at rest;
from him comes my salvation.
He only is my rock and my salvation,
my stronghold; I shall not be disturbed at all.

There are two kinds of faith in conflict in the gospel: faith in money and in the prestige, power, and security that money seems to confer and faith and trust in an all-loving, all-caring God. Sooner or later we have to choose which kind of faith will rule our life. What Jesus is *not* advocating is idleness or shiftlessness. When he says that we should not worry, he does not mean that we are not to care. He is not against reasonable planning, and certainly he is not against caring about the future of one's family, nor would he be against social security.

I think Jesus would agree with this advice: Work and plan and use all your powers as though everything depends on you, and trust and believe in a provident God as though everything depends on the Lord. What Jesus would reject is the kind of planning that dispenses with Providence. He is saying that the Christian life ought to be an act of faith in the Lord who is the author of life, the creator. Does not every creator, anyone who ever makes anything, care for what he or she makes? This is the point Jesus is making today. It is also the point of Reading I. If we think God has forgotten us, he tells us:

> Can a mother forget her infant,
> be without tenderness for the child of her womb?
> Even should she forget,
> I will never forget you.

To worry excessively, Jesus tells us in the gospel, is to risk becoming an unbeliever: "The unbelievers are always running after these things." Then comes the convincer: "Your heavenly Father knows all that you need. Seek first his kingship over you, his way of holiness, and all these things will be given you besides."

The Christian life is a life of faith, of trust, or it isn't a Christian life at all. Can you even remember the worry you had last year at this time? So trust in God, trust in God's never-failing love and care—this is the dare that Jesus extends to each of us today. Does it take a lot of courage to believe in love, especially when the One who makes the dare is the One who made us in the first place?

> The Lord has been my strength; he has led me into freedom.
> He saved me because he loves me (Entrance Antiphon).

84 EIGHTH SUNDAY IN ORDINARY TIME — Cycle B

READING I Hos 2:16-17, 21-22 **READING II** 2 Cor 3:1-6
GOSPEL Mak 2:18-22

Reading I: The Lord uses the symbol of a marrage espousal to express God's great love for Israel.

Reading II: The credential Paul wants more than anything else is his message made evident in the lives of the Corinthians.

Gospel: Jesus answers the objections of the Pharisees and John's disciples to his own disciples' failure to follow the old dietary laws.

It would be hard to find a finer description of love than the Lord gives in today's Reading I:

> I will lead her [Israel, my beloved] into the desert
> and speak to her heart.
> She shall respond there as in the days of her youth.

Love has to be expressed; love has to be responded to. God was speaking to Israel then; today God speaks to us.

The desert into which God leads us so that he can speak to our hearts is Lent. God speaks to us always and in all circumstances; but Lent is a very special time when the Word of love is heard in our hearts and, hopefully, there will be a response from our hearts. What does God say? Return to me. Come back. All is forgiven. We can start life all over again together.

We have often heard that God compares the covenant with Israel to marriage—marriage based on loving fidelity. God never failed in fulfilling his part of the marriage, but Israel, the bride, often strayed into strange beds, into paganism. But the Lord always took her back, forgave her adulteries, never gave up on her. God never gives up on us either, and the desert of Lent is the proof.

So, Lent is God's own idea. More and more I am convinced that everything begins with God—that our praying and praising, our worshiping, our penance, and above all, our morality, and our very living is nothing else than our human response to all that God has done for us out of sheer, unmerited love. God is the eternal suitor, forever wooing us, the beloved, never giving up, always taking us back. So maybe it is time for us to stop running off, time to give our consent to God's deep love for us and to allow ourselves to be swept up into the divine embrace and heart.

But the reality of life has to be faced. Infidelity and divorce abound. Marriage, to be successful, requires a lifetime of hard work and sacrifice on the part of both partners. For a variety of reasons husbands or wives stray. Love is so hard to make, to create, so terribly easy to destroy. Too many partners acquire and concentrate on interests other than the beloved.

There is a movement among the Catholic laity called "Marriage Encounter," which involves husbands and wives getting together on a weekend of prayer and mutual confiding, talking out their problems and difficulties, clearing the air of doubts, bringing into the open secret suspicions, and mutually admitting faults. The result is that they find out how much they mean to each other. They are eager to start over, to renew their marriage vows—their covenant—and to ward off future problems.

Is it unrealistic to think of Lent as a kind of protracted marriage encounter with Jesus, our beloved? We can be frank with him and discuss happenings in our lives that we have difficulty understanding. Most of all, we can be frank with ourselves and bring our infidelities, our sins, back into the forefront of our consciousness. Jesus will speak to our hearts, and he will tell us that no matter how unfaithful we have been, no matter what we have done, he forgives us. He is always eager to take us back into his heart:

> The Lord is kind and merciful.
> He pardons all your iniquities,
> he heals all your ills (Responsorial Psalm).

At the end of our Lenten "marriage encounter," we will renew our baptismal vows. Once again we will pledge our fidelity to Jesus and start life all over again.

> I will sing to the Lord for his goodness to me, I will sing the name of the Lord, Most High (Communion Antiphon).

85 EIGHTH SUNDAY IN ORDINARY TIME Cycle C

READING I Sir 27:4-7 **READING II** 1 Cor 15:54-58
GOSPEL Luke 6:39-45

Reading I: A person's inner convictions, principles, and values come to light in his or her manner of speech.

Reading II: Paul again states his strong belief in our personal resurrection, which, however, does not excuse us from working hard for the Lord.

Gospel: Jesus insists that one's inner being is made manifest in one's speech and behavior.

Both Reading I and the gospel provide us with practical religious deductions from the old Latin adage, *Agere sequitur esse,* which can be variously translated, "Action follows the nature of the being" or "One's inner being determines the way one speaks or behaves or lives." In a word, if one's being is solidly Christian, if Christ is the sole inspiration of our being, then our conduct and speech will be influenced and shaped by Christ. Jesus says in the gospel: "A good tree does not produce decayed fruit any more than a decayed tree produces good fruit. Each tree is known by its yield. . . . A good man produces goodness from the good in his heart; an evil man produces evil out of his store of evil. Each man speaks from his heart's abundance."

We realize, of course, that Jesus is speaking to us. He both warns and encourages us. First the warning. The inner being that we receive from Christ in baptism is Christ himself, his life. It is a conscious, living relationship with him. Like all relationships, this one can grow feeble, disappear, and no longer influence the way we live, speak, and act.

Our relationship with Jesus has to be kept alive and flourishing by means of fervent prayer, holy reading, and reflection—especially on the word of God. Trees, flowers, vegetables, cannot grow and eventually bear fruit unless they are watered and cared for. In our case, Jesus does everything—almost. He gives us our being, he nourishes us on his Word, his Body and Blood, he speaks to us through the great and beautiful sign of nature, he is constantly telling us that he loves us. But we have to *want* to be cared for, to be nourished;

we have to be *open* to his word, his expressions of love; we have to *respond* with grateful hearts. The Responsorial Psalm summarizes all that we are and how we ought to think, speak, and act as persons possessed by Christ:

> It is good to give thanks to the Lord,
> to sing praise to your name, Most High,
> To proclaim your kindness at dawn
> and your faithfulness throughout the night. . . .
> They that are planted in the house of the Lord
> shall flourish in the courts of our God.
> They shall bear fruit even in old age;
> vigorous and sturdy shall they be.

After all that, a bit of moralizing might make us wonder about our own inner being and cause us to ask ourselves: "How Christ-like am I?" This is a question not only for those who preach the gospel but also for those who hear it. The reason is that Christ expects all of his followers to be missionaries by the very fact of their baptism. When one's faith shows forth in one's life, one is bound to attract non-Christians (also the lapsed and lax) to Christ and perhaps cause them to think: What that good Christian is, I want to be. The Alternative Opening Prayer today ought to become our daily prayer:

> Father in heaven,
> form in us the likeness of your Son
> and deepen his life within us.
> Send us as witnesses of gospel joy
> into a world of fragile peace and broken promises.
> Touch the hearts of all men with your love
> that they in turn may love one another.
> We ask this through Christ our Lord. Amen.

347 MONDAY OF THE EIGHTH WEEK IN ORDINARY TIME

YEAR I

READING I Sir 17:19-27
GOSPEL Mark 10:17-27

How great the mercy of the Lord,
his forgiveness of those who return to him! (Reading I)

That phrase not only sums up Reading I, but also contains the entire spirit of the gospel. We cannot be reminded too often that no matter how greatly we have sinned, God's merciful will to forgive can never be denied.

In the gospel Jesus warns, "How hard it is for the rich to enter the kingdom of God!" The evil is that riches are often considered more necessary than God himself. Riches take the place of God; they are preferred to God. Jesus intends his warning here for all of us—rich and poor. We have to ask ourselves, What is my attitude to things, to possessions? Who is number one in my life? Where is my trust: in Christ or in the risky security provided by my possessions?

YEAR II

READING I 1 Pet 1:3-9
GOSPEL Mark 10:17-27

In the first words of his first letter to his flock, our first pope, Peter, gives the proper response of all Christians to what God has done for us in Christ Jesus: "Praised be the God and Father of our Lord Jesus Chirst!" It is a beautiful prayer that ought always to be in our hearts. How exact, too, his observations and his prayer for us: "Although you have never seen him, you love him, . . . you now believe in him and rejoice with inexpressible joy."

If we all have that kind of attitude toward Jesus, we can better understand his warning against the dangers of riches. He warns against trusting in riches, that is, in trying to find security in possessions, preferring them to God. We all have to ask ourselves: Who, what is supreme in my life—God or possessions? Where do I place my trust, in the person of Jesus or in the risky security provided by possessions? Our whole happiness in this life and the next depends on our answer to those questions.

348 TUESDAY OF THE EIGHTH WEEK IN ORDINARY TIME

YEAR I

READING I Sir 35:1-12
GOSPEL Mark 10:28-31

Reading I emphasizes the inner attitude we ought to have in our worship of God. What pleases God more than the size or worth of our offerings is the sincere generosity and the cheerful gladness with which we give. No amount, however great, can win God's favor if our hearts are not right. We simply cannot bribe the Lord!

Jesus also recognizes this fact in the gospel. To leave everything and follow Christ, if it is done for Jesus' sake and the cause of the gospel, will be splendidly rewarded in this life and above all in the next. But the condition that it be based on love, not on desire for gain, is essential. And that is the important thought for all of us: no matter what we have given up, if our motivation is love for Jesus, if our giving is cheerful, our entire life fulfills the necessary condition for ideal worship laid down in Reading I.

YEAR II

READING I 1 Pet 1:10-16
GOSPEL Mark 10:28-31

"Set all your hope on the gift to be conferred on you when Jesus Christ appears," Peter tells us today; and he goes on to suggest that we be holy in our conduct, for it is to holiness that we are called as Christians. We have to remind ourselves that we cannot be holy by any effort of our own, other than by willing acceptance of the grace of Christ and loving cooperation with that grace.

In the gospel, Jesus promises eternal life to those who leave all things for his sake and the sake of the gospel. That is an essential condition, for it is based on love, not desire for reward. We may not be terribly fascinated by the promise of eternal life until we realize that it is possessing and being possessed by Love in person. It is knowing Jesus and his love for us without any fear of that love being lost. That is the salvation the Lord has made known to us.

349 WEDNESDAY OF THE EIGHTH WEEK IN ORDINARY TIME

YEAR I

READING I **Sir 36:1, 5-6, 10-17**
GOSPEL **Mark 10:32-45**

Reading I is a beautiful prayer in which Sirach begs God not only for mercy for his people but also that the Lord will manifest himself to the pagans. We can use the prayer, too. "Show us, O Lord, the light of your kindness" (Responsorial Psalm).

How patient Jesus had to be with his apostles! Here he foretells his forthcoming passion, death, and resurrection, and John and James react by requesting a place of honor in his kingdom! But Jesus did not judge them harshly, nor must we. He patiently explains that greatness in his kingdom will consist not in receiving homage but rather in serving the needs of others: "Whoever wants to rank first among you, must serve the needs of all." Whenever we feel unappreciated in whatever community or parish we are, may we always remember the ideal Jesus laid down and lived himself: "The Son of Man has not come to be served but to serve—to give his life in ransom for the many."

YEAR II

READING I **1 Pet 1:18-25**
GOSPEL **Mark 10:32-45**

It is said that there is a great difference between knowing Christ and knowing about him. In the gospel Jesus describes his coming passion to his disciples, but he has to submit to the disappointment of being completely misunderstood by his closest friends. Even worse, of seeing two of them try to use him for their own advancement. It is terribly important for us to *know* this Jesus with our minds and our hearts and to try to get into his mind, for then we will see how essential it is for us to make our own the principle that has guided his whole life: "The Son of Man has not come to be served but to serve. . . ."

Then, too, we will understand the theological description of the total work of Jesus and the conclusions for our own lives contained in Reading I: "The word of the Lord endures forever." Praise the Lord!

350 THURSDAY OF THE EIGHTH WEEK IN ORDINARY TIME

YEAR I

READING I **Sir 42:15-25**
GOSPEL **Mark 10:46-52**

The deep meaning of Reading I is that this world of ours is the realization of God's creative word and that it reflects the glory of God. The world of nature is a sacrament, a sign, that reveals the beauty and wisdom of God, its creator. "By the word of the Lord the heavens were made," says the psalmist.

Jesus is the greatest of all divine sacraments. He is the revelation of God's creative power, above all, of God's merciful compassion; and the miracles, or signs, he works are always creative. The blind man cries out, "Jesus, Son of David, have pity on me. . . . I want to see." And as it happened at the beginning of creation, so now it happens again. By the word of the Lord the heavens were made; by the word of the Lord Jesus sight is restored to the blind man. "Give thanks to the Lord. . . . Sing to him a new song" (Responsorial Psalm).

YEAR II

READING I **1 Pet 2:2-5, 9-12**
GOSPEL **Mark 10:46-52**

Who, what, is a Christian? Who, what, is the Church? No one has a better answer to those questions than St. Peter. Christians are living stones who make up a spiritual house. We are a chosen race, a royal priesthood, a holy nation, God's own people; but this tremendous dignity also entails privileged obligations, namely, to declare the wonderful deeds of him who called us out of darkness into his marvelous light.

What Christ did for us in baptism is even more wonderful than what he did in restoring sight to the blind man of the gopsel. As sharers of his very own royal priesthood, we have the power to offer spiritual sacrifices to God. What Peter is telling us is, Christian, know your dignity! From this knowledge will flow the highest Christian morality and loftiest praise of God. "The Lord is good: his kindness endures forever" (Responsorial Psalm).

351 FRIDAY OF THE EIGHTH WEEK IN ORDINARY TIME

YEAR I

READING I **Sir 44:1, 9-13**
GOSPEL **Mark 11:11-26**

Today's Responsorial Psalm, "The Lord takes delight in his people," might well be one of the sweetest verses in all Scripture. But Scripture also indicates that there are a few conditions that need to be filled. In the gospel, Jesus is not very delighted with the merchants in the temple, and I doubt that the Lord is very happy with nations that deprive people of their rights. The people the Lord delights in are those who never forget that they are creatures and that God is creator—who show that remembrance by worship.

But a people cannot give delight to the Lord unless they also remember with gratitude their own ancestors, who contributed labor and sacrifice to the making of that people. Think of our own country. What would we be like without our founders and forefathers? What would our Church be without the great saints, missionaries, and martyrs? The Lord can only take delight in a grateful people.

YEAR II

READING I **1 Pet 4:7-13**
GOSPEL **Mark 11:11-26**

Peter tells his people today that there is only one way to be ready for Christ's coming in judgment, and that is to love our neighbor and to practice hospitality. But Peter does not want charity motivated by fear of judgment. He says, "As generous distributors of God's manifold grace, put your gifts at the service of one another, each in the measure he has received." The old saying holds here: you cannot keep what you do not share. Whatever talents the Lord gives us, he wills that they be developed and used not only for our own satisfaction but for the good of the whole Church. Those who do not develop their talents are like the barren fig tree of the gospel.

Among the many important lessons of the gospel, the one we need most is perhaps the most difficult: "When you stand to pray, forgive anyone against whom you have a grievance." Without forgiveness, no one is ready to meet Christ.

352 SATURDAY OF THE EIGHTH WEEK IN ORDINARY TIME

YEAR I

READING I Sir 51:12-20
GOSPEL Mark 11:27-33

In this last reading from Sirach, the author sums up the joy and profit his lifelong search for wisdom has brought him:

When I was young and innocent,
I sought wisdom.
She came to me in her beauty,
and until the end I will cultivate her.

Wisdom is not mere knowledge of facts, not mechanics. It is rather entrance into the mystery of God and the meaning of life—but only an entrance. The exploration goes on through life, through eternity, for the God we really are seeking is infinite, limitless in truth, love, life. The important thing is to *seek,* and it is never too late to begin. The tragedy of human nature is that so few people really desire wisdom. All they want is facts—facts that will be financially rewarding—whereas wisdom gives lasting joy with no danger of a recession. Or, as the psalmist puts it in today's Responsorial Psalm:

The precepts of the Lord give joy to the heart.
They are more precious than gold,
than a heap of the purest gold.

That's wisdom. Seek and you shall find.

YEAR II

READING I Jude 17, 20-25
GOSPEL Mark 11:27-33

Jude again reminds us of our priorities: the Lord God is our greatest need. Therefore "Glory be to this only God our savior, through Jesus Christ our Lord." Deep in our hearts we know this, and no one has better expressed the heart's deepest thirst than today's psalmist:

My soul is thirsting for you, O Lord my God.
O God, you are my God whom I seek;
for you my flesh pines and my soul thirsts.

Everyone has ambitions, both immediate and distant. The goal might be an education leading to a profession or a vacation or just the coming weekend. The human heart feeds on desire, but desire seldom feeds the heart unless it is—or includes—a desire for God, who alone is the answer to all of life's seeking. We seek God, but we often forget that he also seeks us, our love. When our desire for God and his desire for our love finally come together, we have found the answer to the meaning of life.

86 NINTH SUNDAY IN ORDINARY TIME — Cycle A

READING I Deut 11:18, 26-28 **READING II** Rom 3:21-25, 28
GOSPEL Matt 7:21-27

Reading I: Moses tells the people that the Lord will bless their obedience to his law and punish their disobedience.

Reading II: All people are sinners and are deprived of the glory of God, but all are undeservedly justified by Christ Jesus.

Gospel: Good words and good works apart from total dedication to God's will are useless.

There is one attitude the Lord cannot stand. It is the external show of religion in people whose hearts are not in what they say and do when they stand before the Almighty. "None of those who cry out, 'Lord, Lord,' will enter the kingdom of God but only the one who does the will of my Father in heaven" (Gospel).

Free, intelligent creatures have to acknowledge that the Creator-God is Lord of all life, above all, their own. That is what religion is all about. The acknowledgment has to be a free, conscious conviction arising from the heart, finding expression in a person's external words and actions. Worship is the deliberate giving of one's life into the hands and care of one's creator and Lord.

Worship that is genuine has its source in God, as Reading I indicates: "Take these words of mine into your heart and soul. Bind them at your wrist as a sign." The Jews used to do just that. The "bandage" of divine words on their wrists was a constant reminder of their creaturehood, their total dependence on God for all that they were and possessed.

God speaks to us as much as God spoke to the chosen people. We hear the Lord's word Sunday after Sunday, and hopefully, we also have that divine word in Bibles in our homes. Unfortunately, too many Catholics do not read, study, and reflect on the word of God. We don't really see God's word to us as an essential element in our religious practice. But God was speaking to us as much as to the Jews: "Take these words of mine into your heart and soul." The divine word possessing our hearts, our hearts possessing the divine word, is the best possible prevention for keeping far off the superficial, mechanized acts of prayer and worship that Jesus condemned so vehemently in the gospel.

We need to remind ourselves that God's words are addressed to a community of people. And it is to a people, of which we are members, that God continues to speak today. A people, a community, is made up of individual members, each of whom is expected to make a personal acknowledgement of God's lordship. The people, the parish, the religious community, together worship the Lord. The more wholehearted and genuine the contribution of the individual members, the more perfect the community worship of the whole community.

Finally, it is good to recall the old teaching that God doesn't need our worship. Worship does not benefit the Lord. It benefits us, makes us more human, makes us share in God's own divine life. Worship knits the community together more and more and makes us a people dear to the heart of the Lord.

> Lord,
> as we gather to offer our gifts
> confident in your love,
> make us holy by sharing your life with us
> and by this eucharist forgive our sins (Prayer over the Gifts).

87 **NINTH SUNDAY IN ORDINARY TIME** Cycle B

READING I Deut 5:12-15 **READING II** 2 Cor 4:6-11
GOSPEL Mark 2:23–3:6

Reading I: The Lord commands the people to keep holy the Sabbath by refraining from work and remembering how the Lord had rescued them from slavery in Egypt.

Reading II: The Christian life is a daily dying with Jesus, but it is also a rising and living with him.

Gospel: Jesus corrects the rigid legalistic and mistaken ideas of the Pharisees concerning the Sabbath observance.

Unfortunately, this Sunday liturgy is seldom celebrated because of the varying dates of Easter and the Lenten observance leading up to it. It is unfortunate, because this Sunday's deep meaning is so necessary for most American Christians. What is the Sabbath observance all about?

At the very beginning of Christianity, the traditional Sabbath observance on the seventh day of the week was transferred to Sunday, the first day, the day of Christ's resurrection. But the idea was the same: resting from labor *and* remembering what the Lord had done for them. God had directed the Jews to remember how he had delivered them from slavery in Egypt. Christians were inspired to remember the even greater deliverance that Jesus had achieved for them by his death and resurrection—deliverance from eternal separation from God.

Today's liturgy provides modern Christians with some timely thoughts about what Sunday ought to mean. The ideas are timely, for we all know what has happened to the observance of the Lord's day in our time. Only God knows how many moderns completely ignore the Sunday observance and how many more are ignorant of its true meaning. Many Catholics give it mere lip service, like going to Mass "because we have to." We can only wonder how much "remembering" they do.

And we can wonder, too, how many imitate the extreme legalism that characterized the Pharisees' observance. The correctives Jesus gave to offset the Pharisees' legalism still hold: strict observance of the Lord's Day has to take into account basic human needs.

People need meals that have to be prepared, and that is work. There are other kinds of employment that are necessary, the most common being care of the sick. Trains, busses, planes, have to run and fly. Jesus' words still hold: "The sabbath was made for man, not man for the sabbath" (Gospel).

Faithful observance of the Sabbath is like worship: it is not God who benefits by the observance, it is we ourselves. Thoughtful, loving observance makes us more human, more open to God's indwelling in our hearts.

There is one aspect of our Sunday observance that many may forget—even those who try to observe its spirit faithfully: it is the idea of *remembering* what the Lord has done for us. The Jews were to remember God's freeing them from Egyptian slavery. Christians are to remember Good Friday and Easter. The wonderful thing about our remembering is that in the Eucharist *the original event is made present for us here and now*. And that ought to make us want to

> Blow the trumpet at the new moon,
> at the full moon, on our solemn feast (Responsorial Psalm).

88 NINTH SUNDAY IN ORDINARY TIME — Cycle C

READING I **1 Kgs 8:41-43** **READING II** **Gal 1:1-2, 6-10**
GOSPEL **Luke 7:1-10**

Reading I: Solomon begs the Lord to hear the prayers of non-Jews when they come to the Temple to pray.

Reading II: Paul sternly condemns anyone who preaches a gospel that differs from the one he has preached.

Gospel: Jesus rewards the faith of a pagan centurion by healing the man's servant from a distance.

The gospel features a decent, caring man, a Roman army officer, who asks Jesus to come and heal his dying servant. We can speculate on whether or not he believed Jesus to be divine. It seems obvious that he thought of him as more than a medical wonder worker. He sends friends to tell Jesus: "Sir, do not trouble yourself, for I am not worthy to have you enter my house. That is why I did not presume to come to you myself. Just give the order and my servant will be cured."

Jesus sees the man as a true believer, for he says to the crowd, "I tell you, I have never found so much faith among the Israelites." And he heals the man's servant from a distance. A pagan's faith stirs up the healing power of the Savior.

God loved the world so much, he gave us his only Son,
that all who believe in him might have eternal life (Alleluia Verse).

We see another caring man in Reading I—Solomon (before he became involved with a multitude of wives). His is a remarkable prayer for a member of God's chosen people, many of whom thought that they alone had direct communication with the Lord. Solomon had built his glorious Temple, and one day he went there to beg God to hear the prayers of foreigners when they came from distant lands to honor the Lord: "Do all that the foreigner asks of you, that all the peoples of the earth may know your name, may fear you as do your people Israel."

What is remarkable about Solomon is his universalism. He wanted God to be acknowledged as Lord by all the peoples of the earth. Little wonder that he is known as "Solomon the wise." He obviously loved God and showed his love by praying that God would be loved by people everywhere. That would also be the inspiration of St. Paul in Christian times. Love for Christ impelled him. That kind of universality continues to inspire missionaries and all thoughtful Christians today.

There are important deductions to be drawn from both readings, the main one being that God's self-revelation is not confined to any particular people or to followers of any particular religion. Solomon prays for non-Jews; the centurion, is a pagan, a very decent man. Christians need to observe that pagans often respond to God's divine love and self-revelation better than they do themselves.

When we pray before receiving Communion: "Lord, I am not worthy to receive you, but only say the word and I shall be healed," may we remember that it was the Roman centurion who said it first.

Go out to all the world,
and tell the Good News.
Praise the Lord, all you nations;
glorify him, all you peoples! (Responsorial Psalm)

353 MONDAY OF THE NINTH WEEK IN ORDINARY TIME

YEAR I

READING I Tob 1:1, 2; 2:1-9
GOSPEL Mark 12:1-12

"Happy the man who fears the LORD," says the psalmist; and Tobit was such a man. Not only did he revere the Lord, he sought to do God's will in all things. Today's reading shows his thoughtfulness and charity. First he wants to share his meal with a poor man, and then he goes out of his way to bury a murdered man—a work of mercy then, even as it is now.

As with Tobit, so with Jesus. His enemies are out to get him and he knows it. He even taunts them by telling this story. Their ancestors have abused and killed the prophets. The owner of the vineyard decides to send "the son whom he loved." Jesus' enemies know he is talking about himself and them. They want to arrest him, but they fear the crowd. But it won't be long. Jesus will be "the stone rejected by the builders." He will become the cornerstone of the Church, his body, of which we are the members. That's how Jesus and his Father cared for us!

YEAR II

READING I 2 Pet 1:2-7
GOSPEL Mark 12:1-12

The author of Reading I sees the Christian life as one of gift and growth. We receive our salvation and our talents from God, but it is up to us to use our human powers to develop God's gifts to the ultimate of human perfection—love for one another and eternal union of life and love with God.

In our reading from Mark we are not far from Jesus' passion. Jesus uses a parable to illustrate what the Pharisees and scribes have done to the prophets and what they will do to him. We know by hindsight what they actually did. We are now those "others" to whom the Lord has given the vineyard. And Jesus is the "Beloved Son" whom the Father has sent to care for the vineyard. If we ask why the Father sent the Son to save us by dying for us, there can only be one answer: "Love does such things" (Guardini). May we always gratefully receive such love.

354 TUESDAY OF THE NINTH WEEK IN ORDINARY TIME

YEAR I

READING I Tob 2:9-14
GOSPEL Mark 12:13-17

For all his virtues, Tobit was human after all, vulnerable like all the rest of us. His blindness and dependency on his wife finally "get to him," and he refuses to believe her. Moreover, he does it on religious grounds: he suspects her of violating God's commandment against stealing. But she puts him in his place. Knowing she is telling the truth, she tells him off: "Where are your charitable deeds now? Where are your virtuous acts? See! Your true character is finally showing itself!" She has the last—and the best—word, and he will have to admit it. Happiness not only in marriage but also in all our relationships with God depends on mutual trust. No relationship is safe without it. "The heart of the just man is secure, trusting in the Lord" (Responsorial Psalm). And we can add, trusting in your wife, your husband, your friend.

YEAR II

READING I 2 Pet 3:12-15, 17-18
GOSPEL Mark 12:13-17

Peter's second letter concludes with exhortations for Christians that are as valid today as they were in that first century. Our translation urges us to look for "the coming of the day of God" and try to hasten it, but I prefer another translation: that we "earnestly desire" that coming, for only when we are finally with God will our deepest desires for love and joy be fulfilled. The best way to prepare for our personal encounter with our God, Peter tells us, is to grow in grace, that is, in God's immense love and in knowledge of Jesus.

In the gospel Jesus advises us to "give to Caesar what is Caesar's, but give to God what is God's." In other words, loyalty to civil authority and loyalty to God can coexist in us. There need be no conflict. The only tribute God wants from us is our hearts and our love. Let's overpay God!

355 WEDNESDAY OF THE NINTH WEEK IN ORDINARY TIME

YEAR I

READING I **Tob 3:1-11, 16**
GOSPEL **Mark 12:18-27**

"To you, O Lord, I lift up my soul" (Responsorial Psalm). What a perfect lesson on the nature of prayer! The psalm is based on trust in God, for no one who waits for God will be put to shame. It also becomes specific: "Your ways, O Lord, make known to me; teach me your paths . . . for you are God my savior." That is, tell me what meaning there is in what is happening. Then comes the "clincher": "Remember that your compassion, O Lord, and your kindness are from of old."

Reading I is also about prayer, specifically about the prayer of a man and a woman, each with problems that overwhelm them to such an extent that they ask God to let them die. God hears their prayer, but not in the way they desire. God will give them not death but life: a new life with joys and gifts far exceeding all their expectations. "God," says Jesus, "is the God of the living, not of the dead."

YEAR II

READING I **2 Tim 1:1-3, 6-12**
GOSPEL **Mark 12:18-27**

From his prison in Rome the apostle Paul writes a touching pastoral letter to his young convert Timothy, whom he has placed at the head of the Church at Ephesus. It is a letter full of loving and solid advice. Timothy is to "stir into flame" the grace that he has received by the laying on of Paul's hands in ordination. Paul reminds Timothy again of his foremost conviction: we are saved by God's grace, not by any works of our own.

The Sadducees, not believing in the resurrection, try to ridicule Jewish belief in it. The crucial words in Jesus' mysterious answer are his conclusion: by the power of God our resurrected bodies will be a new creation. Our God is the God of the living, not of the dead. To God we lift up our eyes in hope and love.

356 THURSDAY OF THE NINTH WEEK IN ORDINARY TIME

YEAR I

READING I **Tob 6:11; 7:1, 9-14; 8:4-7**
GOSPEL **Mark 12:28-34**

Reading I tells the fascinating story of Tobit's son Tobiah's romance with Sarah, the girl whose seven husbands had been killed by a demon before the marriage was consummated. The reading contains excerpts from several chapters; if you want all the details, you can look them up in your Bible. What is essential for us is reflection on the beauty and nobility of Tobiah's prayer, which could be summarized in the Responsorial Psalm: "Happy are those who fear the Lord, who walk in his ways!" This kind of fear is not slavish. Tobiah and Sarah stand before God in full awareness of their dignity as God's children, called by God to holiness. Their prayer is essentially one of praise, ending with a presentation of their needs as they enter upon their marriage. Marriage, founded on mutual trust, can be a perfect way of fulfilling the first and greatest commandment of the Lord.

YEAR II

READING I **2 Tim 2:8-15**
GOSPEL **Mark 12:28-34**

The word of God is not fettered or chained or shackled—not when it possesses and is possessed by a person as passionate and dynamic as Paul. Paul may be imprisoned, but even in chains he preaches by word and by joining his sufferings to those of Christ. Paul is saying here that suffering with and for Christ is itself redemptive; it generates saving grace. "If we hold out to the end we shall reign with him."

It is easier to *recite* the greatest of all commandments than to put it into practice. To love God with our whole heart, mind, and strength means loving him with the full measure of our devotion. Our greatest problem is with the second commandment—love of neighbor. Love and suffering go together. St. Paul would understand. Maybe that is why he was such a great lover.

357 FRIDAY OF THE NINTH WEEK IN ORDINARY TIME

YEAR I

READING I Tob 11:5-15
GOSPEL Mark 12:35-37

"The LORD gives sight to the blind. . . . The LORD loves the just" (Responsorial Psalm). The love of the Lord for all people, but especially those who are in need, is a fact of life. God may ask individuals to share his Son's passion by personal suffering for a while, but in the end "The LORD raises up those that were bowed down." This principle is perfectly illustrated in Tobit's life. Accompanied by the Angel Raphael, Tobiah and his new bride return home, and Tobiah anoints his father's cataract covered eyes with the fish gall Raphael had told him to acquire. And Tobit's sight is restored! What is instructive for us is the construction and content of Tobit's prayer: "Blessed be God, and praised be his great name!" We may not forget Tobit's wife, the faithful, loving, and trusting Anna. As she shared her husband's suffering, she now shares his grateful praise. That's what marriage is all about: by the sharing of joys and sorrows, wife and husband are brought closer to God.

YEAR II

READING I 2 Tim 3:10-17
GOSPEL Mark 12:35-37

Paul almost seems to be boasting here, but he is actually giving a good illustration of true humility. Humility is knowing oneself and neither overestimating nor underestimating one's achievements and accomplishments. Paul gives all the credit to the Lord. "You know what persecutions I have had to bear, and . . . the Lord saved me from them all." He proposes his way of life to Timothy, begging him to found his manner of acting on the Scriptures and to draw his strength therefrom. "All Scripture is inspired of God [that is, it has God for its principal author] and is useful for teaching . . . that the man of God may be fully competent and equipped for every good work."

The Jesus in whom Paul has believed and lived for insists in the gospel that the Messiah is more than a blood descendant of David:

he is Lord. "The majority of the crowd heard this with delight," says Mark. That's the only way to hear him!

358 SATURDAY OF THE NINTH WEEK IN ORDINARY TIME

YEAR I

READING I Tob 12:1, 5-15, 20
GOSPEL Mark 12:38-44

Tobit's integrity continues to manifest itself. He tells Tobiah to overpay Raphael, his traveling companion. The latter, having finished his work, is now ready to reveal his identity—but not before he gives a little homily to the two men. Angels don't usually preach, but Raphael is worth listening to, even now. As is to be expected from an angel, his chief advice is that they never cease praising the Lord. He also gives practical council for daily living: prayer and fasting are O.K., but almsgiving is better—if done with "righteousness," which undoubtedly includes unselfish love (as is illustrated by the poor widow in the gospel). Actually, the entire sermon can be reduced to two words, praise and almsgiving, which shouldn't be too hard for us to remember.

His homily finished, Raphael reveals his identity. He is a healer, "one of the seven angels who enter and serve before the Glory of the Lord." Is it any wonder that Raphael is the patron saint of so many hospitals and health centers?

YEAR II

READING I 2 Tim 4:1-8
GOSPEL Mark 12:38-44

There is quite a contrast between the scribes condemned by Jesus and the apostle Paul, whom Jesus was to convert. The scribes sought only self-glorification, but Paul spent himself for Christ and the gospel. And he expects his man Timothy to do the same. "I charge you to preach the word, to stay with this task whether convenient or inconvenient . . . constantly teaching and never losing patience."

Is there a more important virtue than patience, not only for teachers but for parents and all of us?

In the gospel Jesus tells us that God was more pleased with the love with which the poor widow gave her two coins than with the big contributions of the wealthy. It is still a good rule, which modern Catholics may not forget, although most pastors would prefer a combination of large sums together with generous love. St. Paul gave his life, his all, and he gave with love. What—and in what spirit—do we give?

89 TENTH SUNDAY IN ORDINARY TIME Cycle A

READING I **Hos 6:3-6** **READING II** **Rom 4:18-25**
GOSPEL **Matt 9:9-13**

Reading I: Hosea tells the Israelites that what God desires of them is love, not sacrifice.

Reading II: Paul proposes Abraham as the model of Christian faith. Abraham never doubted God's promises.

Gospel: Matthew accepts Jesus' invitation to follow him and celebrates with a banquet at which Jesus is present.

The key idea in today's readings comes from Jesus: "It is mercy I desire and not sacrifice. I have come to call not the self-righteous, but sinners."

Jesus sees Matthew, a despised collector of taxes for the Romans, and says to him: "Follow me." Without hesitation, Matthew gets up and follows him. He is so delighted with his new vocation that he puts on a banquet for Jesus, which naturally attracts other tax collectors and other sinners.

When the Pharisees see Jesus and his disciples in the midst of that kind of company, they are properly shocked. They don't dare confront Jesus, so they complain to his disciples: "What reason can the Teacher have for eating with tax collectors and those who disregard the law?" Jesus overhears the question and makes the memorable comment: "People who are in good health do not need a doctor; sick people do. Go and learn the meaning of the words, 'It is mercy I desire and not sacrifice.' I have come to call not the self-righteous, but sinners."

Those words are almost identical with the words of God spoken by the prophet Hosea, who lived in the eighth century before Christ. The people were executing all the externals of worship, but God complained: "Your piety is like a morning cloud, like the dew that early passes away." Then the Lord tells them what worship ought to be: "It is love that I desire, not sacrifice, and knowledge of God rather than holocausts."

So the Pharisees had "forefathers" who thought as they did (and there is always danger that we might inherit their "ideals"). The Pharisees who criticized Jesus in today's gospel have forgotten or misunderstood their Scripture. Above all, they have failed to grasp what the promised Messiah was to be and do and preach, how he was to fulfill his mission. So they created a Messiah after their own false ideas, and worse still, they practiced a religion based on strict observance of the letter of the Mosaic Law—the exact performance of the externals of worship with little concern for the whereabouts of their hearts.

All this is background for today's readings. Again Jesus tries to remind the Pharisees (and us) of the true nature of his messiahship ("I have come to call not the self-righteous, but sinners") and how he is to go about his work—by identifying himself with sinful people. Later St. Paul will write about Jesus: "For our sake God made him who did not know sin, to be sin, so that in him we might become the very holiness of God" (2 Cor 5:21).

As always, these readings speak to our hearts now. The warning against the Pharisaic mentality is always in order; but perhaps the most valuable idea for us is in what Jesus says and does. He has called us to follow him as he called Matthew (although in less distinguished vocations than that of apostle). Having become one with us, he knows what it means to be human. His only motivation for all that he was and did was his all-out *love* for each of us.

Today's readings provide us with the only response Jesus wants from us: "It is love that I desire, not sacrifice." And again, "It is mercy I desire and not sacrifice." Our deep, personal love for him, our mercy and compassion for others, especially for sinners. Is it too much to ask, after all that he has done for us?

TENTH SUNDAY IN ORDINARY TIME Cycle B

READING I Gen 3:9-15 **READING II** 2 Cor 4:13–5:1
GOSPEL Mark 3:20-35

Reading I: The temptation of Adam and Eve, their fall and expulsion from the garden of Eden.

Reading II: Speaking from personal experience, Paul comforts those who suffer infirmities with the conviction that God will welcome them into their eternal dwelling.

Gospel: Jesus, accused of being possessed by Beelzebul, justifies his ministry and reveals the identity of his brothers and sisters.

Reading I is a stark account of the fall of Adam and Eve and the entrance of evil into the world. The account is full of mystery and hard-to-answer questions. For example, How, why, does all humankind have to suffer because our first parents disobeyed God? Why do we get the stomachache when they ate the apple?

God made our first parents free, made them in God's own image. But of what use is freedom if it is not exercised? Again, is love genuine if it is not freely given? Only free persons are capable of loving. What is more important in God's eyes than freely given love? A final note about this reading: In condemning the devil in the guise of a serpent, God tells him:

> I will put enmity between you and the woman,
> and between your offspring and hers;
> He will strike at your head,
> while you strike at his heel.

Traditionally, this has been considered to be the first gospel, the first promise of redemption, a promise that will be fulfilled in Jesus, offspring of the woman Mary.

In today's gospel, we see Jesus in action against Satan. Irony of ironies, his enemies accuse him of being possessed by the ancient enemy who had seduced our first parents. It isn't difficult for Christ to refute the stupid charges of his enemies. "How can Satan expel Satan? . . . If Satan has suffered mutiny in his ranks and is torn by dissension, he cannot endure."

The final incident in the gospel seems at first to be unrelated to the rest of it, but it is the key to understanding not only Christ's work but the Fall itself. Jesus, having been told that his mother and brothers are asking for him, replies: "Who are my mother and my brothers?" Then, gazing on the crowd of people around him, he makes this memorable statement: "These are my mother and my brothers. Whoever does the will of God is brother and sister and mother to me."

It is an amazing observation, but heartwarming and challenging for all of us. For when we place our lives in God's hands and give over our wills to the Lord, we are one with Jesus, and we are more closely akin to him than any physical relative.

There is another truth in Jesus' word that might easily pass unobserved. It relates to the fall of Adam and Eve. Their refusal to do the will of their creator was their essential sin, the sin that Jesus was to counteract. He freely chose to do what they had refused to do. He obeyed the Lord's will and so became the world's Redeemer, the new head of the human race. All who strive to obey God's will are not only his sisters and brothers but fellow redeemers as well.

It's a long time since the events described in Reading I and the gospel. We are present *now,* in this moment of history, and we've lived long enough to know that life isn't always a joy ride. In Reading II, St. Paul has some excellent counsel for those of us who suffer pain of any kind, who experience the infirmities and anxieties of old age: "We do not lose heart because our inner being is renewed each day, . . . The present burden of our trial is light enough and earns for us an eternal weight of glory. . . . Indeed, we know that when the earthly tent in which we dwell is destroyed we have a dwelling provided for us by God, . . . to last forever."

Implicit in the reading is the one attitude that will make this life not only bearable but redemptive and joyous as well: the desire to live each day in total obedience to the will of our beloved creator and Lord. Maybe the secret of life, which Adam and Eve did not realize, is to be found in today's Communion Antiphon:

> God is love, and he who lives in love, lives in God, and God in him.

91 TENTH SUNDAY IN ORDINARY TIME Cycle C

READING I **1 Kgs 17:17-24** **READING II** **Gal 1:11-19**
GOSPEL **Luke 7:11-17**

Reading I: Elijah begs God to restore life to the son of a widow and the Lord grants his request.

Reading II: Paul tells the story of his life before and after his conversion.

Gospel: With a word Jesus raises a widow's dead son to life.

We see Jesus at his most human and his most divine when he is face to face with pain, especially the pain of a poor widow who has just lost her only son to death. We can almost hear him say to the mother, "Do not cry." It's the same thing any of us would say in a similar situation. But unlike our expressions of sympathy, which, though well meant, are just words, Jesus *does* something about the situation. He touches the litter, the men carrying it stand still, and he commands, "Young man, I bid you get up." The young man obeys, he returns from the dead and begins to speak. The evangelist does not reveal the mother's reaction. No need to. He leaves that to our imagination, our own feelings.

What we do not have to try to imagine is the reaction of the people: "Fear seized them all and they began to praise God." First fear, then praise. It is the ancient human reaction to the realization that one is in the presence of the divine. Fear, awe, but not terror. It is rather a sense of one's unworthiness in the presence of the all-holy Lord. But it doesn't last; it gives way to praise and cries of joy. "God has visited his people!" they cry, and how right they are! Jesus most human, Jesus most divine. That's who and what he is.

The mother's reaction might well have found expression in the Responsorial Psalm:

> You changed my mourning into dancing;
> O Lord, my God, forever will I give you thanks.

Those words also belong to the widow in Reading I. She too has lost an only son. She appeals to the man of God, Elijah, or rather she blames him for having killed her son, but actually the accusation is an appeal for help. It is interesting to contrast Elijah's efforts to revive the dead man with those of Jesus. Jesus simply commands. Elijah goes through a series of actions, beginning with a prayer to

God. Then he stretches himself out upon the body, not once but three times, again calling out to the Lord, "O Lord, my God, let the life breath return to the body of this child." And his prayer is heard. Elijah brings the child down from the upper room and restores him to the grateful, joyous mother. And the psalmist anticipates her joyous reaction:

> I will praise you, Lord,
> for you have rescued me.

The key idea in both readings (less obvious in Reading I) is in the words "God has visited his people." God in the person of the prophet Elijah; God in the person of the God-man Jesus. And there can be only one motive for God's visitation: compassionate love. The old refrain should always be present in our minds and hearts: "God so loved the world that he gave his only Son" (John 3:16).

That divine Son is still with us, still moved with pity whenever we are in difficulty or pain. His presence, of course, is not as obvious and visible as it was to the widow of Naim. And his comforting is not as dramatic. His healing now is mostly in the hands of the humans he has commissioned, the ministers of the sacraments. He alone knows how many millions, including ourselves, he has restored to life by means of the sacrament of reconciliation.

> I can rely on the Lord; I can always turn to him for shelter. . . . My God, you are always there to help me! (Communion Antiphon)

That is one reaction; but there is another that may surprise us. Have we ever thought of giving our personal consent to allowing God to love us? Scripture often compares God to a loving mother who longs to grasp her child to her breast—a beautiful image of how God feels about us. Our problem may be a false humility, an inferiority complex arising from our sins, that makes us stand aloof from divine love.

The women in today's readings had no such hesitations. We might well take a lesson from them.

359 MONDAY OF THE TENTH WEEK IN ORDINARY TIME

YEAR I

READING I **2 Cor 1:1-7**
GOSPEL **Matt 5:1-12**

"How blest are the poor in spirit, . . . the sorrowing, . . . the lowly, . . . the persecuted. . . ." What does Jesus mean? The virtues he extols do not seem particularly desirable to Americans. But why not, especially when you understand what the virtues entail? Christ is not proposing a list of nice attitudes for his followers to strive for by mighty effort; rather he proposes a mentality for them, a mentality of which he himself is the best exponent. The Beatitudes "have in view persons who have nothing to hope for from the world and who look to God for everything, . . . who are totally open to God" (*A New Catechism,* p. 99).

Acquiring such a mentality is the work both of God and of human effort. Mostly, it is a sharing in the life of grace Paul describes in Reading I.

> Taste and see how good the Lord is;
> happy the man who takes refuge in him (Responsorial Psalm).

YEAR II

READING I **1 Kgs 17:1-6**
GOSPEL **Matt 5:1-12**

Now we are back in the Old Testament again, to a period in Jewish history when true religion was threatened. But the Lord watches over his prophet Elijah and feeds him. Elijah expresses the universal truth that is ours as well:

> Our help is from the Lord
> who made heaven and earth (Responsorial Psalm).

The Beatitudes are familiar and dear to all Christians, but they have to be understood. They summarize a way of life that is quite different from our American ideal. As *A New Catechism* (p. 99) puts it, the Beatitudes "have in view people who have nothing to hope for from the world and look to God for everything, . . . people who are totally open to God." Actually, what Jesus is proposing is the way of life that he himself has lived. He alone completely fulfills the ideal, but he invites us to follow him and promises to be always at hand for those who feel their need for him and hope in him. That ought to include us all.

360 TUESDAY OF THE TENTH WEEK IN ORDINARY TIME

YEAR I

READING I **2 Cor 1:18-22**
GOSPEL **Matt 5:13-16**

The word "yes" might well be the most important word in any language. It characterized the entire life of Jesus and his mother, Mary. It expresses the ideal attitude to our God that Jesus proposes to us by his life and his word. It expresses our willingness to hear and obey the Lord's desires for us. Above all, it expresses our willingness to allow ourselves to be loved by our God.

It is our yes to God more than anything else that makes us the salt of the earth and the light of the world, which is precisely what Jesus desires us to be. But we are free and fragile. Our fervor can grow cold. If our yes loses its love, we diminish as persons. May we keep ourselves salty and keep ourselves all lit up by making yes the chief prayer of our lives. "Lord, let your face shine on me" (Responsorial Psalm).

YEAR II

READING I **1 Kgs 17:7-16**
GOSPEL **Matt 5:13-16**

In the gospel, Jesus uses salt and light to illustrate the effect he wishes Christianity to have both on Christians and on those with whom they associate. Christians are supposed to have the same seasoning effect on humankind that salt has on food: when they live their faith, they enhance the value of life for others. They give meaning to life—meaning that can preserve it from the living death of boredom. So, too, Christians who live their faith have the same enlightening effect that a lighthouse has for sailors at sea.

But as salt can spoil and lose its power to season food and as light can be concealed, so can Christians who lose their sense of the presence of Jesus, the Light of the world. Our constant prayer must be:

> Lord, let your face shine on us. . . .
> O Lord, let the light of your countenance shine upon us!
> (Responsorial Psalm)

361 WEDNESDAY OF THE TENTH WEEK IN ORDINARY TIME

YEAR I

READING I 2 Cor 3:4-11
GOSPEL Matt 5:17-19

The Law of Moses meant everything to the Jews. They saw it as the expression of Yahweh's loving will. In his lifetime, Jesus often came into apparent conflict with the Law, rather, with certain interpretations of the Law proposed by some Pharisees. For many of them, strict obedience to the letter of the Law was the essence of religion. By such obedience a person achieved salvation. It was this false interpretation of the Law that gave rise to Christ's conflict with the Pharisees. If they were right, what need was there of his saving passion and death? Paul tells us today: "It is not that we are entitled of ourselves to take credit for anything. Our sole credit is from God." What God asks of us is total, passionate receptivity to God's love and salvation. God wants our hearts, our love.

> Extol the Lord, our God,
> and worship at his footstool;
> holy is he (Responsorial Psalm)!

YEAR II

READING I 1 Kgs 18:20-39
GOSPEL Matt 5:17-19

> Keep me, O God, for in you I take refuge;
> I say to the Lord, "My Lord are you" (Responsorial Psalm).

Elijah believed that God was indeed his hope and actually staked his life on his belief. Reading I tells how God rewarded his faith.

Today's gospel puts Jesus' attitude towards the Mosaic Law in its true perspective. He tells us that he has not come to destroy the Law and the prophets, but to fulfill them. The secret of the problem of contrast between the old Law and the new is in the word "fulfill." The word connotes not simply the end fulfillment of prophecy, but an ever deeper and deeper understanding and meaning in the Law and the prophets. It is precisely this that Jesus brings us. In himself, in his life and preaching, in his deeds, he teaches us how to live. Can there be a higher purpose for any law? We live by following him.

362 THURSDAY OF THE TENTH WEEK IN ORDINARY TIME

YEAR I

READING I 2 Cor 3:15–4:1, 3-6
GOSPEL Matt 5:20-26

Today's gospel is a fine example of how Jesus perfects and gives deeper meaning to the Law. The true spirit of the Law demands avoidance not only of awful crimes like murder but also of anger and any kind of hateful action or attitude towards one's neighbor. Jesus drives the point home by insisting that reconciliation with one's brother or sister takes precedence over divine worship itself. The reason is that a divided, angry heart cannot possibly be a worshiping heart in love with a loving God. Worship is not for God, but for us: it makes us more human, more whole. Going through the motions of worship with anger or antagonism in our hearts (or being the cause of others' anger towards us) is a waste of time. We always have to ask ourselves if, in the light of Christ's principles, we have any right to be here at Christ's own worship of the Father.

YEAR II

READING I 1 Kgs 18:41-46
GOSPEL Matt 5:20-26

Sin is in the heart before it is in the deed. Jesus tells us today that being angry with a brother is self-destructive: it hurts us more than it hurts our neighbor. Are we surprised at the link Christ makes between worship and our inner relationship with our neighbor? He tells us that worship is a waste of time if our neighbor has something against us.

That is strong stuff. Can he be serious? Indeed he is. For a Jew there is no more sacred duty than worship of God. But Jesus tells us that even worship has to be put off in favor of reconciliation; and, says the *Jerome Biblical Commentary* (p. 71), it maks no difference who started the quarrel. When are we going to take our Lord seriously in this matter?

363 FRIDAY OF THE TENTH WEEK IN ORDINARY TIME

YEAR I

READING I 2 Cor 4:7-15
GOSPEL Matt 5:27-32

When we think of ourselves and all our weaknesses, we can marvel at the risk God takes in entrusting such great responsibilities to us. Paul says that "This treasure we possess in earthen vessels to make it clear that its surpassing power comes from God and not from us." We cannot take credit for anything; God gives all. We can all verify Paul's description of the Christian life—the afflictions, doubts, temptations to despair, persecutions. These are facts of daily life. But how grateful must we be to Paul for providing us with the meaning of these facts: "Continually we carry about in our bodies the dying of Jesus, so that in our bodies the life of Jesus may also be revealed." Christians never suffer alone; it's always we and Christ together. Like Jesus, we can say, "To you, Lord, I will offer a sacrifice of praise" (Responsorial Psalm).

YEAR II

READING I 1 Kgs 19:9, 11-16
GOSPEL Matt 5:27-32

"I long to see your face, O Lord. . . . Your presence, O Lord, I seek." Today's Responsorial Psalm was Elijah's prayer, but it belongs to us and to all humankind. It expresses the deepest desire of the human heart—our need for God. The wonderful thing is that the prayer is sure to be answered. God never disappoints anyone who sincerely seeks him. He may speak and manifest himself through any of nature's phenomena; but most often the divine voice is gentle and quiet, like "a tiny whispering sound." There is no limit to the number of voices available to our God. Perhaps the one we take most for granted is the voice of conscience, inviting us to do or say or think what is right, warning us about our nearness to driving God out of our lives by serious sin. Jesus tells us today: "Anyone who looks lustfully at a woman has already committed adultery with her in his thoughts." In all of us there is an inner voice telling us what to do, what not to do or think. It may well be the voice of God.

364 SATURDAY OF THE TENTH WEEK IN ORDINARY TIME

YEAR I

READING I **2 Cor 5:14-21**
GOSPEL **Matt 5:33-37**

In his letter to the Romans, Paul tells us that through baptism we are baptized into the passion and death of Jesus, and this is a very real experience, not just a pious hope. Today Paul carries his thought even deeper: "If anyone is in Christ, he is a new creation." In other words, what Christ does for us in baptism is every bit as great and marvelous as the very beginning of life itself. Then Paul returns to his most constant conviction: "All this has been done by God, who has reconciled us to himself through Christ and has given us the ministry of reconciliation." But God's gift to us instructs us in our own way of life, which must be a reconciling life. Paul implores us to be reconciled with God; Jesus tells us there is no way of being reconcilied with God without being reconciled with our neighbor. As the Lord is kind and merciful, so must we be kind and merciful. That's Christianity!

READING I 1 Kgs 19:19-21
GOSPEL Matt 5:33-37

"You are my inheritance, O Lord" (Responsorial Psalm).

Whether he is fully aware of it or not, this psalm verse expresses Elisha's mind when the great prophet Elijah throws his cloak over the young man who then leaves his old life behind and becomes Elijah's helper and eventually his successor. The incident, followed by this psalm, is a good example of every vocation. A vocation is a call from God to carry on God's own work. Any vocation is a call from God, not just to the priesthood or the religious life, but also to the vocation of marriage or single life outside a religious order. No matter what the vocation, the proper response on our part is:

"You are my inheritance, O Lord."

One's own preference has to give way to what the Lord wants.

"I set the Lord ever before me.
Therefore my heart is glad and my soul rejoices" (Responsorial Psalm).

92 ELEVENTH SUNDAY IN ORDINARY TIME Cycle A

READING I Exod 19:2-6 **READING II** Rom 5:6-11
GOSPEL Matt 9:36–10:8

Reading I: The Lord speaks to Moses on Mount Sinai, reminding him of the people's rescue from slavery in Egypt and expressing the hope that they will be faithful to the covenant.

Reading II: Paul relates how Jesus proved his love for all peoples by dying for all.

Gospel: Moved by pity for the shepherdless crowds, Jesus commissions his apostles to preach to them, heal the sick, and expel demons.

The theme that runs through all of today's readings is that of God's compassionate love and pity for all peoples. The first manifestation of this divine pity is beautifully described by God himself in Reading I. The Lord asks Moses to tell the people how he bore them up on eagle wings and brought them here to Sinai: "Therefore, if you hearken to my voice and keep my covenant, you shall be my special possession, dearer to me than all other people, though all the earth is mine."

The kindness, compassion, and pity of the Lord is made visible in the greatest of God's gifts to the world, Jesus Christ. Today's gospel shows this Jesus giving voice and realization to his pity. "At the sight of the crowds, the heart of Jesus was moved with pity." The people obviously need help, healing, love. In a word, they need shepherding, for "they were lying prostrate from exhaustion, like sheep without a shepherd." The gospel goes on to relate what Jesus does about the situation. He chooses a group of twelve apostles, each listed by name, and gives them instructions to care for the people: "cure the sick, raise the dead, heal the leprous, expel demons."

The gospel concludes with a significant remark: "The gift you have received, give as a gift." It is significant because it puts into words the essence of the theology of redemption: salvation begins with God, who bears up all humankind on eagle wings. It is gift, sheer gift, prompted by love and compassion; it cannot be earned or merited. The only thing God wants of us is eager openness to the gift, gratitude, and the willingness to share what has been given to us. In our own way, our own situation in life, we are to try to share the gift we have received. We are to "give as a gift."

The person who probably best understood that statement of Jesus was St. Paul, author of Reading II. Paul's personal experience of conversion, his hearing Jesus speak to him as he lay on the road, his years of meditation in the Arabian desert, all added up to the firmest possible conviction that everything was gift: his very life, his vocation, above all his faith. Divine gift prompted by divine love.

Reading II is an excellent summary of Paul's convictions, especially the statement: "It is precisely in this that God proves his love for us: that while we were still sinners, Christ died for us."

Few followers of Christ ever strove to share God's gift more zealously and successfully than Paul. He was a driven man, driven by the desire to share the faith, the love, the mercy, that Jesus had showered upon him.

We can't all be missionaries as Paul was, and God does not expect us to go out preaching on street corners. But we can all show our gratitude to God by being merciful and by caring for those in need, by praying and suffering for missionaries, and by fidelity to the covenant God made with us when he rescued us from the slavery of sin and gifted us with our faith. We are indeed his people, the sheep of his flock.

> Sing joyfully to the Lord, all you lands;
> serve the Lord with gladness;
> come before him with joyful song. . . .
> The Lord is good:
> his kindness endures forever (Responsorial Psalm).

93 ELEVENTH SUNDAY IN ORDINARY TIME Cycle B

READING I **Ezek 17:22-24** **READING II** **2 Cor 5:6-10**
GOSPEL **Mark 4:26-34**

Reading I: The Lord compares the messianic kingdom to a tender shoot that will grow and bear much fruit.

Reading II: Paul's message is that we live by faith, not by sight. We may long to be with God, but meanwhile we live in hope.

Gospel: Jesus uses the imagery of seeds to give some idea of how the kingdom of God is to mature and grow.

Reading I finds fulfillment in the Church, which is compared to a majestic tree that will bear fruit and give shelter to birds of every kind. The Lord is, of course, thinking about people, not forestry or orchards. Thinking about us. We can see ourselves in two ways—as the birds that find shelter in the branches and as tender shoots from the main tree that God plants and expects to bring forth fruit. The fruit, of course, is intimacy with Jesus and holiness as well as the important fruit of prayer and sacrifice for the spread of Christianity, for vocations, for peace. We have been chosen because God loved us from all eternity. So,

> It is good to give thanks to the Lord,
> to sing praise to your name, Most High, . . .

They that are planted in the house of the Lord
  shall flourish in the courts of our God.
They shall bear fruit even in old age (Responsorial Psalm).

In Reading II, Paul examines our life as shoots off the main tree, as members of the Church. "We walk by faith, not by sight." We might long for deliverance, but we continue to live in hope and patience until the Lord is ready for us.

The gospel is again about growth, not about numerical or physical growth, but about spiritual maturity, growing in love for Jesus.

The seed is the word of God; the sower is Christ;
everyone who finds him will live forever (Alleluia Verse).

Not only all who come to him, but those who receive the divine word with eager openness and allow it to expand their hearts. The reign of God that Jesus speaks about so often is, on our part, a recognition of God's lordship over all of life and of God's undying, everlasting love and concern for us all. The Christian life is, or ought to be, an ongoing maturing in this recognition.

The Christian life is also family, community life. The branches on a tree all live on the life of the trunk. Branches and trunk are one. So, too, the Church. We are all one in Christ. Our problem is to remain and grow together. But because we are human and each of us is free, we are often tempted to live our own lives with little or no concern for the rest of the community. So we need today's Alternative Opening Prayer:

God our Father,
we rejoice in the faith that draws us together,
aware that selfishness can drive us apart.
Let your encouragement be our constant strength.
Keep us one in the love that has sealed our lives,
help us to live as one family
the gospel we profess.

The Eucharist is our family feast. The nourishment of this family is God's holy word *and* the Body and Blood of Christ. Jesus is the bond of unity that keeps us one. May we never forget the great truth contained in the Prayer after Communion:

Lord,
may this eucharist
accomplish in your Church
the unity and peace it signifies.

ELEVENTH SUNDAY IN ORDINARY TIME

READING I **2 Sam 12:7-10, 13** **READING II** **Gal 2:16, 19-21**
GOSPEL **Luke 7:36–8:3**

Reading I: The prophet Nathan lists David's sins; David responds with sorrow and is forgiven.

Reading II: Paul summarizes his doctrine on justification: it is God's gift that cannot be earned by observance of the law.

Gospel: A sinful woman repents her past and washes Jesus' feet with her tears. Her sins are forgiven.

Lord, forgive the wrong I have done (Responsorial Psalm). Forgiveness of sin is what today's liturgy is all about. Both David and the nameless woman of the gospel were sinners. They had forgotten God and given in to shameful self-indulgence. Why did they repent? Because God refused to forget them. God went after them, tracked them down as a shepherd tracks down a lost sheep.

David came to his senses and repented when Nathan told him the story of the rich man who took his servant's prize lamb and made a meal for a guest. In today's Reading I God, speaking through Nathan, gives a detailed account of all the Lord had done for the king. Nevertheless, David has committed adultery and murder. But now David sees himself as he is, and God forgives him. "I have sinned against the LORD." David's contrition is universal. He epitomizes the human condition.

We don't know exactly how the woman recognized her sinful condition and repented, but obviously God's grace had been working in her. Perhaps she had seen Jesus and heard him preach. Now she hears that Jesus is dining at Simon's home, and she decides that this is the moment for her confession. It is perhaps the most dramatic confession in history. Her tears flow over Jesus' feet, and she dries his feet with her beautiful hair. Her actions tell all the world, especially Jesus, how she feels about her sinful past.

The Pharisee Simon is the only one who refuses to understand what has really happened. He sits in judgment over both Jesus and the woman. To himself he says, "If this man were a prophet, he would know who and what sort of woman this is that touches him—that she is a sinner." Jesus can't resist this very special and necessary teaching moment. He contrasts the woman's heroic and dramatic expression of love and repentance with Simon's thoughtless, even deliberate disregard for courtesy. Then Jesus makes the Pharisee reluctantly admit that the person who receives the largest forgiveness of a debt has to be the most grateful.

What is intriguing about this gospel is that Jesus is more understanding of and kinder to the sinful woman than to the self-righteous Pharisee. It's hard to know if his attitude was an evaluation of the degree of the two parties' sinfulness or not. The man is respectable, he fulfills all the religious obligations, he obeys all the laws, but Jesus seems to indicate that something is missing, most probably his heart. The woman knows she is a sinner. The man refuses to admit his sinfulness. "Little is forgiven the one whose love is small," Jesus tells him.

Paul continues Jesus' lesson: a person is not justified by legal observance or good works. The reason for God's acceptance and forgiveness is simply God's loving generosity and mercy. We can never have a claim on God. God has a claim on us, on our faith and gratitude, and it is total.

Jesus tells Simon that the woman's many sins are forgiven "because of her great love," and he says to the woman: "Your faith has been your salvation. Go now in peace." For Jesus, love and faith belong together. Faith is the joyous receptivity to love that allows it to take over one's entire life. That sinful woman has a lot to teach us all!

365 MONDAY OF THE ELEVENTH WEEK IN ORDINARY TIME

YEAR I

READING I 2 Cor 6:1-10
GOSPEL Matt 5:38-42

Christians through the ages have striven to ignore or explain away Jesus' recommendation in today's gospel. Retaliation and revenge seem to have been instinctive in primitive peoples, and moderns are not much better. Jesus' concern is the rescue and salvation of sinners—*all* sinners—those who injure as well as those who are injured. His words today are words of grace, especially to those who are hurt by the deliberately evil or the merely thoughtless actions of others. The one who offends against another hurts that person, but he hurts himself even more. Christ's argument is especially to the injured one who wishes to take revenge by any kind of retaliation: why double the injury? You may get even, but you hurt yourself in so doing. Jesus not only preached this doctrine: he lived it. His word is a lamp for our feet and a light for our path.

YEAR II

READING I 1 Kgs 21:1-16
GOSPEL Matt 5:38-42

The old Exodus Law, "An eye for an eye, a tooth for a tooth," sounds harsh to us, but who of us does not at times succumb to the temptation to get even when someone hurts us? Jesus does not approve of getting even. In today's gospel, he presents his followers with an ideal—not of insistence on legitimate rights granted by civil law, but of forgiving love. It is hard, of course, but whoever claimed that being his follower is easy?

The ideal is not so hard when you think of the example Jesus himself set. None of us has to endure anything like the abuse our Lord and the apostles endured. They successfully resisted all desire for revenge. The same forgiving grace is available to us through the Eucharist *if we desire it.* "Behold, now is the acceptable time, now is the day of salvation." Now, at this Mass!

366 TUESDAY OF THE ELEVENTH WEEK IN ORDINARY TIME

YEAR I

READING I 2 Cor 8:1-9
GOSPEL Matt 5:43-48

Like a shrewd pastor, Paul praises the generosity of one of his former parishes in order to increase the charity of the Corinthians: "Beyond our hopes they [the Macedonians] first gave themselves to God and then to us by the will of God." Paul had given the Macedonians a deep understanding of the whole Church as the body of Christ: they understood that what they did for others they did for Christ, so they voluntarily begged Paul for the privilege of helping other members, even though they themselves were poor. Paul hopes that the example of the Macedonians will instruct the Corinthians about the true nature of the Church and will encourage them to a similar outpouring of charity. "I am not giving an order but simply testing your generous love against the concern which others show." And if the example of the Macedonians is not enough, then perhaps they will be moved by the selfless generosity of Jesus. May we also be moved!

YEAR II

READING I 1 Kgs 21:17-29
GOSPEL Matt 5:43-48

Today Jesus again contrasts current Jewish law and practice to the ideal he sets forth for his followers: "My command to you is: love your enemies, pray for your persecutors. This will prove that you are sons of your heavenly Father." Is he serious? Most of us probably violate this commandment more than any other. The reason is our failure to appreciate the creative power of love. To love someone is to invite him or her to grow, it is to summon a person to new life. And to love someone is to become a new being oneself.

Now I think I understand why Jesus added that last sentence, "You must be made perfect as your heavenly Father is perfect." But how? Because love has that kind of power. It can turn us into new beings like unto God himself. Love implies decision and commitment. Isn't it time we make that decision?

367 WEDNESDAY OF THE ELEVENTH WEEK IN ORDINARY TIME

YEAR I

READING I **2 Cor 9:6-11**
GOSPEL **Matt 6:1-6, 16-18**

Reading I and the Responsorial Psalm could give the impression that the desire for reward is the best motivation for generosity to the poor. Such an attitude would contradict all of Christ's and Paul's teaching. Our charity must never be considered a price we pay for divine favor. Rather, God's unceasing generosity to us ought to make us eager to give and give and give. "God loves a cheerful giver." If anything, then, whatever we give to the poor ought to be thought of as a thanksgiving offering to God.

In the gospel, Jesus reinforces this teaching and extends it to other religious acts like praying and fasting. Perfectly good and praiseworthy acts like prayer and fasting can be spoiled and rendered useless if we do them to be rewarded by those who see us. God loves not only a cheerful giver, but a cheerful *pray*-er and *fast*-er as well. True love is its own reward.

YEAR II

READING I **2 Kgs 2:1, 6-14**
GOSPEL **Matt 6:1-6, 16-18**

Reading I depicts the dramatic passing on of prophetic power, divine favor, and divine responsibility from Elijah to Elisha. Elisha, the disciple, learned in pain the valuable lesson that we may all benefit by—that human sentiment and affection, holy and good though it be, must give way to divine responsibility and the good of the people. But fulfilling divine responsibility as Elijah did and as Elisha had to learn brings its own compensation:

> Let your hearts take comfort,
> all who hope in the Lord (Responsorial Psalm).

Those words are now addressed to all of us here.

Almsgiving, prayer, and fasting are holy and necessary Christian tasks that can be spoiled by vanity. The only remedy for such vanity is a loving intimacy with the Lord, taking comfort in him and hoping in him.

368 THURSDAY OF THE ELEVENTH WEEK IN ORDINARY TIME

YEAR I

READING I **2 Cor 11:1-11**
GOSPEL **Matt 6:7-15**

God knows I love you, Paul tells his people at Corinth, and we know he means it. But like every zealous pastor or chaplain, he is worried about them, his chief concern being the false doctrine about Jesus being preached by some of his rivals whom he calls "super apostles." He vigorously defends himself against their false charges, almost to the point of giving the impression that he is suffering from hurt feelings. But Paul is too big a man for that. He simply loves his people, and he has spent himself for them. Who can blame him if he becomes vehement in defending both them and himself against false accusations?

The noteworthy point in today's gospel about Matthew's version of the "Our Father" is that Jesus relates the greatest prayer of Christians to the greatest need we have as Christians—the need to forgive. "If you do not forgive others, neither will your Father forgive you."

YEAR II

READING I **Sir 48:1-14**
GOSPEL **Matt 6:7-15**

Reading I is a beautiful meditation on the lives of the prophets Elijah and Elisha. Both were God's men, instruments for recalling God's people and their kings to their basic obligation of dependency on and trust in the Lord. They did not foretell the future. In their lives and words they simply proclaimed that

> Let good men rejoice in the Lord.
> The Lord is king; let the earth rejoice (Responsorial Psalm).

Their message is as valid today as it was then.

But Jesus tells us in the gospel that the Lord is also Father, OUR FATHER, and so our prayer to God must primarily be one of joyous, childlike glorification and praise. Jesus reminds us, however, that there is no point in praying to our Father unless we are willing to forgive our neighbor who can also say "Our Father." There is no praise of God without forgiveness of neighbor.

369 FRIDAY OF THE ELEVENTH WEEK IN ORDINARY TIME

YEAR I

READING I 2 Cor 11:18, 21-30
GOSPEL Matt 6:19-23

Judging by the vehemence of Paul's defense, the attack on his reputation must have been vicious. Paul lists his achievements as well as the hardships he has endured. It might sound like bragging; I prefer to call it an exercise in humility, which is knowing the truth about oneself, accepting it, and giving all the credit to God. The Responsorial Psalm reflects Paul's thought:

> I sought the Lord, and he answered me
> and delivered me from all my fears.
> Look to him that you may be radiant with joy.

What the Lord did for Paul, the Lord is just as willing to do for us. But it helps to have one's heart in the right place. "Where your treasure is, there your heart is also." That's for us, too. If our treasure is our possessions, we will be possessed by them—and ruined. If our treasure is Jesus, we will be possessed by him. What greater joy is there than that?

YEAR II

READING I 2 Kgs 11:1-4, 9-18, 20
GOSPEL Matt 6:19-23

Queen Athaliah's weakness was lust for power. It caused her to destroy all her rivals, and in the end it destroyed her. In the gospel, Jesus speaks of a weakness that many of us give in to: the unholy and unhealthy need to possess things, often to the extent of being possessed by them. Wealth, land, clothing, antiques, and all manner of earthly junk can ensnare our hearts and prevent their being centered on Jesus, the only treasure that can give our hungry hearts true and lasting satisfaction. It is not what we *have* but what we *are* that counts in God's view—what we are above all in relation to Jesus. "Where your treasure is, there your heart is also," says our Lord. And we say, Dear Lord, please stabilize these wandering hearts of ours, and help us to center them on Christ alone.

370 SATURDAY OF THE ELEVENTH WEEK IN ORDINARY TIME

YEAR I

READING I 2 Cor 12:1-10
GOSPEL Matt 6:24-34

A divided heart is a sad heart, because it is a worried heart—maybe an impossible heart. Jesus says, "No man can serve two masters. . . . You cannot give yourself to God and money." Why not? Because each demands the fullness of loyalty and dedication. God demands that fullness not for his sake but for ours. We simply cannot be whole and happy apart from God who is the answer to all the yearnings of our desiring hearts.

Paul knew this truth as few others have. He continues his "autobiography" today, as he reveals God's greatest favor to him—his momentary glimpse of heaven. We do not know the nature of "the thorn in the flesh" that kept him from becoming proud, but we can be grateful both to Paul and to Jesus for the words we need as much as Paul: "My grace is enough for you, for in weakness power reaches perfection."

YEAR II

READING I 2 Chr 24:17-25
GOSPEL Matt 6:24-34

No matter how often the people abandoned the Lord and worshiped idols, God never gave up on them. So too with us. The words of the

Responsorial Psalm have not changed their meaning over the centuries. God says, "For ever I will keep my love for him."

But the basic lesson of history also endures. Jesus insists in the gospel, "No man can serve two masters." We Christians can no more serve God and possessions than could the Jews serve both God and idols. The evil in our trying to duplicate loyalty lies in our failure to trust in our Father's loving care. Rather than take refuge in God, we try to find security in possessions and riches. God wants us to keep our values straight—not for his sake but for ours. Remember, "For ever I will keep my love for him."

95 TWELFTH SUNDAY IN ORDINARY TIME — Cycle A

READING I Jer 20:10-13 **READING II** Rom 5:12-15
GOSPEL Matt 10:26-33

Reading I: As a prophet of God, Jeremiah is threatened with persecution, but he is not afraid because the Lord is with him.

Reading II: If all share in the sin of one man, Adam, so all share in the gracious gift of salvation won for us by one man, Jesus.

Gospel: Jesus tells the apostles to expect persecution, but they are not to fear, for the Father protects them.

The man of God, Jeremiah the prophet, was God's witness even at the risk of and eventually the cost of his life. He is aware of his ultimate doom, for almost without exception the vocation of prophet was a call to martyrdom. We need to remind ourselves that the essential task of the Old Testament prophets was to bear witness to the supremacy of God, not to foretell the future.

Jeremiah accepts the Lord's commission, and he is not afraid:

> But the Lord is with me, like a mighty champion:
> my persecutors will stumble, they will not triumph. . . .
> Sing to the Lord,
> praise the Lord,
> For he has rescued the life of the poor
> from the power of the wicked!

Jeremiah eventually gave his life in witness to his faith, but he lives on: his life and his book of prophecy have been the inspiration of countless millions of Jews and Christians through the centuries.

The gospel is a continuation of Jesus' commissioning of his apostles: "Do not let men intimidate you. . . . Do not fear those who deprive the body of life but cannot destroy the soul. . . . Whoever acknowledges me before men I will acknowledge before my Father in heaven." It is much the same message as the one to Jeremiah. The kingdom of God, God's cause, is founded primarily on persecution, on suffering. The history of Christianity bears witness that the Church has always flourished under persecution and suffering. And that continues to be the case in our time. The Church is healthiest today where it is most persecuted.

What about us? Are we to provoke persecution, go looking for it? Hardly. Persecution may give strength to the Church, but perhaps equal to it in efficacious results is the suffering, endured with love, of individual Christians. We can find much satisfaction in St. Paul's mysterious words: "Even now I find my joy in the suffering I endure for you. In my own flesh I fill up what is lacking in the sufferings of Christ for the sake of his body, the church" (Col 1:24).

Every community of Christians, has its full quota of ill, aged, lonely, and dying persons. These people need caring, encouragement, and the conviction that their lives are as worthwhile for the welfare of the Church as when they were actively engaged in full and busy lives. What are we doing for them? Do we ever visit them, make them feel wanted? They need to hear and be convinced of Jesus' words in today's gospel: "As for you, every hair of your head has been counted; so do not be afraid of anything. You are worth more than an entire flock of sparrows."

Suffering people need to know that God cares, and often the only way they can realize that is by the comforting visits from stand-ins for God who remain healthy and active. It is especially to sufferers like these that the words of today's Responsorial Psalm are intended:

> See, you lowly ones, and be glad;
>   you who seek God, may your hearts be merry!
> For the Lord hears the poor,
>   and his own who are in bonds he spurns not. . . .
>   Lord, in your great love, answer me!

96 TWELFTH SUNDAY IN ORDINARY TIME Cycle B

READING I Job 38:1, 8-11 **READING II** 2 Cor 5:14-17
GOSPEL Mark 4:35-41

Reading I: The Book of Job is concerned with the problem and mystery of human suffering. God reminds Job today that God controls the universe, but does not reveal all his ways.

Reading II: Since Christ died for all, we are to live, no longer for ourselves, but for him.

Gospel: Jesus, awakened from sleep, calms a stormy sea with a word and criticizes the apostles for their lack of faith.

We all need today's liturgy. The background of it all—God's words to Job, the Responsorial Psalm, especially the gospel—is God's all-embracing love and concern for people.

> God is the strength of his people. In him, we his chosen live in safety (Entrance Antiphon).

It is this background of God's caring that is behind Jesus' words and actions in the gospel.

Job has gone through terrible suffering, both physical and mental. He may be weakening in his trust in the Lord; so here God reassures him of God's creative power, his control over the elements—especially the sea, the ancient symbol of destructive power. The Lord convinces Job of his faithfulness, and Job comes through the test of faith successfully.

The sea is also featured in the gospel, and today we see it in one of its ugly moods. But it is not the wind and waves that awaken the tired Jesus, asleep on a cushion in the stern of the boat. It is the frightened apostles: "Teacher," they cry, "doesn't it matter to you that we are going to drown?" Of course, it matters. He rebukes the wind and the wind falls off. But he does not let the incident pass without rebuking the apostles: "Why are you so terrified? Why are you lacking in faith?"

They are filled with awe at this manifestation of divine power, and they ask one another: "Who can this be that even the wind and the sea obey him?" Who indeed but the Lord God! This is a perfect example of Jesus' method of teaching the apostles who and what he is. He does it not by coming right out and telling them he is God, he does it rather by his deeds. And in the course of witnessing many more of his marvelous deeds, they will finally draw their own conclusions.

But there is another lesson in this gospel, one that is especially valuable for us. Jesus *sleeps* despite the howling wind, the tossing of the boat. He is tired after a day of preaching and healing. The obvious conclusion is that he is also human. Jesus: God-man, beloved Savior. As he taught the apostles by his power over nature, he now teaches us how to face the storms and turmoil and worries of life. Perhaps the chief lesson is that concern for the problems of others takes precedence over one's own comfort.

The passenger list in Christ's boat can now be counted in the millions, and there is still room. Each of the passengers is troubled in greater or lesser degree. Everyone has worries—deep, personal, frightening, many apparently without solution. We often feel like crying out to Jesus as the apostles did: "Teacher, doesn't it matter to you that we are going to drown?"

And Jesus, still in the boat with us, sadly says to us: "Why are you so terrified? Why are you lacking in faith?" Perhaps the most essential prayer we can pray is: Lord, increase our faith, our hope, our love, so that we can again cry out with the apostles:

> A great prophet has appeared among us;
> God has visited his people (Alleluia Verse).

He is not going to leave us.

We might also want to remember the words of the Entrance Antiphon:

> God is the strength of his people. In him, we his chosen live in safety. Save us, Lord, who share in your life, and give us your blessing; be our shepherd for ever.

97 TWELFTH SUNDAY IN ORDINARY TIME — Cycle C

READING I Zech 12:10-11 **READING II** Gal 3:26-29
GOSPEL Luke 9:18-24

Reading I: A prediction of a person whose death, inflicted by the people of Jerusalem, will be a source of grace for them.

Reading II: Having been baptized into Christ, we are clothed with him, we are children of God, we are all one in Christ Jesus.

Gospel: Assured by the apostles that he is the Messiah, Jesus predicts his passion, death, and resurrection.

"Who do the crowds say that I am?" Jesus asks the apostles. "Who do you say that I am?" There are some scholars who actually believe that Jesus didn't really know who he was, and that is why he asks these questions. Today's gospel hardly bears out any such doubts on his part. After Peter's answer that he is "the Messiah of God," he goes on to predict his passion, death, and resurrection. He may have had in mind the prophecy of Zechariah in Reading I that the inhabitants of Jerusalem "shall look on him whom they have thrust through."

Do we ever ask a question like that about ourselves? Who do people say that I am? What do people really think of me? I suspect that most human beings are curious about their "image." If we ever wonder about what God thinks of us, St. Paul provides us with the answer in today's Reading II: "Each of you is a son of God because of your faith in Christ Jesus. All of you who have been baptized into Christ have clothed yourselves with him."

And Paul goes on to remind us that, as members of Christ, we are to make no distinctions based on race, nationality, social standing, or gender because "All are one in Christ Jesus."

We as a Church, as a nation, as individual Christians, might well examine ourselves on our observance of that divine standard. And in answer to our personal question, Who am I? Jesus provides us with another standard: "Whoever wishes to be my follower must deny his very self, take up his cross each day, and follow in my steps." In other words, carrying the cross of daily life determines our identity as disciples of Christ.

This standard of discipleship may frighten us and make us wonder what the Christian life is all about. What does Jesus mean by "the cross?" Certainly, it includes suffering of any kind, our own or that of those we love. "The cross" is the daily life we all live, in whatever vocation God has called us to. It is fidelity to all the demands and ideals of our particular vocation, fulfilling its requirements to the best of our ability; it is fidelity to the ideal of the Christian life Jesus has sketched for us in the gospels. Above all, it is placing our daily life, our present and our future, in the Lord's hands, relinquishing personal control. Practically speaking, it involves striving to gain command over attachments to food, drink, or other habits that so often direct our lives. We are to prefer nothing whatsoever to the love of Christ.

Is Jesus asking too much? Maybe our answer depends on our reply to the question he asks the apostles today, "Who do you say that I am?" The answer may require reflection in and serious reading of the gospels. It may help to reflect on how well Jesus has "lasted" these two thousand years, on the vast number of followers for whom he meant so much that they literally gave up their lives for him.

Who do *you* say that I am? We simply have to answer that question. Please God that, with Peter, his fellow apostles, and with all Christ's faithful followers through the centuries, we may cry out from the depths of our hearts: You are the Messiah of God. You are the Christ, the Son of the living God!

371 MONDAY OF THE TWELFTH WEEK IN ORDINARY TIME

YEAR I

READING I Gen 12:1-9
GOSPEL Matt 7:1-5

The realistic account of Abram's call in Reading I hardly reveals the interior drama that took place in the hearts of Abram and Sarai. The Lord calls Abram to a new mission, and the old man accepts the call without hesitation. The call—and the promise—made no sense from the human point of view. But Abram trusted God; he believed; he put his whole life and future in God's hands. The result? "Happy the people the Lord has chosen to be his own" (Responsorial Psalm). That is as true of us as it was of Abram. God has also chosen us to be his own. Are we happy to be chosen? Are we even aware of it? May the example and prayers of Abram, our father in faith, inspire us to let go our hold on the past, our hold on all possessions, and launch out into the unknown homeland of God's everlasting love for us.

YEAR II

READING I **2 Kgs 17:5-8, 13-15, 18**
GOSPEL **Matt 7:1-5**

Reading I relates the dramatic moment of the fall of the northern kingdom of Israel and the deportation of its people to Assyria. The author gives the idolatry of the people as the reason for the punishment. But God is not an avenging God. If the people suffer, it is not because God is taking revenge on them but rather that their apostasy brings its own "reward." If they wish to live without God, let them try and see how they like it.

The Responsorial Psalm puts their sad situation into words: "O God, you have rejected us, broken our defenses; you have been angry; rally us!" That is a typically human way of speaking to God. But is it the right way? God does not reject us; we reject God. When we decide that we cannot live without God, when we return to God with all our hearts, we can be sure God will receive us.

372 TUESDAY OF THE TWELFTH WEEK IN ORDINARY TIME

YEAR I

READING I **Gen 13:2, 5-18**
GOSPEL **Matt 7:6, 12-14**

"Treat others the way you would have them treat you; this sums up the Law and the prophets." In the abstract that principle does not seem very noble; however, when it is evident in the thought and practice of a noble person like Abram, it takes on considerable attractiveness. A quarrel between the herdsmen of Abram and Lot brings about a showdown between the two. Conflict is abhorrent to Abram, and he comes to the decision described in the Reading I. As the head of the clan, he could have had first choice of the land. He gives that choice to Lot. This generosity, based undoubtedly on his reverence for Lot as a person, adds to the stature of Abram as one of the world's most attractive of all God's creatures. He presents an ideal for every Christian. Following his example and making Abram's values our own is one of the best ways for all of us to enter through the narrow gate that leads to life.

YEAR II

READING I **2 Kgs 19:9-11, 14-21, 31-35, 36**
GOSPEL **Matt 7:6, 12-14**

"God upholds his city for ever." This verse from the Responsorial Psalm sums up the Lord's undying concern for his people. No matter how often and how seriously they desert him, he always comes to their rescue, especially in response to the kind of faith-inspired prayer prayed by Hezekiah.

The gospel collects several of the sometimes unconnected maxims that make up the Sermon on the Mount. "Treat others the way you would have them treat you." Such good common sense is easier to proclaim than to follow. The question is, how do we want to be treated? We all want our rights, but most of all we want respect, we want recognition as human persons, we want equality, we want love. Christ's guiding principle sounds very nice in the abstract. Our problem is putting it into practice when we deal with members of different races, religions, and (Lord, help us!) a different sex!

373 WEDNESDAY OF THE TWELFTH WEEK IN ORDINARY TIME

YEAR I

READING I Gen 15:1-12, 17-18
GOSPEL Matt 7:15-20

"Any sound tree bears good fruit, while a decayed tree bears bad fruit." Jesus might well have had Abram in mind when he proposed this truth. God's choice of Abram as the father of his people is justified in Abram's thinking and his whole manner of life. His finest fruit is his faith, his trust in the Lord's promise. Humanly speaking, there wasn't a chance in the world that God's promise could be fulfilled. But God speaks divinely, and Abram accepts the promise. To bolster his faith the Lord enters into a solemn covenant with Abram, telling him: "To your descendants I give this land. . . ." God's covenant with Abram is sealed in the blood of animals. At the Last Supper, Jesus will make a new covenant with us, God's people now, and he seals it in his blood. "The Lord remembers his covenant forever" (Responsorial Psalm). And he wants us to remember it, too. That's why Jesus says, "Do this in remembrance of me." Let us do it now.

YEAR II

READING I 2 Kgs 22:8-13; 23:1-3
GOSPEL Matt 7:15-20

By virtue of the covenant Yahweh had established between himself and his people, the Jews, they were to be his very own possession, chosen out of all the peoples of the earth to be heirs of his promises and blessings. Because the Lord loved and chose them, they were to be holy to the Lord God. Unfortunately, the Hebrews often failed to keep their part of the covenant. They worshiped false gods—which is the same as trying to live without God—and learned the hard way that the only result of that kind of living is unhappiness and frustration. Such is the background of today's Reading I.

At this moment in their history even the text of the covenant had been lost. But now it is recovered, the covenant with God is solemnly renewed, and Yahweh is as pleased with them as when the covenant was first made. That is the way God always deals with sinners. God never gives up on anyone. "There is more joy in heaven over one sinner doing penance. . . ."

374 THURSDAY OF THE TWELFTH WEEK IN ORDINARY TIME

YEAR I

READING I **Gen 16:1-12, 15-16**
GOSPEL **Matt 7:21-29**

Marriage customs change as humankind develops. What was approved for Abram then would hardly be acceptable today. Abram's lifelong desire for a son is gratified at long last, and he may well cry out, "Give thanks to the Lord for he is good" (Responsorial Psalm). It's a good prayer for us all. But what about poor Sarai? Just wait (till tomorrow). She who laughs last . . .

Christ's words in the gospel might well be the most terrifying warning he ever uttered. He tells us that following him is a way of life consisting not in pious words but in acceptance of all that the Father chooses to ask of us. Being his followers implies being responsible for the faith he has given us and allowing that faith to shape our lives. "Anyone who hears my words and puts them into practice is like the wise man who built his house on rock." Building the house of religion on any other foundation makes no sense at all.

YEAR II

READING I **2 Kgs 24:8-17**
GOSPEL **Matt 7:21-29**

Today we see the tragic consequences of Hebrew violation of the covenant. The people are led off into captivity in Babylon where in grief and sorrow they face the sad results of having tried to live without God. "For the glory of your name, O Lord, deliver us" (Responsorial Psalm). Yahweh will hear their plea, but only after they have learned by experience that living without God is a living death.

In the gospel Jesus reveals the one and only criterion for discipleship. It is not lofty words, but doing God's will: "None of those who cry out, 'Lord, Lord,' will enter the kingdom of heaven but only the one who does the will of my Father. . . ." Without the Father's will in the midst of our hearts and lives, we run the risk of hearing those chilling words at the end of our lives: "I never knew you. Out of my sight, you evildoers!" May we always want God's will above all else.

375 FRIDAY OF THE TWELFTH WEEK IN ORDINARY TIME

YEAR I

READING I Gen 17:1, 9-10, 15-22
GOSPEL Matt 8:1-4

The rite of circumcision was a sign with the very special religious meaning that Abram's descendants would be God's very own people. At last the moment has arrived for the fulfillment of God's promise to Abraham. Abraham's disbelieving laughter may seem disappointing after all the praise we have heaped upon him. But put yourselves into his 99-year-old shoes. People his and Sarah's age do not ordinarily produce offspring. The Lord insists, however, and soon Abraham is going "to see how the Lord blesses those who fear him," as he has feared and loved the Lord all his life.

From preaching Jesus now turns to healing. "Sir," the leper cries to him, "if you will to do so, you can cure me." Jesus touches him and says, "I do will it. Be cured." That saving, healing will of Jesus continues today. Jesus still holds out his healing hand in all the sacraments.

YEAR II

READING I 2 Kgs 25:1-12
GOSPEL Matt 8:1-4

By the streams of Babylon
we sat and wept
when we remembered Zion (Responsorial Psalm).

This poignant cry expesses the feelings of the stricken Jews in exile in Babylon. All that remains to them of their former glory is a memory that is penetrated with regret, sorrow, pain of loss.

It is good for us to enter into that sad situation and in our hearts make it our own, for experiences like theirs can help us realize how precious is our Christian treasure—our loving, forgiving Jesus. Such an experience can also warn us of what can happen to us when we lose sight of our goals, our Christian values. Because of Jesus, deliverance for us is easier than for them. We need only go to confession and say to him, Lord, if you will, you can make me clean. He will say, I will. Be clean.

376 SATURDAY OF THE TWELFTH WEEK IN ORDINARY TIME

YEAR I

READING I Gen 18:1-15
GOSPEL Matt 8:5-17

God tells Sarah that she is going to have her promised child, and Sarah laughs. When God asks why she laughed, she says, "I didn't laugh." But God says, "Yes, you did." I think God laughed, too. Actually, the meaning of the name Sarah is to give her child Isaac is "God has smiled." I like that. I suspect that God does more smiling than we think. I think he smiled on the centurion, too. He was not even a descendant of Abraham and Sarah, but he had faith, which makes him a very special relative. "Just give an order," he says to Jesus, and all will be well.

The last verses of today's gospel fulfill a messianic prophecy and sum up Christ's life: "It was our infirmities he bore, our sufferings he endured." What we suffer, he suffers. He walks by our side, and at the most difficult times he carries us in his arms. This is the good news of the Lord!

YEAR II

READING I Lam 2:2, 10-14, 18-19
GOSPEL Matt 8:5-17

It would be hard to find a more pitiful description of grief than this lament of the Jews as they experienced the destruction of Jerusalem in 586 B.C. It is a lament out of the very heart of humanity that we can well make our own, for sorrow belongs to all who, through malice or mere human weakness, forsake the Lord's will.

> To what can I liken or compare you,
> O daughter Jerusalem? . . .
> For great as the sea is your downfall.

These words of Reading I are applied to Mary when she holds her crucified son in her arms. It is all right for us to make that application if it will make us love Mary and Jesus more. But what Jesus wants from us is more: he wants faith, the admission of our guilt, the will to amend our lives. Only such a disposition will bring his saving words, I will come and heal you.

98 THIRTEENTH SUNDAY IN ORDINARY TIME — Cycle A

READING I 2 Kgs 4:8-11, 14-16 **READING II** Rom 6:3-4, 8-11
GOSPEL Matt 10:37-42

Reading I: A barren woman shows hospitality to the prophet Elisha and is rewarded with the promise of a son.

Reading II: Baptized into Christ Jesus, we die with him so as to rise and live a new life with him.

Gospel: The gospel treats of the cost of discipleship and continues the theme of hospitality and its rewards.

There are several themes in today's readings, each of which deserves serious consideration: the theme of hospitality, as demonstrated by the woman who welcomed Elisha and by Jesus' own words in the gospel; the theme of the cost of discipleship, which Jesus comments on in the first part of the gospel; and the theme of who and what we are as baptized Christians, as defined by Paul in Reading II. Baptized into Christ's death and resurrection, we must consider ourselves dead to sin but alive to God in Christ Jesus.

Perhaps the three themes coalesce into one, namely, the identity with Christ brought about by our baptism. That identity is the objective fact. How we live it out is what touches at the heart of our daily life as followers of Christ. It involves relationships with others, the preferences we face, who and what is of chief worth and value to us. In a word, it is the *cost* of discipleship that Jesus forces us to consider today: "He who will not take up his cross and come after me is not worthy of me. He who seeks only himself brings himself to ruin, whereas he who brings himself to nought for me discovers who he is."

The Cost of Discipleship is the title of a book by Dietrich Bonhoeffer, a Lutheran pastor who was hanged by the Nazis a week before the end of World War II in Germany. In his book he popularized the terms "cheap grace" and "costly grace." "Cheap grace" is a counterfeit following of Christ, a deeply felt commitment to Christ is absent from it. It is mainly an external practice of religion without any backing from the heart.

In contrast, "costly grace" demands one's accepting the cross of daily life with all its worry and pain. It involves wholehearted obedience to the will of God, giving up every trace of self-will. It is "preferring nothing to the love of Christ" *(Rule of St. Benedict)*.

Today's readings force us to examine our priorities as followers of Christ, to determine whether our following of Christ is cheap or costly. We might ask ourselves if our religious practice has become a loveless, thoughtless routine, a dull gliding along day by day. How seriously do we take our Lord's demands for mutual love, compassion, forgiveness? How concerned are we about Jesus' prayer for unity in our parishes, our communities, our families?

> Father, I pray for them; may they be one in us, so that the world may believe that it was you who sent me (Communion Antiphon).

Does our faith remain on a purely intellectual level, or does it penetrate into and involve our whole being? Have we surrendered ourselves wholly to Christ? And how about our Lord's demands for service and hospitality, welcoming others into the homes of our hearts?

Does this self-examination frighten us, cause us to lose heart? Jesus does not want that. What he does want is that we strive to be honest with him and true to our identity as his disciples. He wants our personal love. A mother who watches all night at the bedside of a beloved child does not consider the cost. All that matters is the child. All that matters for us is Christ. He first loved us and chose us to be his disciples.

> You are a chosen race, a royal priesthood, a holy people. Praise God who has called you out of darkness into his marvelous light (Alleluia Verse).

If we look back over our lives with all God's favors to us, above all his having called us to be his disciples, we have to cry out:

> For ever I will sing the goodness of the Lord (Responsorial Psalm).

99 THIRTEENTH SUNDAY IN ORDINARY TIME Cycle B

READING I Wis 1:13-15; 2:23-24 **READING II** 2 Cor 8:7, 9, 13-15
GOSPEL Mark 5:21-43

Reading I: God formed humans to be imperishable, but death entered the world through the envy of the devil.

Reading II: For our sakes Jesus became poor so that we might become rich by his poverty.

Gospel: Jesus restores a woman to health and brings a dead girl back to life.

Once again there is an obvious relationship between Reading I and the gospel. Today we have a perfect example of how Jesus, the promised Messiah so long awaited by the Jews, was to undo the devastating damage wrought by the devil in the garden of Eden. The two miracles Jesus worked in today's gospel are signs with deep meaning: a woman is restored to health, a dead child is brought back to life.

These two miracles also illustrate how our sacraments fulfill their purpose, especially the sacraments of healing: the sacrament of reconciliation (penance) and the sacrament of the anointing of the sick. "Jesus was immediately conscious that healing power had gone out from him," says the gospel. I believe that he is still conscious of that healing power whenever these two sacraments are administered.

A sacrament is a *sign:* it points to healing, feeding, forgiving, strengthening. But above all, it is a sign that reveals Jesus, reveals how he feels about anyone who suffers in any way. Suffering touches his heart, stirs his compassion.

The human condition that we all share is generally in need of healing. There is a lack of wholeness in us. It may be physical, mental, spiritual, or a combination of them all. We are often fearful, insensitive, unforgiving, vengeful, unappreciative of goodness and beauty in others or in the world of nature. Each of us knows our own weakness. And we want to be healed, made whole again.

But there are certain requirements on our part, too. It is obvious from today's gospel that our first requirement is faith: "Fear is useless" Jesus says. "What is needed is trust." "Daughter, it is your faith that has cured you." It is hardly necessary to insist that faith in Jesus is essential. But we also need faith in ourselves: we have to believe that we are *worth* being healed. And that is not always easy, for a variety of reasons. A poor self-image can result from national origin, lack of education, even physical infirmities or sins we may have committed in the past. But not a single one of these causes is valid. All that matters is who we *are:* we are persons whom God has called into existence because God has known and loved us from all eternity. God cares for *us,* not for where we come from or what we look like.

So we need faith in ourselves, but above all in Jesus. We have to believe that *he* believes in us and that he is eager to heal us of our infirmities, whatever they are. The whole gospel is evidence of this truth. Jesus does want people to believe that they are worth being healed.

Will this twofold faith (in oneself and in Jesus) automatically bring physical healing? Maybe not the kind of wellness we usually think of as healing, although it is probably rare that we do not experience an inner sense of relief and comfort after a good confession.

Millions of people go to places of pilgrimage every year—shrines like Lourdes, Fatima, and more recently, Medjugorje. Very few are physically healed, but most of them depart with a new understanding of their lives and the meaning of suffering as part of life. Many of them come to grasp the meaning and implications of St. Paul's mysterious message to the Colossians: "Even now I find my joy in the suffering I endure for you. In my own flesh I fill up what is lacking in the sufferings of Christ for the sake of his body, the church" (1:24).

This may be the ultimate act of faith: that we with all our human weaknesses and imperfections are not only worthwhile, we are *essential* to Christ, to the Church, and to our world, because through our suffering and dying *we share Christ's redemptive mission.* Because of us, this has to be, it will be, a better world.

We could hardly find a better prayer with which to conclude:

> Lord God,
> Through your sacraments
> you give us the power of your grace.
> May this eucharist
> help us to serve you faithfully.
> (Prayer over the Gifts).

100 THIRTEENTH SUNDAY IN ORDINARY TIME Cycle C

READING I **1 Kgs 19:16, 19-21** **READING II** **Gal 5:1, 13-18**
GOSPEL **Luke 9:51-62**

Reading I: Obeying God's command, Elijah anoints Elisha as his successor, and Elisha leaves all to follow Elijah.

Reading II: Christ has called us to live in freedom; therefore we must serve one another out of love.

Gospel: Jesus decides to go up to Jerusalem and invites others to follow him without looking back.

"As the time approached when Jesus was to be taken from this world, he firmly resolved to proceed toward Jerusalem." That is a sinister phrase; this will be no ordinary visit. Jerusalem will be the place of his crucifixion and death. It is a phrase that conditions everything in our readings today.

As Jesus walks along, he invites some men to follow him. They are willing, but they lay down certain conditions. One wants to bury his father first, another wants to say goodbye to his family. The inhabitants of a Samaritan town will not even allow him to come near. Jesus rejects all excuses and delays. "Come after me" is an invitation, a call, that demands a radical response. It cannot be softened by any human conditions, no delays. "Come after me." Where? To Jerusalem where he will die.

Jesus' call takes precedence over all other obligations, even the courtesy of saying goodby to parents. And he asks us to follow him too. He challenges all of us—not just a few, an elite—to make up our minds about him. We Catholics have allowed some Protestant denominations to take over one of the most crucial phrases of Christianity: "To make a decision for Christ." To make a decision for Christ is the duty of each of us; it is inescapable. And we make it over and over again. Actually, every time we go to confession we make, or ought to make, a new decision for Christ.

When Jesus says, "Come after me," he calls us to follow him to Calvary and to die with him. This is not an invitation to be crucified, as he was, it is not an invitation to martyrdom; rather, it is an invitation to carry with love the cross of daily living and suffering, and more than anything else, an invitation to die to self-love, self-will.

St. Paul has something to say about this in Reading II. He talks about "spirit" and "flesh." By his use of those terms, Paul does not mean "body" in opposition to "soul." He's not talking about human sexuality. "Flesh" for Paul is simply a symbol of all that is fallen in us. It means fallen, unredeemed humanity with all its evil inclinations.

Thus, "fallen humanity" would include not only unlawful sexual acts but also pride, jealousy, anger, gossiping, tearing down reputations, failure to practice works of charity, and failure to love and care for one's neighbor.

Paul goes into great detail about the opposition in us between spirit and flesh. He tells us that Jesus has freed us from slavery to all the manifestations of the flesh. But we do not exercise our freedom in order to choose Jesus and his will against the selfish and sinful indulgence in our own will. Our problem is that we do not seem to realize that Jesus has made us free.

Paul answers such reasoning:

> It was for liberty that Christ freed us. So stand firm, and do not take on yourselves the yoke of slavery a second time! . . . Remember that you have been called to live in freedom—but not a freedom that gives free rein to the flesh. Out of love, place yourselves at one another's service. The whole law has found its fulfillment in this one saying: "You shall love your neighbor as yourself" (Reading II).

What St. Paul is telling us is what we already know from Jesus: there can be no Christianity apart from love of neighbor. Paul is simply emphasizing what he has already said in his letter to the Romans: that the whole law has found its fulfillment in a single command: "You shall love your neighbor as yourself."

Have we strayed from Christ's invitation to "come after me," from our need to "make a decision for Christ"? Hopefully, we have not. That decision is ours to make day by day. It should now be evident that the place to begin is with those around us who are most in need of our loving concern.

And nothing can help us make a decision for Christ more than the realization that he made that journey to Jerusalem and to Calvary—for no other reason than his love for us.

377 MONDAY OF THE THIRTEENTH WEEK IN ORDINARY TIME

YEAR I

READING I **Gen 18:16-33**
GOSPEL **Matt 8:18-22**

There are several ways of looking at the story told in today's Reading I. We could try to determine the enormity of the sins of the people of Sodom and be properly shocked at their wickedness. Or we might consider the social awareness and wonderful charity of Abraham in trying to rescue them. But what appeals most to me is the attitude of the Lord—how eager and anxious God is to forgive the people, despite their degradation. This is our God, then, now and always—our God, whose eagerness to forgive and forget is as available to us now as it was to the people of Sodom then. It is incomprehensible that so many Christians seem to want to concentrate more on their sins than on God's loving kindness.

> Bless the Lord, O my soul;
> and all my being, bless his holy name. . . .
> He pardons all your iniquities,
> he heals all your ills (Responsorial Psalm).

YEAR II

READING I Amos 2:6-10, 13-16
GOSPEL Matt 8:18-22

The word "prophet" is a bit misleading. To us, a prophet is one who foretells the future. But that is only a minor function. Amos, in his life and preaching, illustrates the chief function of the prophet, which is to be the "conscience of the people," reminding them constantly of all that God has done for them and recalling them to renewal of life as partners in their covenant with Yahweh. Often, as is the case today, the prophet threatens them with the consequences of their disloyalty unless they amend.

We Christians need to remind ourselves that the prophets speak to our condition, too. Our sins may or may not be as sensational as those of the Israelites, but when love is the basis of our relationship with God, even the smallest sin is a betrayal. Prophets are the voice of God constantly calling us back.

378 TUESDAY OF THE THIRTEENTH WEEK IN ORDINARY TIME

YEAR I

READING I Gen 19:15-29
GOSPEL Matt 8:23-27

Satchell Paige once said, "Don't look back. Somebody might be gaining on you." The Lord told Lot and his family not to look back to

Sodom, but Lot's wife looked back and was turned into salt. Not only did she disobey God but she did not want to leave the past behind and launch out into a new life. How typical she is of many of us! The past is important to us, and those who forget the past are condemned to repeat its mistakes. But we cannot remain in the past. Life is ongoing. Life is adventure. Every new day, every new year, presents new challenges. The Responsorial Psalm tells us, "Your kindness, Lord, is before my eyes, and I walk in your truth" hand in hand with you, day by day. Unlike the apostles, who do not realize the power of your presence, we fear nothing. So remember Lot's wife. But most of all, remember Jesus who never forgets us.

YEAR II

READING I **Amos 3:1-8; 4:11-12**
GOSPEL **Matt 8:23-27**

Yahweh makes use of every kind of persuasion to bring his people back to him: he tells them of his great love for them in choosing them as his very own, he threatens them, reminds them of the sad results of past infidelity, and finally confronts them with the awful summons: "Prepare to meet your God, O Israel!" We need to remind ourselves that the prophets and their warnings are *our* conscience. Fear of punishment may not be the most noble kind of motivation for an upright life, but at times that is the only thing we heed.

So much the better if, in our stormy voyage through life, we realize that we are in the same boat with Jesus, whose loving care for us protects us against the worst of storms. Think of the deep love behind those words to us: "Where is your courage? How little faith you have!" Why, indeed, *are* we afraid?

379 WEDNESDAY OF THE THIRTEENTH WEEK IN ORDINARY TIME

YEAR I

READING I Gen 21:5, 8-20
GOSPEL Matt 8:28-34

The gospel depicts one of the strangest incidents in the New Testament, strange because it takes place in a pagan land. A herd of swine is destroyed, and the people beg Jesus to leave their neighborhood. Maybe we shouldn't try to seek out some deep meaning, but simply settle for the fact that Christ's mercy and compassion refuse to be confined to any place, any people, any time.

This truth is also illustrated in Reading I. Ishmael, Abraham's son by the slave girl, is exiled by a jealous Sarah. But "the Lord hears the cry of the poor" (Responsorial Psalm). God takes care of Ishmael and promises to make a great nation of him. The Arabs today claim Ishmael as their father. If the Lord hears the cry of poor Ishmael, may we not expect similar loving care?

YEAR II

READING I Amos 5:14-15, 21-24
GOSPEL Matt 8:28-34

"To the upright I will show the saving power of God." These words of the Responsorial Psalm describe Jesus and his life perfectly. In today's gospel, Jesus delivers two demoniacs from satanic influence. That was his entire life; it still is. He continues to exercise that same divine healing power in his Church today, especially in the sacrament of reconciliation.

The best way to thank Christ for his favors is by worship. But not just any kind of worship, as Yahweh indicates by his criticism of his people's public worhsip. That was the problem: it was only public, only external worship. It did not spring from loving hearts, and worst of all, it did not promote justice. God does not need our worship. We need it in order to be whole (and holy). Without it, all God's people suffer, ourselves most of all.

380 THURSDAY OF THE THIRTEENTH WEEK IN ORDINARY TIME

YEAR I

READING I **Gen 22:1-19**
GOSPEL **Matt 9:1-8**

How could anyone put into words the anguish of Abraham, whose hopes and life are dashed by the Lord's command? But God commands and Abraham will obey, even though this particular command will negate all God's promises. It is the ultimate test of faith and Abraham passes it gloriously. I don't pretend to try to solve whatever mystery there might be here. The whole incident may be a kind of preview of what God the Father will some day go through when his own Son Jesus will be sacrificed. It is not for nothing that we see Isaac carrying the wood of the sacrifice. If you desire a moral from the incident, then, when the time comes in your own life that darkness covers all your hopes, just remember Abraham, our father in faith. Call upon him and your faith will flower, and in his name you will be blessed.

YEAR II

READING I **Amos 7:10-17**
GOSPEL **Matt 9:1-8**

Today we see Amos suffering from the harsh lesson in genuine worship he delivered in yesterday's reading. The priest Amaziah accuses Amos of conspiring against the king, predicting Jeroboam's death and the exile of his people. As Amos goes off into exile in the land of Judah, he actually does exercise his prophetic power and foretells what Amaziah accuses him of. The king has refused Amos' warning; thus he opens himself to the penalty deserved by those who refuse to acknowledge the Lord's sovereignty over all life.

> The judgments of the Lord are true,
> and all of them just (Responsorial Psalm).

Jesus meets the same kind of opposition in his lifetime, and like Amos, he refuses to be intimidated. He forgives sins and proves he is God by making a paralytic whole. He continues to do the same thing for us in the sacrament of reconciliation. "God was in Christ, to reconcile the world to himself" (Alleluia Verse).

381 FRIDAY OF THE THIRTEENTH WEEK IN ORDINARY TIME

YEAR I

READING I **Gen 23:1-4, 19; 24:1-8, 62-67**
GOSPEL **Matt 9:9-13**

Reading I relates the continuing unfolding of God's promises to Abraham. Abraham loses Sarah, his wife, and arranges for his son Isaac's choice of a bride. Rebekah will be a worthy mate for him.

The Pharisees wonder why Jesus eats with tax collectors and sinners. The substance of his reply is, "That's where I belong. That's where I feel most at home." And he still does. The Eucharist is the family meal for sinners over which Jesus presides. The Church teaches that the Eucharist forgives sin. If tickets were required for Mass, they might read on one side, "Admit one sinner." And on the other: "Lord, I am not worthy to receive you, but only say the word and I shall be healed."

> Give thanks to the Lord, for he is good,
> for his kindness endures forever (Responsorial Psalm).

YEAR II

READING I **Amos 8:4-6, 9-12**
GOSPEL **Matt 9:9-13**

"Why does your master eat with tax collectors and sinners?" The question is still valid. And the answer is: "That's where I belong. I am savior. It is not the healthy who need a doctor, but the sick." The only ticket we need for any Mass is the one which says, "Admit one sinner." The whole penitential rite of the Mass is based on this premise. Before Communion we cry, "Lord, I am not worthy to receive you, but only say the word, and I shall be healed."

It is good for us to think of this occasionally. I know that I am a sinner. I need Jesus and his healing word and love. If there is anyone here who is not a sinner, let him or her leave and the rest of us will proceed to eat with Jesus and he with us.

382 SATURDAY OF THE THIRTEENTH WEEK IN ORDINARY TIME

YEAR I

READING I Gen 27:1-5, 15-29
GOSPEL Matt 9:14-17

In trying to explain the dishonesty of Jacob and his mother in today's Reading I, St. Augustine writes, "It is not a lie, but a mystery." One can disagree. It certainly was a lie, but it may also be a mystery. Perhaps, as the New American Bible indicates (St. Joseph Edition, p. 30), God does make use of weak, sinful humans to achieve his ultimate purpose. I suspect he prefers honesty at all times.

If the disciples of John are a little troubled at the laxity of Jesus' disciples, one can hardly blame them. Their master John was a true man of God who prepared the Jews for Jesus and his teaching by preaching penance. Fasting was John's way of life. Jesus does not dispute that claim. Fasting is important and necessary for the follower of Christ, but it is not the whole of religious practice. The time will come when Jesus will be taken from the apostles, and then, as a sign of their longing to be reunited with Jesus, they can fast.

YEAR II

READING I Amos 9:11-15
GOSPEL Matt 9:14-17

In the first reading the prophet challenges the Jews to believe that Yahweh will fulfill his promises of happier times to come. "The Lord speaks of peace to his people" (Responsorial Psalm).

In the gospel, Jesus corrects current ideas about the purpose of fasting. Fasting is a penitential exercise—a token of longing desire and hope. People do not fast at weddings. Jesus, the bridegroom, is now with his people. The time will come when he will leave them; then they can express their longing desire and love by fasting. In the second part of the gospel, Jesus touches on the power of his gospel to break out of the previous conceptions of religion the Jews may have had. The good news he brings is going to require a new morality and outlook. We must never fear the new, because the Lord continues to speak of peace and love to his people, to us, if we turn to him in our hearts.

101 FOURTEENTH SUNDAY IN ORDINARY TIME — Cycle A

READING I **Zech 9:9-10** **READING II** **Rom 8:9, 11-13**
GOSPEL **Matt 11:25-30**

Reading I: The prophet predicts the arrival of Jerusalem's king, who will proclaim peace to the nations.

Reading II: Since the Spirit of God dwells in us, we must put to death the evil deeds of the body.

Gospel: Jesus invites the weary to come to him, to take his yoke upon their shoulders and learn from him who is humble of heart.

Reading I is familiar to us from the Palm Sunday liturgy. It shows us a humble king riding into Jerusalem not on a warrior's horse but on a humble donkey. The prophecy is fulfilled in the messianic king, Jesus, who rode into Jerusalem on the first Palm Sunday and who rides into our midst today bringing a message of peace and salvation. He thanks and praises God for what God has hidden from the learned and clever and revealed to little children (see gospel).

But what is the message? The words "hidden from the learned and clever" could be interpreted as a criticism of the Pharisees, who knew all about the Law but whose knowledge did not bring them closer to God or God closer to them.

Jesus is not anti-intellectual, and he is definitely not opposed to the study and interpretation of Scripture, which the Pharisees excelled in. But he is opposed to those who make intellectual achievement an end in itself, the essence of salvation. Salvation for Jesus is not just the acquisition of human wisdom, it is a matter of mind and heart, of the whole personality.

What many of the Pharisees missed is the certain realization that the Lord is a *loving* God—that everything in our life that has meaning depends on our understanding how much God really does love us. With all your heart open yourselves up to this undeserved, unmerited divine love, and I will make you whole. This is Jesus' message for us today. On our part, the key that opens the gates of divine love is trust. Trust God as little children trust their parents. Be expectant as a child, taking it for granted that the Lord who loves us will not let us down or disappoint us. "Come to me, all you who are weary and find life burdensome, and I will refresh you. Take my yoke upon your shoulders and learn from me, for I am gentle and humble of heart. Your souls will find rest, for my yoke is easy and my burden light" (gospel).

The rest for your souls that Jesus promises is not passivity, not a "pie in the sky" kind of Christianity. Following Jesus makes sense—it is the authentically human way to live. People have always found Jesus attractive, even fascinating, because in him life has achieved its highest and most beautiful expression.

The good news of Jesus invites us not to try to live in another world than this but simply to become integrated, whole human persons as Jesus himself was. What makes us whole human beings?

There are two bodies of water in the Holy Land: the Sea of Galilee and the Dead Sea. The Sea of Galilee is beautiful, mainly because it receives water and it releases water into the Jordan River. The Dead Sea is ugly and lifeless, because it retains all the water that it receives. So with us. We all receive very much, especially from God, but only if we share what we have received will we be integrated and whole beings. Everything in our life is gift. Every day we receive our life from God, we receive light, the trees and flowers, the song of birds, and the smiles of friends, loved ones, and children.

"Learn from me, for I am gentle and humble of heart." Jesus is telling us to take him, his gift of divine love and life that he gives us daily and share it all with others, especially with those who seem to lack hope and love. Within the laughter and tears of life, sharing takes many forms. If someone has hurt you, sharing is forgiveness. If you are abrupt with people, sharing is being considerate. If you are not speaking to others, sharing is a friendly greeting. If you tend to use others, sharing is reverence for them.

Jesus says to us today: "Take my yoke upon your shoulders and learn from me, for I am gentle and humble of heart. . . . My yoke is easy and my burden light." The yoke he asks us to accept and to share is his love, his compassion, his caring. Jesus, the most perfect and beautiful person who ever lived, is calling us all to be perfect and beautiful too. And he has taught us by his own life how to achieve that sublime goal.

> Taste and see the goodness of the Lord; blessed is he who hopes in God (Communion Antiphon).

102 FOURTEENTH SUNDAY IN ORDINARY TIME — Cycle B

READING I **Ezek 2:2-5** **READING II** **2 Cor 12:7-10**
GOSPEL **Mark 6:1-6**

Reading I: God sent Ezekiel to preach repentance to the rebellious people, and "they shall know that a prophet has been among them."

Reading II: After God tells Paul that divine grace is sufficient for him, Paul settles for his weakness and all difficulties "for the sake of Christ."

Gospel: Jesus teaches in the synagogue in his hometown and is rejected by his fellow townspeople.

Adam and Eve rejected God. Their sin was the source of the giant river of evil flowing through human history, a stream to which we all make our personal contribution.

Today we see original sin reenacted in God's commissioning of Ezekiel and, above all, in the Nazarenes' rejection of Jesus. "They took offense at him" (Revised Standard Version). "They found him too much for them" (New American Bible). Actually Jesus was a "scandal," a stumbling block, to them. Luke tells us that they even wanted to kill him.

There are many possible reasons. Perhaps they believed that no good could come out of Nazareth. They may have found him too ordinary. "Isn't this the carpenter?" They lacked faith, not only in Jesus, in the Lord, but also in themselves. But most of all, they saw him as a threat to their old way of life. They were satisfied with what they had. They did not trust God enough to believe that this old companion of theirs could possibly have anything new or original to say to them.

So much did their lack of faith distress Jesus that, apart from healing a few who were sick, "he could work no miracle there." Jesus was always responsive to need and faith. He did not find faith and need in his hometown. So he left, and there is no record in the gospels that he ever went back. Jesus was human. He must have been terribly hurt by this rejection, for it was also a rejection of his Father.

What is all this to us? We probably do not do anything as openly offensive as what the Nazarenes did that Sabbath morning. We do not take offense at Jesus or find him too much for us. We just take him for granted. We ignore him or, more likely, explain away his teaching, for example, about the need to love and care for one another.

Or like the Nazarenes, we may be satisfied with ourselves and our old way of life, our never-changing routine. There is nothing more detrimental to a genuine, loving relationship with Jesus than mindless, loveless routine. We do not see our religious practice and way of life as a process of growth and development—progress in penetrating more and more deeply into the mystery of God and the meaning and mystery of the Church. Above all, progress in an ever-deepening and loving intimacy and friendship with Jesus.

Life does not stand still. We all have a past, a present, and a future. So, too, the Church and religious practice. We must learn from our history unless we want to repeat the mistakes of history. We should cherish traditions, but we can't freeze them. And we can't live in the past; the only past event we can make present again is the life, death, and resurrection of Jesus, which takes place in every Holy Mass.

God's creation is always in the process of development, of never-ending new discoveries. So, too, the Church. It is in a process of constant change and progress, yet in essentials it will always remain the Church of Christ. And what *is* essential *is* the Church: Christ, the sacraments, above all the Eucharist. The Church will always be the body of Christ into which we were baptized. The Church is a living organism, and we live and grow with and in it.

There are some married men and women who are the loneliest people in the world. A man and a woman may live under the same roof, eat and sleep together, but they never get to know each other. They take each other for granted, never communicate. Their lives follow a deadly routine that they never allow to be broken.

But there are other marriages in which, because of loving communication, care, and understanding, love ripens and is more beautiful when husband and wife are old than when they first fell in love.

Either of these possibilities is open to us in our relationship with Jesus. This relationship has to grow through conversation (prayer), holy reading, and constant openness to his goodness, beauty, and love.

> Come to me, all you that labor and are burdened, and I will give you rest, says the Lord (Communion Antiphon).

These words are for us. They are uttered by one who loves us more than we will ever know.

103 FOURTEENTH SUNDAY IN ORDINARY TIME — Cycle C

READING I **Isa 66:10-14** **READING II** **Gal 6:14-18**
GOSPEL **Luke 10:1-12, 17-20**

Reading I: Isaiah compares the holy city to a nursing mother who nourishes and comforts her children.

Reading II: The only thing that matters for Paul is the cross of Christ through which he has been crucified to the world.

Gospel: Jesus appoints disciples to go out and preach the reign of God. They are to depend on their hearers for sustenance.

For the Jews (and for the Lord) Jerusalem is more than a city. It is perhaps the most important symbol of the presence of God. In Reading I Jerusalem is pictured as a mother, lovingly nursing her children at her abundant breasts, and it is this image that the Lord assumes for himself:

> As nurslings, you shall be carried in her arms,
> and fondled in her lap;
> As a mother comforts her son,
> so will I comfort you.

God wants to be known, experienced, and loved by us all, so Scripture uses imagery that is familiar to us, that will stir up a response of loving dedication and self-giving. The main idea is that all that is good, loving, beautiful, desirable, and wonderful in our human understanding of mothers and fathers can be attributed to God and still not fully describe God. "God has no body, of course, and so body metaphors, whether masculine or feminine, remian only approximations to the life of God, as in all our language" (Nicholas Ayo).

The evangelist John describes God by what God is and does: "God is love, and whoever abides in love abides in God, and God in him" (1 John 4:16). Nevertheless, the symbolism of God as "mother" or "father" did not seem to touch the hearts of many of the Hebrews despite the preaching of the prophets. Many, especially among the scribes and Pharisees, missed the point of the Lord's age-long instruction and came to see religion and salvation in terms of their own personal success in a loveless observance of the letter of the Mosaic Law. We know how they plagued Jesus all through his public life and how he condemned them.

Strangely, many of these types became Christian and tried to carry their Pharisaic principles with them into Christianity. They tried to impose the obligations of the old Law on the new Christian converts from paganism. St. Paul opposed them vigorously because he saw them and their efforts as a destructive force—a threat to the very heart of Christianity—and as opponents of the preaching and work of Jesus. This is the background of today's Reading II.

Paul was very angry when he wrote this epistle. The Pharisees and some of the Jewish converts boasted about their strict observance of the Law. Paul says: "May I never boast of anything but the cross of our Lord Jesus Christ! . . . it means nothing whether one is circumcised or not." Paul is saying, It is *Christ* who saves. We cannot save ourselves by anything we do. The Christian's only task is to receive what Jesus has done for him or her with deepest gratitude and to respond with joy by a worthy apostolic life of sharing Christ's love.

The many times the Sunday readings return to this problem during the year indicates that the Church believes that Paul's problem with the "Judaizers" is still wtih us. We know from personal experience how easy it is to slip into what might be called a law-and-order mentality in the practice of our Catholic religion.

Rules and regulations are necessary in any society, religious or secular. But when we make the observance of laws and rules the heart of our Christianity, we ignore what God tells us today in Reading I. Above all, we ignore what Jesus says to us about concern and love for one another—especially the poor, the needy, the sick, and the aged. We observe laws and practice self-denial not with the purpose of putting God in debt to us but solely out of love and gratitude.

"May I never boast of anything but the cross of our Lord Jesus Christ!" And may we all allow Mother Church to gather us into her loving arms and fill us at her glorious breasts with the milk of her word and sacraments! Above all, may we allow ourselves to be loved by her and by Jesus, who suffered and died out of love for us! Then we will know how to respond with our own love, and our religious observance will be to the honor and glory of God rather than to ourselves.

Let all the earth cry out to God with joy! (Responsorial Psalm)

383 MONDAY OF THE FOURTEENTH WEEK IN ORDINARY TIME

YEAR I

READING I **Gen 28:10-22**
GOSPEL **Matt 9:18-26**

Reading I indicates in a mysterious way how eager God is to give himself to Jacob and be part of his life. God wants to be part of our life, too. May we make our own the verse of the Responsorial Psalm: "In you, my God, I place my trust."

The most normal way in which God, through Jesus, enters our lives is in the sacraments. Today's gospel shows the true nature of the sacraments. A woman touches Jesus' garment with faith, and she is healed of a hemorrhage. A man pleads with Jesus to come and heal his daughter. What Jesus did for these two, he is more than anxious to do for us. We come to him in all of life's crises and needs, saying in our hearts, If I can only touch the tassel of his cloak, I shall get well. In the sacraments, the mercy and love of Christ are made flesh. Through them he enters into our lives now and lives with us. The Lord, indeed, is kind and merciful!

YEAR II

READING I Hos 2:16, 17-18, 21-22
GOSPEL Matt 9:18-26

Hosea, writing in the eighth century B.C., uses marriage as an image of the covenant relationship between Yahweh and his people. When they forsake the covenant, they are like a spouse who commits adultery. But Yahweh never gives up on them. The Lord abounds in steadfast, forgiving love, always ready to take them back.

That same forgiving love is made flesh in Jesus. A woman holds out her hand in faith to touch his garment and is healed. A dead child returns to life when Jesus takes her by the hand. This incident tells more about the nature of the sacraments than a whole book. No evil we have ever done can stop Jesus from loving and forgiving us. All we have to do is to hold out our hand to him in faith, go to meet him in confession, and he will say to us, Take heart, my child; your faith has made you well.

384 TUESDAY OF THE FOURTEENTH WEEK IN ORDINARY TIME

YEAR I

READING I Gen 32:23-33
GOSPEL Matt 9:32-38

Our encounters with God may not be as exciting as Jacob's, but if our eyes are open, we can meet God in our daily life, our work, above all we can meet God in any kind of service to his flock.

The gospel is about vocation. The first thing to know about vocation is that it is a call from God to carry on the work of him who called himself the Good Shepherd. The Church needs priests and sisters and brothers, but she needs others as well. She needs anyone who is willing to serve people in need. Jesus just tells us to pray for laborers to serve his little ones. The first need is for men and women of all ages to recognize that God calls them and then to follow through. As Jesus was concerned about the needy and poor, so must the Christian be concerned. We may grow old and ill, but concern for people never ceases. May that concern haunt us always—even after we have received our final vocation—to live with our God forever!

YEAR II

READING I Hos 8:4-7, 11-13
GOSPEL Matt 9:32-38

The preaching of Hosea is old and familiar: idolatry not only violates the covenant, it simply does not make any sense, as the Responsorial Psalm spells out. Idols are made by men, and they look like men. But they have mouths that do not speak, eyes that do not see, noses that do not smell. What sense does worshiping such gods make? "Their makers shall be like them, everyone that trusts in them" (Responsorial Psalm).

The condition described in the gospel is still true today. There simply are not enough priests and sisters to do Christ's work of teaching, preaching, healing, and caring for the great crowds who are harassed and helpless, like sheep without a shepherd. Is Jesus' remedy still valid: "Beg the harvest master to send out laborers to gather his harvest"? Are we really praying and sacrificing? Do we truly share in Christ's compassion? Do we really trust in the Lord to answer our need?

385 WEDNESDAY OF THE FOURTEENTH WEEK IN ORDINARY TIME

YEAR I

READING I **Gen 41:55-57; 42:5-7, 17-24**
GOSPEL **Matt 10:1-7**

Our readings from Genesis cover only the high points in Jewish history, and one of the greatest is the history of Joseph, sold by his brothers to slavery in Egypt. But God uses Joseph to rescue his brothers and father from famine. Joseph is one of the most perfect foretypes of Jesus the Savior in the whole Old Testament.

This is the beginning of the 400 years' sojourn of the Hebrews in Egypt; it becomes a story that shows how God is the master of history. It will end with another rescue of his people by God working through Moses at the time of the Exodus, the Passover, and the covenant God will make with the people of Sinai. God still works in the world. We can make our own the prayer: "Lord, let your mercy be on us, as we place our trust in you" (Responsorial Psalm).

YEAR II

READING I **Hos 10:1-3, 7-8, 12**
GOSPEL **Matt 10:1-7**

The Israelite rulers' declaration of independence from Yahweh is bound to bear tragic fruits, "since they do not fear the Lord" (Reading I). The time will come when they will cry out to the mountains, "Cover us," and to the hills, "Fall upon us." The prophet's words are a meaningful spiritual directive: "Sow for yourselves justice, reap the fruit of piety; . . . for it is time to seek the Lord, till he come and rain down justice upon you."

"Seek always the face of the Lord" (Responsorial Psalm). May we reenforce our seeking by singing to him, singing praises to him, telling of all his wonderful works. We must not forget that the Lord is also seeking us. One of these days we are going to have to slow down in our rush through life and allow ourselves to be caught!

386 THURSDAY OF THE FOURTEENTH WEEK IN ORDINARY TIME

YEAR I

READING I Gen 44:18-21, 23-29; 45:1-5
GOSPEL Matt 10:7-15

The Joseph story continues to unfold in the Reading I, and it is not hard for us (as it was for the Jews) to "remember the marvels the Lord has done" (Responsorial Psalm).

In commissioning the apostles Jesus says to them, "The gift you have received give as a gift." That charge holds good for us today. Can we attribute our gospel, our faith, to anybody but to God? Has it cost us anything? The message for us is the same as for the disciples: "The reign of God is at hand!" We have to translate the gospel into our lives and then hand it on as a gift to others. This is our obligation both as individuals and as a parish community. It is only in handing the gospel on that we can keep it and grow in its spirit.

YEAR II

READING I Hos 11:1, 3-4, 8-9
GOSPEL Matt 10:7-15

Man of God that he is, Hosea makes use of every kind of argument to bring his people back to their original condition: that of being a child cradled in the loving arms of the Father. It is impossible to imagine a more compassionate, loving, and forgiving testimony from the heart of God:

> When Israel was a child I loved him,
> out of Egypt I called my son.

It was I who taught Ephraim to walk,
who took them in my arms;
I drew them with human cords,
with bands of love;
I fastened them like one
who raises an infant to his cheeks; . . .
My heart is overwhelmed,
my pity is stirred.
I will not give vent to my blazing anger, . . .
For I am God and not man,
the Holy One present among you (Reading I).

When we hear the Lord speaking to us now with that kind of loving concern, is it possible for us to cling to our self-hatred, our fears of not being forgiven for our sins, our wallowing in self-pity? His love could rescue us from any danger if we would only let it.

387 FRIDAY OF THE FOURTEENTH WEEK IN ORDINARY TIME

YEAR I

READING I Gen 46:1-7, 28-30
GOSPEL Matt 10:16-23

Today we have another wonderful example of the meaning of vocation, a theme that runs all through the Bible and into our own lives as well. If we remember that "The salvation of the just comes from the Lord," if we "trust in the Lord and do good," (Responsorial Psalm) we can always take delight in the Lord and his call to us. Jacob's vocation is remarkable because it comes in his old age. God calls Jacob to a completely new life in a foreign land, and Jacob believes and obeys.

To leave behind an old way of life is never easy: to leave is to die a little. Like Jacob, we all have many calls from God. Perhaps the most important and valuable one is the call to old age and retirement. The great temptation then will be to think that our life is no longer worthwhile, because we can do nothing. Then we have to remember, as Jacob did, that it is not what we do that counts in God's eyes, it is what we are. And we are his beloved children.

YEAR II

READING I **Hos 14:2-10**
GOSPEL **Matt 10:16-23**

Today Hosea lends his heart and voice to the Lord who composes an invitation to the people to return to God in sorrow and repentance for their desertion. If they are truly repentant, Yahweh will heal their faithlessness, will love them and make them a flourishing people again.

We need to remind ourselves that this scriptural expression of sorrow is now ours and that the Responsorial Psalm is even more modern: "Have mercy on me, O God, in your goodness; . . . Thoroughly wash me from my guilt and of my sin cleanse me." The psalmist recognizes the source of evil within us, our inmost heart, and again we can make his prayer our own: "A clean heart create for me, O God, and a steadfast spirit renew within me." Best of all, the psalmist recognizes the chief purpose and best result of a heart renewed, namely, a greater facility in praising and worshiping the Lord God.

388 SATURDAY OF THE FOURTEENTH WEEK IN ORDINARY TIME

YEAR I

READING I **Gen 49:29-33; 50:15-24**
GOSPEL **Matt 10:24-33**

Joseph's resemblance to Jesus emerges again today. As Jesus forgave those who crucified him, Joseph forgives his brothers for selling him into slavery. He also gives a hint of understanding into the mystery of evil when he says, "Even though you meant harm to me, God meant it for good, to achieve his present end, the survival of many people. Therefore have no fear." And his promise to "provide for you and for your children" is marvelously fulfilled in Christ's establishment of his Church, whose purpose is to provide for people's needs to the end of time.

One of our greatest needs is for freedom from fear, and this is what Jesus, *our* Joseph, promises us in today's gospel. He assures us that the Father cares for us, really cares, so "do not be afraid of anything," practically the same words Joseph used. "Give thanks to the Lord, invoke his name" (Responsorial Psalm).

YEAR II

READING I **Isa 6:1-8**
GOSPEL **Matt 10:24-33**

Reading I describes one of the great religious moments of all time. The young Isaiah lifts up his eyes to the holy of holies in the Temple and experiences a vision of the most high Lord. The infinite majesty and holiness of Yahweh is reflected in the attitude of the seraphim, who cover their faces. Isaiah demonstrates the normal human reaction to God's holiness: aware of his sins, he cries out, "Woe is me, I am doomed! For I am a man of unclean lips." His confession brings immediate forgiveness, whereupon he hears Yahwah's voice saying, "Whom shall I send? Who will go for us?" Isaiah answers, "Here am I . . . Send me."

It is not given to everyone to have such a blessed vision. But all of us can make Isaiah's attitude our own: Here am I! Send me. That generous response is much more important for our spiritual life.

FIFTEENTH SUNDAY IN ORDINARY TIME

READING I **Isa 55:10-11** **READING II** **Rom 8:18-23**
GOSPEL **Matt 13:1-23**

Reading I: The Lord sends us the saving word, which is intended to bear fruit in our lives.

Reading II: Paul tells us that the sufferings of our lives are nothing compared with the glory that will be revealed in us.

Gospel: The parable of the sower and the different kinds of soil on which the seed falls.

I once read a story about a captured eagle that was chained in a store window. It attracted many customers and business flourished. An old mountaineer heard about the chained eagle and came to buy it. The owner quoted an enormous price. The mountaineer drew all his savings from the bank and bought the eagle. He took off the chains and set the eagle free. It soared into the sky, dipped its wings, and flew off into the mountains. Someone asked, "Why did you do that?" The old man answered, "That eagle was not meant to be chained. God made it to soar into freedom."

This story can provide us with an insight into Paul's message in today's Reading II. We are like the eagle. Our God never intended that we should live in bondage to anyone or anything. Like the old mountaineer, God paid the enormous price of his Son's death in order to set us free from bondage. Our problem is to remain free and not allow ourselves to be recaptured. Perhaps the other two readings can help us stay free.

Both Reading I and the gospel are about the sowing of seed and about the various kinds of soil and the kind of harvest the divine Sower expects from the soil.

> So shall my word be
> that goes forth from my mouth;
> It shall not return to me void,
> but shall do my will,
> achieving the end for which I sent it (Reading I).

The seed of God's word is all powerful, but it is within our capability to obstruct the divine Sower's purpose and prevent or curtail its growth. Jesus identifies the human weaknesses that can frustrate the seed of God's word: pride, arrogance, self-righteousness, superficiality, faintheartedness, worldly possessions, anxiety.

It is up to us to identify the obstacles in our own hearts that can frustrate the growth of the seed of God's word, for it is only when we know and remove those obstacles that the word can send out its roots, grow, and bring forth the expected harvest. The seed is the word of God. Do we hear and understand? What kind of soil are we?

What really does God want us to hear and understand with our hearts? Well, we can go back to the old mountaineer. He gave up all that he had in order to free the eagle. So too with our God. Because God loves us so much, he wants us to be free from our chains, wants us to be whole human beings and disciples of his Son and—to change the imagery—wants us to be seed planted in the lives of others. "So shall my word be that goes forth from my mouth; it shall not return to me void, but shall do my will" (Reading I).

Jesus says nothing about the mystery of germination. To germinate is defined as "beginning to develop into a higher form." Every farmer knows that there can be no germination, and certainly no growth, without fertilizing and cultivating the soil and pulling out the weeds—and, of course, there has to be water and plenty of sunshine.

So, too, with us. The seed of God's word has to germinate in our hearts by means of meditating (mulling over it, "chewing" it), welcoming it, applying it to our lives. Most of all, we need the "sun" of God's love and grace, and that sun is always shining. With this kind of germination in the soil of our hearts, there is bound to be a bountiful harvest of holiness in us, in our parish community, in our Church. Our prayer today couldn't be more perfect:

> May your love make us what you have called us to be (Alternative Opening Prayer).

FIFTEENTH SUNDAY IN ORDINARY TIME

READING I **Amos 7:12-15** **READING II** **Eph 1:3-14**
GOSPEL **Mark 6:7-13**

Reading I: Amos is sent to the land of Judah to prophesy to the people.

Reading II: Paul tells us that God chose us before the world began to be holy and blameless in his sight, to be full of love and worthy of being redeemed by the blood of Christ.

Gospel: Jesus sends out his apostles to preach repentance, expel demons, anoint the sick, and work cures.

I. A. McClaren tells the story about a young, newly ordained preacher about to preach his first sermon in his new parish. Naturally, he wanted to impress everyone, so he spent hours preparing. He was living with his old aunt, who was very proud of him. When he finished preparing his sermon Saturday night, he went downstairs to talk to his aunt about it. She said: "You'll say what is right, and everybody will be pleased with you. But, O Laddie, be sure and say a good word for Jesus."

He went upstairs, tore up the sermon, and started all over. As he wrote, he "came upon a whole new understanding of the Christian reality: that one of the most fulfilling and the most creative things he will ever do is to say a good word for Jesus."

When you think of it, isn't that the chief purpose of every homily? A good word for Jesus, especially about his great love for us all. Actually, that was Paul's whole apostolic life: saying and writing good words for and about Jesus and bolstering the words with good works. What he says today is pretty deep, and we all need his prayer:

> May the Father of our Lord Jesus Christ
> enlighten the eyes of our hearts
> that we might see how great is the hope
> to which we are called (Alleluia Verse).

We need that enlightening to get some insight into Paul's statement: "God chose us in [Christ] before the world began, to be holy and blameless in his sight, to be full of love; he likewise predestined us through Christ Jesus to be his adopted sons—such was his will and pleasure—that all might praise the divine favor he has bestowed on us in his beloved" (Reading II).

Have you ever thought how astonishing this is? From all eternity, before the universe existed, God *knew* us, loved us into existence, predestined us to be holy and blameless, to be full of love. More than that, God chose us not only to *be*, to exist, but to share his work—the very work God sent his Son Jesus to perform, that is, to bring all things in the heavens and on earth into one under Christ's headship.

Today's gospel shows us how Jesus went about sharing his work with the apostles: he called them and sent them to do what he had been doing—healing the sick, preaching the good news of God's personal love for all, forgiving sinners, expelling demons. But every Christian shares that call, in greater or lesser degree. We all have a vocation. It may not be a vocation to preside at the Eucharist or to forgive sins; this gospel does not mention those functions.

But all of us, by virtue of our baptism, are called to serve and comfort anyone in need—the poor, the hungry, the homeless, the lonely, the aged. Whatever we do for others is priestly ministry, Christ's own work. I can't think of a better word to say for Jesus than that! He and we are one in ministry, one in striving to bring all things into one under Christ's headship.

But a caution here. A vocation is not so much what one does, it is what one *is* in the various stages of one's life. We've heard a lot about the "Protestant work ethic." I take it to mean that the only thing that makes life worth living is what we do, what we accomplish in our lifetime. The problem with that ethic is that, when one is no longer able to do anything, one feels useless and a burden on society and loved ones. Invalids and aged persons have to be convinced that their whole life is prayer, especially when they can no longer work at a regular job. Their *life* is ministry, a living out of the Mass—not only saying a good word for Jesus but doing a good work for him.

And so we repeat today's Alleluia Verse: "May the Father of our Lord Jesus Christ enlighten the eyes of our hearts that we might see how great is the hope to which we are called."

> Christian is the name and the gospel we glory in. May your love make us what you have called us to be (Alternative Opening Prayer).

106 FIFTEENTH SUNDAY IN ORDINARY TIME Cycle C

READING I Deut 30:10-14 **READING II** Col 1:15-20
GOSPEL LUke 10:25-37

Reading I: Moses tells us that God's command is not far off but in our hearts. We have only to carry it out.

Reading II: Christ is the "blueprint" of all creation, the head of his body, the Church. His task is to reconcile everything in his person.

Gospel: In the parable of the Good Samaritan, Jesus tells us to care for anyone who is in need.

How often have we heard this parable about the Good Samaritan! Perhaps it would be good for us to ask if it has made much difference in our lives. In fact, we have to ask it, for there is no teaching of Jesus that more accurately defines a Christian than the image of the Samaritan going out of his way to help a person in need. Today Christ is talking not to the lawyer but to you and me.

In Reading I Moses tells us that God's command is not up in the sky or over the sea. It is something very near us, it is already in our mouths and in our hearts; *we have only to carry it out.* That's the rub. Jesus says to us, You say you love me. Prove it. "How?" we ask. And Jesus responds, You see that woman, that child, that man? Take care of him. Take care of her. Be compassionate. Meet that person's needs. Why? Because that person is me. What you do for any needy person, you do for me.

We might pause for a moment and identify a person we know who is most in need of being loved and cared for. But can we stop at one?

Seek God where he is to be found. Where is God? In your neighbor, in your neighbor's need. That person is the tabernacle of God's presence. We have only to see and believe and minister to that need.

What this parable really tells us is that the Good Samaritan is Jesus himself, and the human race is the victim. He has taken care of us, bound up the wounds of sin, and lodged us in the inn that is his Church. Now we in turn are called to be and do what he is and does. Is that possible? Surely not by our power alone. But we are *not* alone.

It is significant that both in the Alternative Opening Prayer and in the Prayer After Communion we ask to share in Christ's love. "May your love make us what you have called us to be." "By our sharing in the mystery of this eucharist, let your saving love grow within us."

We are never going to learn how to love unless we first learn how to receive love. So maybe the lawyer asked the wrong question. Instead of asking, What must I *do*? he should have asked, What must I *be*? And Jesus tells us what we must be: Learn how to be a victim, learn how to accept my loving care, my power to care, and then you will be able to love and care in turn.

> Turn to the Lord in your need, and you will live (Responsorial Psalm).

We grow, we become ourselves, we become "other Christs," only by giving ourselves away.

389 MONDAY OF THE FIFTEENTH WEEK IN ORDINARY TIME

YEAR I

READING I **Exod 1:8-14, 22**
GOSPEL **Matt 10:34–11:1**

Reading I relates the beginning of the persecution of the Jews in Egypt, an experience that will lead to the Exodus, the high peak of Jewish history that will lead to their ultimate discovery of their identity as a nation.

To know one's identity and to be able to settle for who one is is essential not only for a people but also for every person. Too many people hate themselves and want to be someone else. Today, Jesus tells us the secret of finding our identity: "He who seeks only himself brings himself to ruin, whereas he who brings himself to nought for me discovers who he is." It is only in our relationship with Christ that we come to know ourselves. And this relationship is one of suffering with him. We can ask, Who am I? And Jesus answers: You share my cross. You are a savior with me. "Blest are those persecuted for holiness' sake; the reign of God is theirs" (Matt 5:10).

YEAR II

READING I Isa 1:10-17
GOSPEL Matt 10:34–11:1

In the gospel, Jesus tells us that there are times when we have to decide who or what is number one in our lives—when we have to make a choice between Christ and someone or something else. Hard? Of course. It is the cross that each Christian is called to share with Jesus. But he who loses his life for his sake will find it restored a hundredfold.

Isaiah's condemnation of external worship not founded on concern for social justice is as valid today as it was then. Like all the prophets, Isaiah insists that worship of God that does not include active concern and care for the needs of our fellow human beings is simply unacceptable. Through worship we acknowledge our total dependence on God for all that we are and have. But worship implies responsibility as Isaiah indicates:

> Cease doing evil; learn to do good.
> Make justice your aim: redress the wronged,
> hear the orphan's plea, defend the widow (Reading I).

390 TUESDAY OF THE FIFTEENTH WEEK IN ORDINARY TIME

YEAR I

READING I Exod 2:1-15
GOSPEL Matt 11:20-24

Today we meet Moses, who has been called the most important person in the Old Testament. He will be God's very own choice as the central figure of the Exodus event wherein God will rescue his people from slavery. Moses is a most intriguing character—one with whom all of us should easily be able to identify. In turn weak and indecisive, strong and self-confident, it took him a long time to grow into an awareness of his vocation and his true identity. Moses' best lesson for all of us is that he allowed God to guide him, form him, use him as the Lord willed. He was God's man all the way, as Jesus is to be, as each of us ought to want to be.

The gospel makes us ask ourselves why we do evil, knowing we will punish ourselves in doing it. This is the mystery of evil. The only remedy is preventive: keeping our eyes on Jesus, opening our hearts to his word, allowing him to love us.

Turn to the Lord in your need, and you will live (Responsorial Psalm).

YEAR II

READING I **Isa 7:1-9**
GOSPEL **Matt 11:20-24**

The message of Reading I and the Responsorial Psalm is that "God upholds his city forever," provided that the city (and each individual inhabitant) *wants* to be upheld and is willing to believe that God is more than willing to do it. It is an essential message in any age.

Today's gospel dramatizes the mystery of human freedom. The mystery lies in the perversity of heart that deliberately rejects divine love, knowing all the time that such rejection is bound to be destructive. This was the case with the towns warned by Jesus. Why did they reject Christ? We can only answer that question by determining why *we* reject him. Apparently, we all have to learn the hard way. I believe the solution lies in seeing Jesus as Love in person. May that vision grow in all of us!

391 WEDNESDAY OF THE FIFTEENTH WEEK IN ORDINARY TIME

YEAR I

READING I **Exod 3:1-6, 9-12**
GOSPEL **Matt 11:25-27**

The exciting drama of God's rescue of his people from slavery in Egypt begins with his call of Moses to leadership. Moses' self-image is not very high, and he wants to know why God chooses him. God's answer is as valid for us as it was for him: "I will be with you. . . ."

In the gospel, Jesus thanks the Father for revealing the secrets of life to little children. What he is actually telling us is what God himself told Moses: it is God and God alone who saves. Salvation, rescue, is God's free gift; it cannot be merited or deserved. It is the "little ones," the humble ones who realize their limitations and are receptive to grace and salvation, who best realize this truth. They are the ones who are dependent, who are willing to listen and receive. Moses eventually learned this lesson. May we do as well!

YEAR II

READING I Isa 10:5-7, 13-16
GOSPEL Matt 11:25-27

History and Scripture bear out the idea that Yahweh chastises those he loves, the purpose being, it seems, to bring them to their senses. I prefer to think that those who abandon Yahweh to live their own lives punish themselves. The Lord never gives up on anybody. "The Lord will not abandon his people" (Responsorial Psalm).

In the gospel Jesus gives us a glimpse into the intimacy of loving communion between himself and the Father. The kind of knowledge he speaks about is not mere intellectual knowledge, it is not knowing *about* God. It is knowledge of the heart, a sharing of divine life and love. It is the heart that experiences God, not the reason." Do you wish to share in the mutual love and knowledge that exists between Jesus and the Father? If so, pray for the grace of being completely dependent on God, open to his love, like a little child.

392 THURSDAY OF THE FIFTEENTH WEEK IN ORDINARY TIME

YEAR I

READING I Exod 3:11-20
GOSPEL Matt 11:28-30

No one has ever improved on the name for God that God reveals to Moses today: "I am who am." It means that everything that exists—tiny as a cell or immense as the universe—has its existence from God. God alone exists in his own right, without dependence on anyone or anything else. He is the infinitely perfect, all holy, all wise, all powerful, all loving supreme being. He is a God who knows and cares for each of us with an everlasting love, a God who became flesh in Christ Jesus and who says to us now as Jesus said then: "Come to me, all you who are weary and find life burdensome, and I will refresh you." As God's creatures, we do have obligations toward God, the chief one being to acknowledge God's lordship over us. We do this best by carrying our daily cross with love, and most of all by allowing God to love us. That shouldn't be too hard to do.

YEAR II

READING I Isa 26:7-9, 12, 16-19
GOSPEL Matt 11:28-30

We, both as a people and as individuals, can make our own the prayer contained in today's Reading I:

> My soul yearns for you in the night,
> yes, my spirit within me keeps vigil for you.

This is a prayer of longing desire right out of the lonely, suffering heart of humanity.

Jesus is part of the prayer and surely its answer. He bids us come to him in our labors and troubles, and he will give us rest. But the rest is not some kind of painkiller or tranquilizer. It is a sharing in more pain, the pain of one who loves, Jesus' very own pain, Jesus whose love for each and all of us is boundless. To share in this love, in this redeeming cross of Jesus—is not this the deepest desire of these hungry hearts of ours? Believe him when he says, "My yoke is easy and my burden light."

393 FRIDAY OF THE FIFTEENTH WEEK IN ORDINARY TIME

YEAR I

READING I **Exod 11:10–12:14**
GOSPEL **Matt 12:1-8**

Reading I describes the heart of Judaism—the Passover meal that preceded and celebrated the Israelites salvation from Egyptian slavery. The blood of the Passover lamb saves their firstborn from death, and they themselves feed on the lamb's roasted flesh. "This day shall be a memorial feast for you, which all your generations shall celebrate . . . as a perpetual institution." Through the centuries, Jews have been faithful to that divine command, even as Christians have been faithful to the command of Jesus, who transformed the ancient Passover meal into the Eucharistic meal wherein we feed on the Body and Blood of the true Lamb of God, by whose blood we are saved from slavery to our sins. At the Last Supper, his last Passover meal on earth, Jesus changed bread and wine into his Body and Blood and then commanded, "Do this in commemoration of me." We gladly obey, crying out, "I will take the cup of salvation, and call upon the name of the Lord" (Responsorial Psalm).

YEAR II

READING I **Isa 38:1-6, 21-22, 7-8**
GOSPEL **Matt 12:1-8**

Jesus makes use of every occasion to show how silly and childish are the religious attitudes of the Pharisees. He turns every one of their protests against him or his disciples into an opportunity to bring them to face up to what is essential in religion, namely, God and his rights—rights which in the long run always benefit us, God's children.

One of our great temptations as Christians is to imitate the Pharisees—to make essentials out of accidentals like not eating an ear of grain on the Sabbath or not washing one's hands before eating. Why can't we learn from Christ's condemnation of the Pharisees' mistaken interpretations? What God wants is mercy, not sacrifice; that is, God wants our love, our total acceptance of his will, our willingness to receive his love. God wants our hearts!

394 SATURDAY OF THE FIFTEENTH WEEK IN ORDINARY TIME

YEAR I

READING I Exod 12:37-42
GOSPEL Matt 12:14-21

The Passover meal has been eaten, and the Hebrew people begin their journey toward the Red Sea and ultimate freedom. The Responsorial Psalm expresses the gratitude to God that is in their hearts and at the same time gives a brief history of what the Lord has done for them:

> Give thanks to the Lord, for he is good,
> for his mercy endures forever;
> Who remembered us in our abjection, . . .
> with a mighty hand and an outstretched arm, . . .
> Who split the Red Sea in twain, . . .
> And led Israel through its midst.

We can use the same psalm to thank and praise the Lord for what God has done for us in Christ Jesus—that Suffering Servant foretold by Isaiah, the true Lamb of God who takes away our sins and the sins of the world. "In his name the Gentiles will find hope." We are now those Gentiles. In all our problems, Jesus is our hope. "His love is everlasting."

YEAR II

READING I Mic 2:1-5
GOSPEL Matt 12:14-21

Like Isaiah, Micah is an eighth-century prophet who emphasizes the prophetic role of condemning public immorality and trying to recall the people to their covenant with God. "Woe to those who plan iniquity, and work out evil on their couches" (Reading I). The same warning is repeated in the Responsorial Psalm. If the message speaks to our hearts, let us not turn it away!

The kind of person Jesus would be, what kind of work he would do, and how the Father feels about him were foretold by Isaiah. "Here is my servant whom I have chosen, my loved one in whom I delight" (gospel). Such testimony ought to warm our hearts, especially when we consider how Jesus has dealt with us: "The bruised reed he will not crush; the smoldering wick he will not quench." We are the Gentiles who now hope in his name.

107 SIXTEENTH SUNDAY IN ORDINARY TIME Cycle A

READING I **Wis 12:13, 16:19** **READING II** **Rom 8:26-27**
GOSPEL **Matt 13:24-43**

Reading I: God is master of all, but God judges with clemency. God teaches by deeds that we must be like him.

Reading II: We do not know how to pray as we ought, but the Spirit intercedes for us.

Gospel: Matthew recounts the parables of the wheat, the mustard seed, and the yeast.

Paul tells us today: If you have trouble praying, if you are dissatisfied with your praying, don't give up. Don't let it get you down. "The Spirit makes himself intercession for us with groanings which cannot be expressed in speech." That could mean that our groanings can also be prayer. So, too, our smiles and other manifestations of joy. Our best praying might well be the response we experience to the word of God that we hear or read.

"The Spirit too helps us in our weakness." This might also mean that it is more than our prayer life that is the concern of the Spirit. It is the whole of our life as Christians. This is also the concern of Jesus in today's gospel, in fact, in all his preaching. He speaks to us, tells us God's will for us in the hope that we will respond with a determination to change and become more like to him.

But Jesus has another intent in today's gospel: it has to do with those of us who sometimes get impatient and disturbed with members of our parish family who do not come up to our standards of what we think Christianity ought to be. Too many of us are like the servants who ask, "Do you want us to go and pull them [the weeds] up?"

Jesus tells these perfectionists to be patient with God, patient with those they consider weeds among the wheat; this is also the lesson of Reading I and the Responsorial Psalm. God has the care of all, God is lenient to all, God judges with clemency, and gives his children good grounds for hope that he will stir up repentance for their sins.

> You, O Lord, are good and forgiving,
> abounding in kindness to all who call upon you (Responsorial Psalm).

Our chief concern must be ourselves, whether we are good grain or weeds, whether our influence on others is healthy or not, whether or not we possess the mind of Christ, his sympathy and compassion for sinners, his total dependence on the will of the Father.

There may be a certain amount of self-righteousness in those of us who would like to have a Church or parish in accordance with our own ideas. The kind of Church Jesus is talking about in today's parable is a Church that is both divine *and* human, a Church *of* sinners, *for* sinners. A Church that, like her founder, never gives up on anybody, who says to the perfectionists: "What's your hurry? As long as they are alive, they have the possibility of responding to Christ's love and grace and converting."

And to all of us today Jesus says: Your concern is in becoming good grain or good yeast that will influence others as yeast acts on dough. How do we implement that concern? I can't think of a more effective way than to pray again our prayer of last Sunday: "May your love make us what you have called us to be."

We cannot change ourselves by mere willpower and determination. Only Christ can change us in the depths of our being. And that he will do if only we learn to look intently on him, keep our eyes fixed on him, and respond more and more generously to his love for us.

But those are human words. The inspired verse of the psalmist in today's Communion Antiphon puts the ideal more pointedly:

> The Lord keeps in our minds the wonderful things he has done. He is compassion and love; he always provides for his faithful.

May the Lord make us all into good grain, powerful yeast!

108 **SIXTEENTH SUNDAY IN ORDINARY TIME** Cycle B

108 SIXTEENTH SUNDAY IN ORDINARY TIME — Cycle B

READING I Jer 23:1-6 **READING II** Eph 2:13-18
GOSPEL Mark 6:30-34

Reading I: After warning those who failed to shepherd the people, God promises to raise up a good shepherd who will rule wisely.

Reading II: By shedding his blood, Christ has made it possible for all peoples to be reconciled with one another and with God.

Gospel: Jesus takes pity on a large crowd who were like sheep without a shepherd and he begins to teach them at great length.

Shepherding is the theme of today's Mass. Reading I is both a warning to bad shepherds and a prophecy of a wise and good shepherd to come. That reading, together with the Responsorial Psalm, insists that the real shepherd is none other than the Lord God.

"The Lord is my shepherd; there is nothing I shall want." God's shepherding is made flesh in Jesus. "Upon disembarking Jesus saw a vast crowd. He pitied them, for they were like sheep without a shepherd; and he began to teach them at great length." It is significant that Jesus sees teaching as the main way to care for the bewildered flock.

But what is shepherding? We usually think of it in terms of a person who leads, guides, protects, feeds, and cares for his flock. The shepherd knows his flock and the sheep know him, his voice. Jesus called himself "the Good Shepherd." And we may recall one of the post-Easter Masses when Jesus tells us that he "lays down his life for his sheep."

The term "shepherding" also applies to the clergy, especially to bishops. The crozier, used by bishops in pontifical Masses, was originally a shepherd's crook or staff. He used it to gather in the flock.

But shepherding is by no means restricted to the clergy. Parents are the first shepherds of their children; they have the same function as that of Jesus himself: they are to tend, watch over, protect (but not overprotect), teach, and lead. Above all, they are to love, to care for, to be willing to lay down their lives for their flock.

Teachers are shepherds in the true sense. I am sure we all have had teachers who knew the green pastures of wisdom, knowledge, and high ideals to which they led us. It is no accident that the gospel today describes Christ's shepherding in terms of teaching.

Nurses, administrators, cooks, are all shepherds; there is hardly any profession that does not include some shepherding. And some of the best shepherding of all can be done by the aged and retired who, by their prayers and sufferings, can do so much to gather into oneness in Christ the scattered members of any flock. No responsible Christian is absolved from the obligation and privilege of being a stand-in for Christ, the Good Shepherd, carrying on God's work in his or her own way.

The end purpose of all shepherding is "that all may be one," according to the final prayer of Jesus at the Last Supper. It is the building of a family, a community. The words of Jeremiah in Reading I are a terrible warning not only to popes, bishops, and pastors but for all Christians. To say or do anything that scatters, disrupts, or destroys the unity of any flock is to make oneself deserving of the words of the prophet: "Woe to the shepherds who mislead and scatter the flock of my pasture, says the Lord" (Reading I).

But we always come back to Jesus, our Good Shepherd—to his caring for us, leading us, feeding us with his word and sacraments, his loving concern for each of us without exception. We are now that crowd on whom he continues to take pity. It is on us that he has compassion. He looks for us if we stray and get lost. He never gives up on any of us.

The heart of all shepherding is love. Love is what made Jesus a good shepherd. And his love is his best gift to us. May we always respond to his love and, above all, may we give up all fear of being loved by him. May his love make us what he has called us to be—joyous, loyal, receptive, loving members of the flock of those redeemed by the blood of Jesus, our own good shepherd!

109 SIXTEENTH SUNDAY IN ORDINARY TIME Cycle C

READING I **Gen 18:1-10** **READING II** **Col 1:24-28**
GOSPEL **Luke 10:38-42**

Reading I: Abraham shows gracious hospitality to three strangers, who reward him with the promise of a son.

Reading II: The mystery of Christ in us is the message Paul preaches to the Gentiles.

Gospel: Martha shows hospitality to Jesus by preparing a meal for him, while Mary listens to his word.

> Even now I find my joy in the suffering I endure for you.
> In my own flesh I fill up what is lacking in the sufferings of Christ
> for the sake of his body, the church (Reading II).

What can St. Paul mean by this mysterious passage? Were Christ's sufferings inadequate? Hardly! What Paul is telling us is that in some mysterious way the Christian is privileged to participate in the passion of Jesus, that there is some "quota" of suffering that the Church and her members must endure before Christ's victory is final and complete. This is the mystery Paul refers to in Reading II: "the mystery of Christ in you, your hope of glory."

What Paul says of himself is certainly true of all of us. The inevitable deduction to be drawn from his words is that the sufferings we endure have redemptive value: we are "saviors" with Jesus. Someone has said that the greatest tragedy in the world is not that there is so much suffering in the world, but that so much of it is wasted. It may be endured bravely and stoically, but if it is not accepted with love and, above all, if it is not related to Christ's passion, it may be wasted.

The Christian need not, should not, morbidly look for suffering, it comes to us all in varying degrees. When suffering does happen, a person should make use of all natural means to get rid of it, for example, by consulting doctors; but if natural means fail, one may have to accept and generously endure pain with as much love as possible, always keeping in mind Paul's words in Reading I.

Hospitality, an equally essential guide for Christian living, comes to us in Reading I and the gospel. Both Abraham and the sisters

Martha and Mary opened their homes in hospitality to others: Abraham welcomed strangers, Martha and Mary welcomed an old family friend, Jesus. But the readings indicate that, in welcoming these persons, they were welcoming God himself.

Neither Abraham nor the two sisters thought of receiving a reward, but it came in both cases. God rewarded Abraham's hospitality far beyond any human expectations: his barren wife would have a child.

Martha's reward was of a different nature. It came in the form of a life lesson in relating to Christ. She wanted to do a lot for Jesus, whereas *he wanted to do a lot for her*. That's always the way it is with God. Mary chose the better part because she understood better how God works: she understood that religion is much more what God wants to give us and do for us than what we want to do for God. The English Benedictine monk Aelred Graham writes: "What can we do for God? Nothing at all. It is not by our asceticism that we take possession of God, but rather by our submissiveness that we allow him to take possession of us."

Both Martha and Mary were hospitable. Both loved Jesus very much. But Mary obviously understood better than Martha that true hospitality is *receiving* more than *giving* or *doing*. It is opening oneself to God's self-giving. It is allowing oneself *to be loved* by God more than trying to show the degree of our love by overdoing one's deeds of kindness. Our Lady is the best exemplar of true hospitality: she opened her whole being, her life, her heart, to God's gift of his Son, and so she was able to say: "God who is mighty has done great things for me" (Luke 1:49).

Perhaps now we can understand Jesus' words to Martha: "Martha, Martha, you are anxious and upset about many things, . . . Mary has chosen the better portion and she shall not be deprived of it."

It may well be that the shortest and best definition and secret of Christianity is contained in the simple word "hospitality." It is opening our whole being to him who is divine Love in person, Jesus Christ our Lord.

> I stand at the door and knock, says the Lord. If anyone hears my voice and opens the door, I will come in and sit down to supper with him, and he with me (Communion Antiphon).

395 MONDAY OF THE SIXTEENTH WEEK IN ORDINARY TIME

YEAR I

READING I **Exod 14:15-18**
GOSPEL **Matt 12:38-42**

We are on our way with the Hebrews to the Red Sea and trouble is brewing. We get our first glimpse of the fickleness and timidity of the people. They lack even the uncertain faith of Moses and are willing to go back to the bad old days rather than take a risk into the unknown. Moses' answer is worthy of the man of God he really is: "Fear not! Stand your ground, and you will see the victory the Lord will win for you today."

That's good advice for us, too. More and more we see the Exodus of the Hebrews as an act of faith. So what's new? Isn't that what life—all life—is about, above all, our Christian life? Our Moses is Jesus. It is he now who tells us, "Fear not!"

> If today you hear his voice,
> harden not your hearts (Alleluia Verse).

"Let us sing to the Lord, he has covered himself in glory" (Responsorial Psalm). Our faith is in him.

YEAR II

READING I **Mic 6:1-4, 6-8**
GOSPEL **Matt 12:38-42**

The Church puts these words in Jesus' mouth on Good Friday when we see him hanging on the cross: "My people, what have I done to you? How have I offended you? Answer me!" I hope that our answer is worthier than that of Micah's contemporaries who think they can make up for their offenses simply by offering more sacrifices to the Lord. The prophet's conclusion is as valid today as it was then: there is only one thing they (and we) can do that can restore our love-relationship with Yahweh: we must repent and return to the Lord our God. What Yahweh desires is a change of heart. And he ends with a program for our religious life that challenges us in the depths of our being:

You have been told, O man, what is good,
and what the Lord requires of you:
Only to do the right and to love goodness,
and to walk humbly with your God (Reading I).

396 TUESDAY OF THE SIXTEENTH WEEK IN ORDINARY TIME

YEAR I

READING I **Exod 14:21–15:1**
GOSPEL **Matt 12:46-50**

Today's incident in Reading I is the high point in Hebrew salvation history. We must not allow ourselves to brood over God's methods of saving his people by drowning their enemies and lose sight of the essential fact, namely, that it was God and God alone who did the saving, as Moses and the people recognize when they sing: "I will sing to the Lord, for he is gloriously triumphant; horse and chariot he has cast into the sea."

It is always God and God alone who saves—a lesson that Jews and Christians alike have had a hard time accepting. We all want to do the saving ourselves, but it can't be done. This is the lesson of Jewish history; it is the lesson of Jesus' whole life. It is a lesson that his mother Mary understood as no one else ever did. "Whoever does the will of my heavenly Father is brother and sister and mother to me." She put it this way: "Let it be done to me as you say" (Luke 1:38). Either expression is an excellent prayer.

YEAR II

READING I **Mic 7:14-15, 18-20**
GOSPEL **Matt 12:46-50**

Jesus tells us in the gospel that there are different ways of being related to him: by blood, as was Mary; by faith, which involves total commitment to and trust in the will of the Father; and by a combination of the two. Obviously none of us can be related to Jesus by blood. But being his brother or sister through obedience to the will of the Father is open to any one of us who is courageous enough to desire it. And it is a deeper relationship than by blood.

Mary, of course, is related to Jesus both by blood and by the most perfect obedience to the Father's will. She is the perfect Christian who not only inspires us by her example but also helps us to make her prayer our own: "I am the servant of the Lord. Let it be done to me as you say" (Luke 1:38).

397 WEDNESDAY OF THE SIXTEENTH WEEK IN ORDINARY TIME

YEAR I

READING I Exod 16:1-5, 9-15
GOSPEL Matt 13:1-9

Perhaps we would not be so tempted to look down on the unbelieving Jews if we put ourselves in their place. They had been uprooted, they were in the desert, on their way into the unknown future. God understands their condition and continues to care for them. He feeds them daily with miraculously multiplied meat and bread—food for their journey on their way to the Promised Land.

The food he provides for our journey is so much more satisfying—it is the Body and Blood of Jesus himself. The Lord gives *us* bread from heaven to eat. More than that, he gives us his word, a divine seed that Jesus the Sower wishes to plant in our hearts. The yield of happiness and peace this seed will bring forth depends on the kind of soil we are. If we are a bit rocky now, we can always become good soil with a bit of fertilizing and harrowing. Or shall we just say, a bit of penance?

YEAR II

READING I Jer 1:1, 4-10
GOSPEL Matt 13:1-9

We may not all be called by God to be prophets as Jeremiah was, but what God said to Jeremiah is surely true of us: "Before I formed you in the womb, I knew you." From all eternity each of us has been in God's mind, and because we were also the object of his love, God chose us to be made flesh, to be born as human beings. Each of us is chosen.

To realize and appreciate that fact is the greatest aid we can have in becoming aware of our identity. We all need to know who we are and, above all, to know that we are loved. Reading I tells us that fact. Our response has to be:

> For you are my hope, O Lord;
> my trust, O God, from my youth. . . .
> My mouth shall declare your justice,
> day by day your salvation.
> O God, you have taught me from my youth,
> and till the present I proclaim your wondrous deeds (Responsorial Psalm).

398 THURSDAY OF THE SIXTEENTH WEEK IN ORDINARY TIME

YEAR I

READING I Exod 19:1-2, 9-11, 16-20
GOSPEL Matt 13:10-17

> Blessed are you in the temple of your holy glory, . . .
> Blessed are you on the throne of your kingdom, . . .
> Blessed are you in the firmament of heaven,
> praiseworthy and glorious forever (Responsorial Psalm).

These inspired words provide some idea of the human reaction to the manifestation of the Lord God to his people on Mount Sinai. The all-perfect, all-holy, all-loving God is on the verge of speaking to his people through Moses and revealing to them his desire to be with them forever.

In the gospel, we see the fullness of God's self-revelation in Jesus, whose healing words continue to be balm for our hearts—but only on condition that we are open to receive his words, willing to assume the consequences of his teaching and allow it to shape our lives.

What is indispensable is the inner readiness to give ourselves, to be converted. How receptive are we?

YEAR II

READING I **Jer 2:1-3, 7-8, 12-13**
GOSPEL **Matt 13:10-17**

Today's gospel is a continuation of the parable of the sower, which began yesterday. Some seed fell along the path, some on rocky ground, some among thorns, and some on rich soil, which alone brought forth a good harvest. When the disciples ask why Jesus speaks in parables, his answer is mysterious. It may be that he is hinting at the mystery of human receptivity to divine truth. Powerful though divine truth may be, it is within our human power to resist it. We shall not hear and understand—the word will not take root in us—unless we are receptive. What is indispensable is the inner readiness to give oneself, to be converted, to have an ear for the inner message. Without that readiness we hear only the story, not its meaning. May the rain of divine grace soften the hard crust of our hearts and open them to divine truth!

399 FRIDAY OF THE SIXTEENTH WEEK IN ORDINARY TIME

YEAR I

READING I **Exod 20:1-17**
GOSPEL **Matt 13:18-23**

"The law of the Lord is perfect, refreshing the soul" (Responsorial Psalm). Those words of the psalmist give quite a different view of the Ten Commandments than most of us are accustomed to. They are not mere negative prohibitions: they "rejoice the heart." In the commandments, God is simply telling us what we must do and what we must avoid if we are to be fulfilled and happy human persons.

> The command of the Lord is clear,
> enlightening the eye; . . .

> The ordinances of the Lord are true,
> all of them just.
> They are more precious than gold, . . .
> sweeter also than syrup
> or honey from the comb (Responsorial Psalm).

It is how we observe the commandments that matters. If we keep them out of fear and not from a motive of love, we defeat God's whole purpose in giving them. Christian morality is our response to God's love for us, expressed in the commandments. It is love in action.

> Happy are they who have kept the word with a generous heart (Alleluia Verse).

YEAR II

READING I Jer 3:14-17
GOSPEL Matt 13:18-23

In Reading I we see why some commentators describe the writings of the prophet Jeremiah as a sort of scrapbook or anthology of passages from various periods in his life rather than the orderly, chronological collection we might expect. Here at the beginning of his work, for instance, where he deals mainly with prophecies from his early career, we find a passage that apparently relates to a period nearly forty years later—the Babylonian Exile in 587 B.C. We hear the Lord call the exiles to a glorious reunion at Jerusalem, which will become the religious center of the nation once again—indeed, for all nations. This theme also appears in the Responsorial Psalm: "He who scattered Israel, now gathers them together." In the gospel parable of the sower and the seed, Jesus explains how people respond in different ways to the word of God, which invites them into the kingdom.

400 SATURDAY OF THE SIXTEENTH WEEK IN ORDINARY TIME

YEAR I

READING I Exod 24:3-8
GOSPEL Matt 13:24-30

Today's Reading I tells of one of the high moments in Jewish history. It describes the "engagement ceremony" that would unite God with his people and they with him. Moses relates God's proposal and the people's consent: "We will do everything that the Lord has told us." It's as though God has said, Will you be my bride? and they respond: We will. Next day Moses seals the vows, the covenant, by the extremely symbolic ceremony of throwing part of the blood of the sacrifice on the altar, which stands for God. Then he reads the Book of the Covenant (the marriage agreement) and the people again respond: "All that the Lord has said, we will heed and do." Then Moses sprinkles the blood on the people, and the marriage is sealed. All this is background for the Eucharist. When Jesus instituted the Eucharist at the Last Supper, he said over the cup of wine: "This cup is the new covenant in my blood. Do this, whenever you drink it, in remembrance of me" (1 Cor 11:25). We obey Jesus at every Mass, and there, too, we renew our marriage vows with our God. The Mass is our sacrifice of praise and thanksgiving.

YEAR II

READING I Jer 7:1-11
GOSPEL Matt 13:24-30

Jeremiah warns his people that the presence of God's temple in their midst is no guarantee of their survival as a nation. Amend your ways, he says. Do not trust in these deceptive words: "This is the temple of the Lord! The temple of the Lord."

In the gospel, Jesus describes the Church as a field in which weeds and wheat grow together. We sometimes get impatient with the Church. Wouldn't it be nice, we think, if every member were as good and holy as we are? At times we would like to throw out the sinners. Jesus is more realistic—and patient. He knows that his Church is the home of sinners; and what he did in his lifetime when he ate and drank with sinners, the Church continues to do now. I think that he really means it when he says, "I tell you, there will be more joy in heaven over one repentant sinner than over ninety-nine righteous people who have no need to repent" (Luke 15:7).

110 SEVENTEENTH SUNDAY IN ORDINARY TIME — Cycle A

READING I **1 Kgs 3:5, 7-12** **READING II** **Rom 8:28-30**
GOSPEL **Matt 13:44-52**

Reading I: The Lord is pleased with Solomon's request for an understanding heart—"to judge people and know what is right."

Reading I: God makes all things work together for the good of those who love him.

Gospel: Jesus uses several images to describe the reign of God.

Recall the gospel story about the rich young man who asked Jesus what he had to do to gain eternal life. When Jesus told him that if he wished to be perfect he would have to sell what he had, give the money to the poor, and then come and follow him; the young man went away sad because he had great possessions (see Matt 19:16ff.).

Today's readings are about the values, the priorities, that determine the way we live out our lives. A man finds a treasure buried in a field; he sells all that he has and buys the field. A merchant finds a pearl of great value. He puts up all that he has and buys it.

What is a value? Philosophers tell us that a value is that for which we will sacrifice all other things. A value is the groundroot of our being, it is the heart of our life (Father Carr).

The one gift Solomon asked of God was an understanding heart. What he was really requesting was a share in God's own heart, he wanted a heart that would help him perceive the ideal relationship with his creator, namely, the realization of God's lordship over all of life. He also wanted to know the right relationship he should have with his fellow humans, with possessions; he wanted a deeper understanding of the Torah, God's Law, God's wisdom in Scripture.

Unfortunately, Solomon's value was only temporary in his life. His understanding heart gave way to lust and tyranny. God was no longer the Lord of his life. His own will replaced the will of the Lord. What happened to Solomon is a most valuable lesson and warning to everyone. We all need to be aware of the danger of losing our values including the greatest value and priority of all, namely, Jesus and our relationship, our intimacy, with him and our relationship with others. The Opening Prayer today is full of wisdom:

> God our Father and protector,
> without you nothing is holy,
> nothing has value.
> Guide us to everlasting life
> by helping us to use wisely
> the blessings you have given to the world.

We acquire our values from a variety of sources: parents, teachers, peers, our culture and environment, television, books, people we admire and look up to. The greatest source of all is Holy Scripture, above all, the life and preaching of Jesus. All other priorities should be evaluated according to that best of sources.

Are we aware of the sources of false values that threaten our understanding hearts? Can we recognize the practices, ideas, ideals, omissions, attachments, and prejudices that might cause us to lose our most precious value—eternal companionship with Jesus and all our loved ones?

I wish I could recall the name of the author who wrote: "The supreme value is to seek a personal awareness of the love that Jesus has for each of us. This love is the hidden treasure, the pearl of great price, a value worth risking everything for."

Life is a quest, a search. But it is a two-way search. God's search for us, our love, our dedication, far surpasses in intensity our search for God. Allowing God to find and possess us is the greatest value of all.

111 SEVENTEENTH SUNDAY IN ORDINARY TIME Cycle B

READING I 2 Kgs 4:42-44 **READING II** Eph 4:1-6
GOSPEL John 6:1-15

Reading I: The prophet Elisha feeds two hundred men with twenty barley loaves.

Reading II: Since we make up one body and one spirit, we must make every effort to preserve unity.

Gospel: Jesus feeds a crowd of five thousand with five barley loaves and a couple of dried fish.

> The hand of the Lord feeds us;
> he answers all our needs (Responsorial Psalm).

The gospel writers and the early Church obviously considered the miracle of the multiplication of loaves one of the most important of all Jesus' signs. Each of them mentions it, two of them twice. Hunger is the most basic of all human needs. Hunger for bodily nourishment, hunger for truth, for love, for life and the meaning of life. Hunger for God. Today's readings are all about hunger.

The miracle of the mutliplication of loaves is important for many reasons, but mainly, I believe, because it prepares for the institution of the Eucharist. The Church wants us to meditate on the Eucharist today and on some of the following Sundays. Today's readings provide insights into the Eucharist that are not always prominent in our thinking.

What purpose did Jesus have in mind when he instituted the Eucharist? Certainly it was to satisfy human hunger for God; but I am convinced that he had another intention as well—one that St. Thomas Aquinas understands when he writes that the first effect of the Eucharist is the *unity of the mystical body,* the Church. Do we not all receive the same Christ? Is Christ divided? "May all of us who share in the body and blood of Christ be brought together in unity by the Holy Spirit" (Eucharistic Prayer II).

And this helps us to understand Paul's message to us today: "Make every effort to preserve the unity which has the Spirit as its origin and peace as its binding force. There is but one body and one Spirit, . . . There is one Lord, one faith, one baptism; one God and

Father of all, who is over all, and works through all, and is in all" (Reading II).

We need to be reminded often of the relationship between the Body and Blood of Christ which we receive in the Eucharist and the body of Christ which is the Church. Holy Communion is a deeply personal experience of Jesus, but we may miss much of its deeper meaning if we fail to allow it to bring us to a greater understanding and awareness of the whole Church and of the other members of this parish family, this community of the baptized. The Mass is no place for the solitary diner who wants to be cut off from others.

We hunger for God, and Jesus satisfies that hunger in the Eucharist. But there exists an even deeper hunger—God's hunger for us, for our love, our total commitment to Jesus Christ.

> The eyes of all look hopefully to you, . . .
> You open your hand
> and satisfy the desire of every living thing (Responsorial Psalm).

But the eyes and heart of the Lord look hopefully to us, too. God asks for our hearts so that they may be "clear channels of the stream of his love flowing like a shiny wave over all our fellow humans" (Caryll Houselander) to the end that through the Eucharist we may live "a life worthy of the calling you have received, with perfect humility, meekness, and patience, bearing with one another lovingly" (Reading II).

It is only in becoming one body with Jesus and with one another that we can share his blessings with our sisters and brothers who do not know him and experience the lasting joy of his presence.

SEVENTEENTH SUNDAY IN ORDINARY TIME

READING I **Gen 18:20-32** **READING II** **Col 2:12-14**
GOSPEL **Luke 11:1-13**

Reading I: Abraham bargains with God for the salvation of the wicked cities of Sodom and Gomorrah, and the Lord spares the cities.

Reading II: In baptism we are buried with Christ but also raised to life with him.

Gospel: Jesus teaches the disciples to pray the Lord's Prayer and to pray with persistence for all our needs.

Reading I depicts Abraham arguing with God, trying to bargain with him. The incident tells us a lot about Abraham, a lot about God. Both God and Abraham loved sinners. It's all right to argue with God, so long as you do not try to put God in debt to you. Above all, it's all right to pray with persistence. The real emphasis in Reading I is perseverance and the simplicity of deep faith.

Perseverance in prayer and the simplicity of deep faith also characterize the gospel. As always, the main ideas of Reading I are implemented, perfected, and fulfilled in the gospel. Specifically, today's gospel is about the Our Father. Jesus says: "When you pray, say: 'Father, hallowed be your name. . .'" The Our Father is precious for many reasons, but most of all because it is Jesus' own prayer.

I wonder if the Our Father is not the most used, the *most recited,* but the most *poorly prayed* prayer that we know. Our problem may be that we *say* or *recite* it with little realization of its deep meaning. Fr. Godfrey Diekmann is a theologian who has specialized in the study and teaching of the early Church Fathers—the theologians who lived in the centuries immediately following the life of Jesus. These Fathers are the source of Father Diekmann's teaching on the Lord's Prayer.

The first idea is that Jesus gives a completely new way of thinking about God. Jesus calls God "Abba," which is usually translated "Father." But, rather, it is a name connoting the intimacy, the love, the dependency, the tenderness and profound familiarity of a child with his or her daddy. "Abba" indicates the very intimacy of Jesus himself—the way he feels about his heavenly Father. When he speaks about "my Father and your Father," he is expressing a desire to share his own attitude with us.

A second point Father Godfrey makes is that the Our Father is the epitome of all Christ's teachings: it sums up the good news of the gospel. In the early Church, handing over the Our Father was an essential moment in the instruction of new converts. This rite told them that, after their baptism, they too could call God Father, Abba, for then they would share in the very life and sonship of Jesus himself. The prospective Christians were told that whenever they prayed the Lord's Prayer, they renewed their baptism. Do we ever think of that when we pray it?

Third, each of the petitions of the Our Father imposes obligations on the ones who pray them. For example, if we rejoice in calling God "Father," let us give God the right to rejoice in us. When we pray, "Thy kingdom come," we pray that God's lordship will be acknowledged not only in Russia and in our nation but in our own hearts. When we say, "Forgive us our trespasses as we forgive those who trespass against us," we have to mean what we say. Put another way, if we refuse to forgive others we are asking God *not* to forgive us. If we refuse to forgive, we can't even pray the Our Father. Forgiveness is the special prerogative of the Father, which he wants to share with us.

When we pray "Thy will be done" we are making our own Christ's most intimate prayer, the prayer that motivated his entire life.

The Lord's Prayer, with its request for daily bread and forgiveness, is the best possible "table prayer" for the banquet of the Lord at Holy Mass. We shall try to recall these ideas when we pray the Our Father at our Eucharist today.

A child needs a father and a mother who really care. It is very difficult to live and mature without them. Unfortunately, it sometimes happens that human fathers and mothers disappoint their little ones and let them down in one way or another.

But Jesus tells us that there is one Father who never lets us down, who can always be counted on. We have a Father who is good, who is love in person, a Father who knows each of us by name, who cares, who is always for us, who is gracious and forgiving. Above all, a Father who is lavish in his love for us, who never gives up on us, who *believes* in us.

With one mind and one heart, as a family of God our Father's chosen daughters and sons, let us pray slowly, thoughtfully, lovingly: "Our Father, who art in heaven . . ."

401 MONDAY OF THE SEVENTEENTH WEEK IN ORDINARY TIME

YEAR I

READING I Exod 32:15-24, 30-34
GOSPEL Matt 13:31-35

"You know well enough how prone the people are to evil" (Reading I). This judgment of Aaron explains a lot, both about Israel's infidelities to their covenant with God and about our own. It is Adam's sin, his denial of God's supremacy, and the results of that sin and all sins ever since. We are all prone to evil. This has to do with the mystery of free will. "They forget the God who saved them, who had done great deeds in Egypt" (Responsorial Psalm). But sin is not just ordinary forgetting. It is deliberate, free refusal to remember our God, our creator. The only remedy is love—honest, genuine, personal love for God that penetrates our minds, our hearts, our very bones, as yeast penetrates dough and makes it rise (see gospel). It is only with that kind of love that the reign, the true lordship of God will be established. May we all contribute to it!

YEAR II

READING I Jer 13:1-11
GOSPEL Matt 13:31-35

Jeremiah's imagery is explicit. As a cloth is spoiled when buried in the ground, so is a people ruined that refuses to admit its total dependency on God. Yahweh had made the Jewish people cling to him that they might be for him a people, a name, a praise, and a glory; but, he says sadly, "They did not listen." As the Responsorial Psalm has it, "You have forgotten God who gave you birth." We may forget God, but God never forgets us.

Christ's emphasis today is on the spread of his kingdom, both in numbers and in influence. As yeast permeates dough and makes it rise, so does he desire his word, his love, his very being, to permeate us and transform society. We have to ask ourselves how much we have allowed Jesus to permeate our lives and how much of Christ Jesus others have absorbed from us.

402 TUESDAY OF THE SEVENTEENTH WEEK IN ORDINARY TIME

YEAR I

READING I Exod 33:7-11; 34:5-9, 28
GOSPEL Matt 13:35-43

A cloud is the most common Old Testament symbol of God's presence. From the midst of the cloud God speaks to Moses face to face, and here Moses pleads for his people. No matter how often and how greatly they have sinned, God yields to Moses' prayers for their forgiveness; for God is and always will be "a merciful and gracious God, slow to anger and rich in kindness and fidelity, continuing his kindness for a thousand generations" (Reading I).

And how necessary is that forgiveness! Jesus tells us in the gospel that his Church is like a field in which weeds grow along with good grain. The Church is a Church of sinners, for sinners. But it is also the dwelling place of merciful forgiveness.

> As a father has compassion on his children,
> so the Lord has compassion on those who fear him" (Responsorial Psalm).

We may lose hope in ourselves and in one another; our Father never loses hope in us.

YEAR II

READING I Jer 14:17-22
GOSPEL Matt 13:35-43

Reading I is a perfect illustration of a fact of life and religion that we know from personal experience. People turn to God when disaster makes them come to their senses.

> Help us, O God our savior,
> because of the glory of your name;
> Deliver us and pardon our sins
> for your name's sake (Responsorial Psalm).

In the gospel, Jesus uses the image of the weeds growing with the wheat to explain the existence of sinners in the Church. It is a condition and a situation that he is not happy about. He knows that sin destroys persons whom he loves. In fact, he sometimes seems to love sinners more than saints. He is more eager to forgive than we are to be forgiven. With sinners everywhere and in every age, may we cry out:

> Remember not against us the iniquities of the past; . . .
> Let the prisoners' sighing come before you (Responsorial Psalm).

403 WEDNESDAY OF THE SEVENTEENTH WEEK IN ORDINARY TIME

YEAR I

READING I Exod 34:29-35
GOSPEL Matt 13:44-46

Moses' radiant face tells us a lot about Moses, but more about God. The face reflects God's glory, his majestic holiness. Moses' face was radiant not because of what he said to God but because he knew how to listen to God. "Holy is the Lord, our God" (Responsorial Psalm). Holy, too, those who converse face to face with God in prayer. Our conversation with God may not make our faces as radiant as Moses' was, but it can do much more: it can fire our hearts with divine love. In the Alleluia Verse Jesus tells us more about the power of Prayer:

> I call you my friends, says the Lord,
> for I have made known to you all that the Father has told me.

Intimacy with God like that of Moses is truly a great treasure, a priceless pearl that is worth more than any other treasure. And it is available free to anyone who opens his mind and heart to God's radiating word.

YEAR II

READING I Jer 15:10, 16-21
GOSPEL Matt 13:44-46

Because the loneliness and hardship of his prophetic vocation made Jeremiah feel sorry for himself, the Lord reassures him, "I will free you from the hand of the wicked, and rescue you from the grasp of the violent." We have as much right to that reassurance and to Yahweh's consoling words as Jeremiah had: "God is my refuge on the day of distress" (Responsorial Psalm).

In the gospel Jesus compares the kingdom to a treasure hidden in a field or to a pearl of great price. He is telling us that no sacrifice is too great in order to acquire a place in the Church, but he goes on to say that membership in the Church is of no value to us unless we acknowledge in hearts and minds and, above all, in our lives that God and God alone is the Lord of our lives. In God's will and only in God's will is our peace.

404 THURSDAY OF THE SEVENTEENTH WEEK IN ORDINARY TIME

YEAR I

READING I **Exod 40:16-21, 34-38**
GOSPEL **Matt 13:47-53**

The word "church" can have at least two meanings. For Jesus "church" is people of all kinds, good and bad (see gospel). For the Jews on their way to the Promised Land, the Temple (church) is the dwelling place of the most High God in their midst. The cloud is the symbol of God's presence. The Jews cannot *see* God, but they *experience* God's being-with-them on their way; and this experience of his presence makes them cry out, "How lovely is your dwelling-place, Lord, mighty God!" The experience of God's presence causes people to become aware of their sinfulness, and it fascinates them, causing a desire to remain forever in that Holy Presence.

> My soul yearns and pines
> for the courts of the Lord.
> My heart and my flesh
> cry out for the living God (Responsorial Psalm).

As Catholics we need and we can have both understandings of "church." Without them our faith is incomplete.

YEAR II

READING I Jer 18:1-6
GOSPEL Matt 13:47-53

"Can I not do to you, house of Israel, as this potter has done?" Yahweh asks in Reading I. And the answer is yes, if we permit it. God wishes to shape each of us according to his divine plan, as a potter shapes his clay. The end result can be a beautiful, holy, happy person, like Mary, the mother of Jesus, and the saints. But we are free and we can resist God's will. However, God is patient. He may take a lifetime to shape us; he never gives up.

Perhaps our resistance to God's plan will diminish as we gradually come to realize that

> Happy he whose help is the God of Jacob,
> whose hope is in the Lord, his God.
> Who made heaven and earth,
> the sea and all that is in them (Responsorial Psalm).

God did a marvelous job in *that* creative act. Why are we so hesitant to become pliable and supple in his hands?

405 FRIDAY OF THE SEVENTEENTH WEEK IN ORDINARY TIME

YEAR I

READING I Lev 23:1, 4-11, 15-16, 27, 34-37
GOSPEL Matt 13:54-58

To remember and to celebrate the remembrance was the heart of the Jewish religion, as it is also the heart of our religion. Feasts are God's idea. "These are the festivals of the Lord which you shall celebrate at their proper time with a sacred assembly" (Reading I). Note the words "sacred assembly." Feasts are community celebrations that do more than anything else to make a people into a people, a parish or religious community into a true community. God does not need our worship or our celebrations: *we* need them in order to grow as individuals and as a people into our full human and divine stature and potential. Not to celebrate is to lose our personal and communal identity. It was in this tradition that Jesus instituted the Mass, when at the Last Supper (a *Passover* celebration) he told his Church, "Do this in memory of me." Today again, thanks be to God, we can fulfill his command!

YEAR II

READING I Jer 26:1-9
GOSPEL Matt 13:54-58

There are as many ways of rejecting God as there are persons in the world. The people of Nazareth rejected Jesus because of their poor self-image: they could not believe in him because they could not believe in themselves.

Jeremiah's contemporaries rejected Yahweh's warning of the coming destruction of their beautiful Temple. They had lost sight of the very idea of the Temple as a holy place where Yahweh dwells and where he gathered them together to give voice to their worship, their common admission of God's lordship over them. The Temple had become only a national monument, and in their pride they were offended at the very idea of its destruction. The Responsorial Psalm expresses Jeremiah's grief at his failure to convince them of their coming defeat. We can make his prayer our own: "Lord, in your great love, answer me."

406 SATURDAY OF THE SEVENTEENTH WEEK IN ORDINARY TIME

YEAR I

READING I Lev 25:1, 8-17
GOSPEL Matt 14:1-12

God wanted time to be hallowed for his people. Days like the Sabbath, feasts like the Passover, and years like the Year of Jubilee (in Reading I) were to remind the people not only of God's past deeds of mercy towards them but also of his ongoing care. Today's description of the Year of Jubilee also reveals the divine desire that religion should have social and ecological implications, too. Even the land was to have its rest: "The earth has yielded its fruits; God, our God has blessed us" (Responsorial Psalm).

Today's gospel relates the gruesome death of John the Baptizer. His work of preparing the way of Jesus comes to a bloody end, but no sword, no vengeful spirit, can kill his call to repentance. John confronts each of us today even as he did his contemporaries to turn to God, to be converted. It's never too late to listen!

YEAR II

READING I **Jer 26:11-16, 24**
GOSPEL **Matt 14:1-12**

In both of today's readings, a man of God confronts death at the hands of enemies of God. Both vigorously defend God's law. Jeremiah wins and saves his life—for the time being. John the Baptizer loses both his argument and his head. But both live on and both continue to accuse us today when we prefer our wills and way of life to God's.

Both John and Jeremiah in their own way give us a preview of Jesus, whom they prepared for and prefigured. "Behold, I am in your hands," says Jeremiah. Jesus will voice practically the same sentiment in Gethsemani the night before he dies. The conviction of being God's chosen ones, the certain knowledge that they are doing God's will, destroys fear and gives both a stature and presence that will remain forever. Please God some of their courageous conviction will rub off onto us!

113 **EIGHTEENTH SUNDAY IN ORDINARY TIME** Cycle A

EIGHTEENTH SUNDAY IN ORDINARY TIME

READING I Isa 55:1-3 **READING II** Rom 8:35, 37-39
GOSPEL Matt 14:13-21

Reading I: The Lord's invitation to the people to come and eat and drink without payment.

Reading II: Nothing in heaven or on earth can separate us from the love of God that comes to us in Christ Jesus our Lord.

Gospel: Jesus has pity on the crowds, cures their sick, and feeds them with miraculously multiplied loaves and fishes.

"Something beautiful for God" is the way Mother Teresa describes her work. The work, of course, is with the poor and dying: she gives them loving care and helps them to die with dignity. "As often as you did it for one of my least brothers, you did it for me" (Matt 25:40). Mother Teresa believes that.

Most good Christians want to do things for God, and that's fine, unless they do their good deeds with the idea of placing God in debt to them, trying to buy or merit their salvation. But how many of us realize that the chief message of Scripture is that God wants to do great things for us? God has given us life, family and loved ones, faith. God has given us his Son Jesus to be our Savior. Jesus has given us salvation, guidance, the sacraments, above all, the Eucharist. Try to imagine what life would be like without these gifts.

To put it plainly, religion does not consist in the great or small things we do for God but rather in what God has done and continues to do for us. Religion is allowing oneself to be served and loved by God. Nothing evil that we ever do can prevent God from loving and serving us. This idea should not discourage good works, especially for the poor. We do good works *out of grateful response* for all that God has done for us.

Consider how this concept of religion is verified in today's Alternative Opening Prayer:

> Gifts without measure flow from your goodness. . . .
> Our life is your gift.
> Guide our life's journey,
> for only your love makes us whole.

Then there is the beautiful Reading I;

> All you who are thirsty,
> come to the water!
> You who have no money,
> come, receive grain and eat;
> Come, without paying and without cost,
> drink wine and milk!

In a word, all we have to do is to open our hands and hearts, and God will fill us with all divine life and love.

The theme of God's mercy continues in the Responsorial Psalm:

> The Lord is gracious and merciful,
> slow to anger and of great kindness.
> The Lord good to all
> and compassionate towards all his works. . . .
> You open your hand
> and satisfy the desire of every living thing.
> The hand of the Lord feeds us; he answers all our needs.

And so, too, in Reading II. St. Paul asks, "Who will separate us from the love of Christ?" And the answer is, nothing. We can conquer any human trial, come to terms with any suffering, even death. In short, we are conquerors "because of him who has loved us." The love is free for the taking. All we have to do is to open our hands and hearts.

Finally, there is the gospel, which is about the multiplication of loaves and fishes. People are hungry. Touched with pity for them, Jesus blesses five loaves and a couple of fish, breaks the loaves, and gives them to the apostles, who distribute them to the people, about five thousand of them. They all have their fill, and twelve baskets of fragments are left over. Obviously, Jesus intended this miracle to prepare the apostles (and us) for the greatest of all God's love-gifts, the Eucharist. The essential meaning of "eucharist" is "gift." The Eucharist is Christ's gift of himself, his gift of love.

And so with all the sacraments: God comes to us in every one of life's needs, out of sheer, undeserved love. This is true not only of the Eucharist but also of the wonderful sacrament of reconciliation. The entire Bible demonstrates God's eagerness to forgive—not just once but again and again. And this is especially true of Jesus, Son of God. There is nothing we can do to keep God from forgiving us.

But we have to accept God's love into our lives and hearts. Once we realize fully how very much God loves us, anything can happen. We might even become saints!

> Only your love makes us whole.
> Keep us strong in your love (Alternative Opening Prayer).

114 EIGHTEENTH SUNDAY IN ORDINARY TIME — Cycle B

READING I **Exod 16:2-4, 12-15** **READING II** **Eph 4:17, 20-24**
GOSPEL **John 6:24-35**

Reading I: The people complain about lack of food, and the Lord feeds them daily with manna and quail.

Reading II: To be a Christian means learning Christ and laying aside one's former way of life.

Gospel: Jesus tries to make the people understand that he is the true bread from heaven.

The great French novelist Francois Mauriac says that through much of his life he was aware of Christ, but with writing and lecturing and the many other things he did, had been really too busy for him. He says: "I preferred the radical anguish of my youth to Christ, I suppose. But now Christ has become the great love of the evening of my life." He says he is amazed to have discovered that God is never so close to us as when we think God is absent. But most importantly, he tells about all the intellectual problems he has had through the years. Then he says, "God has never answered my questions which were laden with despair. All he has ever done is to give himself to me in Christ" (quoted in *Sunday Sermons,* Vol. 12, No. 4).

Well, today's Mass is an urgent, earnest effort to help make Christ the great love, not of the evening of our lives, but of life here and now and from now on.

Once again Reading I, which tells about God feeding his people manna and quail during their journey, and the gospel, in which Jesus calls himself the "bread of life" link up. And Paul in Reading II has practical advice on what Christianity ought to mean for us. Both Reading I and the gospel tell us that people get hungry, as we all know from personal experience. To be human is to be hungry, says Monika Hellwig. The body's hunger for food is a sign of a deeper hunger for love, truth, for insight into the mystery of life, suffering, and death—in a word, for God made flesh in Christ Jesus. "I myself am the bread of life," he tells us today. "No one who comes to me shall ever be hungry, no one who believes in me shall thirst again."

At the end of his life Mauriac discovered that Jesus is life's chief value, the central love of life. But why wait till old age? Many try to submerge the heart's deep hungers and try to satisfy them in a variety of superficial ways—the acquisition of great possessions, power, social or political acclaim. Jesus challenges all of us today: "You should not be working for perishable food but for food that remains unto life eternal."

And Paul also has strong, pertinent words: "I declare and solemnly attest in the Lord that you must no longer live as the pagans do—their minds empty. That is not what you learned when you learned Christ!" Paul's concern is for an ongoing, never-ending conversion for his people, a progressive acquiring of the mind and heart of Christ. "You must lay aside your former way of life and the old self which deteriorates through illusion and desire, and acquire a fresh, spiritual way of thinking. You must put on that new man created in God's image, whose justice and holiness are born of truth" (Reading II).

Christ gives himself to us in the Eucharist; but he can do nothing for us, he cannot give us his mind and heart, unless we are willing to commit our entire self to him. "Unless we give ourselves to him, he cannot give himself to us," says Father Carr.

> I myself am the bread of life.
> No one who comes to me shall ever be hungry,
> no one who believes in me shall thirst again.

In Jesus and only in Jesus can our hunger, our thirst for the wholeness of life, be satisfied. "This is the work of God: have faith in the One he sent."

And we may not forget that if Christ satisfies our hungers, if we feed on him, we also take on his hunger for justice, his deep concern for mutual love and for those who suffer in any way, but above all for those who suffer starvation.

This gospel, along with the "confession" of Mauriac, makes me ask myself if Jesus Christ is the central and ultimate value, the chief love, of my life. Please God that we shall not have to wait till the evening of our lives to become convinced that in Christ, and only in him, will all the hungers of our lives find fulfillment!

> God our Father, . . .
> Guide our life's journey,
> for only your love can make us whole.
> Keep us strong in your love (Alternative Opening Prayer).

115 EIGHTEENTH SUNDAY IN ORDINARY TIME Cycle C

READING I Eccl 1:2, 2:21-23 **READING II** Col 3:1-5, 9-11
GOSPEL Luke 12:13-21

Reading I: Life makes no sense if it has no deeper goal than achieving worldly success.

Reading II: Having been raised up with Christ, we are to keep God at the center of life and avoid anything that endangers eternal joy.

Gospel: Jesus' parable about the rich man who grows rich for himself instead of growing rich in the sight of God.

The story is told about a wealthy man who was dying. The priest at his bedside urged him to be sorry for the sins of his life, especially the sin of avarice. The priest told him that he didn't have long to live. Was he prepared to meet his God? Thinking he could soften the man's heart and move him to sorrow, he held a beautiful silver crucifix before the man's eyes. For a moment the man's expression softened, and the priest thought he had been touched by the image of Christ crucified. But too long the man had been accustomed to evaluating things by their material value. He asked the priest, "Father, how much do you think that crucifix is worth?" And then he died.

A Minneapolis Star Tribune columnist once wrote about a man who had achieved the pinnacle of his amibition when he became president of a large corporation. One day as he sat in his office, he thought to himself: "Now I have reached the age of retirement. I have everything I ever wanted; but I live in the same house as my wife, and we never learned to talk together. I don't know my own children, and they don't know me. I don't know anything about enjoying music, literature, or art of any kind. I'm going to retire in a month, and I don't even know how to fish!"

These two stories might be modern versions of Jesus' parable in today's gospel. They contain a terrible warning about what can happen to a person whose life priorities are upside down, about the frustration and despair of a man or woman who places material success ahead of God in his or her life.

The man in the columnist's story was doubly guilty: first, of a wrong set of values and life priorities and second, of failing to allow life to enrich him with its God-given treasures. He had refused to become educated, refused to grow up into a whole human being. He had organized his life without reference to God, kept God on the fringes of life rather than at the center. Such a life, in the end, can bring a person nothing but frustration, and despair.

But it isn't only material riches and the unholy search for them that today's readings warn against. Seeking intellectual knowledge without reference to benefiting others can also be dangerous, as Reading I indicates. The wrong search for wisdom, condemned in Reading I, is an attempt to presume knowledge and control over God. This is the "vanity of vanities" ridiculed by Qoheleth. This is not to downgrade education and study, but simply to point out that no matter how intelligent one is, the ways of God are God's ways—a mystery that always beckons us to more study, more prayer.

Avarice, possessiveness, greed for either riches or unholy knowledge—all are self-destructive. May we all learn this truth before we end up like the dying man who asked what the silver crucifix was worth. "If today you hear his voice, harden not your hearts" (Responsorial Psalm).

What does our Lord mean by "growing rich in the sight of God"? It means placing and keeping God at the center of one's life rather than on the fringes. It means self-giving, living for others rather than for oneself. It means friendship and intimacy with Jesus and learning to appreciate all those things that the rich man in the *Star Tribune* story had neglected: music, poetry, literature, maybe even learning how to fish.

"Growing rich in the sight of God" means learning how to love, having love at the very center of our being—love for God over all else and love for one another. You can't have the one without the other. And love has to be worked at, it has to be created by sacrifice, learning to live for others. We have to give love, but before it can be given we have to learn how to receive love—receive it above all from God. That is the true meaning of hospitality—being open to the Lord's desire to be at home in us. Today's Alternative Prayer sums it all up:

> God our Father,
> gifts without measure flow from your goodness,
> to bring us your peace.
> Our life is your gift.
> Guide our life's journey,
> for only your love makes us whole.
> Keep us strong in your love.

407 MONDAY OF THE EIGHTEENTH WEEK IN ORDINARY TIME — Cycle A

YEAR I

READING I **Num 11:4-15**
GOSPEL **Matt 14:22-36**

We must not look down on the Israelites (or Moses) for their complaints against God. We've outdone them more than once. Hardened hearts flourish in every age. God himself provides the only remedy in today's Responsorial Psalm: "If only my people would hear me, and Israel walk in my ways."

Since those days, we also have the word and, above all, the example of Jesus to elicit our love and gratitude. But we have to respond to him and his word with faith. As long as Peter keeps his eyes fixed on Jesus and concentrates on him, he does the impossible. But as soon as his concentration on Jesus gives way to the distractions of the wind and waves, he begins to sink. We must not be too hard on Peter. How often has his experience been ours! The obvious lesson is: Keep your eyes fixed on Jesus, your ears open to his word, "Come." Let us go!

YEAR II

READING I **Jer 28:1-17**
GOSPEL **Matt 14:22-36**

The apostles' boat was being tossed about like a cork. Is it any wonder that they were terrified? Well, there are times in our lives when we too seem to be tossed about by terrifying winds of adversity. And we seem so alone, so helpless. But we are not alone. The very same Jesus who walked toward his friends that stormy night is walking by our side now. And the same voice reassures us: "Get hold of yourselves! It is I. Do not be afraid."

What Jesus desires of us is faith in him and in his presence, even when we do not see him. Twice in this incident today he complains gently of the apostles' lack of faith. "How little faith you have," he says to Peter. "Why did you falter?" It's a good question. Why do *we* falter? Is it because of our failure to stay close to Christ as he speaks to us in these daily gospels? Or because we never even read or think about the gospels? He's always there.

407 MONDAY OF THE EIGHTEENTH WEEK IN ORDINARY TIME Cycles B & C

YEAR I

READING I **Num 11:4-15**
GOSPEL **Matt 14:13-21**

We are now with the Hebrew people as they begin their journey through the desert to the Promised Land. It is not going to be an easy or pleasant experience for us, mainly because it is so true to life. The people have been delivered from slavery in Egypt. God has chosen them as his very own people, he gives them an allotment of daily food, but they complain. "My people heard not my voice, and Israel obeyed me not" (Responsorial Psalm). Moses gets so disappointed with them that he asks to be allowed to die.

It's all a rather sorry picture, and it tempts us to judge the Jews rashly. But then comes the sobering question: how would we have done in their situation? How do we do now? The Old Testament tells the history of the Hebrew people, but let us not forget: history repeats itself. Their history is our history now. May we do half as well as they did.

YEAR II

READING I **Jer 28:1-17**
GOSPEL **Matt 14:13-21**

Today Christ's loving compassion drives him to heal the sick among the crowds that follow him and then to feed them by miraculously multiplying five loaves and two fishes, so that more than five thousand persons have enough to eat.

Jesus teaches who and what he is not so much by what he says but by what he does. He does works that belong to God alone. Great as was the miracle he performed that day, it cannot compare with the feeding of hungry hearts, prefigured in that miracle, which he continues to do for us day after day in the Mass. His love is everlasting. If at times in our lives we become too used to the miracle of the Eucharist, the best thing for us to do is to retire to a lonely place with him and let him speak to our hearts about his love made flesh in the Eucharist.

408 TUESDAY OF THE EIGHTEENTH WEEK IN ORDINARY TIME Cycle A

YEAR I

READING I **Num 12:1-13**
GOSPEL **Matt 15:1-2, 10-14**

Jealousy of their brother Moses poisoned the hearts of Aaron and Miriam, even as it can poison our hearts. Their jealousy also poisoned their relationship with him. Moses may have his faults, but he is also God's man, God's choice as leader of his people; in complaining about that choice, they are trying to play God. And that's precisely what sin is. Sin cannot hurt God but only those guilty of it, as today's incident illustrates.

Moses, like Jesus, pleads for his brother and sister, and they are healed—but only on condition that they repent. The Responsorial Psalm is as universal as sin. It belongs to Miriam and Aaron, it belongs to us. It admits guilt, it begs for forgiveness, it acknowledges the God whom sin offends, but best of all it recognizes the only real remedy against sin:

> A clean heart create for me, O God,
> and a steadfast spirit renew within me (Responsorial Psalm).

YEAR II

READING I Jer 30:1-2, 12-15, 18-22
GOSPEL Matt 15:1-2, 10-14

The "pecking process" is again at work: the pecking of the scribes at Jesus for the failure of his disciples to wash their hands before eating a meal. Jesus' reply is disturbing: "It is not what goes into a man's mouth that makes him impure; it is what comes out of his mouth." When Peter warns Jesus that he has scandalized the Pharisees, Jesus calls his critics blind. And in later verses, he explains that what comes out of a person's mouth comes forth from the mind, for it is the mind that generates evil thoughts, murder, adultery, theft, false witness, and slander. We all know that from personal experience. It is the mind that brews all the evil desires and ideas that result in sin and crime. A person may appear to be entirely respectable, but if his mind is filled with hatred and lust, that person's "religion" has taken flight. And that's tragic.

408 TUESDAY IN THE EIGHTEENTH WEEK IN ORDINARY TIME Cycles B & C

YEAR I

READING I Num 12:1-13
GOSPEL Matt 14:22-36

Jesus has just fed the multitudes with miraculously multiplied bread. He withdraws up the mountain to pray after sending the apostles off in their boat. Soon he sees that they are in trouble, so he takes after them, walking on the water. They are frightened, but he calls out: "Get hold of yourselves! It is I. Do not be afraid!" On an impulse Peter says, "Lord, if it is you, tell me to come to you across the water." "Come!" says Jesus. All goes well till Peter notices the high waves. Frightened he begins to sink. Jesus saves him, but not without a rebuke for his lack of faith.

Dear Peter! He may have his faults, but Jesus chooses him as head of his Church. Peter helps us to know ourselves as we are. When we fail to remember Peter's humanness, we cease to realize what it means to be a Christian. With all his faults, Peter does have a spirit of adventure, and that might well be one of Christianity's essential virtues.

OR

The following gospel and commentary may be substituted especially in Year A when Matthew 14:22-36 is used on Monday.

GOSPEL Matt 15:1-2, 10-14

The gospel shows Jesus again in conflict with the Pharisees and scribes. They complain about the disciples' neglecting to wash their hands before eating, but actually they are attacking him. Again he tries to show them that being religious is not a matter of externals like washing hands; it is a matter of the heart, of a person's inner being, and how that inner being is oriented towards God. Mark has Jesus putting these words in God's mouth: "This people honors me with their lips, but their hearts are far from me." It is a terribly strong accusation. It was originally addressed to the Pharisees, but if we are not watchful, it could easily be true of any one of us. Wounded human nature is not restricted to any historical era or any class of people.

YEAR II

READING I Jer 30:1-2, 12-15, 18-22
Either Matt 14:22-36 OR
Matt 15:1-2, 10-14

"Incurable is your wound, grievous your bruise," God tells his people through the prophet Jeremiah, and he goes on to list many of their former crimes (which God compares to adultery in marriage). The people has endured its punishment by being exiled from their homeland. But God never gives up on them, just as he never gives up on us, no matter what sins we have committed. "See! I will restore the tents of Jacob, his dwellings I will pity. City shall be rebuilt upon hill, and palace restored as it was. From them will resound songs of praise. . . . You shall be my people, and I will be your God."

This reading is a warning to all of us, as a nation, a Church, as individual Christians. We too can refuse to remember that God is Lord of our lives, and if we do, we have to accept the consequences. But, I repeat, God never gives up on us. He is always ready to take us back into his loving heart.

409 WEDNESDAY OF THE EIGHTEENTH WEEK IN ORDINARY TIME

YEAR I

READING I Num 13:1-2, 25–14:1, 26-29, 34-35
GOSPEL Matt 15:21-28

The sin of the Israelites in today's Reading I is lack of trust in God. He has brought them to the edge of the Promised Land, and now they succumb to fear. The Responsorial Psalm reviews their faithless history, but it is our history as well: "We have sinned, we and our fathers. . . . They forgot the God who had saved them. . . ."

The Canaanite woman in the gospel belonged to the pagan people the Israelites defeated. She is surely one of the most fascinating figures in the gospel. She refuses to take no for an answer to her pleading. Her daughter is troubled, so she cries to Jesus, "Have pity on me." Like all mothers, like Mary, like Jesus himself, she suffers with the suffering of the one she loves. Her persistence wins Jesus' admiration and the cure of her daughter. "Lord, remember us, for the love you bear your people" (Responsorial Psalm). We must never give up praying for the ones we love.

YEAR II

READING I Jer 31:1-7
GOSPEL Matt 15:21-28

To realize that one is really and truly loved is one of the greatest needs of the human heart. This realization is also the foundation of all true morality. Today God tells his people, us included, that he has loved us with an "age-old love" and that he has been and always will be merciful to us. It is one of life's mysteries that we have such difficulty believing in God's love for us. Too often we allow the temporary setbacks and pains of life to blind us to that fact. Too often in the past the God we were told about inspired terror rather than grateful love. God was used as a threat to make us behave. The words and deeds of the Lord and, above all, his giving us Jesus who is the sign of God's love give the lie to that teaching. "With age-old love I have loved you," he tells us. Isn't it time we begin to believe in that love?

410 THURSDAY OF THE EIGHTEENTH WEEK IN ORDINARY TIME

YEAR I

READING I Num 20:1-13
GOSPEL Matt 16:13-23

Many priests, on reading today's gospel, will quite naturally speak about Jesus appointing Peter the head of the apostles and the rock foundation of his Church. But there may be something very important for all of us in Jesus' question, "Who do you say that I am?" He really wants to know, because if we have not made up our minds about him by now, there is danger that our Christian faith has little or no foundation. Have we ever really tried to reflect on the question "Who is Jesus for me"? If we have not yet done so, there's no time like the present to start. And so much the better if we write down our convictions, so that we can compare them with what, hopefully, we will write again and again in years to come. Please God that there will be deeper insights into our relationship with him as we live, love, suffer, work, and grow in intimacy.

YEAR II

READING I Jer 31:31-34
GOSPEL Matt 16:13-23

"The days are coming," says the Lord, "when I will make a new covenant with the house of Israel." At this and at every Mass the priest will say, "This cup is the new covenant in my blood, the blood of the new and everlasting covenant." The Mass fulfills Jeremiah's prophecy; but more than that, it points to and helps us advance toward an ultimate fulfillment, which we will enjoy when the Lord's words are fulfilled: "I will place my law within them, and write it upon their hearts; I will be their God, and they shall be my people." Our prayer now and always must be, "Create a clean heart in me, O God, and a steadfast spirit renew within me" (Responsorial Psalm).

Do we realize how essential Jesus and the Mass are to that fulfillment? What would be our answer to the question Jesus asks today: "Who do you say that I am?"

411 FRIDAY OF THE EIGHTEENTH WEEK IN ORDINARY TIME

YEAR I

READING I **Deut 4:32-40**
GOSPEL **Matt 16:24-28**

More and more it becomes apparent that *remembering* is about the most essential element in religion. The history of the Jewish people we have been following reminds us of how often God insisted on it. Moses does the same today. He simply reviews that history and insists that it was God's personal love for his people that was responsible for their having been chosen. And he concludes, "This is why you must now know, and fix in your heart, that the Lord is God in the heavens above and on the earth below, and that there is no other."

Jesus wanted to be remembered, too, and that is one of the reasons he gave us our seasons and feasts, with the Mass as the remembering which makes the past deeds of the Lord present to us and for us. We can each make our own the word of today's Responsorial Psalm: "I remember the deeds of the Lord" in our own life. "O God, your way is holy; what great God is there like our God?"

YEAR II

READING I **Nah 2:1, 3; 3:1-3, 6-7**
GOSPEL **Matt 16:24-28**

The prophet Nahum today rejoices over the fall of Nineveh, the city that so cruelly treated the captive Jews. The judgment on Nineveh is a warning to the chosen people of what will happen to Jerusalem if they scorn their covenant with Yahweh.

In yesterday's gospel Jesus foretold his coming death. Today he lays out his expectations for us: "If a man wishes to come after me, he must deny his very self, take up his cross, and begin to follow in my footsteps." We all have our own cross. No two are alike, because no two of us are alike. What is certain is that love—our love responding to the love of Jesus—can turn any cross into triumph. What is essential in the intention of Christ is not so much that we suffer as he did but that we love as he did. Not suffering but love redeems and gives joy.

412 SATURDAY OF THE EIGHTEENTH WEEK IN ORDINARY TIME

YEAR I

READING I Deut 6:4-13
GOSPEL Matt 17:14-20

What Moses said in this conclusion to his sermon to his people is as valid today as it was then: "Hear, O Israel! The Lord is our God, the Lord alone. . . . You shall love the Lord your God with all your heart. . . . Drill [these words] into your children." I might add: drill them into your hearts. And if you need words with which to express the love of your hearts, today's Responsorial Psalm provides them: "I love you, O Lord, my strength, O Lord, my rock, my fortress, my deliverer."

Jesus is offended by the lack of faith on the part of his countrymen and apostles because it implies a repudiation of his Father. We, too, beg for healings. But do we really believe? Is there in our lives a failure to take Jesus seriously not only as a healer but as the be-all and end-all of our lives? Lord, help our unbelief!

YEAR II

READING I Hab 1:12–2:4
GOSPEL Matt 17:14-20

In his prophecy, Habakkuk complains gently to Yahweh about the way he runs the world, and Yahweh's answer is as applicable to us now as it was to the Jews then: "The just man, because of his faith, shall live." Loyalty and trust in God do not go unrewarded; so with infinite assurance we make our own the psalmist's confession of faith: "You will never abandon those who seek you, Lord."

Faith that gives life is also Jesus' concern in the gospel. Nothing is impossible to him who has faith in the love and pity of the Lord. Faith is essentially a human response of confident trust in God's tender care. Jesus' complaint about lack of faith is still valid today. We can always make our own the anguished plea of the father: Lord, I believe; help my unbelief!

NINETEENTH SUNDAY IN ORDINARY TIME

READING I **1 Kgs 19:9, 11-13** **READING II** **Rom 9:1-5**
GOSPEL **Matt 14:22-23**

Reading I: Elijah hears the Lord's voice, not in any of nature's spectacular manifestations but in a tiny, whispering sound.

Reading II: Paul tells us that he would risk any calamity for the sake of his own people, the Israelites.

Gospel: Both Jesus and Peter walk on the water, but Peter begins to sink when he becomes aware of threatening waves.

Faith in Christ that is real and deep means trusting God all the way. It's like giving up all human resources and putting one's life and future entirely in God's hands. We may never lose sight of the fact that the One in whom we place our trust is the Lord who loves and cares for us as only God can love and care.

A boat riding the stormy waves is a striking and well-known image of the Church riding the stormy waves of history. The Church is the people *of God,* and it is constantly being threatened by every possible influence, good and bad, in every age. Older Catholics may remember how the Church was persecuted in Mexico in the first decades of this century. She often had to go underground.

What about the Church today? Compared to the Church of pre-Vatican II days when everyone seemed secure in the faith, when we knew where we were with Catholic teaching and morality, this modern Church often no longer seems to be the same Church. Many are terribly disturbed, and they all have their favorite characters to blame, rightly or wrongly. Pope John XXIII, the Pope who was inspired by the Holy Spirit to hold the Council, is often blamed. He may have surmised that he would be criticized, for in his very first address to the Council Fathers, he spoke about the "prophets of doom." He never realized how exactly his description would fit so many disturbed Catholics of our day.

Recall the details of today's gospel. Jesus has not abandoned his ship. He's simply been up on the mountain praying for his flock, and today he is walking on the waves, coming to the ship. Get hold of yourselves! It is I. Do not be afraid! In other words, trust in me and in my promises that I will be with you till the end of the world, and the gates of hell shall not prevail against you.

This does not mean that we may not be troubled about some of the outrageous practices sometimes propagated by a few members of the Church, whether of the far left or the far right. There are some of the latter who would like to reverse history and return to the "good old days." Well, there are no longer any "good old days"; there are only "good new days," because the Church has to keep pace with our world and all its human and scientific developments.

We might even question the so-called security we used to talk about in the old days. Was security a healthy condition? I doubt it very much. The life of the Church and of her individual members has to be a life of faith, and faith is all-out *trust* in God our Father and in his Son Jesus Christ. It is the exact opposite of security.

> I hope in the Lord.
> I trust in his word (Alleluia Verse).

To those who worry and complain about the direction the Church is taking in our time, Jesus cries out: "Get hold of yourselves! It is I. Do not be afraid!" Jesus did not found his Church and intend it to remain anchored offshore through the centuries. Rather, he intended it to ride the waves of history, serving the needs of people of every age, including our own.

It is true, he did not intend that the doctrines contained in his Gospels should ever change in substance or be done away with. But he surely had no objection to the Church and her theologians meditating on the gospel truths and acquiring ever-new insights into those truths. The contents of the Gospels can never be exhausted.

What about us? Does this gospel have any special meaning for us, for our personal lives? It surely does. There are times in all our lives when the waves of misfortune, sickness, family tragedy, seem about to engulf us. There are times when our Christian faith is deeply tried and we feel like giving up in despair. Then it is that Jesus, who loves us more than we will ever know, says to us: Why are you faltering? I am with you always. Do not be afraid.

Then it is time for an act of faith and trust, rising from the depths of our hearts:

> I hope in the Lord,
> I trust in his word (Alleluia Verse).

NINETEENTH SUNDAY IN ORDINARY TIME

READING I **1 Kgs 19:4-8** **READING II** **Eph 4:30–5:2**
GOSPEL **John 6:41-51**

Reading I: Nourished by bread from heaven, Elijah walked forty days and forty nights to the mountain of God, Horeb.

Reading II: Paul tells us to imitate God as his dear children and follow the way of love.

Gospel: Jesus claims to be the bread of life, the bread he will give for the life of the world.

I have always seen chapter six of John's Gospel as Jesus' preparation of the apostles for the Last Supper and the institution of the Eucharist. I still do. But recently I came across another idea: that todays' section of chapter six is really about Jesus as the special revelation of God. The idea is that the *notion* and *reality* of God is best manifested in Jesus. God is life-giving. Jesus is living, life-giving bread.

In Jesus and his gospel, the Lord God shares himself, his infinite divine wisdom, the way of life he would have us follow. Jesus is the bread of understanding. So Jesus is nourishment, food for the way to Horeb, the mountain of God, nourishment along the way of life. He is food both in word and in sacrament. He is the bread of understanding.

If Jesus is the bread of understanding, the special revelation of God, we are forced to ask ourselves how well we really know and understand him. Not just facts about him as the Gospels reveal him but in our hearts; know him, as far as possible, in his intentions, his emotions, his attitudes toward people—how he feels about his enemies, his mother, his friends. What he would think of life in our world today. We cannot know the reality of God without knowing Jesus, or, more exactly, we cannot know God well wihtout knowing Jesus.

The wisdom of Jesus is conveyed not only in the Gospels but in other parts of the New Testament as well. For example, in today's Reading II Paul gives us some very practical advice about living according to the mind of Christ. First there are some negative imperatives: do nothing to sadden the Holy Spirit; get rid of all bitterness, passion and anger, harsh words, slander, and malice of every kind.

Then the positive: be kind, compassionate, forgiving. In a word, be imitators of God as his dear children. Follow the way of love, even as Christ has loved us. Jesus gave himself for us as an offering to God, a gift of pleasing fragrance.

The key words are "compassion" and "forgiving, just as God has forgiven you in Christ." Forgiving may be the most difficult. To be hurt, offended, threatened, and then to wipe away the hurt with a word of honest forgiveness is difficult if not impossible by our own power alone. But we are not alone. We have the example of Jesus, who suffered the greatest of all hurts, praying on the cross: "Father, forgive them, they do not know what they are doing." It is that Jesus who gives himself and his forgiving impulse and power to us in the Eucharist.

"Compassion" means "suffering with." Jesus himself had and still has compassion on us. Please God we have experienced it. One of the finest examples of compassion is recorded in the story of three young nurses who decided to spend the first year after finishing their training in a big city slum. One day one of the nurses was holding a dirty, wounded bum in her arms and washing his wounds. A man passing by exclaimed, "I wouldn't do that for a million dollars!" "Neither would I," she replied. But she was doing it because she saw Christ in the wounded man. Whatever you do to the least of these you do to me.

Jesus gives himself to us in the Eucharist as divine wisdom—a way of life. The gift will be wasted unless we accept it with grateful, loving, open hearts. Our response is best expressed in the Alternative Opening Prayer:

> Father,
> we come, reborn in the Spirit,
> to celebrate our sonship in the Lord Jesus Christ.
> Touch our hearts,
> help them grow toward the life you have promised.
> Touch our lives,
> *make them signs of your love for all men.*
> Grant this through Christ our Lord. Amen.

NINETEENTH SUNDAY IN ORDINARY TIME

READING I **Wis 18:6-9** **READING II** **Heb 11:1-2, 8-19**
GOSPEL **Luke 12:32-48**

Reading I: "That night" (of the Exodus from slavery in Egypt) was known beforehand by the Jewish fathers Abraham, Isaac, and Jacob; and the people waited in faith for their deliverance.

Reading II: The reading exalts the faith of the great leaders of the Jewish people and their descendants.

Gospel: Jesus tells us that we know not the day or the hour of the coming of the Son of Man; therefore, we must always be prepared.

What is your idea of God? There are probably as many ideas of God as there are people. The Book of Genesis tells us that God created us in God's own image and likeness (see 1:26), but the cynical French writer Voltaire is supposed to have reflected that man got revenge and created God in man's own image.

False ideas of God may be responsible for the loss of faith of many young people in our day. A God of sanctions, a kind of super highway policeman in the heavens always trying to catch someone in wrongdoing is common enough. A God who is against everything that is pleasant and enjoyable is another false idea.

Father Burtchaell of Notre Dame once pointed out that many young people grow out of these false ideas of God, and having nothing left, give up believing in God at all. The loss of any sense of sin among so many Catholics today can probably also be attributed to the false ideas of God that many grew up with.

What is the true, biblical idea of God? Almighty, supreme Lord and creator of the universe and all in it, yes. But also a God who is a loving Father, who cares for every single one of us, including sinners. A God who chose us to be his own, who never ceases to love us, no matter what wrong we have done in the past or will do in the future. A forgiving God whom Jesus described so perfectly in the parable of the prodigal son. It might better be described as the parable of the prodigal father, who gathered his wayward son in his arms and wept for joy.

"God so loved the world that he gave his only Son, that whoever believes in him may not die but may have eternal life" (John 3:16).

This is our God! God is the fullness of love. Human love is from God. God is a love-sharing, life-sharing, truth-sharing Lord.

I have asked, what is your idea of God? But what is your idea of an ideal Christian? Some may think that the ideal Christian is one who obeys all the rules and commandments, in short, a "practicing" Catholic. That may be an important part of the ideal. I do not know the origin of this description of the ideal Christian, but it deserves serious consideration: A Christian is one who believes, really believes, in love; really believes that God loves and cares for her or him and is willing and eager to receive that divine love. Christianity is not so much a matter of doing great things for God but of believing that we are loved by God and allowing God to do great things for us.

> Happy the people the Lord has chosen to be his own (Responsorial Psalm).

There is nothing we can do to merit God's love. It's free for the taking. God loves us no matter what. God loves us not for what we have *done* or continue to do but for who we *are*—chosen beloved members of his flock.

The ideal Christian is a person of deep faith. Real faith is not trusting in the security provided by possessions and wealth but rather confident trust in God's loving care. It is a kind of entrance into a daring adventure, the best example of which is the Patriarch Abraham. Abraham left his old, established life behind, as God had requested and struck out for a new land, starting a family at an advanced age, his wife being barren and almost as old as he. God had promised Abraham that he would be the father of a new nation, and Abraham took God at his word.

The best example of great faith is Mary, mother of Jesus. God had promised that she would be the mother of the Messiah. Mary didn't understand how it could happen; she simply believed. "I am the servant of the Lord. Let it be done to me as you say" (Luke 1:38).

God doesn't ask such great things from us. God doesn't ask us to give up everything and start a new life in a foreign land. All God asks is that we live from day to day doing the best we can to be faithful to our particular vocation, trusting in God's caring, hoping in God, desiring God with all our hearts. There is no better way than this to be ready to meet the Lord at the moment of death.

Our lives, like those of the saints, involve suffering and pain. Is there anyone who is entirely free of worry? There are degrees of worry, but worry diminishes the more we believe that God cares, that God loves, that God will not allow us greater trials than we can bear.

> Our soul waits for the Lord,
> who is our help and our shield.
> May your kindness, O Lord, be upon us
> who have put our hope in you (Responsorial Psalm).

413 MONDAY OF THE NINETEENTH WEEK IN ORDINARY TIME

YEAR I

READING I **Deut 10:12-22**
GOSPEL **Matt 17:22-27**

Moses again reminds his people of God's majesty and lordship over all creation: "The heavens . . . belong to the Lord, your God, as well as the earth and everything on it." They cannot bribe him or win his favor in any other way than to love and serve him and to be kind to the aliens, widows, and orphans. Moses insists that the Lord wants us to serve him—not out of fear of punishment or to buy his favor but with all our hearts and souls. And he insists: This is not for God, but "for your own good."

That's what Jesus wants, too. He expects his followers to pay their just taxes as citizens, but he hopes for and expects our love and gratitude for all that *he* has done for us—much more than any state, modern or ancient, can do. He hopes for our love and gratitude. Is that expecting too much?

YEAR II

READING I **Ezek 1:2-5, 24-28**
GOSPEL **Matt 17:22-27**

"Heaven and earth are filled with your glory." This Responsorial Psalm depicts the reality of the majesty of Yahweh glimpsed by Ezekiel. When he saw the vision of the Lord, he fell on his face, as any creature does in the presence of the all-holy Lord. During the next couple of weeks we will be hearing Ezekiel preach Yahweh's lordship to his compatriots in Babylon.

The all-holy, all-perfect Lord seen by Ezekiel became man in Jesus, who today takes to himself the title, "Son of Man," first used by Ezekiel. We can hardly blame the disciples for being distressed at his prediction of his forthcoming passion and death. And they probably are not too reassured by the miracle he works. Jesus expects us to pay our own taxes as citizens, but he expects more from us as members of his body. He hopes for our love and gratitude. Is that expecting too much?

414 TUESDAY OF THE NINETEENTH WEEK IN ORDINARY TIME

YEAR I

READING I **Deut 31:1-8**
GOSPEL **Matt 18:1-5, 10, 12-14**

Moses, like all saints, was God's own creation. He became holy and great because he gave himself over to God and allowed God to shape him, as a potter shapes his clay. His deepest wish was to lead his people into the Promised Land, but God willed otherwise. He is now ready to hand over his command to Joshua. Both to his people and to Joshua he insists that it is the Lord who marches before and with them, and he will not fail them or forsake them. Therefore, they must not be afraid. That's good advice for us as well, especially when we add to it Jesus' own description of his Father in the gospel: God is a shepherd whose love for his sheep drives him to seek out and find any one of the flock that strays. "Just so," says Jesus, "it is no part of your heavenly Father's plan that a single one of these little ones shall ever come to grief." He was thinking and talking about you.

YEAR II

READING I **Ezek 2:8–3:4**
GOSPEL **Matt 18:1-5, 10, 12-14**

The truth that God's word is nourishment for the soul is wonderfully illustrated in Reading I. God asks Ezekiel to eat the scroll, and the prophet testifies, "I ate it; and it was as sweet as honey in my mouth." But the divine food has to be shared with others: "Son of man, go now to the house of Israel, and speak my words to them."

In the gospel Jesus speaks of the Father as a good shepherd who rejoices more over one recovered sheep than over ninety-nine that never went astray. One of the best means the Lord has in recovering lost sheep is a Christian who "eats" the word of God and then shares it with those who have yet to discover its sweetness and fascination. The only Scripture some people ever get to taste is what they read in the lives of people who love it.

415 WEDNESDAY OF THE NINETEENTH WEEK IN ORDINARY TIME

YEAR I

READING I Deut 34:1-12
GOSPEL Matt 18:15-20

Moses dies, but like all good men and women, he lives on in the memory of his people. He also lives today with us, showing us not so much by word but by his way of life how to allow God to lead us through life's stages. It is significant that "no one knows the place of his burial." If the people had known it, they might have wanted to make a shrine there—the last thing this God-centered man would have wanted. They might also have wanted to remain there, whereas God wanted them not to live in the past but to go on into the Promised Land, learning and loving more and more, growing into greater and greater intimacy with him. That's what he wants us to do, too. History is a guide to life; it warns us of possible mistakes, but most of all, it is an invitation to all of us to make new history. "Say to God, 'How tremendous are your deeds!' " (Responsorial Psalm)

YEAR II

READING I Ezek 9:1-7; 10:18-22
GOSPEL Matt 18:15-20

The glory of the Lord is higher than the skies. . . .
From the rising to the setting of the sun
is the name of the Lord to be praised.

High above all nations is the Lord;
above the heavens is his glory (Responsorial Psalm).

The exiled Jews refuse to accept any such teaching. Today's Reading I tells the results of their apostasy. Only those who have received a mark on their forehead are to be saved. They are the ones who "moan and groan over all the [idolatries] that are practiced within [the city]."

According to one scholar, the mark on the foreheads of the just ones was in the form of the letter *tau,* a cross. May we who are signed with the sign of the cross in baptism always be grateful for the love of Jesus who has saved us from eternal death by his cross, death, and resurrection.

416 THURSDAY OF THE NINETEENTH WEEK IN ORDINARY TIME

YEAR I

READING I Josh 3:7-10, 11, 13-17
GOSPEL Matt 18:21–19:1

History has a habit of repeating itself. Forty years before today's incident, the Israelites walked to liberation through the waters of the Red Sea. Today they walk to their new home through the walled waters of the Jordan. Sacred history will go on, but God will continue to be with his people, guiding them, forgiving their sins, always taking them back.

What the wicked servant in the gospel does seems contemptible to us until we stop and think, I've done the same thing again and again. If God acted according to our standards, no one would ever be pardoned. We make no sense, least of all to ourselves. We persist in maintaining hardened hearts. Nowhere is human frailty more obvious. Create a new and clean heart in me, O Lord. Only with a new heart can we learn that the greatest love is forgiving love, the kind of love God has for us.

YEAR II

READING I **Ezek 12:1-12**
GOSPEL **Matt 18:21–19:1**

Reading I is about hearts that rebel against Yahweh's will and his love. Through the prophet, God warns the people of impending doom, but it will do no good. The Responsorial Psalm echoes the tragic situation of those, then and now, who "tempted and rebelled against God the Most High."

The wicked servant in the gospel seems ridiculous to us until we face up to the truth that we do what he did again and again. God forgives our sins—no matter how enormous and numerous—but we refuse to forgive a neighbor who hurts our feelings or even slightly offends us. Why is this? Mainly because we have not yet allowed Christ's life and love to invade our inner being. When will we learn that the greatest love is forgiving love, because that is the kind of love God has for us?

417 FRIDAY OF THE NINETEENTH WEEK IN ORDINARY TIME

YEAR I

READING I **Josh 24:1-13**
GOSPEL **Matt 19:3-12**

Reading I is a perfect example of God's favorite method of instructing his people in religion. All details of his favors to them are reviewed, and they can only conclude in the words of today's Responsorial Psalm: "His love is everlasting. . . . Give thanks to the Lord. . . for his mercy endures forever."

All love should be everlasting. That's the message of the gospel, which treats of the indissolubility of marriage. But if love can be as powerful as a tempest, it is also delicate and fragile. It can be wounded and destroyed. *Any* human relationship can be ruined unless both partners have a conscious ideal of love, of self-giving, of selflessness. That kind of ideal can see us through any possible threat to a love relationship. Without it we are doomed. With it we can become saints in any vocation.

YEAR II

READING I Ezek 16:59-63
GOSPEL Matt 19:3-12

In the Old Testament God often used the marriage union as a symbol of the covenant between him and his people. Whenever the people violated the covanent, God used the term "adultery" to characterize their infidelity. However, no matter how often they were unfaithful, the Lord never gave up on them. He always took them back and restored the covenant. Today God promises to set up a new covenant with them: "I will set up an everlasting covenant with you" (Reading I).

It is a promise that Jesus fulfills at the Last Supper when he says over the cup of wine: This cup is the new covenant in my blood. Do this in remembrance of me. Every time we celebrate Mass we renew our marriage vows with our God, and thus we fulfill the chief purpose of all the covenants, namely, greater and greater intimacy with our God.

418 SATURDAY OF THE NINETEENTH WEEK IN ORDINARY TIME

YEAR I

READING I Josh 24:14-29
GOSPEL Matt 19:13-15

The covenant relationship between God and his people had its ups and downs. The temptations to adore strange gods were much stronger for the Jews of that time than we imagine; some of the false worship was very attractive, and besides, Israel was a solitary island of true worship in a sea of idolatry. So they often fell away from the covenant. Then they would remember all God's goodness to them, and they repented and returned to God. Such was the rhythm of their lives.

Joshua has lived and suffered with his people all his life, and now, as he is about to die, he makes a final effort to solidify their resolve to be faithful. "We will serve the Lord, our God, and obey his voice," they say. The old covenant is renewed in a very solemn manner. "You are my inheritance, O Lord. Keep me, O God, for in you I take refuge" (Responsorial Psalm). This beautiful prayer is as valid for us as it was for the Jews. Apart from God, we have no good.

YEAR II

READING I Ezek 18:1-10, 13, 30-32
GOSPEL Matt 19:13-15

In today's Reading I, the Lord warns his people and us not to try to "pass the buck" and blame anyone but ourselves for the punishment our sins bring upon us. The heart of the message is: Grow up. Act your age. "Cast away from you all the crimes you have committed, and make for yourselves a new heart and a new spirit."

Those are strong words, and knowing our weaknesses, we can only pray: "A clean heart create for me, O God, and a steadfast spirit renew within me (Responsorial Psalm). God is more than willing to answer that prayer. Perhaps an even more basic prayer for us is that we be willing to receive the clean heart and the steadfast spirit that the Lord is more than anxious to create within us.

119 TWENTIETH SUNDAY IN ORDINARY TIME Cycle A

READING I Isa 56:1, 6-7 **READING II** Rom 11:13-15, 29-32
GOSPEL Matt 15:21-28

Reading I: Observing what is right, doing what is just, loving the name of the Lord, keeping God's covenant—this is the way to salvation.

Reading II: The Jews' rejection of Christ made salvation of the Gentiles possible. But God will never abandon the chosen people.

Gospel: The faith of the Canaanite woman wins Jesus' consent to heal her daughter.

> Almighty God, ever-loving Father,
> your care extends beyond the boundaries of race and nation
> to the hearts of all who live.
> May the walls which prejudice raises between us,
> crumble beneath the shadow of your outstretched arm
> (Alternative Opening Prayer).

This prayer summarizes the main ideas of today's readings, which have to do with the ancient question of who is going to be saved. It is a problem that troubles many Christians today. There has always been a tendency to want to be exclusive about salvation. For example, many of the chosen people didn't think the Gentiles had much of a chance.

In our time there are some Christian denominations who would like to limit salvation to those who have "received Christ." They base their judgment on a quote from the Gospel of Mark: "The man who believes in it [the good news] and accepts baptism will be saved; the man who refuses to believe in it will be condemned" (16:16). This shortsighted view isolates a single verse from the Bible and constructs an entire theology on it that contradicts the content and context of the rest of the Bible.

What does the Bible say about salvation? Today's readings give some good answers:

> The foreigners who join themselves to the Lord,
> ministering to him,
> loving the name of the Lord,
> and becoming his servants . . .

Them I will bring to my holy mountain
    and make joyful in my house of prayer; . . .
For my house shall be called
    a house of prayer for all peoples (Reading I).

In Reading II Paul says that he glories in his ministry to the Gentiles, although he deeply regrets the rejection of Christ by some of his own people, the Jews. And God will not give up on them either.

In the gospel, Jesus at first seems to go along with the exclusiveness of the Jews: "My mission is only to the lost sheep of the house of Israel." But the Canaanite woman refuses to be put off. "Help me, Lord!" she cries. And he gives in: "Woman, you have great faith! Your wish will come to pass." One does not have to be a member of the chosen people in order to have faith and be saved.

Three great and comforting truths can be derived from Scripture:

a. God *wills* the salvation of all people.
b. Jesus lived and died for the salvation of all people.
c. No one is lost except by his or her own free, deliberate, and malicious choice.

We simply cannot limit God's ways of saving people. We cannot put bounds around God's saving will and love. Are we to believe that all those billions of persons who lived before Christ and who have lived since but who have never heard of Jesus, have never been baptized, are lost? That is not the teaching of the Bible or of Catholic theology.

If people are true to themselves, if they follow their consciences, if they do what they believe is right, they can be saved. The essential condition for both non-Christians and Christians is openness to God and God's love. What is necessary is faith and trust, like that of the Canaanite woman in the gospel, faith that is an absolute dependence on God. For Christians, that stems from a realization of our helplessness without Jesus. We have to remember that religion does not consist in what we do for God but what God does and has done for us. Religion is not a lot of doing or giving; more than all else, religion is the grateful receiving of Jesus' love and all that he has done for us.

Our faith is God's great gift to us. We have it without in any way having earned it or deserved it. Faith implies the responsibility of being open to all peoples of all faith or of none at all. Christianity is not yet complete. It is in the process of evolving into a Church that will someday be enriched by the special treasures of all religions, all cultures and liturgical practices and ways of worshiping God. God is working among non-Christian peoples, and the inspirations God gives them must not be lost or rejected. We can learn from all, and the more we learn the most Christian we become. May we never forget that

> With the Lord there is mercy, and fullness of redemption (Communion Antiphon).
>
> O God, let all the nations praise you! (Responsorial Psalm)

May we in every Mass share in joining our praise to theirs!

120 TWENTIETH SUNDAY IN ORDINARY TIME Cycle B

READING I **Prov 9:1-6** **READING II** **Eph 5:15-20**
GOSPEL **John 6:51-58**

Reading I: Wisdom is personalized as a woman who invites guests to come to her banquet and partake of nourishing food and drink.

Reading II: Paul spells out positive and negative details on what it means to watch over one's conduct.

Gospel: Jesus continues his discourse on the bread of life. His flesh is real food and his blood is real drink.

There are various kinds of hunger in human beings: for food and drink, for love, for truth, for understanding of the meaning of life, for hope, for acceptance, for recognition. Above all, there is our hunger for God.

> Taste and see the goodness of the Lord (Responsorial Psalm).

And there are various kinds of nourishment: the food and drink we take at our meals, the love we receive from loved ones and friends, the wisdom and knowledge that come from education and literature, the beauty of nature, music, poetry, people.

We need all these kinds of nourishment, but the one we need most is the kind Jesus speaks about:

I myself am the living bread
come down from heaven. . . .
the bread I will give
is my flesh, for the life of the world (gospel).

Last Sunday we said that John 6 is not only preparation for the Eucharist but a special revelation of God: the truth that the idea, the *notion* and the *reality* of God is best manifested in Jesus Christ. Jesus is infinite wisdom, the bread of understanding, the way, the truth, the life. This idea is continued in Reading I of today's Mass:

Wisdom has built her house, . . .
She has dressed her meat, mixed her wine, . . .
Come, eat of my food,
  and drink of the wine I have mixed!

"Taste and see the goodness of the Lord." The food and wine that Lady Wisdom speaks about points to the Eucharist, but also to the nourishment of truth, beauty, and all that a person needs for wholeness of life. We need not fear getting drunk on this kind of wine, rather, we are filled with the desire to "Give thanks to God the Father always and for everything in the name of our Lord Jesus Christ" (Reading II).

The special nourishment that Jesus promises is "my flesh, for the life of the world." This bread of life is the fullest possible meaning of nourishment. "The man who feeds on my flesh and drinks my blood remains in me, and I in him."

When we eat our daily meals, the food and drink we consume become us, they add to our being, we grow up and sometimes grow out! When we partake of the Body and Blood of Christ in the Eucharist, he takes us into himself. This means that we share in him, in his presence in the world. We share in his thinking, his emotions, his attitudes of compassion toward those who are poor, sick, homeless, or oppressed. We share in his redeeming work of reconciling humankind to the Lord, of building the Church. Above all, we share in the hunger of Christ for humans, his hunger for love and for a wholehearted response to his self-giving.

Please God we will soon come to realize and appreciate the full meaning of the Eucharist that is so available to us. And for that grateful appreciation we pray:

God of mercy,
by this sacrament you make us one with Christ.

By becoming more like him on earth,
may we come to share his glory in heaven (Prayer after Communion).

121 TWENTIETH SUNDAY IN ORDINARY TIME Cycle C

READING I **Jer 38:4-6, 8-10** **READING II** **Heb 12:1-4**
GOSPEL **Luke 12:49-53**

Reading I: Jeremiah is cast into a cistern, but Ebed-melech pleads for his rescue and the king grants the prayer.

Reading II: Putting away sin, we are to keep our eyes fixed on Jesus who inspires and protects our faith.

Gospel: Jesus predicts that he will be a cause of division among his followers.

Years ago a popular song began with the words:

I don't want to set the world on fire,
I just want to start a flame in your heart.

The author undoubtedly did not intend his song to be understood in any theological way, but the song actually does describe the desire of Christ. He wants to set the world on fire, and he wants to do it by assemblies of flaming hearts. In today's gospel, Jesus says to his disciples: "I have come to light a fire on the earth. How I wish the blaze were ignited!"

The good news of God's universal desire to give divine life and love to all the world and to reconcile all humanity to himself cannot be spread except by human hearts afire with love for Jesus and with the desire and determination to share in his saving work. Such fiery hearts are their own witness.

The fiery hearts Jesus wants are not our own creation. Recall how essential the original Pentecost was for the completion of Christ's redeeming life, work, and preaching. The Church would never have spread had it not been for the fired-up hearts of the apostles.

Recall what happened on that first Christian Pentecost: The disciples were all gathered in one place, and "suddenly from up in the sky there came a noise like a strong, driving wind. . . . Tongues as of fire appeared, which parted and came to rest on each of them. All were filled with the Holy Spirit" (Acts 2:1-4).

This was the fulfillment of Jesus' desire to light a fire on the earth. He just wanted to start a flame in their (and our) hearts. We recall how the apostles reacted: they rushed out into the city to spread the good news of Jesus' love with fired-up hearts, and some three thousand persons were added to the fold (Acts 2:41).

What the apostles experienced we have all experienced, but in a less sensational way: We have been baptized into the death and resurrection of Christ; we have received that same Holy Spirit in confirmation, and year by year we receive the Spirit in our celebration of the great feast of Pentecost.

Our chief task in life is to keep the divine fire burning bright in our hearts. How? By keeping our eyes fixed on Jesus, "who inspires and perfects our faith" (Reading II), and by receiving into our hearts the word that Jesus shares with us.

> My sheep hear my voice.
> I know them,
> and they follow me (John 10:27).

I am not proposing that we all rush out into the city and start preaching on street corners. May we just be what Jesus has called us to be: an assembly of hearts on fire with love for God and one another, hearts burning with the desire of Christ for the spread of his gospel. A gathering of fired-up hearts cannot but attract the attention of others and make them want to share that same kind of love. And for that end we pray:

> Almighty God, ever-loving Father,
> Your care extends beyond the boundaries of race and nation
> to the hearts of all who live.
> May the walls, which prejudice raises between us,
> crumble beneath the shadow of your outstretched arms (Alternative Opening Prayer).

And may we all always keep our eyes fixed on Jesus!

419 MONDAY OF THE TWENTIETH WEEK IN ORDINARY TIME

YEAR I

READING I Judg 2:11-19
GOSPEL Matt 19:16-22

The period of the Judges covers 150 years and marks another stage in the evolution of the Jewish people. Today's Reading I tells us that these charismatic leaders had their problems. The people did not listen to them: "They were quick to stray from the way their fathers had taken." The people had to learn the hard way that no one can live without God. We can't either.

The young man in the gospel asked the wrong question. It would have been better if he had asked, "What must I *be*. . . . ?" For the answer Jesus gives him is that he must be detached from earthly possessions and be totally dependent on God for everything. Being a true follower of Jesus means being totally open to God's loving gift of himself to us. The tragedy of the young man is that he preferred some*thing* to some*One*. But do we not often do the same?

YEAR II

READING I Ezek 24:15-24
GOSPEL Matt 19:16-22

Preferring something to God is what we do whenever we sin, and it is what the Israelites did. Again and again the Lord forgave them and took them back (just as he does for us), but they forgot the God who gave them birth (see Responsorial Psalm), and when you forget the God who gave you birth, you put God out of your life and you are on your own. Why do we always have to learn the hard way that living on our own, without God, is to live in death?

Jesus invites the young man in the gospel to become a perfect follower of his, but when he learns the conditions, the lad went away sorrowful, "for his possessions were many." Those possessions now under his control seemed more desirable than a promised perfection still to come. The tragedy is that he preferred some*thing* to some*One,* namely, the God of all joy.

420 TUESDAY OF THE TWENTIETH WEEK IN ORDINARY TIME

YEAR I

READING I **Judg 6:11-24**
GOSPEL **Matt 19:23-30**

Gideon was one of the most popular of the Judges. He reluctantly accepts his call from God and asks for a sign of God's presence. God's answer to him is also for us: "Be calm, do not fear." "The Lord speaks of peace to his people" (Responsorial Psalm).

In the gospel we hear Jesus' terrifying words, "Only with difficulty will a rich man enter into the kingdom of God." When the disciples ask, "Then who can be saved?" Jesus responds with the key words of the incident, the basic theology of salvation: "For man it is impossible; but for God all things are possible." In other words, we do not save ourselves. We even need God's help to recognize and remove the obstacles to his saving grace, one of the greatest being our possessiveness. What obstacles do we have?

YEAR II

READING I **Ezek 28:1-10**
GOSPEL **Matt 19:23-30**

To want to be like God, to want to be able to control our life and destiny is the first, the original sin—the sin of our first parents and the sin of us all. Reading I spells out the sin and its tragic consequences. "You are a man, and not a god, however you may think yourself like a god." It is Lord who deals death and gives life. And may we never forget it!

Who or what holds first place in my life—my possessions or Christ? The things I own, including my own opinions, or the will of God? I have to answer those questions. There is no escaping them. Jesus himself tells us that he knows how hard it is to make the choice; in fact, it is impossible without God's help. With humans this is impossible, but with God's help—and only by God's help—it can be done.

421 WEDNESDAY OF THE TWENTIETH WEEK IN ORDINARY TIME

YEAR I

READING I Judg 9:6-15
GOSPEL Matt 20:1-16

For Abimelech to become king would be like placing a leafless thornbush over other trees for shade. The point of the fable may be that the dignity of any office does not guarantee the worthiness of the occupant.

The main idea of the gospel is again the total gift of salvation, a gift that cannot be earned by anything we do. Not an hour or a week or a lifetime can deserve the greatness of God's gift of salvation in Christ Jesus. Moreover, the amount of time we work is God's affair and God's alone. Deathbed conversions, even of the greatest sinners, are events to rejoice in, not to pout about. "Are you envious because I am generous?" It's a good question for us, too. We might also ask ourselves if we are sufficiently grateful for having been called by God to do his work and if we are working up to our full potential.

YEAR II

READING I Ezek 34:1-11
GOSPEL Matt 20:1-16

In Reading I God, through Ezekiel, tells us that the awful dignity and immense responsibility of a shepherd derives from the fact that any human shepherd—pope, bishop, pastor, parent—is a stand-in for the Good Shepherd, God himself. The Lord have mercy on those who fail through malice or neglect to fulfill that responsibility!

The gospel parable contains the whole theology of redemption. Salvation is a free gift that not even a lifetime of labor can merit or deserve. It is possible for us to loaf on the job or fail to work up to our potential for Christ, misusing our talents, above all failing to be sufficiently grateful for our having been hired to work in the vineyard. The only thing that can keep us on the job is love; and it is not too difficult when we remember that "The Lord is my shepherd, I shall not want."

422 THURSDAY OF THE TWENTIETH WEEK IN ORDINARY TIME

YEAR I

READING I Judg 11:29-39
GOSPEL Matt 22:1-14

Jephthah's vow was not very wise and surely not one to be imitated. One does not bargain with God, especially with the lives of others. "Here am I, Lord; I come to do your will" (Responsorial Psalm). You can't find a better prayer than that.

In the gospel Jesus is telling his enemies that their rejection of him is like their forefathers' rejection of the prophets. But God's desire to give himself will not be thwarted. He practically forces his guests to come to the banquet. The affair of the wedding garment reminds us that we are guests at the banquet of salvation, but being a guest implies responsibility on our part. We have to wear the wedding garment of fidelity to God's word, of being a servant to all, of practicing the works of mercy. Again, the best possible wedding garment for us is in those words, "Here am I, Lord; I come to do your will."

YEAR II

READING I Ezek 36:23-28
GOSPEL Matt 22:1-14

Yahweh's promise to give the people a new heart and a new spirit and to substitute a heart of flesh for a heart of stone has actually been fulfilled in each of our lives. In baptism, God poured clean water over us and made us new creatures; he invited us into the wedding feast of his Church. He chose us for membership in the wedding feast because he loved us.

Have we responded to that love? Unfortunately, too many Christians reject God's love (which is another name for sin). It is possible for us to lose the wedding garment of divine grace—that new heart and new spirit that God gave us in baptism. And so our constant prayer, the most human of all prayers, is

> A clean heart create for me, O God,
> and a steadfast spirit renew within me.

Cast me not out from your presence,
and your holy spirit take not from me (Responsorial Psalm).

423 FRIDAY OF THE TWENTIETH WEEK IN ORDINARY TIME

YEAR I

READING I Ruth 1:1, 3-6, 14-16, 22
GOSPEL Matt 22:34-40

The Book of Ruth tells the charming story of a wonderful woman whom God chose to be a character in the great drama of salvation. Ruth is a foreigner, a Moabite, who insists on being kind to Naomi, her mother-in-law. Upon the death of her husband, Naomi decides to go home to Bethlehem. One daughter-in-law decides to stay in Moab, but Ruth makes up her mind to go with Naomi. She utters a beautiful profession of faith, one that seems to give a kind of foretaste of the *fiat* of our Lady: "Wherever you go I will go, wherever you lodge I will lodge, your people shall be my people, and your God my God." Few people have ever obeyed the great commandment of love of the Jewish Law more lovingly than Ruth, a non-Jew. She loved the Lord with her whole heart. She loved Naomi even more than she loved herself. Tomorrow we'll see how well she is to be rewarded.

YEAR II

READING I Ezek 37:1-14
GOSPEL Matt 22:34-40

Restoration, resurrection, reconciliation—this is the meaning of Ezekiel's fantastic vision today. A people that had doomed itself to death by forsaking its God is rescued by God, restored to life, and reconciled with him. This is God's promise to his people. "Let them give thanks to the Lord for his kindness and his wondrous deeds" (Responsorial Psalm).

Once again, we who are Christians see the perfect fulfillment of the vision in the renewal of the body of Christ, the Church, year after year in her celebration of the death and resurrection of Christ. We also see it fulfilled in each of us when, having died through sin, we are brought back to life and reconciled with Christ through the sacrament of reconciliation. With all this in mind, is it hard to refuse to "give thanks to the Lord, his love is everlasting."

424 SATURDAY OF THE TWENTIETH WEEK IN ORDINARY TIME

YEAR I

READING I Ruth 2:1-3, 8-11; 4:13-17
GOSPEL Matt 23:1-12

Today's Reading I condenses the last three chapters of the Book of Ruth. It reveals only the essentials of the manipulations whereby Naomi brings Ruth and Boaz together as husband and wife. The remarkable love story behind it all is only hinted at in the reading. Both Ruth and Boaz are noble characters, each recognizing the worth of the other. This kind of "mixed marriage" was forbidden to Jews, but one has the impression that the whole affair unfolded under the directions of divine Providence; for the offspring of this marriage is Obed, father of Jesse, the father of King David, most illustrious ancestor of Jesus.

Ruth fulfilled perfectly Jesus' own prescription for holiness in today's gospel: "The greatest among you will be the one who serves the rest. Whoever exalts himself shall be humbled, but whoever humbles himself shall be exalted." "See how the Lord blesses those who fear him" (Responsorial Psalm).

YEAR II

READING I Ezek 43:1-7
GOSPEL Matt 23:1-12

What would we do without the visions of the majesty, the power, the beauty, the wonder, and the glory of God provided by the prophets? Ezekiel's vision today is one of the most graphic in the

Bible—"I heard a sound like the roaring of many waters, and the earth shone with his glory." The vision causes the prophet to fall on his face in awe, aware of his sinfulness—like Peter, James, and John when they see Jesus transfigured. Like the apostles, Ezekiel is lifted up by the Spirit and assured that the real dwelling place of God on earth is in his people, not in temples of stone.

While we rejoice in God's presence in our midst, may we not forget that our Emmanuel, our God-with-us, is also the all-perfect, all-holy, all-loving, all-powerful God whose glory filled the Temple!

122 TWENTY-FIRST SUNDAY IN ORDINARY TIME Cycle A

READING I Isa 22:15, 19-23 **READING II** Rom 11:33-36
GOSPEL Matt 16:13-20

Reading I: The Lord promises to grant authority to Eliakim, clothe him with a robe, and place the key of the House of David on his shoulder.

Reading II: Paul extols the inscrutable mystery of God, creator and Lord of all that exists. To him be glory forever.

Gospel: Peter answers Jesus' question about his identity and is established as the rock foundation of the Church Christ will build.

Of all the gospel selections we hear, today's is perhaps the most familiar to Catholics. Jesus chooses Peter to be the rock foundation, the head of his Church. It is the great proof text of the primacy of the pope, since Peter went to Rome where he established his episcopal See, and all his successors have claimed the title "Bishop of Rome."

Few Catholics realize that there was an Old Testament prophecy (Reading I today) that Jesus would fulfill by his words recorded in today's gospel. "I will place the key of the House of David on his shoulder" prepares us for Christ's words to Peter: "I will entrust to you the keys of the kingdom of heaven."

What is essential is the one who does the appointing. If he has no authority, how can he confer authority? If the one who made Peter the rock foundation of his Church is only human, then the foundation is weak. Belief in Christ as the Son of God is what makes the Church the Church established by Jesus on Peter and his successors.

So the question Jesus asks is important to him; he needs to know "Who do people say that the Son of Man is?" "Who do you say that I am?" Jesus now asks each of us that question, and we have to answer. Peter's response came out of his personal experience of Jesus over a period of almost three years. During those years of hearing Jesus, seeing evidences of his loving compassion in his miracles, praying with him, Peter came to know Jesus as a dear friend, as a very wonderful man, but as much more than a man. "You are the Messiah, . . . the Son of the living God!"

As with Peter, so our answer to the question Jesus asks us has to come from our personal experience of Jesus, our deep faith in him. Is this possible? Not in the same "see, touch, and hear" way that was Peter's experience. We live now, some two thousand years later. But we do have the Gospels. They bring Jesus to us. We can hear him, witness the same miracles seen by the apostles and the thousands of his contemporaries, we can absorb his values and make them our own. And we can share in his sacrificial banquet, the Last Supper, the Eucharist. He is our personal food and drink. He is present to us and dwells in us. Prayer is essentially becoming aware of his loving presence; it is our being present to him.

Some years ago, poet Catherine de Vinck edited a book containing a collection of answers from some sixty women and men of different faiths to the question "Who do you say that I am?" The answers were deeply personal and heartfelt. All were variations of Peter's answer, but with each person's experience of Jesus in his or her own life. Cardinal Suenens' answer is typical and beautiful: "Christ is NOW; he is past, present and future. Little by little he becomes the breathing of my soul" (The Christophers, New York, 1981, 88).

It is good for all of us to answer the question and to write it down. The more personal our response and the more it springs from our inmost being, the more it will shape our lives. Day by day Jesus asks us, Who do *you* say that I am? May we reply directly to him, may it spring from our personal experience of him. May it shape our life! You are Jesus, Messiah. You are the heart of my heart, you are the breathing of my soul!

We are told that prayer begins with God. God speaks to us in Scripture, in the great sacramental sign of nature, in the smile of a child, in any number of ways. Today Jesus' voice reaches us across the centuries: Who do you say that I am? We respond: You are Jesus, God's Son, you are the life of my soul! That's prayer.

123 TWENTY-FIRST SUNDAY IN ORDINARY TIME — Cycle B

READING I **Josh 24:1-2, 15-18** **READING II** **Eph 5:21-32**
GOSPEL **John 6:60-69**

Reading I: Joshua urges the people of God to make their choices between the God of their fathers and the god of the Amorites. They choose to renew their covenant with the one true God.

Reading II: Paul writes about the ideal relationship that should exist between members of Christ.

Gospel: The conclusion of Jesus' instruction on the Eucharist. Some disciples leave him, but the Twelve remain faithful.

Today's readings bring us to the climax of Jesus' teaching on the Bread of Life. They touch on covenant, Church, the Real Presence, and the personal commitment Jesus requires of each of us who want to be his followers. In Reading I Joshua asks his people to renew the covenant alliance God made with Moses and them on Mount Sinai. It was God himself who had compared the covenant between himself and his people to the marriage contract; and he accused them of adultery whenever they violated the covenant by worshiping false gods. So the covenant often had to be renewed, and that's what happens in today's Reading I.

Reading II is also about a covenant, that of marriage and the ideal relationship that should exist between husband and wife. Taken out of their context, Paul's words are offensive to many modern Christians. And they are misunderstood, for example, by husbands who think Paul is giving them the right to lord it over their wives and children. That is definitely *not* what Paul had in mind.

Paul is using the image of marriage to describe the Church, the body of Christ, and the relationship that members should maintain toward one another and toward Christ. The norm of this relationship is *love*, mutual respect, service, and recognition of the equal dignity of each member of Christ. "Defer to one another out of reverence for Christ," says Paul. We might add, out of reverence for one another.

The Jews renewed their covenant with God again and again. They needed to not only because it helped them to remain faithful but because it helped keep them alert to their obligations to one another. Every marriage needs renewal for the same reasons. That is why celebrating wedding anniversaries is so important.

If every marriage needs renewal, so too does the Church, the body of Christ. This is what we do at every Mass: we plunge our oneness with Christ and with one another back into its source, its roots. The Mass is a celebration of unity, of our covenant with Christ and with one another, as well as a celebration of Christ's living presence in our midst. It is the making present again here and now of his entire life, death, and resurrection.

Every sharing in the Eucharist implies a decision on the part of each of us like the decision Jesus puts to the apostles in today's gospel. He asks us now, "Do you want to leave me too?" Peter's words are ours: "Lord, to whom shall we go? You have the words of eternal life. We have come to believe; we are convinced that you are God's holy one."

There are many Catholics who have given up the Church, given up the Eucharist. Perhaps it is because they have never understood the true meaning either of Church or of Eucharist. There is only one way to bring them back and also to bring all Christians together into one fold, and that is the Eucharist. We will pray in the Prayer after Communion:

> May this eucharist increase within us
> the healing power of your love.

Love, and only love, can heal, especially when it is the divine love that Jesus holds out to us in the Eucharist.

> Taste and see the goodness of the Lord (Responsorial Psalm).

TWENTY-FIRST SUNDAY IN ORDINARY TIME

READING I Isa 66:18-21 **READING II** Heb 12:5-7, 11-13
GOSPEL Luke 13:22-30

Reading I: Isaiah foretells the universality of God's saving desires.

Reading II: We are not to lose heart because of trials, for they are the Lord's way of disciplining us.

Gospel: Jesus tells us that salvation depends on God's saving will rather than on membership in the chosen people and mere external obedience to the Law.

The main theme of God's word to us today is not only the number but the quality of the persons who are to be saved. It is a problem that troubles a lot of Christians. There are some fundamentalist followers of Christ—both Catholic and Protestant—who insist, "You can't be saved unless you belong to us." That's rather like playing God.

In Reading I Isaiah tells of God's universal will to save all people: "I come to gather nations of every language; they shall come and see my glory." And we can recall the old theological teaching that God gives all sufficient grace to be saved, that Jesus died for the salvation of all, and if anyone is lost, it is because he or she deliberately and maliciously resists God's saving will.

But salvation is not automatic. In the gospel Jesus tells us that being members of the Jewish people (and by extension, being members of any Christian denomination) is no guarantee of salvation. That would make salvation too mechanical, it would dehumanize it, it would make Christianity a spectator sport.

Salvation has indeed been won for us by Christ, and there is nothing we can do to earn or deserve it. Nevertheless, the faith that Christ freely gives us imposes responsibilities on us. We may never take it for granted. Faith results in a living relationship with Jesus, and a relationship with any person, especially with Jesus, can never be static. If one does not grow in intimacy, the relationship deteriorates and can easily be lost. The result could be hearing the frightening words of Christ: "I tell you, I do not know where you come from. Away from me, you evildoers!"

Actually, the Lord himself sees to it that we do not take our faith for granted. Today's Reading II tells us how very much, and in what ways, God wants to be involved in our personal work of fidelity to our faith: "My sons do not disdain the discipline of the Lord nor lose heart when he reproves you; for, whom the Lord loves, he disciplines." There are probably times in our lives when we wish the Lord wouldn't love us quite so much.

How often are we tempted to think, what kind of love is it that insists on making things miserable for those I care for so much? It may be what some counselors of families of alcoholics call "tough love." It is a love that says, I love you enough that I refuse to make it easy for you to grow.

No one denies that suffering is difficult to understand and even more difficult to accept, especially when we see it in the lives of those we love. Nevertheless, I believe we instinctively recognize that suffering is an essential element in our growth and maturing as Christian men and women, that it is the best possible grateful response to the salvation Jesus won for us by his life, death, and resurrection. But *only* if it is motivated by love. Bitterness and complaining can totally vitiate its value.

To be a Christian means *to follow Christ* "while making his way toward Jerusalem" where he will be crucified. May we never forget Christ's words, "He who will not take up his cross and come after me is not worthy of me" (Matt 10:38). It is a little hard to explain that away.

According to Fr. J. J. Hughes, Reading II tells us that life's trials and troubles are signs not of God's absence but of his presence. "Everything that threatens our peace of mind, or even life itself, is a challenge, an opportunity to grow. Our trials and sufferings are the homework we are assigned in the school of life."

I am confident that we are never alone in suffering. Jesus is with us, suffering with us, holding us up, sharing his courage. We have to be patient with God as God is patient with us. We remember, too, that Jesus died, but he also rose again. And that is our destiny also, as he himself tells us in today's Communion Antiphon: "The man who eats my flesh and drinks my blood will live for ever; I shall raise him to life on the last day."

425 MONDAY OF THE TWENTY-FIRST WEEK IN ORDINARY TIME

YEAR I

READING I **1 Thess 1:2-5, 8-10**
GOSPEL **Matt 23:13-22**

"The Lord takes delight in his people" (Responsorial Psalm). One is almost tempted to exclaim, Really? Isn't that an exaggeration? Surely, it can't be the general rule. How about when his people forsake him and go after false gods? This has to be about the weirdest verse in all the psalms. Well, St. Paul tells the Thessalonians why the Lord takes delight in them. They have received the gospel, which has become for them "not a mere matter of words for you but one of power" (Reading I). O.K. but what about those same people if they become careless and no longer live the way of the gospel? Will God still take delight in them? Probably much more than we think. For God judges hearts, he understands human weakness. He never gives up on anyone. God forgives again and again. Lord, "Behind me and before, you hem me in and rest your hand upon me. Such knowledge is too wonderful for me" (Ps 139:5-6). Wonderful indeed! May we remember it always, especially when we sin and give way to self-disgust. "The Lord does indeed take delight in his people" (Responsorial Psalm).

YEAR II

READING I **2 Thess 1:1-5, 11-12**
GOSPEL **Matt 23:13-22**

What Jesus condemns in today's gospel was the smugness that resulted from a rigid observance of the Law that characterized some of the Pharisees. Jesus teaches that the heart of true religion is love: the Father's love for us, his children, a love to which we will respond if we are in the least bit sensitive. This is the heart of religion. Being religious cannot be measured by the number of laws and rules we keep or the amount of money we contribute to churches and charitable causes. The only possible test of genuine religion is the love of God manifested in loving concern for our neighbor. This is a lesson we need today as much as the Pharisees did then.

One of the best ways of responding to God's love for us is by joyful worship. So

> Sing to the Lord a new song;
> sing to the Lord, all you lands;
> sing to the Lord; bless his name (Responsorial Psalm).

426 TUESDAY OF THE TWENTY-FIRST WEEK IN ORDINARY TIME

YEAR I

READING I **1 Thess 2:1-8**
GOSPEL **Matt 23:23-26**

The First Epistle to the Thessalonians places some stress on the early Christian hope for the Second Coming of Christ. In general, it is a peaceful, pastoral letter in which Paul offers guidance and concern for his community; but Paul also comes through as a vulnerable and very human person, an enviable trait in any pastor.

In the gospel Jesus is again in conflict with the scribes and Pharisees. His harsh warning to the Pharisees is never outdated. Who of us does not at times act and think like them? In any age there is danger of a person's being so preoccupied with matters of external cleanliness and externals in general that we lose the most necessary concern of all: a pure, sincere, honest heart.

> The word of God is living and active;
> it probes the thoughts and motives of our heart (Alleluia Verse).

The word can also keep us honest, and who doesn't need that?

YEAR II

READING I **2 Thess 2:1-3, 14-17**
GOSPEL **Matt 23:23-26**

St. Paul's letters to the Thessalonians are down-to-earth, pastoral letters containing fatherly advice and warnings. Today he counsels his people not to allow themselves to become disturbed or terrified at the thought of the Second Coming of Christ.

Paul believed that the Second Coming was near at hand, but that did not stop him from working his heart out to spread the gospel of Jesus. He longed for that coming, was not afraid of it, and did not use it as a threat to try to make his people behave, as some modern preachers do. He was more concerned with helping his people to share his desire, his love, for Christ, and to respond to Christ's love with worship and joyous song. Yes, the Lord is indeed going to come "to judge the earth. . . . Let the heavens be glad and the earth rejoice!" (Responsorial Psalm)

427 WEDNESDAY OF THE TWENTY-FIRST WEEK IN ORDINARY TIME

YEAR I

READING I **1 Thess 2:9-13**
GOSPEL **Matt 23:27-32**

Paul is not boasting today, but simply making clear to his flock that, even though he was responsible for their spiritual guidance, he pulled his weight in practical matters as well.

> you have searched me
> and you know me, Lord.
> Where can I go from your spirit?
> from your presence where can I flee? (Responsorial Psalm)

This reminder of the "everywhereness" of God is so essential for our spiritual growth. Simply to be conscious of God's presence to us and in us is prayer, it is communion. May we be as present to him as he is to us!

Christ's conflict with the Pharisees continues. We are warned not to see the conflict in isolation from the rest of the gospel. Jesus uses the conflict to help us to see religion not as purely human effort and the performance of external deeds but as it ought to be, namely, complete openness to what God has done and wishes to continue to do for us.

YEAR II

READING I 2 Thess 3:6-10, 16-18
GOSPEL Matt 23:27-32

There is no question but that the Lord is more understanding of sins committed in moments of human weakness than of those resulting from deliberate efforts to deceive God, one's fellow citizens, and oneself. Jesus never condemned sins of the flesh as harshly and violently as he condemned the hypocrisy of the Pharisees and scribes. Essentially, these men were hypocritical showoffs. Judged by external appearances they were walking saints, but inwardly they were full of deception and idolatry.

Phariseeism, or hypocrisy, is incomprehensible. Whether practiced by the Pharisees of Jesus' time or by us today, it makes no sense. I will have to remind myself of that the next time I see myself going through the motions of religious observance without any backing from my inmost heart.

428 THURSDAY OF THE TWENTY-FIRST WEEK IN ORDINARY TIME

YEAR I

READING I 1 Thess 3:7-13
GOSPEL Matt 24:42-51

> Be watchful and ready:
> you know not when the Son of Man is coming (Alleluia Verse).

Both readings speak of that coming. And we all know there is nothing more inevitable than meeting Christ at the moment of death. But what does Jesus mean by telling us to be watchful and ready? He surely doees not want us to be filled with fear and dread. The example of the early Christians tells us that the best preparation is eager desire to be with him, our beloved Lord. It is desire for God that makes us human, but also love. I don't know who said that "the best preparation for the Second Coming is solidarity with one another," but that's what it is all about. Paul says the same thing: "May the Lord . . . make you overflow with love for one another and for all." So our best prayer is: "Fill us with your love, O Lord, and we will sing for joy!" (Responsorial Psalm)

YEAR II

READING I **1 Cor 1:1-9**
GOSPEL **Matt 24:42-51**

The prospect of the Second Coming of Christ is very real to the first Christians. It is evident in the epistles of St. Paul, and Jesus himself refers to it in today's gospel: "Stay awake, therefore! You cannot know the day your Lord is coming." But how are we to be ready either for the Second Coming of Christ at the end of time or for our meeting with him at the moment of our death? Judging by the whole spirit of the gospel, Jesus does not want our preparation to be motivated by fear of being found wanting, fear of eternal punishment. He wants our preparation to be motivated by eager desire to meet the Beloved.

If all our life we have been seeking and longing for God with eagerness and love, our ultimate meeting with God will be a moment of happiness and fulfillment. In the meantime we pray, "Fill us with your love, O Lord, and we will sing for joy!" (Responsorial Psalm, Year I)

429 FRIDAY OF THE TWENTY-FIRST WEEK IN ORDINARY TIME

YEAR I

READING I **1 Thess 4:1-8**
GOSPEL **Matt 25:1-13**

The main point of the gospel is simple: the Christian must always be ready for the unpredictable coming of Christ as well as for his own encounter with him at death. Paul's advice to the Thessalonians has to be understood in the light of the loose moral conditions of his time. Sexual license and immorality of every kind were simply regarded as normal and inevitable. But Paul reminds them of their new *being* as members of Christ: they have put on Christ. Their bodies are temples of the Holy Spirit. Therefore, they must live according to their being, their having been born again in Christ. They have only one destiny, one vocation—to become holy by allowing Christ's values, his own holiness, to take over in their lives. The temptations we might have may not be of the same intensity as those of Paul's converts; but our vocation is the same—holiness. May God's will and ours coincide.

YEAR II

READING I 1 Cor 1:17-25
GOSPEL Matt 25:1-13

St. Paul contrasts God's idea for saving and reconciling us to himself with that of the world: "Jews demand 'signs' and Greeks look for 'wisdom,' but we preach Christ crucified, a stumbling block to Jews, and an absurdity to gentiles; but to those who are called, Jews and Greeks alike, Christ the power of God and the wisdom of God." Paul insists that it is God who saves and he does it in his own way. It is the only way in the end that can stir up the only thing God desires from us—our love, our gratitude, our praise.

The earth indeed "is full of the goodness of the Lord. Exult . . . in the Lord." Not fear but grateful love penetrated with ardent desire for Christ is the best, the only way to ready ourselves for our personal encounter with the Lord at our death.

430 SATURDAY OF THE TWENTY-FIRST WEEK IN ORDINARY TIME

YEAR I

READING I 1 Thess 4:9-12
GOSPEL Matt 25:14-30

The verses of today's Reading I follow immediately after Paul's reminder to us yesterday that the vocation of every Christian is holiness. God calls each of us to become saints. This call follows from our having put on Christ in baptism, our having been baptized into him. Today comes his second conclusion: *Christians must love one another*. There is simply no growth in holiness, in love for God, without mutual charity among Christians.

The point the gospel makes can also be tied in with our call to holiness. We must develop and use our gifts and talents not only that we might become more whole but that God's kingdom may expand on earth. This may imply risk, but without risk and the faith it implies there can be no vital Christianity. "Love one another as I have loved you," says Jesus. That may require the greatest risk of all.

YEAR II

READING I 1 Cor 1:26-31
GOSPEL Matt 25:14-30

"Consider your own situation," Paul tells us today. Consider the fact that, having known and loved you from all eternity, God has chosen you and called you to share his own divine life in Christ Jesus. Yes, indeed, "Happy the people the Lord has chosen to be his own" (Responsorial Psalm).

But Jesus in the gospel indicates that the gift of divine life he has given us is also a responsibility: it is to be shared with others along with the additional talents God has given us through our parents. We may not bury them or leave them undeveloped, for it is only by working at and perfecting our talents that we become more human—which is another way of saying that we become more redeemed, more divine.

Our soul waits for the Lord, . . .
For in him our hearts rejoice;
in his holy name we trust (Responsorial Psalm).

125 TWENTY-SECOND SUNDAY IN ORDINARY TIME Cycle A

READING I **Jer 20:7-9** **READING II** **Rom 12:1-2**
GOSPEL **Matt 16:21-27**

Reading I: Jeremiah is human and weak: he complains to the Lord because God's love is painful.

Reading II: Paul tells us to offer our bodies as a living and holy sacrifice to God and to refrain from being influenced by our world.

Gospel: Jesus foretells his death and resurrection and then tells his disciples that his followers must take up their cross and follow him.

According to an old story, a professor wrote on the board the topic of an essay he wanted his class to write: "Is Life Worth Living?" One student's answer was just one line: "It depends on the liver." His mark was an *A*.

How would we compose our essay on that question? I would begin this way: It depends on how the liver fulfills the requirements for discipleship that Jesus lays down in today's gospel, and it depends on how much thirst for God there is in our souls and how we try to satisfy that thirst.

Recall last Sunday's gospel from this same chapter of Matthew: Jesus asks the apostles, "Who do you say that I am?" Peter answers: "You are the Messiah, the Son of the living God!" Jesus calls Peter "blest," and promises to make him the rock foundation of his Church. He will endow Peter with all the powers that he himself possesses.

Today's gospel follows immediately. Jesus predicts his coming death and resurrection, and Peter tries to talk him out of it. Jesus' response is vehement: "Get out of my sight, you satan!" And then he lays down the conditions for discipleship: "If a man wishes to come after me, he must deny his very self, take up his cross, and begin to follow in my footsteps."

There it is—the answer to the question, "Is life worth living?" Life will be worth living if we really try to take up our particular cross and carry it with the same love with which Jesus carried his. For Jesus, the cross meant embracing his Father's will, placing his life completely in his Father's care. We have to want, we have to try, to do the same. Practically, this makes me ask myself: What attitude, what attachments do I have that hinder my all-out following Christ? There's no escaping that question.

The cross means suffering in varying degrees. Each of us has his or her own suffering. The suffering of a teenager differs from that of an aged resident in a nursing home. Just desiring to carry our cross makes us followers of Jesus, *and* it makes life worth living.

But taking up our cross and following Christ also, thank God, is filled with hope, and that hope is given us in the knowledge that sharing in Christ's cross means that we are also sharers in Christ's *saving* mission, we are coredeemers with him. Paul's plea in Reading II fits in with our theme: "I beg you through the mercy of God to offer your bodies as a living sacrifice holy and acceptable to God, your spiritual worship. Do not conform yourselves to this age, but be transformed by the renewal of your mind, so that you may judge what is God's will, what is good, pleasing and perfect."

But we must not forget the second condition for making life worth living. Today's Responsorial Psalm provides it: "My soul is thirsting for you, O Lord my God." This thirst, this desire for God, is planted deep in our hearts by the very God who created us in his own image and likeness. It is the echo of God's own thirst for us, for our love. Life is definitely not worth living without it. "My soul is thirsting for you, O Lord my God" can be one of our finest, most productive prayers.

> May the Father of our Lord Jesus Christ
> enlighten the eyes of our heart
> that we might see how great is the hope
> to which we are called (Alleluia Verse).

To that prayer we can all cry, Amen!

TWENTY-SECOND SUNDAY IN ORDINARY TIME

READING I **Deut 4:1-2, 6-8** **READING II** **Jas 1:17-18, 21-22, 27**
GOSPEL **Mark 7:1-8, 14-15, 21-23**

Reading I: Moses asks his people to obey the Lord's commandments and thus to give evidence of their wisdom.

Reading II: Jesus tells us that by humbly welcoming God's word, we will be saved. We must act on the word.

Gospel: Jesus criticizes the Pharisees for imposing man-made laws on people and disregarding God's commandment of love.

No one has ever equaled Jesus as one who could put down those who needed it, especially certain members of the Pharisee or scribe classes who were constantly out to "get" him for teachings that seemed to them to threaten their customary way of life and worship. Jesus calls these men "hypocrites" and applies to them the condemnation of Isaiah:

> This people pays me lip service
> but their heart is far from me.
> Empty is the reverence they do me
> because they teach as dogmas mere human precepts.

And Jesus adds his own word: "You disregard God's commandment and cling to what is human tradition."

What is the commandment they disregard? We hear it in Reading I: "In your observance of the commandments of the Lord, your God, which I enjoin upon you, you shall not add to what I command you nor subtract from it." There was nothing wrong with the old Law that God gave to Moses and the people. On the contrary, it was an expression of God's loving concern and constant presence. But in the course of centuries many human interpretations were added to the Law and made equal to it. This is what Jesus condemned.

Some of the scholars had made the Law an end in itself rather than a means to bring the people closer to God. The Law was supposed to be an *aid* to holiness, not the essence, the heart, of religion. Jesus taught that there are times when laws, especially the rabbinic traditions, can become obstacles to justice and decency in human relations. Consequently, the laws were subject to development, enrichment, and sometimes even abandonment.

There was nothing wrong with the Jewish purification rule, but Jesus saw the Pharisees' insincerity in citing the rule to him. They complained not because they loved God but because they were out to "get" Jesus, whom they saw as a threat to their personal security. So they plotted to get rid of him.

In all his contacts with these experts in the Law, Jesus was constantly putting his finger on the real problem with all religious regulations: you can legislate what people can do or cannot do, not what they think and what is in their hearts. Without personal, freely given love as a response to God's will expressed in his Law, law runs the danger of becoming mere formalism, and that's what it was for Jesus' enemies.

There are two possible misuses of religious laws that we have to beware of: the first is *minimalism*—the mentality that says: "How far can I go without committing mortal sin? How can I stretch the law without getting God angry with me?" The other misuse is *maximalism.* "They think they are putting God at the center of their lives. In reality their lives are centered on law. By going beyond their minimum obligations they believe they can establish a claim which God is bound to honor" (John Jay Hughes in *The Priest*, August, 1982).

Maximalism is a temptation that is as strong today as it was in Jesus' time, especially for very religious people. All of Scripture teaches that one cannot earn or buy what *God insists on giving,* namely, himself, his love, his very own Son to be our guide, our beloved Savior. Our fulfillment of religious regulations must simply be our loving response to what God has done and continues to do for us.

Our problem is, where are our hearts? Who and what is essential in our religious observance? Does our observance of laws spring from loving gratitude, does it bring us to greater intimacy with Jesus, make us love him and our neighbor more, help motivate us to practice the spiritual and corporal works of mercy, "[looking] after widows and orphans in their distress" (Reading II)?

It is our *heart* that Jesus is concerned about. The whole life of a Christian has to be an affair of the heart. Our Christian life involves constant purification of our hearts, ongoing conversion, ever-growing intimacy with Jesus. It is when we stop growing in love for Christ and concern for the poor and become satisfied with our religious "condition" and observance that we are in danger of withering and dying. So we pray without ceasing:

> I call to you all day long, have mercy on me, O Lord.
> You are good and forgiving, full of love for all who call to you (Entrance Antiphon).
> Lord,
> you renew us at your table with the bread of life.
> May this food strengthen us in love
> and help us to serve you in each other (Prayer after Communion).

127 TWENTY-SECOND SUNDAY IN ORDINARY TIME Cycle C

READING I **Sir 3:17-18, 20, 28-29** **READING II** **Heb 12:18-19, 22-24**
GOSPEL **Luke 14:1, 7-14**

Reading I: Worthy religious advice about our need for humility and being attentive to God's word.

Reading II: For the author of Hebrews, Mount Zion (Jerusalem) is an image of the heavenly Jerusalem to which we draw near without fear.

Gospel: Jesus illustrates true humility and hospitality: invite those who cannot return the favor.

When St. Augustine was asked which was the most necessary of all the virtues he is supposed to have said, "Humility." What was the second? "Humility." And the third? "Humility." It would seem that humility contains all the virtues. Jesus would undoubtedly agree. In today's gospel he sees the guests pushing their way to the most prominent seats at a meal, obviously because they want to be recognized as important. Jesus says, "Everyone who exalts himself shall be humbled and he who humbles himself shall be exalted."

But what *is* humility? Humility is truth: it is knowing and appreciating the truth about yourself; it is integrity, sincerity, honesty. It neither overestimates nor underestimates yourself, your talents and abilities. The humble person knows his or her strengths and weaknesses. The humble person seeks to develop the strengths and talents he or she possesses.

In accepting the truth about yourself, you give the credit to God who endowed you with talents and gave you the obligation of developing and using them for the good of others. You may certainly take pleasure in work well done, so long as you realize that the very impetus to *do* the work comes from God.

So, be who you are and what you are: no more, no less. And yet never be satisfied with your knowledge, especially of Jesus, with your ability to love, your generosity and spirit of service.

While humility may be the most elusive of the virtues, the most difficult to capture and retain, pride is the most subtle and sneaky of the vices. Our first parents wanted to be more than they were; they wanted to be like God. Their pride was the beginning of the wide stream of evil to which we all contribute whenever we sin.

The proud person is self-centered, not God-centered or people-centered. The proud person cannot be told anything, because he or she has all the answers. The proud person is completely satisfied with himself or herself and completely dissatisfied with life as lived by others. Pride is essentially destructive: both self-destructive and destructive of family and community or parish life. The proud person never wants to receive anything from others. He or she wants to give not out of generosity but in order to gain control over others.

Despite appearances to the contrary, the proud person is basically *insecure* and tries to make up for his or her insecurity by boasting and vainglory in all its manifestations.

We probably all know the danger and evil of pride. The problem is, how do we overcome pride? How do we become humble? Certainly, not by merely *willing* to be humble. Humility is a virtue, and all virtue comes from God. God is more than willing to give us this virtue, but only on condition that we *desire* it—desire it with the same strong desire with which we desire and seek God himself.

Once again we are back to the basic human and Christian attribute that we have considered so often these past weeks: open hands signifying open, hungry, eager hearts.

Becoming humble is the work of a lifetime, at least for most of us, so we have to learn from our failures and mistakes and be patient with ourselves, as God is. The real answer to our quest for humility may lie in Christ's own words to us today:

Take my yoke upon you;
learn from me for I am gentle and lowly of heart" (Alleluia Verse).

Notice the words: first, "Take my yoke upon you." Only *then* comes Christ's recommendation, "Learn from me. . ."

It is bearing the cross of life's anxieties, pains, worries that best helps us to learn humility from Jesus. Maybe it is time for all of us to allow Jesus to live his life in us *daily,* and then we, like him, will be gentle and lowly of heart. And maybe we won't even know it!

431 MONDAY OF THE TWENTY-SECOND WEEK IN ORDINARY TIME

YEAR I

READING I **1 Thess 4:13-18**
GOSPEL **Luke 4:16-30**

Like any compassionate pastor, Paul tries to console those who have lost loved ones in death. His point is that, like the Christ they believed in and lived for, the departed will rise again on the last day. This may not be very comforting to those who have lost loved ones. They want them back; they don't want to wait for the last day. But they have them back. Not, of course, in their physical presence as before, but in a new presence. Paul tells us elsewhere that all we who have been baptized into Christ are one body with him. Since we are all one in Christ, we are one with one another whether we are still on earth or already departed. As the Preface of the Mass for the Dead has it, in death "life is changed, not ended," which means that our loved ones who are with Christ are also with us. "Console one another with this message" (Reading I).

YEAR II

READING I **1 Cor 2:1-5**
GOSPEL **Luke 4:16-30**

Because the people of Nazareth could not believe in and love themselves, they were unable to believe in Jesus and accept him as Messiah. This rejection may have been the beginning of Christ's passion. How do you think he felt about this? Their disbelief contrasts vividly with the faith of Paul.

St. Paul says that the only knowledge he claimed to have was about Jesus, the crucified Christ—humbled, helpless, despised. All he had to give them was Christ and the power of the Holy Spirit. We need Paul and his enthusiasm about Jesus to bring us back to the one thing necessary—a living, growing, loving relationship with Jesus as our Lord, who is also Christ, the crucified. Then our faith will rest not on the wisdom of men but on the power of God. And that is much better.

432 TUESDAY OF THE TWENTY-SECOND WEEK IN ORDINARY TIME

YEAR I

READING I **1 Thess 5:1-6, 9-11**
GOSPEL **Luke 4:31-37**

There is much talk these days about experiencing Christ, and apparently it is also happening in the lives of many Christians of all denominations. Jesus enters into their consciousness, he touches their lives, even as he touched the life of the possessed man in today's gospel, and they are changed. I wonder if we do not all—whether we realize it or not—have a deep-seated yearning for such an experience. Does not today's Responsorial Psalm express a universal desire rising from every human heart?

> One thing I ask of the Lord;
> this I seek:
> To dwell in the house of the Lord
> all the days of my life,
> That I may gaze on the loveliness of the Lord. . . .

That prayer was intended to be heard. To experience Jesus is indeed a great grace. But I wonder if it might even be a greater grace to live by faith—to believe *without* seeing and experiencing.

YEAR II

READING I 1 Cor 2:10-16
GOSPEL Luke 4:31-37

God is the impenetrable mystery whose riches we shall enjoy forever and ever. "The Spirit scrutinizes all matters, even the deep things of God" (Reading I). The more we share in the life of the Spirit, the more we can come to understand our God, even in this life. Paul says, "The Spirit we have received is not the world's spirit but God's Spirit, helping us to recognize the gifts he has given us."

Worldly wisdom speaks to the mind. The spiritual things Paul mentions speak to the heart—to the whole person, heart, mind, and will. I think that what Paul is talking about here is *experiencing Christ,* having a vivid sense of intimacy with him. To experience Jesus is indeed a great grace. But might it not be an even greater grace for us to live by faith—to believe without seeing and without feeling?

433 WEDNESDAY OF THE TWENTY-SECOND WEEK IN ORDINARY TIME

YEAR I

READING I Col 1:1-8
GOSPEL Luke 4:38-44

Paul wrote to the Colossians at least in part to correct false teaching, but you will find his message appealing and full of deep spiritual nourishment. The gospel shows us Jesus in his most natural element—as the friend, the healer of the sick. But it is also significant in that it shows us Jesus retiring for prayer in the open country. These periods of solitude are essential to him and to his work of proclaiming the good news and healing. We must learn from Jesus how to balance our lives between action and prayer. By his entire life, including work and teaching, he shows us that it is not so much what we do that matters; it is what we are. And what we are results mostly from the Father's restoration of our being when we are alone with him in prayer.

YEAR II

READING I 1 Cor 3:1-9
GOSPEL Luke 4:38-44

In the gospel we see Jesus where he most loves to be—in the midst of the sick and suffering, healing, comforting, consoling. But this gospel is especially significant in that it shows Jesus retiring for prayer after a day of consuming activity. These lonely places in his life, these periods of solitude, are essential for him and for his work.

We must learn from Jesus, not only from what he says but from how he lives, how he sees the need to balance his life between action and prayer. He shows us that it is not so much what we do that matters but what we *are;* and what we are results mostly from the Father's restoration of our spiritual being while we are at prayer.

> Happy the people the Lord has chosen to be his own.
> Our soul waits for the Lord,
> who is our help and our shield (Responsorial Psalm).

434 THURSDAY OF THE TWENTY-SECOND WEEK IN ORDINARY TIME

YEAR I

READING I Col 1:9-14
GOSPEL Luke 5:1-11

Once again Paul returns to one of his favorite themes—the fact that it is Christ and he alone who saves us, without any merit on our part. "Through him we have redemption, the forgiveness of our sins." And the Responsorial Psalm seconds Paul: "The Lord has made known his salvation." Our task is to cry out with grateful hearts: "Sing joyfully to the Lord, . . . break into song; sing praise."

The miraculous catch of fish makes Peter aware that he is in the presence of God. Aware of his sinfulness, he cries, "Leave me, Lord. I am a sinful man." But it is very significant that Jesus does not leave. It is his style to stay with sinners. He never gives up on us. He remains present to us, present in us, with us. All we have to do is to become—and to remain—present to him!

YEAR II

READING I 1 Cor 3:18-23
GOSPEL Luke 5:1-11

Everything is significant in this marvelous gospel. The people press around Jesus to hear the word of God, and he goes up into the pulpit, Simon's boat, where he gratifies their hunger for him and for the word. Then Jesus becomes a perfect fish finder who rewards Peter's trust, "If you say so, I will lower the nets." Peter, realizing he is in the presence of the divine and suddenly aware of his own sinfulness, cries out, "Leave me, Lord. I am a sinful man." He and his companions are convinced: they leave all things to follow Jesus.

They will not be disappointed. Has anyone ever been disappointed in Jesus? Not if they press around him to hear his word, and not if they let down the nets of thier minds and hearts into the sea of Jesus' love. May our nets be always mended and ready!

435 FRIDAY OF THE TWENTY-SECOND WEEK IN ORDINARY TIME

YEAR I

READING I Col 1:15-20
GOSPEL Luke 5:33-39

It is instructive for us to contrast the image of Jesus as we have been observing him in these daily gospels with the image as presented by Paul today. The Jesus of the Gospels is really and truly man; he suffers with people and for them; he is merciful, compassionate, and loving. Paul writes a generation after Jesus' death, and he writes theology more than biography. He tells us that Jesus is the sacrament of God, that he is the blueprint of all creation. All things were created through him and for him, and that includes us and all our works. We are not just accidents of history. From all eternity we have existed in the mind of the Word of God. We are now members of his body, the Church, of which he is the head. Does this give us some idea of our dignity as Christians and the importance of our lives? "Give thanks to him; bless his name" (Responsorial Psalm).

YEAR II

READING I **1 Cor 4:1-5**
GOSPEL **Luke 5:33-39**

The disciples of Jesus joyfully celebrate the presence of Jesus, Israel's Messiah and bridegroom, and Jesus is blamed because they do not fast. Fasting is a penitential exercise—a token of longing and hope. Christ will be taken from the disciples, and then they will fast until they join him in the eternal wedding feast of heaven.

Jesus uses the imagery of mending and wine bottling to compare an old era of Messiah-*expected* with the new era of Messiah-*present*. He is referring to the difficulty of reconciling religion as practiced by the Pharisees with the new religion as preached by Jesus and exemplified in his life. For the Pharisees, salvation results from their literal fulfillment of the Law. For Jesus, "The salvation of the just comes from the Lord" (Responsorial Psalm). That makes all the difference in the world!

436 SATURDAY OF THE TWENTY-SECOND WEEK IN ORDINARY TIME

YEAR I

READING I **Col 1:21-23**
GOSPEL **Luke 6:1-5**

The Sabbath was God's own idea. It makes sense from every possible point of view. Breaking into a routine of work is both physically and mentally necessary for human persons. It is, above all, spiritually necessary and healthy. It gives us an opportunity to stop and reflect for a few hours on him who is the creator and Lord of all, an opportunity to acknowledge his lordship by worship. "The

Lord sustains my life. Freely will I offer you sacrifice; I will praise your name, O Lord" (Responsorial Psalm). God doesn't need our Sabbath (Sunday) observance. We do. In Mark 2:27 Jesus says, "The sabbath was made for man, not man for the sabbath." The Pharisees had forgotten this basic truth when they enclosed the Sabbath in countless restrictive rules. Jesus rebukes them, but he would also rebuke us if we excused ourselves from Sunday Mass without a good reason.

YEAR II

READING I 1 Cor 4:9-15
GOSPEL Luke 6:1-5

Far be it from Jesus to diminish the importance of the Sabbath in today's gospel! He would definitely not approve of modern Christians' careless non-observance of Sunday. All he is saying is that human need takes preference over the letter of the Law.

Today St. Paul gives a justification for his life as an apostle by presenting criteria for distinguishing a true apostle. It is by suffering and persecution that an apostle can lay claim to true apostleship. And he has endured plenty of that. He also claims spiritual fatherhood over his converts: they are his very own children, for he begot them to new life through the gospel—a new life of union with Christ and with one another. "It was I who begot you in Christ Jesus through my preaching of the gospel." Paul is our father, too. Without his teaching, we would never really know Jesus.

TWENTY-THIRD SUNDAY IN ORDINARY TIME

Cycle A

READING I Ezek 33:7-9 **READING II** Rom 13:8-10
GOSPEL Matt 18:15-20

Reading I: God's prophet is to be a watchman for the people, warning and correcting anyone who acts wickedly.

Reading: According to Paul, all the commandments are summed up in love of neighbor as oneself.

Gospel: Jesus gives the disciples the principle for correction of a community member who is guilty of offensive acts.

As always, there is a relationship between Reading I from the Old Testament and the gospel. Today's readings are about correcting a brother or sister who commits a wrong against another member of a community of Christians. Correcting others is always difficult, especially so because most of us are aware of our own frailties and tendencies to offend others. Recall that Jesus himself warned against seeing the beam in the eyes of another and failing to see the speck in our own eye.

Why does Jesus give us this command? Why is it important for him? This section of Matthew's Gospel is from Jesus' discourse on the Church. Jesus' great concern is not just for individuals but for the Church, the assembly of his followers. Everything in today's gospel is in the context of any group of Christians who make up the Church in miniature.

What does Jesus mean when he tells us to point out the fault of another person? First of all, it is good for us to realize what correction is *not.* It is not being a morality law-enforcement officer. Jesus says: "If your brother should commit some wrong against you, go and point out his fault, but keep it between the two of you."

There is a great amount of polarization and contention in our modern Church. People take sides on issues, and apparently there is not a great deal of Christian charity in the motivation, words, and actions of the partisans. We know that Jesus tells us that mutual love is the greatest commandment, and today Paul says that "love is the fulfillment of the law." But we often say, "Yes, but . . ." And we proceed to forget or we refuse to remember all that Jesus teaches about mutual love.

But what does Jesus want when he tells us to correct one who harms us? He wants *reconciliation.* Reconciliation is what he came to achieve. Reconciliation between humankind and God, between brother and brother, between sister and sister. What Jesus desires in giving us today's gospel is nothing else but the continuation, the extension, of his redeeming work. And he puts that extension into our charge.

> God was in Christ, to reconcile the world to himself;
> and the Good News of reconciliation he has entrusted to us" (Alleluia Verse).

And may we not forget that reconciliation also involves forgiveness.

One of the mysteries of our life as Christians is that, despite the insistence of Jesus on our absolute need to love and forgive one another as an essential condition for being Christian, we are generally unsuccessful in living according to his ideal. I suspect that the main cause of our lack of success is not only that we do not think our Lord's injunction applies to our particular case but also that we assume we can fulfill his command by our own power alone.

But we don't learn loving and forgiving the way we learn a skill. Loving arises from our being *new creatures in Christ,* as Paul reminds us. By virtue of our having been born again in Christ by baptism, we possess the capability to carry out his command. Christ lives in us; he wants to love and to forgive in and through us. He is ours; we are capable of loving with his heart, because, as St. Paul tells us, "the love of God has been poured out in our hearts through the Holy Spirit who has been given to us" (Rom 5:5). The power to love has been given to us. The secret in learning how to love is growing in awareness of this new being that we are.

So, if we have had trouble observing this greatest of the commandments, may we reflect again and again, beginning today, on who and what we are in Christ and let him take over in us and for us. It is not easy. Learning to love and forgive is ordinarily a lifetime work.

Finally, if we all—we who are offended and we who offend—would see fraternal correction as Christ's command to us to carry on his work of reconciliation, we wouldn't wait for the offended one to correct us; we would initiate the process ourselves with an apology or maybe just a smile. Better than all else, we would be careful never to make correction necessary at all.

If today you hear his voice,
harden not your hearts (Responsorial Psalm).

129 TWENTY-THIRD SUNDAY IN ORDINARY TIME Cycle B

READING I **Isa 35:4-7** **READING II** **Jas 2:1-5**
GOSPEL **Mark 7:31-37**

Reading I: This prophecy, originally intended for the exiles in Babylon, is applied to the marvelous effects of Christ's redeeming act.

Reading II: James strongly objects to any kind of favoritism for the rich over against the poor.

Gospel: Jesus makes use of various healing actions in his cure of a deaf man with a speech impediment.

Many old-time Catholics generally took it for granted that the salvation won for us by Jesus was purely spiritual. Simply stated: he opened heaven for us. But Scripture usually pictures salvation in more realistic, more physical terms. Thus, in today's Reading I Isaiah tells us that our God will come to save us.

Then will the eyes of the blind be opened,
the ears of the deaf be cleared;
then will the lame leap like a stag,
then the tongue of the dumb will sing.
Streams will burst forth in the desert.

It is true that this prophecy was probably intended originally to depict the redemptive deliverance of the Jews exiled in Babylon, but, very early, Christian writers began to see the passage as being perfectly fulfilled by Jesus' life, death, and resurrection.

During his public life Jesus spent much of his time preaching and healing physical ailments, as in today's gospel. He fed the hungry, and even raised the dead to life again. To be sure, he did forgive sins, but his healing was mainly physical. He never said, just be patient; bear your cross, offer it up, and you'll get your reward in the next life. He was concerned for the whole human person, body and spirit, and his or her life in this world.

With that kind of example, it seems strange that, through much of human history, this Christ-like concern for the whole person was obscured and even forgotten by many Christians. It was taken for granted that the poor were poor and the rich were rich, and that's the way God had planned it. The great seventeenth-century French bishop Bossuet once preached a sermon to King Louis XIV and his court on the eminent dignity of the poor, his main argument being that the poor were necessary in order to give the wealthy an opportunity to practice charity.

Jesus was compassionate. He suffered with all his people, he bore their pains and made use of every opportunity to heal. Fidelity to the mind of Christ and his example compels us who call ourselves his followers to follow his example. Practically, this entails a compassionate concern for those in need of any kind—physical, spiritual, mental—and our caring must be motivated by love. The well-known psychiatrist Karl Menninger said: "Love cures. It cures those who give it, and it cures those who receive it." After he had spent many years close to death in a Nazi concentration camp, Viktor Frankl, a Vienna psychiatrist, wrote: "The salvation of men is in love and through love."

Love is kind of mystery and miracle combined, and it is a miracle each of us is capable of working. But it is a miracle that escapes us when we take it for granted, when we do not work at it.

The good news of the Gospels is that God who is love has endowed us with his own creative, healing love. And it is God's love in us that makes us whole human beings. Because we can and do love, we can experience the fullness of our humanity and our commitment to Christ. But without love, we cannot be human at all, and we certainly cannot be Christian.

The French novelist Francois Mauriac wrote about a priest whose lifelong ministry represented a complete giving of himself in love to and for others. He literally wore himself out working for others. Even on his deathbed he could think only of others and their needs. As he died, his final words were "I shall never love enough." Please God we will all make a like statement as we leave this world!

130 TWENTY-THIRD SUNDAY IN ORDINARY TIME Cycle C

READING I Wis 9:13-18 **READING II** Phlm 9-10, 12-17
GOSPEL Luke 14:25-33

Reading I: Human wisdom, acquired by study, needs to be fortified by the gift of divine Wisdom.

Reading II: Paul pleads for Christ-like treatment for a slave he is sending back to the owner, Philemon.

Gospel: Jesus lays down conditions for being his followers.

We probably seldom reflect on how terrible some of Jesus' words must have sounded to those who first heard them. Take today's gospel. How shocking it must have sounded to those Jews for whom the family meant everything. And here he is telling them that *the* condition for following him and becoming his disciples is that they turn their backs on everyone near and dear to them—father, mother, wife, children.

He goes on to say that they have to take up their cross and follow him. The cross is the most despised symbol in all Israel, for it was on a cross that the hated Romans executed troublesome Jews.

I do not believe that Jesus wanted to frighten off potential disciples. But he did want them to know what he expected of them. He wanted to challenge them in the depths of their being. He is saying: what you have to do to follow me as my disciples is to surrender your life to me. You have to be ready to give up any attachment that prevents your *total commitment* to me, whether it be material things that control you or immaterial, such as destructive ideas, prejudices, and enmities. He is saying: there can be no divided loyalties.

This gospel challenges every one of us who claim to be Christian: we have to stand up and be counted. The world is full of people who call themselves Christian. But how many so-called Christians are really committed to Jesus, how many actually live by this gospel (or at least try to), how many have tried to place their lives and future in his care?

In the early days of Christianity, the manner in which people became Christian was different than it is now. In those times people heard the apostles proclaim the good news of Jesus' life, death, and resurrection and were won over and converted to him. They were instructed over a long period of time, then baptized, confirmed, and given the Eucharist.

In contrast, most modern Catholics are born into Catholic families and baptized as infants. They receive basic instruction from parents, priests, and teachers and enter into the life of the parish. They observe all the religious practices. It could well be, however, that they miss that element of personal conversion to Jesus that the first Christians experienced. How many of the people who call themselves Catholic are willing, right now, to make him "number one" in their lives—willing to give up personal attachments to pleasure, possessions, un-Christian enmities, that stand in the way of their following Jesus unreservedly?

When it comes to understanding their Catholic faith, too many modern Christians have never advanced beyond the level of the catechism they learned as children. Religion for many is primarily a matter of "do's and don'ts, rewards and punishments." Theirs is hardly an adult, mature Christianity. But we have to be careful here. Real conversion involves more than knowledge of truths and teachings. It involves total dedication to a person, to Jesus Christ. In a word, it involves turning one's life around.

This conversion may not be as dramatic as that of St. Paul. It is an experience very similar to that which happens when a man and woman fall in love with each other: it is a gradual process that may take years. They *grow into love.* And once they are in love, they live for one another. Each is willing to lay down his or her life for the other. So it can and should be with our conversion to Christ.

Hopefully, most Christians are on their way to a personal conversion to Jesus, if they have not yet experienced a sudden one. But there is a danger we all need to be aware of. We know that, just as husband and wife who take each other for granted and stop communicating with each other can fall out of love, so too we can fall out of love with Christ by taking him for granted, by growing careless about communing and communicating with him, never thinking of him except on Sundays.

This gospel may not have been very pleasant to listen to, but if it has made us ask ourselves: "Who is number one in my life? Who is the Lord of my life? Who is the greatest love of my life? Have I really surrendered my life into his hands?" it could be one of the most important gospels of the entire year. Nothing is too hard for one who loves. And we do not forget that Jesus first loved us!

437 MONDAY OF THE TWENTY-THIRD WEEK IN ORDINARY TIME

YEAR I

READING I **Col 1:24–2:3**
GOSPEL **Luke 6:6-11**

There is great meaning and satisfaction in Paul's statement, "In my own flesh I fill up what is lacking in the sufferings of Christ. . . ." There's a lot of mystery, too. What could possibly be lacking in the sufferings of Christ? It had to be complete and perfect. Nevertheless, Paul seems to indicate that Jesus "lends" a share of his passion to us, his members. And if that is true, then we are all coredeemers with Christ. Which may well be the reason why Paul introduces today's Reading I with the words, "Even now I find my joy in the suffering I endure for you." You may have heard the saying that the greatest tragedy is not that there is suffering but that so much of it is wasted. It is just endured without reference to Christ or to those in need. The one idea that can keep suffering from being wasted is to make our own Paul's words: "In my own flesh I fill up what is lacking in the sufferings of Christ for the sake of his body, the church."

YEAR II

READING I **1 Cor 5:1-8**
GOSPEL **Luke 6:6-11**

Paul's harsh condemnation of the sinful, lewd conduct of his people is better understood when we grasp his vision of the Church (or the parish) as the body of Christ. For Paul, there is no such thing as an isolated sin, injuring only the sinner. Just as yeast has its effect on all the dough, so does the evil of sin endanger the health of the entire Church (or parish). So we have Paul's advice, familiar to us from the Easter liturgy, "Get rid of the old yeast to make of yourselves fresh dough." During Lent we die to sin in order to live unto God, and there is no point in limiting his advice to Lent and Easter. All our lives we are called upon to celebrate Christ's victory over sin, not with the old yeast of corruption and sinfulness but with the unleavened bread of sincerity and truth. Do we have any corruption to get rid of?

438 TUESDAY OF THE TWENTY-THIRD WEEK IN ORDINARY TIME

YEAR I

READING I Col 2:6-15
GOSPEL Luke 6:12-19

Today's readings give us two images of salvation. In the gospel, power goes out from Jesus to heal bodily infirmities, to deliver victims from the bonds of physical and mental diseases. However real this deliverance was for those people, it was a sign and a symbol of a deliverance from an even worse slavery—the power of Satan. Paul gives the theology of this deliverance in Reading I. Once again he insists that deliverance is Jesus' own work and his alone. Paul uses picturesque language to illustrate his point. It is as though we owed Jesus a huge sum of money and gave him an IOU for the amount. Paul tells us that Jesus tears up the IOU and frees us from the obligation of paying the bill. "The Lord is compassionate to all his creatures," says the psalmist today. And he puts into our hearts our personal response to what Jesus has done for us: "I will extol you, O my God and King, and I will bless your name forever and ever."

YEAR II

READING I 1 Cor 6:1-11
GOSPEL Luke 6:12-19

How often do we pray before making important decisions as Jesus did before choosing his apostles? Practical living and prayer belong together. It is only prayer that gives substance and power to any kind of work for God.

Practical living is Paul's concern, too—practical community living. Those early Christians suffered from wounded relationships even as we do, and Paul suffers with them. What Paul says remains valid for us today. Disputes, disagreements, can destroy Christ's most precious possession, the Christian community in which the Lord wishes to take delight. We, like the first Christians, have been washed, sanctified, and justified in the name of the Lord Jesus Christ. Isn't it about time that we all learn to work, to pray, to live, together in love and so make ourselves worthy of the Lord's delight?

439 WEDNESDAY OF THE TWENTY-THIRD WEEK IN ORDINARY TIME

YEAR I

READING I Col 3:1-11
GOSPEL Luke 6:20-26

Paul is very practical in his sermon to the Colossians today. He knows his flock; he knows human nature. He has something for everyone. "Put to death whatever in your nature is rooted in earth," he says, and then he lists the sins against purity. But these are not the only sins. Anger, quick temper, malice, insults, lying, sins of the tongue—all these may not seem so bad, but do they not do real injury to the body of Christ? In baptism, Paul tells us, we stripped off the old self, and we put on a new self, that of Christ himself. Paul begs us to be logical and to live and act out of the fullness of this new being. In a word, he wishes us to think and speak and act as Christ would if he were in our place. In the body of Christ there is no room for distinctions between persons of different races and nationalities. There is only Christ. It is he who makes us all one. He is everything in each and all of us. Let us act accordingly.

YEAR II

READING I 1 Cor 7:25-31
GOSPEL Luke 6:20-26

Let no one become angry at Paul's advice today. It has to be understood in the context of the inadequate position of women in his time, of his personal preference for a life of celibacy in the service of the Lord, and above all, his conviction that the end of the world is at hand. Whatever Paul says anywhere has always to be understood in the light of his fundamental conviction: whether we are men or women *we all have equal dignity and importance in the body of Christ*—Christ, who died for each and every one. Paul's chief counsel today is that the Christian prepare himself or herself for the end by putting heart and soul into living out whatever vocation he or she has. That is good advice for anybody in any age.

The Beatitudes describe the attitude of submissiveness and receptivity that we all need in the presence of the love God has for us.

440 THURSDAY OF THE TWENTY-THIRD WEEK IN ORDINARY TIME

YEAR I

READING I **Col 3:12-17**
GOSPEL **Luke 6:27-38**

Again Paul uses the old principle that action follows the nature of the being to illustrate what he expects of his converts. They have been chosen by God to exist because he loves them. Therefore, as God's own children, they are to act accordingly. They must be compassionate, humble, gentle, patient—as was Jesus. They are to bear with one another and forgive. Above all, they are to love one another. This is the very heart of Christian living. As an aid to the effective carrying out of this program, let them be open to the message, the good news of Christ, and may that message find a home in their hearts. They are to sing psalms, hymns, and inspired songs with gratitude in their hearts, and never say or do anything except in the name of Jesus, giving thanks to God the Father through him. If we love one another, God will live in us in perfect love. That's Christian living!

YEAR II

READING I **1 Cor 8:1-7, 11-13**
GOSPEL **Luke 6:27-38**

Living as a member of the body of Christ in any parish or community requires a mentality of concern for other members based on a deeper concern for the whole body and a personal love for Christ. When our hearts are fixed on that concern, then the details of daily living will follow more naturally. But never easily. Living the ideal parish and community life requires effort, even heroism. Both Paul and Jesus spell out the details in our readings today.

Paul lays down the principle that any action that could possibly lead others to sin should be avoided. Jesus extends the old commandment of love of neighbor to the love of enemies. Help, Lord help!

> Probe me, O God, and know my heart;
> try me, and know my thoughts;
> see if my way is crooked,
> and lead me in the way of old (Responsorial Psalm).

441 FRIDAY OF THE TWENTY-THIRD WEEK IN ORDINARY TIME

YEAR I

READING I **1 Tim 1:1-2, 12-14**
GOSPEL **Luke 6:39-42**

Paul's two letters to Timothy are pastoral: they are mainly about the care church leaders owe their flocks, but we can all find practical, good advice in them.

The gospel demonstrates the irrationality of judging others' motivation. When we do this, we are guilty of the same foolish behavior as the man Jesus ridicules in the gospel. But this seems to be the way we are. What Jesus is telling us is that, with all the evil we are capable of, it is precarious to be the least bit critical of others. Besides it is sheer hypocrisy. It is only when we have succeeded in becoming completely sinless, holy, and perfect that we can assume that prerogative of God and presume to judge others. Do you think that you will ever arrive at that degree of perfection?

> Your word, O Lord, is truth;
> make us holy in the truth (Alleluia Verse).

YEAR II

READING I **1 Cor 9:16-19, 22-27**
GOSPEL **Luke 6:39-42**

Relationships between community and parish members continue to concern both Paul and Jesus today. Paul's example is worthy of our imitation: he has made himself a slave to all and has become all things to all men. "I do all that I do for the sake of the gospel," he says.

Jesus tells us that we have to give up being judgmental because when we judge and condemn others we judge and condemn ourselves. There is an innate desire in most of us to want to make others over into our own likeness—we want to play God. He alone has that right. He wants to make us over into his likeness, wants to make us more merciful, more understanding, more forgiving, more prayerful, more compassionate. How long are we going to resist and reject his loving, creative act?

442 SATURDAY OF THE TWENTY-THIRD WEEK IN ORDINARY TIME

YEAR I

READING I 1 Tim 1:15-17
GOSPEL Luke 6:43-49

In the gospel Jesus is speaking about the genuineness of religious conviction—or the lack thereof. He simply says: you can't be a phoney Christian for long without it becoming apparent. And he illustrates the truth with several examples: a fruit tree has to be healthy and sound if it is to bring forth good fruit. "Each tree is known by its yield." And he draws the conclusion: "A good man produces goodness from the good in his heart; an evil man produces evil out of his store of evil." Christianity requires more than mouthing pious phrases like "Lord, Lord." The life of St. Paul is a living example of how to become honest in religious practice. He admits his sinfulness, but he gave over his life to Jesus and allowed Jesus to live and act in him, to use him as his instrument. "To the King of ages, the immortal, the invisible, the only God, be honor and glory forever and ever! Amen" (Reading I). Let that be our prayer now!

YEAR II

READING I 1 Cor 10:14-22
GOSPEL Luke 6:43-49

Paul's treatment of the Eucharist, written as early as A.D. 55 or 57, is the oldest Christian text we have. It emphasizes that the Eucharist comes from the community and is supposed to build community.

Jesus tells us that every tree can be identified by the fruit it bears. We cannot hear this word without some apprehension. What kind of tree am I? Am I Christian in more than name? To be truly Christian in my inner being, I must be the very incarnation of the dying and rising of Jesus and realize that dying and rising in my own life. Like Christ I must be totally dedicated to the will of the Father. Above all, like Christ I must be a reconciler. What kind of answer do I have for Jesus' question, "Why do you call me, 'Lord, Lord' and not put into practice what I teach you?"

131 TWENTY-FOURTH SUNDAY IN ORDINARY TIME — Cycle A

READING I Sir 27:30–28:7 **READING II** Rom 14:7-9
GOSPEL Matt 18:21-35

Reading I: In place of anger and wrath, which are hateful to God, we are to forgive our neighbors if they wrong us.

Reading II: Both in life and in death we are the Lord's. Ours must be a responsible life.

Gospel: The parable of the unforgiving servant is a warning to all of us who refuse to forgive one another from our hearts.

It is important to remember that today's gospel is a continuation of Jesus' preaching on the Church. The emphasis last Sunday was on fraternal correction as a necessary ingredient for the spiritual health of the Church. Today Jesus insists that there can be no soundness in the body of Christ if its members do not forgive one another again and again. There is no limit to God's forgiveness of us; therefore there can be no limit to our forgiveness of one another. This is today's message from Jesus.

Failure or refusal to forgive easily develops into *vengeance,* one of the most destructive of threats to that kind of peace the Church prays for in today's Entrance Antiphon:

> Give peace, Lord, to those who wait for you. . .

But why are we so unsuccessful in carrying out this divine ideal of compassion and forgiveness? One of the reasons may be that homilists have overemphasized the *threat* implied in today's gospel (if you do not forgive, God will not forgive you). But is the motivation of threat God's normal way of bringing about spiritual health in his Church? Rather, does God not want us to share *his* way? And what is that?

Look at today's Mass. Again and again it places emphasis on the mercy and love of God for all, especially for sinners. For example, in the Opening Prayer:

> May we serve you with all our heart and
> know your forgiveness in our lives.

To *know* here means to *experience.* The Responsorial Psalm is even more explicit:

The Lord is kind and merciful;
slow to anger, and rich in compassion.

This is our God, this is his way of caring for us. And the more we experience God's merciful and compassionate forgiveness in our own lives, the more we will want to love God in return and the more we will do what God wants us to do.

We need to be reminded often that morality for Christians does not consist in obeying a lot of rules and laws; it is primarily our personal response to God's everlasting love for us, God's forgiveness of our sins. Lovers do all they can to avoid offending the beloved. It is quite possible that we are not yet God-lovers to the degree of which we are capable; we may still lack an appreciation of how much God loves us, how *unconditionally* God loves us and refuses to hold our offenses against us.

Awareness of God's love for us in Jesus, above all his having chosen us to be his very own children, must be the motivating principle of our moral life. And it is this kind of awareness of divine love that will enable us to carry out the Lord's command: Be merciful, even as your heavenly Father is merciful. Be compassionate even as your heavenly Father is compassionate.

And it works the other way, too: in the experience of forgiving, trying to love one another with all our hearts, we will truly know the forgiveness of God in our own lives.

In Reading II St. Paul tells us: "Both in life and in death we are the Lord's." Perhaps it is time for us to let the Lord take over our thinking, our deciding, our acting.

TWENTY-FOURTH SUNDAY IN ORDINARY TIME

READING I **Isa 50:5-9** **READING II** **Jas 2:14-18**
GOSPEL **Mark 8:27-35**

Reading I: One of Isaiah's prophecies of the Suffering Servant, applied to Christ who undergoes all manner of suffering.

Reading II: To claim to have faith but not to put it into practice in meeting the needs of others is lifeless and useless.

Gospel: Mark's version of Jesus' desire to know who people think he is and Jesus' own prophecy of his death and resurrection, along with his requirement that his disciples must also bear their cross.

Today's readings seem more appropriate to the season of Lent than to Ordinary Time, but the message fits every period of our life. "Who do you say that I am?" Jesus wants to know. The question requires an answer from every one of us.

But Jesus also wanted to know what idea of the Messiah the people had and what they actually thought of him. He wanted the apostles and the people to know once and for all who he was as Messiah and how he would carry out his work. And equally important, he wanted his followers through the ages to realize what their lives as his followers would be like.

Jesus' life would be the fulfillment of that Suffering Servant song we hear in Reading I:

> I gave my back to those who beat me,
> my cheeks to those who plucked my beard;
> My face I did not shield
> from buffets and spitting.

That was the ancient prophecy. In today's gospel Jesus describes how he will fulfill it: "He then began to teach them that the Son of Man had to suffer much, be rejected by the elders . . . be put to death, and rise three days later." When Peter brashly tries to change and modify that divine plan, Jesus replies with near violence: "Get out of my sight, you satan! You are not judging by God's standards but by man's!"

Then comes the plan for his followers' way of life: "If a man wishes to come after me, he must deny his very self, take up his cross, and follow in my steps. Whoever would save his life will lose it, but whoever loses his life for my sake and the gospel's will save it."

The fact is that no one escapes the cross. Everyone suffers in some way. There is a great variety of crosses, the commonest ones being sickness, worry about loved ones, disgrace, poverty, joblessness, a humiliating habit, and old age. Jesus' words apply to everyone: "He must deny his very self, take up his cross, and follow me." In other words, give up the direction and control over life into the care of God, as Jesus himself did.

It is possible that suffering can become not only endurable but even gratifying when we can see meaning in it, when we know that good will come from it not only for ourselves but for others. It is strangely comforting to realize that, while each person's suffering and cross is personal, perhaps new, to each one of us, it is not really original. It has already been endured by Christ: he bore our griefs and carried our sorrows with him up onto his cross. He suffers with us. There are daily deaths in the life of every living person. Jesus tells us that God is at work in all this, that he brings new life and grace out of our agony and dying.

It seems that God has to hollow us out before he can fill us with new life and love. The paradox of Christianity is that we must empty ourselves to find happiness, deny ourselves to find fulfillment.

All this does not mean that we abandon human means of overcoming ill health. Jesus healed again and again. The medical profession carries on its work. But there comes a time in everyone's life when the inevitability of suffering and dying has to be faced. Then is when Jesus calls us to give free and loving consent to the cross he wishes to share with us. It is then that we can make our own the gratifying meaning of St. Paul's mysterious statement: "Even now I find my joy in the suffering I endure for you. In my own flesh I fill up what is lacking in the sufferings of Christ for the sake of his body, the church" (Col 1:24).

We might wonder, what could possibly be lacking in Christ's sufferings? The only answer is that in some mysterious way Jesus willed to grant us the great grace of being coredeemers with him. But our sufferings must be borne with love, for, as Father Quoist says, "It is not suffering that redeems, only love redeems" (*Christ is Alive,* Garden City, New York, Doubleday and Co., 1971, 102).

Only love can redeem. That's the final word. The greatest tragedy in the world is not that there is suffering, but that so much of it is wasted. Or it is endured stoically and bravely, but *without love.* So, dear God, fill us and keep us filled with that love that will make our suffering redemptive, that will help us glory in the cross of our Lord Jesus Christ which he allows us to carry with him!

133 TWENTY-FOURTH SUNDAY IN ORDINARY TIME — Cycle C

READING I **Exod 32:7-11, 13-14** **READING II** **1 Tim 1:12-17**
GOSPEL **Luke 15:1-32**

Reading I: Moses pleads to God to spare his sinful people, and the Lord grants his prayer.

Reading II: Paul tells Timothy how the Lord forgave his former sinfulness and granted him faith and love.

Gospel: The parable of the prodigal son. Heaven rejoices when a sinner repents and returns home to God.

The theme of God's willingness, even eagerness, to forgive repentant sinners is evident in all three of today's readings. In each reading someone or something is lost, is recovered, and there's a celebration. Jesus' story of the prodigal son is the best known and the most dramatic.

The young son takes off from home, spends his inheritance in sinful living, then repents and resolves to return home and make his confession to his father. But the father waits for the boy, and when he sees him in the distance, he runs to the boy, embraces him, kisses him and doesn't even want to listen to his "confession." There has to be a party, a celebration, because "this son of mine was dead has come back to life. He was lost and is found."

The parable would have been complete if if had stopped there. That's the essential part, for it tells us that nothing can stop God from showing mercy and forgiveness to straying prodigals, to sinners of all kinds and degrees. This parable, more than any other, tells us why Jesus and his gospel is *good news.* Someone has said that if the rest of the four Gospels were lost, except this parable, we would still have the heart of Jesus' message. The parable also gives us an essential insight into the being and heart of our God.

Sinners seemed to love being with Jesus. They felt at home with him. Despite all their past evildoing, they were not in the least uncomfortable with him. *He gave them hope.* They felt instinctively that he cared for them.

In spite of this parable and the insight it gives into the true nature of both the Father and the Son, we Christians often have a hard time believing in God's mercy and eagerness to forgive. We often seem to prefer a stern and vengeful Lord to the Lord depicted by Jesus, not only in today's parable but throughout the Gospels.

This parable also makes us ask ourselves about our own attitude towards sinners. Do we resemble the older brother? His problem is that he had set himself up as a judge. *He* had served his father so faithfully, day in, day out. *He* had never failed in his duty. He was proud of his accomplishments and took all the credit to himself. And as a result of his self-centered attitude, he suffered from what might be called hardening of spiritual arteries; and because of his proud sense of personal achievement, God's compassion and forgiving love could find no place in him.

It is important for all of us to keep the father's words in our hearts: "My son, you are with me always, and everything I have is yours." Those are the Lord's words to us now. We are with him always because he has always been with us, and if we have been faithful it is not by our own strength and courage but only by God's grace in us. All we can do is to celebrate and rejoice and give thanks.

"This man welcomes sinners and eats with them." How true! How gloriously true! Jesus welcomes us into his embrace again and again. He never gives up, never loses hope. And the Eucharist is the party, the banquet. Hopefully, we all feel at home at this celebration that the Lord is giving for us, whether we are repentant sinners or innocent children in the family of God.

> O God, how much we value your mercy. All mankind can gather under your protection (Communion Antiphon).

I am convinced that we will never grow into mature Christians until we realize how much God has loved us and continues to love us, lavishly and prodigally. This parable is the living proof.

443 MONDAY OF THE TWENTY-FOURTH WEEK IN ORDINARY TIME

YEAR I

READING I 1 Tim 2:1-8
GOSPEL Luke 7:1-10

Jesus was always happy to find faith among the Gentiles. Today's gospel is typical: "I tell you, I have never found so much faith among the Israelites." Both readings treat of salvation for the Gentiles. Paul says: "He [God] wants all men to be saved and come to know the truth." In other words, it is possible for many non-Christians, many unchurched people, to be closer to God than some practicing Christians. There can be a great difference between genuine faith in Christ and the strict observance of the rules and practices of Christianity. Religion is more than practicing rules. It is responding with love to the word of God to us: "God loved the world so much, he gave us his only Son, that all who believe in him might have eternal life" (Alleluia Verse). Or, as the Responsorial Psalm has it:

> The Lord is my strength and my shield.
> In him my heart trusts, and I find help.

YEAR II

READING I 1 Cor 11:17-26, 33
GOSPEL Luke 7:1-10

The early Christian custom of celebrating the Eucharist in connection with a love feast called the *Agape* was a fine idea: it meant the sharing of food and companionship among brothers and sisters in the faith. Unfortunately, the idea of building up mutual charity gave way to the abuses Paul condemns in today's reading. In describing the Last Supper, he wishes to point out the close connection between the sacramental Body of Christ and the mystical body. It is no accident that in chapters 11, 12, and 13 Paul treats of the Eucharist, the Body of Christ, and charity. The relationship still exists. Paul's warning and condemnation still hold against those who partake of the sacrificed Body of Christ in Holy Communion but who refuse to practice charity towards their fellow members of the body of Christ, the Church.

444 TUESDAY OF THE TWENTY-FOURTH WEEK IN ORDINARY TIME

YEAR I

READING I **1 Tim 3:1-13**
GOSPEL **Luke 7:11-17**

Reading I might easily cause us to compare our bishops and pastors with the ideal laid down by Paul in the first reading. There are positive and negative qualifications—all adding up to the one thing necessary: that the bishop or pastor be a real pastor, a good shepherd, after the manner of Jesus himself. The Responsorial Psalm beautifully sums up Paul's ideal:

> I will walk with blameless heart.
> He who walks in the way of integrity
> shall be in my service.

If you wonder about the mention of wives for the clergy, remember that the rule of celibacy did not become general until hundreds of years later. While Paul is proposing an ideal for bishops and pastors, is there any reason not to see that same ideal as useful and valuable for fathers, mothers, teachers, and religious superiors? We all need—and can have for the asking—the heart of Christ.

YEAR II

READING I **1 Cor 12:12-14, 27-31**
GOSPEL **Luke 7:11-17**

In Reading I Paul uses the human body, with all its members and functions, to desribe Christ's Church. Paul's main idea is the equality existing between members of the Church: Jews, Greeks, women, men, white, black, red, or yellow—we are all baptized into the body of Christ and all "drink of the one Spirit." Jesus is the head of the body; we the members.

In the human body each member has its own function to perform. Some members may seem more important, but each is essential for the well being of the whole. In the human body it is unthinkable that one member should work against another; so too in the body of Christ. "You, then, are the body of Christ. Every one of you is a member of it." Isn't it time we start thinking of our membership in the Church in those terms?

445 WEDNESDAY OF THE TWENTY-FOURTH WEEK IN ORDINARY TIME

YEAR I

READING I 1 Tim 3:14-16
GOSPEL Luke 7:31-35

Paul's phraseology today is fascinating. He wants Timothy and his flock to "know what kind of conduct befits a member of God's household, the church of the living God. . . ." And he goes on to propose the basis of the conduct he expects, namely, the mystery of the Incarnation: "He was manifested in the flesh, vindicated in the Spirit, . . . preached among the Gentiles, believed in throughout the world." At first sight this might seem strange as a foundation for moral living, until we reflect that love was behind it all: the love of the Father in sending his Son, the love of Jesus prompting him to teach, suffer, die, and rise from the dead for us. Because of that divine love for us, Paul proposes, we ought to respond with the kind of conduct that only love can summon forth.

> Your words, Lord, are spirit and life,
> you have the words of everlasting life (Alleluia verse).

YEAR II

READING I 1 Cor 12:13–13:13
GOSPEL Luke 7:31-35

Learning how to live means learning how to love. This might well be the basic idea of this most famous section of Paul's epistles. Without love, he tells us, all religion is a sham. Nothing can take the place of love.

Perhaps we would be more successful in putting this ideal into practice if we followed the practical directives Paul gives: love is patient, it is kind, it does not insist on its own way, bears all things, endures all things. But we always come back to the basic reason for love—our membership in Christ's body. His Spirit is the bond joining us all together. What we do—or fail to do—to one another, we do or fail to do for him. Happy indeed the people the Lord has chosen to be his own, members of his Body, learning to live by learning to love!

446 THURSDAY OF THE TWENTY-FOURTH WEEK IN ORDINARY TIME

YEAR I

READING I **1 Tim 4:12-16**
GOSPEL **Luke 7:36-50**

"Come to me, all you who labor and are burdened, and I will give you rest" (Alleluia Verse). Few persons have ever obeyed this invitation of Jesus more dramatically than the woman in today's gospel. We don't know her name, and that is as it should be. She is universal, she is "Everyone." Whether we are great and sensational sinners as she was or just ordinary, run-of-the-mill ones (as most of us are), she is our spiritual director in conversion, in learning to live for Jesus, in losing our hearts to him. She is conscious of her sins, but most of all conscious of him and his love. Today's gospel is a celebration of love.

Reading I is instructive in that it indicates the best possible preparation for becoming a priest and an apostle—being an example of love, faith, and purity, reading scripture and preaching—and the manner of ordination—the laying on of hands by a bishop.

How great are the works of the Lord! (Responsorial Psalm)

YEAR II

READING I **1 Cor 15:1-11**
GOSPEL **Luke 7:36-50**

The fact that Paul had a vivid experience of the risen Jesus is the basis of his right to preach the gospel. Christ entered Paul's life through grace, even as he has entered our lives in baptism and the Eucharist; and by the grace of God both Paul and we are what we are.

Jesus also entered the life of the nameless sinful woman in the gospel. He appeared to her as Love in person, infinitely desirable. She responded in the only way she knew how: she wet his feet with her tears of sorrow, kissed them, anointed them with oil. Like Paul, she was converted. She lost her heart to Jesus. Henceforth her heart and her life belong to Jesus. Whether we are saints or sinners, isn't that what all of us really want to do?

Give thanks to the Lord, for he is good,
for his mercy endures forever (Responsorial Psalm).

447 FRIDAY OF THE TWENTY-FOURTH WEEK IN ORDINARY TIME

YEAR I

READING I 1 Tim 6:2-12
GOSPEL Luke 8:1-3

Remember that Paul's letter to Timothy is pastoral. It contains practical directives and counsel for Timothy's task as shepherd of his community, together with warnings about possible destructive dangers. Today's Reading I mentions two of these dangers—false doctrines, which can cause contention, dissension, slander, and evil suspicions in the community; and using religion as a means of personal gain. "The love of money is the root of all evil" may sound like a rather extreme statement, until we recall illustrations of its truth of which we are personally aware or have read about. Paul tells us that this kind of love can even destroy faith and it can cause fatal wounds in individuals and in the community. This warning ought to cause all of us to look into our hearts for destructive symptoms. No one is immune. "Happy the poor in spirit" (Responsorial Psalm). To possess and be possessed by the spirit of Jesus is all that matters.

YEAR II

READING I 1 Cor 15:12-20
GOSPEL Luke 8:1-3

"If Christ was not raised, your faith is worthless. You are still in your sins," Paul tells us today. Let that sink in for a moment. It means that if Christ has not been raised, we have been duped: our own Christian faith and practice have been useless. That is how firmly and strongly Paul believes in and insists on the reality of Christ's resurrection. He stakes everything on it. But, he concludes, Christ has in fact "been raised from the dead, the first fruits of those who have fallen asleep."

Only God knows the number of fruits of the resurrection each of us will be, and he alone knows the nature of the risen body we shall enjoy. But you can bet on it, it will be worth waiting and suffering for.

Lord, when your glory appears,
my joy will be full (Responsorial Psalm).

448 SATURDAY OF THE TWENTY-FOURTH WEEK IN ORDINARY TIME

YEAR I

READING I 1 Tim 6:13-16
GOSPEL Luke 8:4-15

What kind of soil am I? We cannot escape that question after hearing this parable of the sower and the seed. "The seed is the word of God." It is Jesus and his teaching. The soil is our human heart. It is all a question of receptivity on our part, of readiness to receive Christ into our life. It is also a question of the genuineness of our desire to be converted, to be completely won over to Christ. Jesus mentions the various dangers to true receptivity—the cares, riches, and pleasures of life. We can all add a few of our own. Jesus intends the parable both as a warning and an encouragement. It is a plea to lay aside fears of Christ taking over in our lives.

> Happy are they who have kept the word with a generous heart,
> and yield a harvest through perseverance (Alleluia Verse).

We'd better believe that!

YEAR II

READING I 1 Cor 15:35-37, 42-49
GOSPEL Luke 8:4-15

The meaning of a natural symbol like seed is inexhaustible. Jesus compares his word to a seed which, if it finds our hearts to be good soil, can transform us into saints. Paul compares our natural bodies to seed. If the seed is to bear fruit, it has to die. So, too, our natural bodies; when they die the power of God intervenes to give them new life.

Paul tells us that on earth our bodies are animated by a vital principle, the soul. The Spirit is already at work in us, transforming us more and more into children of God. On earth this animation is mainly on our spiritual faculties—will, faith, love; but it has no apparent influence on the body. For Paul, after the resurrection of the body, we will enjoy bodies totally animated by the Holy Spirit. I can hardly wait! We will walk in the presence of the Lord, with the light of the living.

TWENTY-FIFTH SUNDAY IN ORDINARY TIME

READING I Isa 55:6-9 **READING II** Phil 1:20-24, 27
GOSPEL Matt 20:1-16

Reading I: The Prophet tells the exiles in Babylon to turn to the Lord for mercy, for he is generous and forgiving.

Reading II: Paul confesses that he is torn by two desires: to die and be with Christ and to continue working for his people.

Gospel: Jesus' parable is about the workers in the vineyard, all of whom receive the same wage.

The expression "self-made man" or (less frequently) "self-made woman" is current in our country. Such a person always makes his or her own way, never wants anything he or she hasn't earned or can't pay for; and often looks down on anyone on any kind of welfare program. This is the American way, and America was built on that kind of philosophy. Well, such a philosophy may be fine for building a nation, and especially one's ego; but it is not all right for building a spiritual life. And it may be one of our worst temptations.

The readings of the last three Sundays challenge our commonly accepted way of thinking and judging. Three Sundays ago Peter tried to argue Jesus out of accepting his passion and death; the next Sunday Christ's teaching on the need to love one's neighbor and fraternal correction contrasted with our normal way of dealing with others; last Sunday we were told that we have to forgive others as God forgives us. Today Isaiah reminds us of God's word: "My thoughts are not your thoughts, nor are your ways my ways." And Jesus illustrates that principle in today's gospel.

He is not trying to teach a lesson in social or distributive justice. He is not proposing a new kind of wage scale or labor relations. What Christ is teaching is *the infinite, universal mercy and love of God for all people.* It is mercy and love that cannot be earned or merited or bought with any price, even by a lifetime of hard work in the vineyard. Actually, the daily wage Jesus speaks about is *salvation*—God's own gift. Our "work" is to accept it gratefully and respond to it—by fidelity to our Christian life in whatever vocation God has called us to, by caring for one another and for all who are in need of any kind.

Our response is not carried out with any intention of putting God in debt to us, but simply as an expression of grateful love.

Jesus has some of the Pharisees in mind in using this parable. Many of them were hypocritical, but their greatest fault was their conviction that God owed them salvation simply because of their lifelong fidelity to the minutest details of the Mosaic Law.

Years ago the English Benedictine Fr. Aelred Graham asked, "What can we do for God?" And he answered, "Nothing at all. It is not by our asceticism that we take possession of God, but rather by our submission that we allow God to take possession of us." We need to reflect on the words "by our submission." It means opening our hearts, our whole being, to God's grace and love. Only with our self-receptivity can God take possession of us.

This parable and Father Graham's comment give us the authentic idea of what our life as Christians ought to be.

Negatively, the parable tells us that there can be no judging of others—whether they are Roman Catholic or not, lifelong Christians or deathbed converts. We can always remember the parable: those who worked only an hour a day received the same wage as those who labored all day.

It is not for us to judge anyone. We must not begrudge salvation to anyone. That's the Lord's privilege. We must not try to place limits on God's mercy and compassion. But we can be instruments and examples of God's mercy by the kind of grateful, loving, joy-filled lives we lead.

We can all say: If I have been faithful to the Lord, it is only because of God's fidelity to me, God's grace and mercy, which he always holds out to me. I may not take credit for anything I have accomplished. Our greatest need as Christians is to realize fully in our inmost being, in our heart of hearts, how much God has loved and continues to love us, how great has been God's mercy to us.

> I am the Savior of all people, says the Lord.
> Whatever their troubles, I will answer their cry,
> and I will always be their Lord (Entrance Antiphon).

135 TWENTY-FIFTY SUNDAY IN ORDINARY TIME — Cycle B

READING I Wis 2:12, 17-20 **READING II** Jas 3:16–4:3
GOSPEL Mark 9:30-37

Reading I: Opponents of Jews living in Egypt plot their persecution, which anticipates the persecution and death of Jesus.

Reading II: James outlines the potential evils in any group that result from jealousy and "vile behavior."

Gospel: Another of Jesus' prophesies of his death and resurrection.

The similarity between Reading I and the gospel is striking. The pagan Alexandrians' plot against the Jews living in their city is almost a word-for-word prophecy of what Jesus' enemies plan for him: "Let us condemn him to a shameful death; for according to his own words, God will take care of him" (Reading I). Jesus prophesies: "The Son of Man is going to be delivered into the hands of men who will put him to death."

Mark adds: "Though they failed to understand his words, they were afraid to question him." His very own "support group," who had been with him almost three years, who had heard his preaching and seen his miracles, didn't have the faintest idea what he was talking about. Instead, they argued about who was the most important among them. This lack of comprehension was no small portion of his coming passion.

Hard-nosed old James—one of the apostles who was probably most involved in all the arguments about priority in Jesus' kindgom, but one who finally grasped the full meaning of Jesus' prophecies—tells us what the apostles' (and our) problem is: "Where there are jealousy and strife, there also are inconstancy and all kinds of vile behavior. . . . Where do the conflicts and disputes among you originate? Is it not your inner cravings that make war within your members?" (Reading II)

I would imagine that modern psychologists would agree with James, but they would probably add that people get jealous because they are insecure, not sure of themselves, their motives, even their own worth; possibly there is also some sense of guilt, all of which they try to cover up by false accusations against others.

Along with insecurity there is a lack of maturity. Father Carr writes: "To be a Christian one must be mature. To be mature is to have the ability to put another's needs above one's own. It is to be tolerant. It is to realize we live in an imperfect world."

Jealousy prompts us to undermine others and attack them when ever we feel threatened by them. We can justify almost anything—no matter how destructive—under the guise of self-righteousness or what we consider to be the true Christian ideal. There are many Christians who never see themselves as they are and therefore never succeed in coming to terms with their own inner conflicts. They never really grow into maturity.

Jesus understands all this and is saddened by it. But he does not give up, either on the apostles or on us. He does, however, propose a remedy—one which he has personally demonstrated in his own life and which he will illustrate when he washes the feet of his friends before dying for them. He takes a little child, places him in their midst, puts his arms around him and says, "Whoever welcomes a child such as this for my sake welcomes me."

Mark quotes Jesus as follows: "Anyone among you who aspires to greatness must serve the rest; whoever wants to rank first among you serve the needs of all" (10:43). Jesus simply wants to create a new way of living that reflects God's own rule—a rule he reflects in his own life.

But may we remember: the Christian life is more than social service. It involves an interior renewal, a conversion, that goes on all our life. A conversion in which we die with Christ out of love so that we may truly live. And for that conversion, we never cease to need help. And so we pray:

> Father,
> guide us, as you guide creation
> according to your law of love.
> May we love one another
> and come to perfection
> in the eternal life prepared for us (Opening Prayer).

TWENTY-FIFTH SUNDAY IN ORDINARY TIME

READING I **Amos 8:4-7** **READING II** **1 Tim 2:1-8**
GOSPEL **Luke 16:1-13**

Reading I: Amos, a social justice prophet, condemns those who "trample upon the needy and destroy the poor of the land."

Reading II: Paul proposes the ideal of universal prayers for all people, especially those in authority.

Gospel: The first part of the gospel is about the crooked manager who cleverly arranges for his future. The second part contains Jesus' warning that no one can serve two masters—God and money.

Reading I sums up Old Testament teaching about the concern one has to have for the needy and poor. To deprive the needy and poor of their rightful wages, to cheat them in any way, to be indifferent to their plight, is to bring upon oneself the sentence of the Lord: "Never will I forget a thing they have done!"

The gospel, especially the last section, is also concerned with the priorities of the Christian's life. Few, if any, of the Sunday gospels are as essential as this one for the formation of a philosophy of life. It is important for all Christians but especially for the young who are developing the sense of values that will guide them along their way.

In the first part of the gospel, Jesus does not recommend dishonesty. He is simply telling us that we have to be as careful and farsighted about our spiritual growth and our eternal happiness as the crooked manager in the parable. Jesus is also suggesting that riches can endanger our salvation by blinding us to the real, the genuine, values of life. Some of the unhappiest, most insecure people in the world are those who have everything. They are never satisfied, they always want more, and many become grasping, miserly, greedy; they live in terror that they will lose everything they have.

Jesus' message is that human beings are more important than things. You can't buy happiness, love or respect. *Things* don't make you happy; *people* do. In the long run, only possessing God and being possessed by God can make us truly happy. "No servant can serve two masters. . . . You cannot give yourself to God and money."

So it comes down to who and what has priority in our lives. Whom and what do we value most—what we *are* or what we *have?* To answer those questions it may help to remind ourselves of the teaching of Scripture: that we really *own* little or nothing, that everything we earn or possess is ours *only in trust,* that we are stewards of God's riches. It is always good to ask ourselves: Can we take anything with us when we die except what we have become through the stewardship of all our possessions, including our talents and our heart?

What both Amos and Jesus want of us is more than a check to the United Way or Community Chest. They want an *attitude,* a *mentality,* toward the poor or needy; they want compassion that *costs.* They want respect for them as persons, never-ending concern and caring for all the needy. And the needy may include those closest to us—members of our family and parish or school. Perhaps the neediest of all are those without love and recognition, those without friends.

So Jesus tells us today: "Make friends for yourselves through your use of this world's goods." That is, we are called to make friends of the poor by giving alms, food and shelter, but most of all, by giving ourselves, our hearts. And with that kind of giving, there is always an exchange. Maybe it's not so much a question of what we do for them but what they can do for us. And what is that? They help us keep our values pure, prevent us from becoming victims of avarice and greed, help us become more human—which may be the first step to becoming more Christian. They may well be God's own messengers, helping us to serve him in his little ones, helping us make God supreme in our lives.

> Jesus Christ was rich but he became poor,
> to make you rich out of his poverty (Alleluia Verse).

What Jesus has been for us, we must strive to be for others. That's the Christian life. There can be no other way.

> Praise the Lord who lifts up the poor (Responsorial Psalm).

And it is our privilege that the Lord wants to lift up the poor with our hands and hearts.

449 MONDAY OF THE TWENTY-FIFTH WEEK IN ORDINARY TIME

YEAR I

READING I **Ezra 1:1-6**
GOSPEL **Luke 8:16-18**

The Book of Ezra tells of the return of captive Jews to their homeland after their captivity in Babylon. "The Lord has done marvels for us." This verse of the Responsorial Psalm marvelously expresses what God did for his people. How similar that phrase is to Mary's conviction, "God who is mighty has done great things for me" (Luke 1:49). And when we look at our own lives, is not this also our story?

In the gospel Jesus tells us that his truth has to radiate: we may not retain it only for ourselves. "Take heed, therefore how you hear." It is only in hearing the gospel with open, loving, welcoming hearts that it will become ours so that it will overflow from us to others. The very fact that we have heard this gospel and that we are here indicates that the Lord has done marvels for us, as he did for the Jews who were delivered from their captivity.

YEAR II

READING I **Prov 3:27-34**
GOSPEL **Luke 8:16-18**

The Book of Proverbs contains pithy suggestions for moral living; their observance will help to create a kind of noble humanism in us that needs the New Testament revelation of God's love to balance it off.

The Word of God is a divine instrument for helping us to become truly human—which is why Jesus tells us "take heed, therefore, how you hear." Too often we hear but we do not grasp Christ's meaning. Even if the meaning does come through to us, it will vanish unless we meditate on the word and probe its deepest meanings. It is only in hearing the word with open, loving, welcoming hearts that it will become ours and overflow from us to others. How receptive are we to Christ's word?

450 TUESDAY OF THE TWENTY-FIFTH WEEK IN ORDINARY TIME

YEAR I

READING I Ezra 6:7-8, 12, 14-20
GOSPEL Luke 8:19-21

We can look on Mary as the mother of Jesus and the wife of Joseph; we can also look upon her theologically—as the figure or type of the Church. This may be the way Jesus sees her in today's gospel, and surely it is the way Vatican II sees her. She is the model of and for the Church. Seeing Mary, imitating Mary, making Mary's thought her own, the Church becomes the true mother of all the redeemed. If we would truly share in Mary's and the Church's motherhood, there is only one way to do it. We have to hear the word of God, but hear it with our whole being, as she did. Hear it with her kind of receptivity. We can't imitate Mary's physical motherhood. But what Jesus tells us today is that we can share her spiritual motherhood: we can, like her, hear God's word and allow it to govern our lives. "Blessed are they who hear the word of God and keep it" (Alleluia Verse). Blessed, indeed!

YEAR II

READING I Prov 21:1-6, 10-13
GOSPEL Luke 8:19-21

Those who hear the Word of God and put it into practice are mother and brother and sister to Jesus. That includes those of us who at least make some effort to give the direction of our lives over into God's hands. Jesus is not downgrading his mother Mary, for no one has heard God's word and responded to it with greater loyalty and love than Mary. What Jesus does here is establish priorities: great as was Mary's dignity as the physical mother of God, it could not compare with the greatness that was hers by virtue of her total dedication to the will of God. It is in that dignity that we may all share, if we can but bring ourselves to receive heroically the love of God which is behind the Word of God. Jesus does not put Mary down. He puts us up!

451 WEDNESDAY OF THE TWENTY-FIFTH WEEK IN ORDINARY TIME

YEAR I

READING I Ezra 9:5-9
GOSPEL Luke 9:1-6

The Babylonian captivity of the Jews in exile lasted some 70 years, at the end of which God raised up religious reformers who led his people back to Jerusalem, where they were urged to rebuild the Temple. The character of one of these great men, Ezra, comes through to us in the beautiful prayer we have just heard—a prayer including a confession of past national sins, gratitude for God's forgiveness, and a rededication of the people to the service of God. "Blessed be God, who lives for ever" (Responsorial Psalm). Ezra's prayer is universal. It fits every nation and people, it fits the Church, it fits every one of us, whether we are great sinners or small. God does not punish us. We punish ourselves when we try to live without God, when we refuse to remember his lordship over us. The true God is merciful and forgiving. The kingdom of God is always near. "Repent and believe the good news" (Alleluia Verse).

YEAR II

READING I Prov 30:5-9
GOSPEL Luke 9:1-6

There is good sense in the prayer of today's Reading I. Excess of either kind—too much money or too little—can ruin the right relationship one should have with God. Possessions demand responsible use. Too much of anything can cause a person to find his security in that possession rather than in God, the source of all good. And too little of life's necessities can tempt a person to steal and profane God's name. Therefore, moderation—a golden mean between poverty and riches—is a worthy object of prayer for anyone in any age.

But both readings present an even higher ideal for the greathearted: God "is a shield to those who take refuge in him," says Proverbs; and Jesus counsels confidence that God's loving care will not be lacking to those who trust him. This is the word that can be a lamp for our feet!

452 THURSDAY OF THE TWENTY-FIFTH WEEK IN ORDINARY TIME

YEAR I

READING I **Hag 1:1-8**
GOSPEL **Luke 9:7-9**

"The Lord takes delight in his people" (Responsorial Psalm). What an extraordinary statement! Despite all their infidelities and backslidings, the psalmist proclaims that "the Lord loves his people." We could be forgiven for thinking that God is easy to please. In Reading I he has to try to persuade the repatriots that it is time they got that temple rebuilt. They drag their feet. So he sends Haggai to bring them to their senses. It is necessary to insist that God does not want the temple rebuilt for his sake but wants to see and take pleasure in it as a noble human achievement. His chief concern is the people. He knows that they need the temple, that all the people need holy places where they can feel at home with their God, where they can praise his name and thus become what he wants them to be—the crown of his creation.

YEAR II

READING I **Eccl 1:2-11**
GOSPEL **Luke 9:7-9**

The author of Ecclesiastes (third century B.C.) is troubled by the meaning of existence. For him happiness is transitory, vain, and unsatisfying. His time and his world knew little about a world to come, so this world is supposed to supply the answers to life's mysteries, and it cannot. The book is characterized by pessimism; since the author does not know the history of salvation, he cannot know the meaning of life.

The author does have a vision of God, but it is limited and is not seen as an answer to the meaning of life. His thinking is closer to pagan than to Christian existentialism, which demands that we answer Jesus' question, "Who do you say that I am?" If with Peter we can answer, "The Christ of God," then and only then will we know if there is any meaning in our lives.

453 FRIDAY OF THE TWENTY-FIFTH WEEK IN ORDINARY TIME

YEAR I

READING I Hag 1:15–2:9
GOSPEL Luke 9:18-22

Today's gospel relates an incident that is common to all three synoptics: Jesus' demand that the apostles express themselves about him, that they give their personal response to his question, "But you—who do you say that I am?" Peter answers for them all, and I am sure that in their hearts they ratify his confession: "The Messiah of God." We are familiar with Matthew's recording of our Lord's answer to Peter, "You are 'Rock,' and on this rock I will build my church" (16:18). It may seem strange to us now that Jesus insists on the disciples' making this decision. But he does it for their own good. He knows that he can never be real to them, can never be their Lord and Savior unless they come to a personal decision about him. For the same reason, we too have to answer his question, "Who do you say that I am?" Are you ready to answer?

YEAR II

READING I Eccl 3:1-11
GOSPEL Luke 9:18-22

There may be a little too much determinism in the Reading I to suit some Christians; it needs Christ and the spirit of the gospel, and we may have to provide that ourselves.

Jesus believes it is essential that his disciples express openly their opinion about him. "Who do you say that I am?" He knows that he can never be real to them, that he can never be their Lord and Savior and friend unless they come to a personal decision about him. Nor will Jesus ever be real to us unless each of us is able here and now to answer his question: "Who do you say that I am?" If you have never tried to answer that question, try it. And the sooner the better. If you are courageous enough to put your answer in writing, so much the better.

454 SATURDAY OF THE TWENTY-FIFTH WEEK IN ORDINARY TIME

YEAR I

READING I **Zech 2:5-9, 14-15**
GOSPEL **Luke 9:43-45**

Jesus again foretells his forthcoming passion and death, but the apostles have a hard time grasping that idea, and maybe we don't do too well either. He tells them that he is going to be delivered into the hands of men, the implication being that men will do him in. Not only do they fail to grasp his meaning, but they are "afraid to question him about the matter." The Christian life without suffering would be nice, but it wouldn't be Christian. That's what Jesus is telling *us* in today's gospel. Without redemptive suffering in our lives, we hardly qualify as followers of Jesus. The old refrain of the *Way of the Cross* echoes through life: "We adore thee, O Christ, and we praise thee, because by thy holy cross thou hast redeemed the world." By our suffering, our cross, we share in the world's redemption. That's what makes our life worthwhile.

YEAR II

READING I **Eccl 11:9–12:8**
GOSPEL **Luke 9:43-45**

Ecclesiastes' advice to young people today is valid for persons of any age: always keep in mind your God and your relationship of loving dependence on him. The author is aware of the beauty of life, despite his conviction that old age and death are inevitable. His metaphors on the suddenness and finality of death are powerful and poignant, a refreshing honesty in view of our modern efforts to hide death.

There may be reason to indulge in regrets for past mistakes if we have not lived life and youth to the fullest, have not taken advantage of all its potential. But there is one way of returning to and always retaining our youth, and that is by staying young in heart and mind and by staying close to and empathizing with young people as long as we live. They have a lot to tell us.

137 **TWENTY-SIXTH SUNDAY IN ORDINARY TIME** Cycle A

137 TWENTY-SIXTH SUNDAY IN ORDINARY TIME — Cycle A

READING I Ezek 18:25-28 **READING II** Phil 2:1-11
GOSPEL Matt 21:28-32

Reading I: The prophet defends God's way of judging: a person who dies unrepentant is lost; a sinner who dies repentant is saved.

Reading II: Paul pleads for unanimity among his Philippian converts and begs them to make the mind of Christ their own.

Gospel: Jesus tells the chief priests and elders that prostitutes and tax collectors who repent will have a better chance for salvation than they.

Our life as Christ's followers has its ups and downs, its successes and its failures. As one author puts it: "We fall, we falter, we fail, we make mistakes, we hurt others (often the ones we love most). We talk about Christian love and we mean to love, but how we fail!" Every once in a while the thought strikes us: how terribly human we are! How subject to our moods, even to the weather!

And how often we fail in living out the ideal of Jesus, the ideal he himself lived—that of service to those in need. This might be illustrated by an incident in Camus' novel *The Fall.* A respectable citizen is walking along a canal in Amsterdam one night, and suddenly he hears the cry of a woman for help. She had either fallen or been pushed into the canal. "I ought to help her," he says to himself. Then he starts to doubt. What will the implications be? How about personal danger? By the time he has thought it through, it is too late. The cry has been silenced. He walks on, making all kinds of excuses for his failure to help. Camus' conclusion is devastating: "He did not answer the cry for help. That is the man he was."

Has something like that ever happened to us? I'm not sure if Camus actually went on to point out what kind of man he ought have been. That's one of the differences between human authors and Jesus, whose lifetime concern was to show what kind of persons we *ought* to be. This was surely his concern in today's gospel.

The chief priests and elders were all very respectable men in the Jewish community. They fulfilled all their religious obligations to the letter and made the required contributions to the upkeep of the

Temple. And they were very quick to judge and condemn those who did not follow their way of life, especially the tax collectors and the fallen women. But they refused to hear and heed John's call to repentance, and, says Jesus: "tax collectors and prostitutes did believe in [John]. Yet even when you saw that, you did not repent and believe in him."

Jesus does not even mention the fact that the chief priests and elders have refused to accept his own plea for repentance, for true, genuine religion of the *heart,* not just external compliance with rules. That was the kind of men they were.

> My sheep listen to my voice, says the Lord;
> I know them, and they follow me (Alleluia Verse).

The chief priests and elders did not want to be Jesus' sheep; they did not choose to hear his voice and follow him. The inevitable question is, do we want to hear Jesus and follow him? We don't have to be tax collectors or fallen women to hear and follow Jesus. All we need is a bit of dissatisfaction with our past and present life and a genuine desire to want to live as Jesus wants us to live. In short, a desire to be converted to him with all our heart.

We stumble and fall, we shift and fail, but God is always there, ready to pick us up. God never gives up on us, even though we may give up on ourselves. Jesus wants repentance, but the kind of repentance that takes us beyond good intentions. I have often insisted that conversion for most Christians is a matter of a whole lifetime. It is ongoing. It never ceases to challenge us. The final result is that we become the kind of persons we ought to be, not the kind we were. This deep inner change is possible only through the power of God's grace. But we have to want it, open our hearts to it. And that is why we pray:

> Father,
> you show your almighty power
> in your mercy and forgiveness.
> Continue to fill us with your gifts of love.
> Help us to hurry toward the eternal life you promise
> and come to share in the joys of your kingdom (Opening Prayer).

Jesus is always willing and anxious to hear any cry for help, to forgive, to take us back. That is the kind of man he was. That is the kind of man he is. That is the kind of man he always will be.

138 TWENTY-SIXTH SUNDAY IN ORDINARY TIME — Cycle B

READING I Num 11:25-29 **READING II** Jas 5:1-6
GOSPEL Mark 9:38-43, 45, 47-48

Reading I: Moses shares the spirit of prophecy with the seventy elders and rejects Joshua's complaint that the spirit also came upon two men not of their company.

Reading II: A violent condemnation of the rich who exploit the poor.

Gospel: Jesus corrects John for the disciples' efforts to prevent a non-disciple from casting out devils in Jesus' name.

Once again there is a common idea in Reading I and the gospel: one does not have to belong to any privileged group in order to receive God's special gifts and favors. What is necessary is that one be willing to share one's gifts—both spiritual and temporal—with those who do not possess them and are in any kind of need.

The mentality condemned in Reading I and the gospel is still prevalent today: If you don't belong to us, to our denomination, you can't be saved. One wonders what such Christians do about today's texts. These Scripture readings tell us that God's power, love, and special gifts cannot be the exclusive possession of any particular group, people or church.

I am convinced that God chose the Jews to be his very own people and to be the primary bearers of divine revelation. And I am all the more convinced that Jesus established a Church in which he willed to continue to live, to act, to preach the good news of God's saving love through all ages to come. I believe that this Church is the principal means wherein his saving work is carried on. We Catholics have a right to be gratified and happy to be members of this Church, but we have no right to be narrow and arrogant about our having been chosen as its members.

We need to remind ourselves that there is great good, there is compassion, heroism, mercy, holiness, and salvation outside the Catholic Church—precisely because there are women and men who heroically fulfill the requirements for discipleship that Jesus lays down in the Gospels. In today's gospel Jesus tells us,

> Any man who gives you a drink of water because you belong to Christ will not, I assure you, go without his reward."

In simple terms Jesus is saying that we all have to learn how to be sensitive to the needs of others, whether the needs are physical or spiritual. The Christian with the mind of Christ is one who can recognize human needs and minister to them, as Jesus did.

Gifts, both material and spiritual, imply responsibility, as all three of today's readings indicate. We cannot keep what we are unwilling to share, whether it be our faith, our sympathy, or our riches, both spiritual and material. To be Christian and Catholic means having the world vision of Jesus himself. Todays' gospel speaks of the terrible punishment reserved for those who refuse to take this teaching seriously.

Jesus warns us that we shall be called to give an account for the way in which we have used or failed to use, to share, our spiritual and material riches. What our Lord really demands of us is a change in our thinking, if that thinking fails to correspond with his own mind.

I once read a story about a woman named Myra who worked in an office. She had no friends; she seemed to be full of anger; she was just plain disagreeable. "Stay away from her," was the advice given to any new employee. Then came a woman called Margaret. She made a special effort to let Myra know that there was someone who cared for her. Amazingly, Margaret's efforts eventually bore fruit. Myra began to break out of her shell and show interest in others. Then suddenly Margaret died. Myra was inconsolable. She cried, "She was the only Christ I ever knew."

We are reminded of Christ's words: "I assure you, as often as you did it to the least of my brothers [or sisters], you did it for me" (Matt 25:40). We all need fulfillment. Jesus was aware of that basic human need, and he provided us with the best possible means for achieving it, namely, caring for those in need. There is an old Indian proverb: "For the Indian a person of great spiritual power is the person who can give the most things away."

But essential as it is to learn how to do good for others in the name of Jesus, it could be that learning how to receive any manifestation of love and mercy is just as necessary. And it may be harder, because it requires humility, a recognition of our own inadequacy, of our frail human condition. What we need most of all is the willingness to receive *from Jesus,* whose love for us, whose will to give and forgive, is simply inexhaustible.

Maybe we could add a corollary to the Indian proverb and say that the person of the next greatest spiritual power is the one whose heart is open to receive the love and caring of Jesus, the one who is always willing to share that love and caring with others.

May the power of Christ's love fill all our hearts!

139 TWENTY-SIXTH SUNDAY IN ORDINARY TIME Cycle C

READING I **Amos 6:1, 4-7** **READING II** **1 Tim 6:11-16**
GOSPEL **Luke 16:19-31**

Reading I: A stern warning to the complacent people who live luxuriously and neglect the needy.

Reading II: Paul exhorts Timothy to recall and live according to the profession of faith he made at his baptism.

Gospel: The parable of the rich man who lives and feasts sumptuously and ignores the plight of poor Lazarus, who lies at his gate.

Who is the rich man in today's gospel parable? Jesus doesn't give him a name, although he does name the beggar Lazarus who lies at the gate, covered with sores. Jesus lets us give a name to the rich man, and maybe it's our own. Do we identify with him? That possibility is open to each of us.

We have to be clear about the reason why the rich man is condemned to hell. It is not for being rich, but for being *callous and indifferent* to the beggar at his gate. For him Lazarus simply doesn't exist. His self-indulgence and gluttony have blinded his vision.

Eventually both men die. For Lazarus, death is deliverance; for the rich man, it is hell. He reaps the effects of the total lack of values that ruled and ruined his life. He is in "the abode of the dead where he was in torment." Hell, it is said, is not so much where you go as what you become. There is no hope for deliverance—ever. And all because his manner of life had already isolated him from other people, made him completely indifferent to their existence. Especially the poor and starving.

Both parts of today's parable demand our reflection, but perhaps the real core of Jesus' teaching is in the latter part. The rich man says to Father Abraham: "If someone would only go to them [his brothers] from the dead, then they would repent." Abraham replies: "If they do not listen to Moses and the prophets, they will not be convinced even if one should rise from the dead."

Is Abraham right? We probably know from personal experience that he is. When Jesus tells us by word and his own example that we may not become indifferent to anyone, least of all to the Lazaruses, the unloved, unnoticed people around us, do we listen and obey?

For all of us, especially for young people, this gospel contains one of the most essential lessons we have ever heard. Young people who are in the process of forming a philosophy of life—a set of principles and values by which they hope to live and find meaning and happiness in life—are the ones in greatest need of Jesus' teaching today. They will be living in a world where happiness supposedly consists in possessing more and more, in acquiring the latest and best of everything advertised on TV and in magazines. It's a world in which people are easily influenced to resist the need to grow up and face the responsibilities that we all have toward fellow humans and, above all, to God.

It's terribly important that all of us, especially parents, become aware of the insidious influences that can destroy and endanger our future in this world and the next. We are all in the process of *becoming;* we are all on our way either to eternal happiness with God and loved ones or eternal separation. May we never forget that *people,* especially all the "relatives" of Lazarus, are more important than possessions and fun weekends. And God is the most important of all. A life without God and God's Son, Jesus and his Gospels, is a wasted life.

Paul's counsel to Timothy was meant for then and for all ages: "Man of God that you are, seek after integrity, piety, faith, love, steadfastness and a gentle spirit. Take firm hold on the everlasting life to which you were called."

But we always come back to the gospel. The Jesus who speaks to us today is a Jesus who loves us, who is deeply concerned about our personal spiritual growth, but a Jesus who also warns us about what could happen to us if we refuse to listen to him and to take him seriously.

"Woe to the complacent in Zion!" (Reading I) Not only in Zion but everywhere.

455 MONDAY OF THE TWENTY-SIXTH WEEK IN ORDINARY TIME

YEAR I

READING I **Zech 8:1-8**
GOSPEL **Luke 9:46-50**

Zechariah was another of the prophets God raised up to encourage the Jews to rebuild the Temple after their return from Babylon. Reading I contains prophecies about the coming messianic age when God will shower his blessings on the Jews and, through them, on all nations. God's people scattered throughout the world will return to Jerusalem. "They shall be my people, and I will be their God." This prophecy has reference to the Messiah, to Jesus, initiator of the messianic age, but the complete fulfillment will hardly take place until Jesus comes again to establish his kingdom forever. We—and the Church—are in the process of becoming. In the Responsorial Psalm God says:

> The Lord will build up Zion again,
> and appear in all his glory.

We are involved in that great act of becoming the new Jerusalem being built up by the Lord. "Blessed are you, Father, Lord of heaven and earth!"

YEAR II

READING I **Job 1:6-22**
GOSPEL **Luke 9:46-50**

The Book of Job is one of the most profound masterpieces of all literature. It is a great drama whose subject matter is the problem of evil, especially the suffering of the innocent. Today we hear the introduction to the book and watch Job's reaction to the first bad news he receives: the loss of his flocks and the killing of his herdsmen, then, worst of all, the death of all his children. Job says:

> Naked I came forth from my mother's womb,
> and naked shall I go back again.
> The Lord gave and the Lord has taken away;
> blessed be the name of the Lord!

It is a noble reaction, but probably not very satisfying to people who suffer today. We approach an insight into suffering when we follow St. Paul's advice and see our personal suffering as a sharing in the cross of Christ, thus making us coredeemers with him. But in the end we settle for the truth that suffering is a mystery. Some day we'll understand. Meanwhile, Blessed be the name of the Lord! (Reading I)

456 TUESDAY OF THE TWENTY-SIXTH WEEK IN ORDINARY TIME

YEAR I

READING I Zech 8:20-23
GOSPEL Luke 9:51-56

A fascination with the divine, an unquenchable hunger to come into God's presence and remain, is a permanent quality of the human heart. This quality is dramatized in Reading I. "Let us go with you, for we have heard that God is with you," say the foreigners to the Jews. Jesus has come. His name is Emmanuel—God-with-us. One wonders how much this truth shapes our lives as Christians, Christ-bearers. Is there any possibility that a non-Christian will grab us and beg: "Let me go with you, for I have heard that God is with you"? There is no doubt that God wants to be with us. This was the whole purpose of his becoming Man in Christ Jesus. When people can see Christ in our lives, our attitudes and actions, they will be irresistably drawn to him.

> Shine on the world like bright stars;
> you are offering it the word of life (Alleluia Verse).

That's what our being Christian is all about.

YEAR II

READING I Job 3:1-3, 11-17, 20-23
GOSPEL Luke 9:51-56

Job's troubles have been piling up. Today he curses the fact that he was born; and in the last verses he asks the "why" of suffering. He was not the first who asked that question, nor will he be the last. There may be a hint of an answer in the words of today's gospel, "He firmly resolved to proceed toward Jerusalem." In Jerusalem Jesus is going to suffer, die, and rise again; and the Christian who suffers and shares that passion, death, and resurrection becomes a redeemer with Christ. This answer may not satisfy everyone. Many will settle for the theory that Christianity does not give all the answers to the "why" of suffering; it rather provides the strength and courage to bear it and bring good out of it.

> O Lord, my God, by day I cry out;
> at night I clamor in your presence. . . .
> incline your ear to my call for help (Responsorial Psalm).

457 WEDNESDAY OF THE TWENTY-SIXTH WEEK IN ORDINARY TIME

YEAR I

READING I Neh 2:1-8
GOSPEL Luke 9:57-62

Nehemiah was a layman, another of the great restorers of Jerusalem. He was a practical man endowed with deep faith. This book relates his life and work.

In the gospel Jesus lays down the conditions for following him. The life of a disciple of Christ is insecure and uncertain. "Foxes have lairs, the birds of the sky have nests, but the Son of Man has nowhere to lay his head." Jesus invites people to follow him. They seem willing, but then they make their excuses. Jesus' reply may seem harsh to us: "Let the dead bury their dead; come away and proclaim the kingdom of God." It is a question of priorities—of who and what is essential in life: God and his work, his call, his long-range plans, or one's own personal needs and desires. Jesus has called each of us to follow him in a particular vocation. Please God we can say in our hearts: I count all things worthless but this: to gain Jesus Christ and to be found in him.

YEAR II

READING I Job 9:1-12, 14-16
GOSPEL Luke 9:57-62

The drama of Job Everyman continues. In trying to understand the why of suffering, Job's friends are not much help to him. They say that God is fair and Job agrees, but he wonders how a creature can ask the Creator for fair treatment. Job's awareness of the greatness and magnificence of God is praiseworthy, but it may also prevent his coming near to God for a satisfactory answer. He ends up saying,

> "Even though I were right, I could not answer him,
> but should rather beg for what was due me."

The Responsorial Psalm echoes Job's dilemma—and it also provides us with an essential prayer for our own puzzling problems and worries:

> Daily I call upon you, O Lord;
> to you I stretch out my hands. . . .
> Why, O Lord, do you reject me;
> why hide from me your face?
> Let my prayer come before you, Lord.

458 THURSDAY OF THE TWENTY-SIXTH WEEK IN ORDINARY TIME

YEAR I

READING I Neh 8:1-4, 5-6, 7-12
GOSPEL Luke 10:1-12

Today's reading from Nehemiah is reminiscent of the original giving of the Law to Moses on Mount Sinai. The great esteem God's people had for the sacred scroll is indicated by the fact that they prostrate before it as though it were God himself. This rediscovery of the Law is such a great event in their history that it calls for a celebration. Ezra tells them, "Today is holy to the Lord your God. Do not be sad, and do not weep." But the people did weep—surely for joy—as they heard the words of the Law. The Responsorial Psalm is a kind of understatement, but we can well make it our own, especially when we remind ourselves that the old Law is fulfilled in the gospel, the good news of Jesus:

> The precepts of the Lord give joy to the heart.
> The law of the Lord is perfect,
> refreshing the soul" (Responsorial Psalm).

YEAR II

READING I **Job 19:21-27**
GOSPEL **Luke 10:1-12**

"Pity me, pity me, O you my friends," cries Job out of the midst of his misery. But, strong man that he is, he refuses to give in to defeat. He does not lose his faith. "I know that my Vindicator lives . . . whom I myself shall see . . . from my flesh I shall see God; my inmost being is consumed with longing." How beautiful! The world is full of Jobs. Unfortunately, too many of them allow the burden of suffering to crush out their faith, and they give up on their God. Others refuse to concede defeat: their trust in God is too great. If you would like to know the secret of victory over suffering, it may well be in Job's last word today, "My inmost being is consumed with longing." Desire for God is our response to his desire for us. It is its own reward.

> Hear, O Lord, the sound of my call;
> have pity on me, and answer me. . . .
> Your presence, O Lord, I seek (Responsorial Psalm).

459 FRIDAY OF THE TWENTY-SIXTH WEEK IN ORDINARY TIME

YEAR I

READING I **Bar 1:15-22**
GOSPEL **Luke 10:13-16**

The "act of contrition" in Reading I belongs in the hearts of every people, every community, every individual. "We have sinned in the

Lord's sight and disobeyed him . . . We have neither heeded the voice of the Lord, nor followed his precepts . . . Each one of us went off after the devices of his own wicked heart. . . ." The theme running through the whole confession is refusal to heed the voice of the Lord, which is also the theme of the sinful cities of the gospel. The essential lesson for us in reading and hearing God's word is that of attachment to that word. We put ourselves into the experience of the Old Testament people and try to understand that their experiences are our experiences now. Their cry, "For the glory of your name, O Lord, deliver us" (Responsorial Psalm) is now ours. "Deliver us and pardon our sins for your name's sake."

YEAR II

READING I **Job 38:1, 12-21; 40:3-5**
GOSPEL **Luke 10:13-16**

"Guide me, Lord, along the everlasting way" (Responsorial Psalm). This most human and beautiful of prayers belongs to Job when God mentions some of the secrets of the universe which he alone can fathom. Job is now satisfied, he is at peace with himself and is willing to let the Lord direct his life.

If we meditated more on the Book of Job, we could be at peace with ourselves and willing to let the Lord direct our lives, too. No one knows us as God does. He alone knows the needs of our lives, knows how we can best be ourselves.

> O Lord, you have probed me and you know me; . . .
> Truly you have formed my inmost being;
> you knit me in my mother's womb.
> I give you thanks that I am fearfully, wonderfully made;
> wonderful are your works (Responsorial Psalm).

Have you ever heard a more wonderful prayer?

460 SATURDAY OF THE TWENTY-SIXTH WEEK IN ORDINARY TIME

YEAR I

READING I Bar 4:5-12, 27-29
GOSPEL Luke 10:17-24

"You forsook the Eternal God who nourished you," Baruch tells his people; and no better definition of sin has ever been given, from the sin of our first parents to the latest one any one of us committed. Sin is forsaking God, refusing to remember that he is God and we are his creatures. But he continues to forgive, continues to hope in us, even as he did for his people then. "Fear not, my children, call out to God! . . . In saving you [he will] bring you back enduring joy" (Reading I). Why? Because "the Lord listens to the poor" (Responsorial Psalm). We are those poor. All we have to do is to seek him with all our hearts, and then our hearts will be merry. That is the good news that Jesus preached, too.

> Blessed are you, Father, Lord of heaven and earth;
> you have revealed to little ones the mysteries of the kingdom (Alleluia Verse).

The mystery of mysteries that the Father has revealed to us, his children, is his merciful, forgiving love made flesh in Jesus our Lord.

YEAR II

READING I Job 42:1-3, 5-6, 12-16
GOSPEL Luke 10:17-24

Job has passed the test and has vindicated the high esteem God had for him. He has emerged from an ordeal of terrible human pain a wiser and better man—a man who, as he said, knew *about* God by hearing, but now he *knows* God through personal experience. Suffering remains a mystery to him, but he has come to terms with it and has not allowed it to defeat him.

The Responsorial Psalm wonderfully sums up not only the reflections of Job but of all of us who follow him in hanging onto God, no matter what:

> It is good for me that I have been afflicted,
> that I may learn your statutes.

I know, O Lord, that your ordinances are just,
and in your faithfulness you have afflicted me. . . .
The revelation of your words sheds light, . . .
Lord, let your face shine on me.

140 TWENTY-SEVENTH SUNDAY IN ORDINARY TIME Cycle A

READING I **Isa 5:1-7** **READING II** **Phil 4:6-9**
GOSPEL **Matt 21:33-43**

Reading I: The Lord's vineyard is the house of Israel. He hopes it will yield good grapes, but is disappointed.

Reading II: Paul's practical advice on living the Christian life: "Live according to what you have learned and accepted."

Gospel: Jesus uses the parable of the vineyard and its evil tenants to make clear to his enemies what they will do to him.

Both Reading I and the gospel are about vineyards whose vines bring forth grapes, which in turn are made into wine. But it should not be too difficult for us to grasp that what both Isaiah and Jesus are talking about is *people:* the people of God, the house of Israel, in Isaiah's time; the house of Israel as it existed at the time of Christ. And there is also a definite application to the people of God now, the Church.

According to Fr. Dominic Crossan, parables are intended to remove our defenses and make us vulnerable to God. "It is only in such experiences that God can touch us" (quoted in *Homiletic Service,* Ottawa, 1984). Hopefully Jesus is more successful in making us vulnerable to God than he was with his enemies then.

Jesus uses this parable on the chief priests and elders of the people a few days before they put him to death. He reviews the history of how, over the centuries, God had tried through his prophets to make them into a responsible people. Then he talks about himself when he quotes the owner of the vineyard: "They will respect my son." But they kill the son. When Jesus asks his enemies what the owner of the vineyard will do to the murderers they reply: "He will bring that wicked crowd to a bad end and lease his vineyard out to others who will see to it that he has grapes at vintage time." They know Jesus is talking about them, but they refuse to change.

Now it's time to bring ourselves into the picture. Does this parable have any application to us modern Catholics and to our Church today? Does it make us vulnerable to God? The answer to these questions may be found in today's Alleluia Verse:

> I have chosen you from the world, says the Lord,
> to go and bear fruit that will last.

Are we as a Church fulfilling our obligations today? What kind of harvest are we bringing forth? If we are fulfilling our mission as Jesus wants us to, why are we losing so many members, especially so many of the younger ones? Have we been so concerned about our personal salvation that we have forgotten about being members of a universal Church, one which is obligated to bring the good news to all peoples?

Father Carr writes: "It does precious little good to prove theologically that the Catholic Church is the true Church of Christ when the lives of Catholics don't show good fruit. We can prove the Church is true in doctrine, but if the lives of Catholics don't show forth the love of Christ and zeal for God, then we are fighting a losing battle" (Sunday Missal Service, Quincy, Ill.).

What God wants of us as a Church today is a growing awareness of a world in need of Christ. God wants us to know that we are a people on a mission, that of showing forth Christ in our lives and attitudes. God wants a deeper concern for everyone who is in need of any kind. In a word, what God wants of us is *Christ-likeness* and a deep sense of our being loved by Christ with a love that surpasses all our desires.

The Church is, or ought to be, a sacrament of God's love to the whole world, and each of us is a sacrament as well. Are we aware of our power? If not, we need the prayers of our Eucharist today:

> Father,
> your love for us
> surpasses all our hopes and desires.
> Forgive our failings,
> keep us in your peace
> and lead us in the way of salvation (Opening Prayer).

Almighty God,
let the eucharist we share
fill us with your life.
May the love of Christ
which we celebrate here
touch our lives and lead us to you (Prayer after Communion).

I have chosen you from the world, says the Lord,
to go and bear fruit that will last (Alleluia Verse).

141 TWENTY-SEVENTH SUNDAY IN ORDINARY TIME Cycle B

READING I Gen 2:18-24 **READING II** Heb 2:9-11
GOSPEL Mark 10:2-16

Reading I: The Genesis account of the creation of all living animals and birds followed by the creation of woman.

Reading II: Jesus tasted death "for the sake of all men." He was made perfect through suffering.

Gospel: Jesus comes out strongly for the indissolubility of marriage. He then declares that we must become like little children in order to enter the kingdom of God.

Both Reading I and the gospel treat the nature and permanence of marriage. Reading I tells us that in marriage man and woman become one body; Jesus repeats that truth in the gospel. Because of that oneness, Jesus says, "Let no man separate what God has joined."

The inseparability of wife and husband in marriage is the ideal that the Roman Catholic Church has sought to maintain over the centuries. The fact is, however, that divorce is everywhere on the increase and among Catholics almost as much as in other denominations.

Happy and successful marriages are built on the ideal of fidelity, which means that people must be true to themselves, to friends, to their chosen spouses, and above all to God. Without fidelity to God there is serious danger of infidelity in marriage. And the contrary is also true: when people are faithful to God, to themselves, and to friends, the problem of infidelity in marriage greatly diminishes.

Marriage is a true vocation, which means that God calls a woman and man to become holy in and through a loyal living out of every aspect of marriage. Most people are married or will be married in the near future. (We need to be reminded that the single life as a layperson is also a true, God-given vocation. So too the life of widows and widowers). Most marriages are reasonably happy, though none are free from problems or from suffering, worry, and pain. It seems that love and suffering are inseparable companions, and suffering is without limit in its varieties.

In marriage as in all vocations, growing and maturing is the deepest need. And both spouses have to work at the maturing. They have to learn the true meaning of love: that it is living for the beloved rather than for the self. Both have to learn the needs of the other partner, both physical and psychological (the needs of children, too). Perhaps the greatest need any person has is for recognition as a person, beloved and respected. Every person needs to be loved and cherished, to be *told* that she or he is loved, and it can't be too often.

Spouses have to learn how to talk together as equals, to discuss mutual problems. Each has to learn how to listen; each has to learn to recognize personality faults and failings and to work at overcoming them. In a word, spouses have to communicate. One might speculate that most failures in marriage can be traced to failure to communicate as mature, adult, equal human persons.

Marriage is for mature persons who are capable of taking on responsibility for the other as well as for themselves.

Years ago Ann Landers' column had some excellent suggestions for creating a happy married life:

1. Never both be angry at once.
2. Never yell at each other unless the house is on fire.
3. Never meet without an affectionate welcome.
4. Yield to the wishes of the other as an exercise of self-discipline if you can't think of a better reason.
5. If you have any criticism make it lovingly.
6. Neglect the whole world rather than each other.
7. Never bring up a mistake of the past.
8. Don't be afraid to give compliments to the other.
9. Never go to bed mad.

10. When you've made a mistake, talk it out and ask for forgiveness.
11. Remember, it takes two to make an argument. The one who is wrong is the one who will be doing the most talking.

A word to those not yet married. We cannot insist too much on the need for thorough preparation—spiritual, physical, and financial. It has been said that people spend many years preparing for a profession, but when it comes to preparing for the most important profession of all, the vocation of marriage, they think they can do it in a few weeks or months.

Essential to the preparation is finding out what the future spouse thinks about the meaning of life, about religion, about the life to come. What are his or her priorities and values? Are the future spouses both capable of heroic love? Can they talk together and argue without raising their voices? The essential element: What values do each of them have? What is really important to each?

Happy, successful marriages do not happen all at once. Like genuine love they have to be made, created, often at the cost of great effort and sacrifice. Creating this love is a mutual growth process that must continue all through life.

A final warning: marriages break down when the spouses lose sight of one another and begin to live only for themselves, when they refuse to remember the almost divine dignity of the human person and use or treat one another only as objects or as personal property.

May Jesus, who worked his first miracle at a wedding feast, help all married couples by his word, his example, and his sacrificial love to grow and mature together into the fullness of love!

TWENTY-SEVENTH SUNDAY IN ORDINARY TIME

READING I Hab 1:2-3, 2:2-4 **READING II** 2 Tim 1:6-8, 13-14
GOSPEL Luke 17:5-10

Reading I: The prophet cries out to the Lord for help, and the Lord replies: "The just man, because of his faith, shall live."

Reading II: Paul advises Timothy to stir into flame the gift of God and to guard the rich deposit of faith he has received.

Gospel: The apostles ask Jesus to increase their faith, and Jesus places some of the responsibility on them.

It would seem that there isn't a single living person who does not have to face up to the problem of pain and suffering at some time in his or her lifetime. Many are tempted to ask, "If God is really good, if God loves me, why does this tragedy happen to me?" In Reading I the prophet Habakkuk asks: "How long, O Lord? I cry for help but you do not listen."

The popular Anglican theologian C.S. Lewis, wrote a book called *The Problem of Pain,* which provided an intellectual discussion of the problem. Then he discovered the inadequacy of his attempts to find intellectual insights into the problem when he lost his beloved wife. He became inconsolable and bitter. Finally, he wrote another book, *A Grief Observed,* in which he recognized the folly of the reason-alone approach as he described his agonizing search for God's goodness at the deepest level of his being. I suspect that his conclusion resembled that which God suggests to the prophet Habakkuk: "The rash man has no integrity; but the just man, because of his faith, shall live." Lewis died at peace with himself and with the mystery of life and death.

Faith, then, is the key, the only key, that can open a glimpse into the mystery of pain, sorrow, and anguish that afflicts each of us at various times in our lives. But when dealing with mystery, a glimpse, and not a full explanation, is all that one can expect. We know that faith is a gift from God, as the apostles recognize in today's gospel. Jesus had been telling them some hard truths, and they cry out to him, "increase our faith!" That's our prayer, now and always.

But, in Reading II, St. Paul recognizes that, though faith is God's gift, which cannot be earned, it imposes obligations on us, above all the responsibility for its upkeep. He says: "Stir into flame the gift of God bestowed when my hands were laid on you. . . . Guard the rich deposit of faith with the help of the Holy Spirit who dwells within us."

We may wonder how we can stir up our faith, or fan it into a flame, as another translation has it. Surely, one way is to open our senses, our hearts and minds, to the world around us. The world is throbbing with the life, the love, the beauty, of its loving creator. With good reason, the world of nature has been called a sacrament, a sign, of God's goodness, but God can enter into us and stir up our faith only if we know how to see, to listen, to experience. Only the unthinking dullness of mind and heart remains unmoved by a rainbow, a sunrise, or a sunset in all their glory. The flame of faith cannot but burn more brightly with such visions.

Another way of stirring into flame the gift of faith is listening to the word of God, allowing it to penetrate our minds and hearts.

> If today you hear his voice,
> harden not your hearts (Responsorial Psalm).

The evangelists experienced the good news that God loved them. It pulsated through their beings. And it was in their overwhelming experience of God's goodness that they knew that, in its very experience, God was operating—to bring good out of it, to transform it, to bring healing to others through it, to make it part of Christ's redeeming life, passion, and death.

> The Lord is good to those who hope in him, to those who are searching for his love (Communion Antiphon).

With good reason did the apostles ask Jesus, "Increase our faith," for it is faith in God, faith in his love, faith in his fidelity, compassion, and loving kindness, faith in God's all-seeing vision and ability to bring good out of evil, that makes it possible for us to fly above fields of pain—even on broken wings.

Lord, increase our faith so that we can comprehend that

> "You have given everything its place in the world, and no one can make it otherwise. For it is your creation, the heavens and the earth and the stars; you are the Lord of all" (Entrance Antiphon).

> Father of the world to come,
> Lead us to seek beyond our reach
> and give us the courage to stand before your truth
> (Alternative Opening Prayer).

461 MONDAY OF THE TWENTY-SEVENTH WEEK IN ORDINARY TIME

YEAR I

READING I **Jonah 1:1–2:1, 11**
GOSPEL **Luke 10:25-37**

The Book of Jonah contains a deep theological lesson for us all. Jonah is reluctant to obey God's call to preach penance to the wicked pagan city of Nineveh, so he tries to escape. He probably doesn't think these non-Jews are worth saving. Today's Reading I relates the futility of a man who tries to avoid God's summons to be a messenger of mercy and repentance to the Ninevites. He will learn the hard way that divine mercy cannot be limited to a single people.

This, at least in part, is also the message of the gospel. The non-Jew, the Samaritan, member of a people despised by the Jews, best represents ideal obedience to God's universal command of love for him and love for neighbor. As it was then, so it often is now. Very often non-Catholics, even non-Christians, are more concerned about helping the poor and underprivileged than we are. Does this disturb us? If not, it should!

YEAR II

READING I **Gal 1:6-12**
GOSPEL **Luke 10:25-37**

Whether one had to follow Jewish customs and religious practices in order to be a Christian is the subject of the epistle to the Galatians. Even though such a problem is not a concern for us today, the epistle contains important practical advice and essential theology for our spiritual formation.

We can never hear this gospel too often. Jesus could have given a definition of neighborliness in *words.* He does much better; he dramatizes neighborliness in such a way that we can never forget it; and then he tells us, "Go and do the same." I don't think we can forget Christ's important point—that it was a non-Jew, a Samaritan, who best exemplified true love. Would he make the same point today about us Catholics? Why is it that many non-Christians seem to be more concerned about the outcasts than we are?

462 TUESDAY OF THE TWENTY-SEVENTH WEEK IN ORDINARY TIME

YEAR I

READING I Jonah 3:1-10
GOSPEL Luke 10:38-42

God may have chosen the Jews as his very own people, but he also created and loves all peoples. What may well make a people or a person more pleasing to God is not their belonging to a particular religious or national group but the degree of generosity, love, and sorrow in their response to his summons to repentance. Jonah preaches penance in the name of God, and the people respond far beyond his expectations. Tomorrow we shall see how he reacts.

> Happy are they who have kept the word with a generous heart,
> and yield a harvest through perseverance (Alleluia Verse).

These words of Jesus are true not only with regard to the Ninevites, but also to Mary in the gospel who sat at Jesus' feet. We have heard this story so often that the point Jesus wants to make may be lost on us. And the point is: no matter how busy we are, even in doing his work, we simply have to take time out to listen to him when he speaks to us.

YEAR II

READING I Gal 1:13-24
GOSPEL Luke 10:38-42

In Reading I Paul establishes his credentials as an apostle: the fact of his conversion, his years of solitude in Arabia preparing for the apostolate, his early association with the apostles, especially Peter, and the beginning of his apostolic preaching. In the very beginning he sets down a basic concept of his Christian life: that it is God who knew him before he was born, God who called him to his particular vocation. Every one of us can say the same thing. From all eternity God has known each of us, God has loved us, called us into being, called us to be followers of his son.

> O Lord, you have probed me and you know me; . . .
> Truly you have formed my inmost being;
> you knit me in my mother's womb (Responsorial Psalm).

463 WEDNESDAY OF THE TWENTY-SEVENTH WEEK IN ORDINARY TIME

YEAR I

READING I **Jonah 4:1-11**
GOSPEL **Luke 11:1-4**

The smallness of Jonah's religious outlook is illustrated by his anger with God for granting merciful forgiveness to the Ninevites. Ironically, he was God's voice in calling them to repentance! God does not condemn Jonah, he just makes him look a little ridiculous to himself: "You were concerned over the plant which cost you no labor. . . . And should I not be concerned over Nineveh, the great city, in which there are more than a hundred and twenty thousand persons . . . ?" It is people who are precious in God's eyes—no matter what their race, religion, or nationality. How right is the psalmist who gave us today's Responsorial Psalm:

> All the nations you have made shall come
> and worship you, O Lord, . . .
> For you are great, and you do wondrous deeds;
> you alone are God.

And we can add: You are our Father, for we have received the Spirit which makes us all God's children. And the Our Father is our prayer!

YEAR II

READING I **Gal 2:1-2, 7-14**
GOSPEL **Luke 11:1-4**

Remember Paul's problem: there are certain troublemakers in the Galatian community who wanted to define Christianity by limitations—by confining membership to those who did or would adhere to the Old Law. Paul insisted that by his death and resurrection Jesus saved all humankind: *this* is the good news of the gospel. We are saved without merit or good deeds on our part by *Christ*, not by adhering to the Jewish laws and customs.

It was a struggle for the very heart of Christianity, a life and death struggle, with the Judaizers having very important people on their side. If the Judaizers had won the argument, Christianity today would be a tiny Palestinian sect rather than a world-wide religion. What is more important to us—what Christ has done for us or what we do for ourselves?

464 THURSDAY OF THE TWENTY-SEVENTH WEEK IN ORDINARY TIME

YEAR I

READING I **Mal 3:13-20**
GOSPEL **Luke 11:5-13**

The Book of Malachi gives a picture of life in the Jewish community, back from exile in Babylon. Malachi's criticism of abuses was to contribute considerably to reform.

The gospel counsels perseverance in prayer, and who doesn't need that? There may be a certain amount of defeatism in our prayers of petition, or we may even be ashamed of praying for things and intentions we need. This is not Christ's way of thinking. Of course, it is possible that some of the favors we ask for may be a little unworthy or selfish. Why don't we just leave that up to God? Why don't we just take Jesus at his word? Pray unceasingly for what you need and desire, especially if what you desire involves others. And remember: "Happy are they who hope in the Lord" (Responsorial Psalm).

> Open our hearts, O Lord,
> to listen to the words of your Son (Alleluia Verse).

That's a prayer the Lord can hardly refuse!

YEAR II

READING I **Gal 3:1-5**
GOSPEL **Luke 11:5-13**

Judging by today's Reading I, the Judaizers must have won over many of Paul's converts to their false understanding of Christianity. Paul's criticism is devastating. He accuses them of having been bewitched. Did they receive the Spirit by their minute fulfillment of the Law or by joyous, grateful acceptance of what Jesus had done for them?

If mere human works save, then why was Christ and his sacrifice necessary? "How did you receive the Spirit? . . . Is it because you observe the law or because you have faith in what you heard that God lavishes the Spirit on you and works wonders in your midst?" (Reading I)

That Paul has good backing for his teaching in the Old Testament is indicated in the Responsorial Psalm:

> Blessed be the Lord God of Israel,
> for he has visited his people,
> He has raised a horn of saving strength for us
> in the house of David his servant.

465 FRIDAY OF THE TWENTY-SEVENTH WEEK IN ORDINARY TIME

YEAR I

READING I Joel 1:13-15; 2:1-2
GOSPEL Luke 11:15-26

The occasion for the prophecy of Joel and its summons to nationwide fasting and penance was an invasion of locusts that swarmed over Judah about 400 B.C. It was so frightening that the prophet saw it as a symbol of the Day of the Lord, the Last Judgment. This is the Scripture text that the Church has selected to introduce the holy season of Lent. "Proclaim a fast, call an assembly."

But the Day of the Lord that the Church envisions at the beginning of Lent is Holy Easter, which is truly the day the Lord has made, the day of the triumph of Jesus our Lord who became man and lived among us and enabled those who accepted him to become the children of God. Today's gospel shows Jesus in another conflict with the Pharisees, who accuse him of being possessed by Satan, thus accounting for his ability to cast out devils. He tells them and us that if we are not with him, we are against him. That's our choice.

YEAR II

READING I Gal 3:7-14
GOSPEL Luke 11:15-26

Paul keeps insisting: it is faith that saves, not works. But what is faith for Paul? It is not accepting a system of doctrines. It is rather standing before God like Abraham and saying, here I am, Lord. Mary put it in her own words, "I am the servant of the Lord. Let it be done to me as you say" (Luke 1:38). Faith is willingness to allow Christ to love us, to save us from ourselves. The Judaizers insisted that Gentiles could be saved only by fulfilling the Law. Paul, knowing the Law better than they, insisted on the contrary that the Christian's only task (and it is a joyous one) is to stand beneath the cross, look up at Jesus and say: "Here I am, Lord. Let it be done to me as you say."

> I will give thanks to the Lord with all my heart . . .
> Great are the works of the Lord (Responsorial Psalm).

466 SATURDAY OF THE TWENTY-SEVENTH WEEK IN ORDINARY TIME

YEAR I

READING I Joel 4:12-21
GOSPEL Luke 11:27-28

Today's gospel contains the whole doctrine of prayer. A nameless woman in a crowd hears Jesus confound the Pharisees, sees him chase out a devil, and unable to contain her enthusiasm, she calls out in a combination of holy envy and praise of Mary, "Blest is the womb that bore you and the breasts that nursed you!" That beautiful prayer contains praise, gratitude, loving appreciation for Jesus; and it begins with him—he is the one who occasions it, as is always the case. Jesus' reply does not downgrade his mother. As no one else ever did, Mary heard the word of God and kept it. St. Augustine says about this passage: "More blessed is Mary for believing the faith of Christ than for conceiving the flesh of Christ." Jesus' formula for blessedness is available to all of us. Can we not, like Mary, hear the word of God and try to put it into practice in our lives?

YEAR II

READING I **Gal 3:22-29**
GOSPEL **Luke 11:27-28**

Jesus is the decisive event in human history. It is he who makes all things and all conditions new. Today we arrive at the heart of Paul's letter to the Galatians, namely, the unity of all the baptized in Christ. Paul tells us that, through baptism, all secondary differences between persons are stripped away so that our shared unity in Christ may predominate: "There does not exist among you Jew or Greek, slave or freeman, male or female. All are one in Christ Jesus." In the light of that truth, it is hard to understand how it is possible for us Christians to discriminate against others of different races, religions, and sex. Do we not realize that when we give every person or class their rights, we enrich ourselves? Blessed are those who hear *this* word of God and keep it!

143 TWENTY-EIGHTH SUNDAY IN ORDINARY TIME Cycle A

READING I **Isa 25:6-10** **READING II** **Phil 4:12-14, 19-20**
GOSPEL **Matt 22:1-14**

Reading I: A prophecy of the end-time when God will wipe away all tears, and all peoples will recognize God as Lord of all.

Reading II: Paul writes from prison to thank the Philippians for their generosity to him and to assure them that God will reward them.

Gospel: The parable of the wedding feast to which God invites guests, but they refuse to come.

The point of the parable was to inform the chief priests and elders how tragic it was to refuse to accept the invitation to come to the banquet of salvation provided by Jesus. It is a final effort on the part of Christ to win them over. They refuse, and the invitation goes to the Gentiles. The parable also demonstrates the Lord's irresistable determination, his desire, to save all peoples, to invite all to the eternal banquet of salvation.

The parable illustrates the total gratuitousness of salvation. No need to buy a ticket. It's free and completely undeserved. "Everything is ready. Come to the feast." The last part of the parable indicates, however, that those invited should be prepared; they need to wear the wedding garment of grace, unstained by spots of serious sin.

The parable is also an appropriate image of the Holy Eucharist. The Mass is the making present again of the Last Supper and Jesus' death on Calvary; we who now take part in it are as privileged as those originally present at those events.

We are right in believing that the Mass is our best opportunity for giving ourselves to God and acknowledging God's lordship over our lives. But one of the main points of today's readings is that we see the Mass as God's greatest gift to us. Greatest gift because it is Jesus himself whom God gives. We might try to grasp how insignificant our gift is compared to the Lord's.

The Mass tells us clearly that God is all loving and that each of us is worth loving, worth Jesus' giving up his life and dying for us. The Mass, more than anything else, tells us of our great worth in the eyes of God and of Jesus, God's Son. We are often so fragile, so hesitant to believe in our intrinsic value. We so tend to downgrade ourselves. Which is why we have to be reminded so often of God's intense, all-powerful love and concern for us.

> The Lord is my shepherd; I shall not want.
>   In verdant pastures he gives me repose;
> Beside restful waters he leads me;
>   he refreshes my soul (Responsorial Psalm).

One of our greatest needs is to want to love our God, but an equally great need is the willingness and strong desire to be *loved* by God, to be willing to accept divine love and caring. But divine love given and accepted needs to be shared. I do not recall the source of the following appropriate quote: "Our needs for truth and love are never fully satisfied because we never finish growing. We can go to Mass unashamedly to receive, not so much so that we can give back, but that we can give out of the love that we find there. The

Father gives truth and love to his children so that they can pass it on to others."

So we go to the banquet of the Lord because the Lord invites us, because the Lord loves us, because we need to be assured of that divine love, because we need reminding that there are countless others who are also very much worth being loved by the Lord—and by us. Essentially, the Mass is an invitation to deepest intimacy with Jesus—the intimacy of friend with friend, of lover with beloved.

Love is what the Mass is all about. Perhaps this tells us something about the man without the wedding garment at the feast in today's parable. If we refuse to accept God's love, if we refuse to pass it on, if we despise ourselves and others, if we are unwilling to be converted and turn to Christ, then we are not wearing a wedding garment and are in danger of being cast out into the night where we can despise ourselves and refuse love to our heart's content.

Perhaps now we are ready to make today's Opening Prayer our own:

> Lord,
> our help and guide,
> make your love the foundation of our lives.
> May our love for you express itself
> in our eagerness to do good for others.

144 TWENTY-EIGHTH SUNDAY IN ORDINARY TIME Cycle B

READING I **Wis 7:7-11** **READING II** **Heb 4:12-13**
GOSPEL **Mark 10:17-30**

Reading I: The reading emphasizes the great worth of wisdom, which is insight into life's meaning, in knowing how to live.

Reading II: God's word is living; it penetrates into the core of our being and lays bare our inmost thoughts.

Gospel: Salvation lies in observing the commandments, but Jesus says that to be perfect one must give up one's most precious possessions and follow him.

There is a closer connection between Reading I and the gospel than is at first apparent. Reading I exalts the gift of wisdom, which is more than knowledge or any intellectual achievement. True wisdom is a very special insight in how to live; it is a philosophy of life that enables a person to discern life's deep meaning, and most important of all, the ultimate goal of life in the world to come.

The young man in the gospel is good and upright in every way; he had observed the commandments meticulously. But apparently he is not happy, and surely he is not satisfied with his life. Something is missing, and he asks Jesus what it is. Jesus' answer crushes him: "Go sell what you have and give to the poor; . . . After that come and follow me." And he goes away sad, for he had great possessions. He knows in his heart that he is preferring his possessions to Christ; he turns his back on the one thing that could make him happy and give meaning to his life—the love in the face and heart of Jesus.

The man in the gospel is nameless, which might mean that he stands for everyone, for Christians everywhere. This could be the most disturbing gospel for all of us to hear. I mean, *all* Christians, not just the well off with great possessions. The gospel applies to religious women and men who have made a vow of poverty as much as to wealthy persons, for it makes us face up to ourselves and to our unwillingness to relinquish the attachments that prevent us from belonging to Jesus and following him, without any holding back.

The key word in Jesus' statement is "possessions." It has many meanings, the most common being wealth, land, buildings, cars, etc. But the word has a wider meaning, one which can apply to such things as food, alcohol, tobacco, un-Christian opinions and prejudices. Jesus faces each of us today and compels us to face ourselves and our unwillingness to relinquish *any* attachment that prevents us from belonging to him without reservation. It makes us ask ourselves, what is there in my life that possesses me more than Jesus does. What do I find impossible to give up?

Is this hard? Of course it is, and no one understands this better than Jesus himself. And St. Paul, too. He belonged totally to Christ, but he had to give up his entire past, including his hatred of Christianity, in order to follow Christ. He himself had painful experience of the words he writes to us today: "God's word is living and effective, sharper than any two-edged sword. It penetrates and divides soul and spirit."

In her commentary on today's gospel, Lettie Morse writes: "The rich man in today's gospel missed his chance when he turned away from Jesus' love. Have we not often done the same? But the good news is that Jesus doesn't give up on us. Each day is a new chance to repent and believe, a new chance to discover who we are, and to begin to live a rich and full and eternal life—a life of freedom and love."

All this may seem extremely negative and threatening, and that is not my intention. To be sure, religion is not ethics, it is not mere observance of commandments; following Christ *is our personal response in love to the goodness and lovableness of Jesus.* Our most necessary task in life lies in discovering Christ's divine lovableness in all its fullness, and then our total renunciation, our all-out gift of self and all that we have and are, will follow inevitably.

> Fill us with your love, O Lord,
> and we will sing for joy (Responsorial Psalm).

145 TWENTY-EIGHTH SUNDAY IN ORDINARY TIME Cycle C

READING I **2 Kgs 5:14-17** **READING II** **2 Tim 2:8-13**
GOSPEL **Luke 17:11-19**

Reading I: Pleased at his cure from leprosy, Naaman the Syrian believes in God and returns home with two loads of Israel's soil.

Reading II: "There is no chaining the word of God," writes Paul from prison. He will bear his suffering to obtain salvation for others.

Gospel: Jesus cures ten lepers, but only one of them, a Samaritan, returns to give thanks.

There is much drama both in Reading I and in the gospel. In both stories there are healed lepers, there is thanksgiving, and there are persons who are instruments of the healing. In biblical times lepers lived without hope; but in both readings today there is healing. Naaman the Syrian is healed when he follows Elisha's directives, and the ten nameless lepers in the gospel are cured while on their way to show themselves to the priests, as Jesus had directed them.

Naaman's cure results in belief in God, and he wants to show his gratitude with a gift to Elisha. When Elisha refuses the gift, Naaman asks for two mule-loads of soil so that he can worship God on Hebrew soil when he returns home. In the gospel only one person returns to thank Jesus for his cure, and he was a Samaritan, a foreigner.

What God wants us to keep in mind from these readings is:
—his eagerness to heal both physical and spiritual ills;
—the need for human instruments of divine healing;
—God's hope for some expression of gratitude.

I firmly believe that God is as eager to heal now as he was in biblical times. God could do this healing directly, but it has always been his habit to use human instruments. (In Jesus' case, a divine-human instrument.) *Every* Christian, not just the priests and the "saints," has a vocation to be a healer in one way or another. There is no one who could not offer the touch of a caring hand, a kind word, an open ear, a visit to an ill or aged person. There are no limits to the kinds of spiritual healing everyone is capable of. Without willingness to heal and serve, one's Christianity could be a sham. In our Opening Prayer we plead:

> Lord,
> May our love for you express itself
> in our eagerness to do good for others.

Our emphasis on the common vocation of all Christians to be God's healing "mediators" does not take away from the great need of the people of God today for those special instruments of healing—the priests who administer God's own sacraments of healing, especially the Eucharist, the sacrament of reconciliation, and the anointing of the sick. We all need to pray that God will inspire more and more persons to consider preparing themselves for this ministry, for the increasing number of priestless parishes where no sacramental healing is possible is alarming.

A word about gratitude. Today's gospel is really a parable describing redemption, about what Jesus has done for all of us. We are healed, reconciled with our God, just as really as the grateful Samaritan is healed of his leprosy. Christianity isn't authentic without healing and service; it isn't authentic without gratitude. And again we recall that God doesn't need our thanks. We need it in order to be fully and genuinely human.

Because Jesus knew we would want to be grateful, he gave us the Eucharist. The word "eucharist" actually means "thanksgiving." Jesus not only gave us healing by living and dying for us, he gave himself to us in the Eucharist, in the Mass. So he is, at the same time, salvation, healing, and thanksgiving. That's the kind of divine wonder that only God could think up!

> For all things give thanks to God,
> because this is what he expects from you in Jesus Christ (Alleluia Verse).

467 MONDAY OF THE TWENTY-EIGHTH WEEK IN ORDINARY TIME

YEAR I

READING I **Rom 1:1-7**
GOSPEL **Luke 11:29-32**

Today we begin Paul's letter to the Romans—an epistle that has influenced Christian thought perhaps more than any other New Testament writing. In today's Reading I we have mention of many of the key truths of the early Christian faith—Paul's own vocation, the fact that Jesus fulfills Old Testament hopes and prophecies, the Messiah's descent from King David, the resurrection, the necessity of faith, God's call to the Gentiles, and God as our Father. The key idea of both readings today is that Jesus is indeed the one person who brings salvation: "The Lord has made known his salvation" (Responsorial Psalm). Jesus condemns his enemies for rejecting him. He is not even treated as well as the lesser prophet Jonah. We now can hear this letter addressed to us: "To all . . . beloved of God and called to holiness . . ." Our vocation from God is to be saints. How do you like that?

YEAR II

READING I Gal 4:22-24, 26-27, 31–5:1
GOSPEL Luke 11:29-32

In today's difficult passage Paul is still fighting for freedom for his converts from the slavery of the old Law and its legalisms. He uses the comparison between Hagar, the slave girl, and Sarah, Abraham's legal wife—the one a type of the old economy of salvation, and the other the new economy, stemming from Zion, the New Jerusalem. Paul again reminds his enemies that through Christ we are freed from slavery to the old Law.

Paul's final words today are very significant: "It was for liberty that Christ freed us. So stand firm, and do not take on yourselves the yoke of slavery a second time!" Freedom implies responsibility—the responsibility of making personal choices inspired by love. That is the only kind of Christianity Christ is interested in. Blessed be his name forever!

468 TUESDAY OF THE TWENTY-EIGHTH WEEK IN ORDINARY TIME

YEAR I

READING I Rom 1:16-25
GOSPEL Luke 11:37-41

Today's Reading expresses Paul's conviction that Christianity has superseded Judaism and that the old covenant has given way to the new. To be saved, a person only had to believe, to accept joyfully and gratefully the salvation won by Jesus. Paul also describes humanity without Christ, and there was no excuse for its depravity. People should have been able to conclude to the existence of a supreme Being merely by observing the world around them, and to conclude to a law of morality flowing from the existence of a creator. Maybe Paul expected too much. We Christians have Christ, we have his example, his word, his sacraments.

The word of God is living and active;
it probes the thoughts and motives of our heart (Alleluia Verse).

Yes, but if we deliberately close our hearts to his love, even he can't open them. So please, all you hearts, stay open!

YEAR II

READING I Gal 5:1-6
GOSPEL Luke 11:37-41

Both of our readings today provide a double-barreled rejection of Phariseeism. A whole generation separates the Pharisees who attacked Jesus from those who were making trouble for Paul. In any century, including our own, it is the same old evil.

Paul again returns to his main argument: if the Judaizers look to the Law to make them just, then they have separated themselves from Christ. Jesus insists that the inner cleansing of the human heart is more important than the external cleanliness of cups and bowls. For both Paul and Jesus the conclusion is the same: what matters is faith that expresses itself in love. There is not a single person here, including myself, who does not need that advice. Lord, let your loving kindness come upon us all!

469 WEDNESDAY OF THE TWENTY-EIGHTH WEEK IN ORDINARY TIME

YEAR I

READING I Rom 2:1-11
GOSPEL Luke 11:42-46

It sounds as though St. Paul is attacking one of our favorite indoor sports—judging and condemning others. "Every one of you who judges another is inexcusable. By your judgment you convict yourself, since you do the very same things." And if you think that judging others (and may we not include gossiping about others?) is blameless or a minor sin, listen to Paul again: "Do you suppose, then, that you will escape his judgment, you who condemn these things in others yet do them yourself?" But it seems that no threat of punishment will make us stop judging others. We need a complete change of heart, a conversion, and Paul suggests the way to begin it: "Do you not know that God's kindness is an invitation to you to repent?" Only God can change our hearts, and he will do it if our desire for the change is as strong as his.

YEAR II

READING I Gal 5:18-25
GOSPEL Luke 11:42-46

As we hear our last selection from the Epistle to the Galatians, we can sum up Paul's doctrine: we do not save ourselves by obeying the Law; it is Christ who saves us by his death and resurrection. For Paul, obeying the Law is a characteristic of childhood. To become adult Christians, we have to grow out of the obedience-to-law mentality and learn to trust in Jesus. Paul would violently disagree with those Catholics who made obedience to the commandments the heart of religion. For him, the adult Christian is led by the Spirit. Adult Christianity is faith, trust, total gift of one's life into God's loving guidance. If you want to know the difference and contrast, recall Paul's words today: "Since we live by the spirit, let us follow the spirit's lead." It is never too late for us to begin living this new life.

470 THURSDAY OF THE TWENTY-EIGHTH WEEK IN ORDINARY TIME

YEAR I

READING I Rom 3:21-29
GOSPEL Luke 11:47-54

The theme of Reading I is one of Paul's favorites: redemption is a gift of Christ's spontaneous love for us. As the Responsorial Psalm has it, "With the Lord there is mercy, and fullness of redemption."

The gift is totally undeserved on our part. Paul says again, "We hold that a man is justified by faith apart from observance of the law." So we do not boast of our good deeds. Our only duty is to believe in the immensity of God's love for us and to respond to it in our lives, our attitudes:

I trust in the Lord;
my soul trusts in his word (Responsorial Psalm).

That is Christianity. But everything that Paul says in his epistles is summed up by Jesus in a single phrase: "I am the way, the truth, and the life, . . . no one comes to the Father, except through me" (Alleluia Verse). No way of ours can compare with his. It's time to get on it and follow him all the way.

YEAR II

READING I Eph 1:1-10
GOSPEL Luke 11:47-54

The overall theme of Ephesians is unity of the baptized in the risen Christ. Paul opens with a magnificent vision of Christ the Lord, a vision that needs to be compared to the humble man Jesus who walked the roads of Galilee. Today's Reading I contains the whole theology of the relationship between God and us. It tells us of our worth in the sight of God, of our having been chosen by God before the foundation of the world to be holy and blameless before him. God has loved us freely without any merit on our part, loved us as his very own children. In him we have redemption through his blood, the forgiveness of our trespasses according to the riches of his grace that he has lavished upon us. We catch a glimpse of God's eternal plan: to unite all things and all persons in Christ. We still have a long way to go, but even now we can sing to the Lord a new song, for he has done marvelous things.

471 FRIDAY OF THE TWENTY-EIGHTH WEEK IN ORDINARY TIME

YEAR I

READING I Rom 4:1-8
GOSPEL Luke 12:1-7

"Fear nothing, then. You are worth more than a flock of sparrows." So does Jesus reassure his hearers then and us now. It is an ancient, divine message to all mankind—an effort on God's part to establish the kind of relationship with us that God knows we need. Judging by the experience of people through the ages, including us, there is a kind of inner impulse in us to want to earn God's favor and protection by our deeds. It may well be one of the most mysterious effects of original sin. All of Jesus' life is a refutation of that kind of thinking. So too says the psalmist: "Lord, . . . you fill me with the joy of salvation." And especially Abraham, whose heroic faith remains the model for all of us. He believed, he trusted, he did not fear, he knew how much God loved him. Lord, let your mercy be on us, as we place our trust in you.

YEAR II

READING I Eph 1:11-14
GOSPEL Luke 12:1-7

"Happy the people the Lord has chosen to be his own," says the psalmist. Do we have any kind of realization of what it means to be chosen by God as his very own? Do we really *experience* that happiness? I do not believe we can call ourselves Christians without it. Too often Christian life is thought of as the carrying out of various religious practices and regulations. The Pharisees were great at that kind of religion. But Jesus tells us to beware of hypocrisy, the false external show of religion. True religion is based on trust in God's love, in joy at our having been chosen by God out of love. "Fear nothing, then, you are worth more than a flock of sparrows." May the Holy Spirit with whom we have been sealed increase the sense of that happiness in us all!

472 SATURDAY OF THE TWENTY-EIGHTH WEEK IN ORDINARY TIME

YEAR I

READING I Rom 4:13, 16-18
GOSPEL Luke 12:8-12

"The Lord remembers his covenant for ever" (Responsorial Psalm). And that forever includes now. We may forget him and his desire to give himself to us, but he never forgets, never takes back his forgiving love. "You descendants of Abraham, his servants, . . . He, the Lord, is our God" (Responsorial Psalm). God's approach to Abraham involved a request to leave his pleasant retirement and to launch out into the unknown future, and it included the promise that God would be with Abraham forever. Abraham obeyed, he trusted, he never hesitated, to put his life into God's hands and to take God into his life. As Paul puts it today, "Hoping against hope, Abraham believed," and as a result, he "became the father of many nations," including us. "All depends on faith, everything is a grace." That's the whole meaning of Christianity and Christian spirituality. All we need do is to open our hearts to that grace—to him who is *our* grace, Jesus the Lord.

YEAR II

READING I Eph 1:15-23
GOSPEL Luke 12:8-12

What a magnificent prayer: "May the God of our Lord Jesus Christ, the Father of glory, grant you a spirit of wisdom and insight to know him clearly" (Reading I). *Knowing* for Paul is not a matter of knowing or even understanding facts or truths; it's not knowledge of the mind but rather of the heart. Actually, it is the vivid experience of loving and being loved by God. We may all hope that Paul's prayer for us will be granted! Paul goes on to tell us: "He has put all things under Christ's feet and made him head of the church, which is his body: the fullness of him, who fills the universe in all its parts." So all created things contribute to the fullness of Christ. Therefore, the Church is not only people but also all of God's creation. That's really thrilling: it surely helps us to look with reverence and admiration on the world of nature around us. Is that hard to do?

146 TWENTY-NINTH SUNDAY IN ORDINARY TIME Cycle A

READING I Isa 45:1, 4-6 **READING II** 1 Thess 1:1-5
GOSPEL Matt 22:15-21

Reading I: God makes use of the pagan king Cyrus, conquerer of Babylon, to grant freedom to the captive Jews and allow them to return home.

Reading II: Paul thanks the convert Thessalonians for their fidelity and promises prayers that they will continue proving their faith.

Gospel: Trying to entrap Jesus, his enemies send messengers to ask him if it is lawful to pay tax to the emperor or not.

"Entrapment" has long been a favorite device for causing political enemies to lose credibility. Today's gospel is the latest in many efforts on the part of Jesus' enemies to entrap him so that they can deliver him over to the Roman emperor for punishment. Again, he refuses to be taken in; they cannot possibly argue with Jesus' response to their question: "Give to Caesar what is Caesar's but give to God what is God's."

That statement seems to touch on the issue of the relation of Church and State—a prominent issue in any year, especially one in which elections take place. One of the decisions of the bishops who gathered in Baltimore in 1884 was, "Do not in any way identify the interests of our holy Faith with the fortunes of any political party." The prominent Scripture scholar Bruce Vawter says that this passage in today's gospel is not the gospel's final word on Church and State. "The Gospel has no theology on Church and State" (*The Four Gospels,* Garden City, N.Y. Doubleday, 1967, 313).

For me, the real emphasis in Jesus' response in today's gospel is on "Give to God what is God's." This statement belongs to the context of his entire life and teaching, which is essentially that of restoring *the right order between creator and creature,* thus undoing the evil of the first Adam who wished to make himself the equal of God.

Give the Lord glory and honor (Responsorial Psalm).

Jesus' enemies try to trick him into declaring himself on a political matter. He in turn challenges them (and us) to declare themselves on the real issue—the creature's relationship to God, the creator. "Give to God what is God's." And what is that? Everything. "The earth and all its fullness." We—our life, our whole being.

> I am the Lord and there is no other,
> there is no God besides me (Reading I).

The image of a prominent political figure is stamped on the coins of our country. But each of us has another image stamped on our soul. In baptism we are stamped with the seal of Christ. Therefore, we belong to him, to our God, and it is God's will that we personally and deliberately render to God what is his—ourselves, our lives, our service now and forever, so that God may dispose of us as he desires.

"Give to God what is God's." No loopholes there, no deductions, no writeoffs.

> Lord our God, Father of all,
> you guard us under the shadow of your wings
> and search into the depths of our hearts.
> Remove the blindness that cannot know you
> and relieve the fear that would hide us from your sight (Alternative Opening Prayer).

"Give to God what is God's." This is the challenge Jesus presents to his enemies then and to us now. So we keep coming back to Jesus for the answers to all of life's problems. We follow him in his own total dedication of his life to the Father. And we make his dedication our own.

> Give to the Lord glory and honor.
> Give to the Lord, you families of nations, . . .
> give to the Lord the glory due his name! (Responsorial Psalm)

TWENTY-NINTH SUNDAY IN ORDINARY TIME

READING I Isa 53:10-11 **READING II** Heb 4:14-16
GOSPEL Mark 10:35-45

Reading I: A prophecy of the future suffering of the Servant of the Lord who will suffer and bear the guilt of many.

Reading II: Jesus, our great high priest, "was tempted in every way that we are, yet never sinned."

Gospel: James and John ask Jesus for privileged places in his kingdom; Jesus says that those who wish to be great must serve the needs of all.

What does it mean to be a Christian? We can find the answer to that important question in today's readings, especially in the example and words of Jesus. We see Jesus almost at the end of his way up to Jerusalem, his mind undoubtedly filled with what Isaiah had prophesied of him: he is to be crushed with infirmity and to surrender his life; he is to bear the guilt of all sinners of all time; but through his sufferings all peoples will have the freedom to be children of the Father.

Then come James and John. They have left all things to follow him, and now they want to know what's in it for them. The other apostles aren't any better. They are indignant that James and John got ahead of them. How patient Jesus is with them! "You do not know what you are asking. Can you drink the cup I shall drink or be baptized in the same bath of pain as I?" Jesus is applying to himself the servant song of Isaiah we have in Reading I: "The Lord was pleased to crush him in infirmity." In Gethsemani Jesus will pray: "Father, if it is your will, take this cup from me; yet not my will but yours be done" (Luke 22:42).

James and John tell Jesus that they can drink the cup. But they hardly understand its full meaning. It is time for Jesus to clarify for them, for all the apostles, *and for us,* what following him entails: "Anyone among you who aspires to greatness must serve the rest. . . . The Son of Man has not come to be served but to serve—to give his life in ransom for the many." Today's Responsorial Psalm provides us with the spirit in which we are to live our lives of service:

Lord, let your mercy be on us,
as we place our trust in you.

We must be convinced that salvation is God's work alone. We cannot earn it by anything we do, not even by an entire life of service. We can only open our hearts to it, receive it gratefully and lovingly, surrender to it.

Our life of service is our *personal response in love* to Christ's love for us, his gift of his life for us. We do not serve others in order to win divine favor as James and John wanted. We serve out of love as Jesus did. For Jesus it was through death to life; so it must be for us. We have to allow him to free us from any kind of self-seeking so that we can follow where he leads.

Christianity does not consist primarily in following a moral or ethical code; it does not involve abiding by a variety of external observances, as the chief priests followed the laws of Judaism. These observances are important and may not be downgraded. But they are to flow from something vastly more important, namely, surrender in love to Jesus' total self-surrender to the will of the Lord. "Let us confidently approach the throne of grace to receive mercy and favor and to find help in time of need" (Reading II).

Christianity is a pilgrimage, it is God's people following Christ, the new Moses, on a journey through life and often a way of the cross, to the Promised Land. It is listening to him, following his directions, following after him, even when the road ahead appears threatening and full of dangerous curves. Jesus the Lord is the all-important one on this journey. Our prayer for the way is always:

Lord, let your mercy be on us,
as we place our trust in you.
Our soul waits for the Lord,
who is our help and our shield.
May your kindness, O Lord, be upon us,
who have put our hope in you (Responsorial Psalm).

148 TWENTY-NINTH SUNDAY IN ORDINARY TIME — Cycle C

READING I **Exod 17:8-13** **READING II** **2 Tim 3:14–4:2**
GOSPEL **Luke 18:1-8**

Reading I: As long as Moses keeps his arms raised to God in prayer, his people are successful in battle.

Reading II: All Scripture is inspired by God; it is the source of wisdom. Paul charges Timothy to preach this inspired word always.

Gospel: To emphasize perseverance in prayer, Jesus tells the parable of the widow who refuses to give up demanding her rights.

I call upon you, God, for you will answer me; bend your ear and hear my prayer. Guard me as the pupil of your eye; hide me in the shade of your wings (Entrance Antiphon).

The lesson of Reading I and the gospel is perseverance in prayer. We must never become defeatist in our prayer of petition. As long as Moses keeps his arms raised in prayer to the Lord, his people are victorious in battle. When he drops his tired arms, they lose. Besides perseverance there are other important lessons in Reading I. It is obvious that God *wants* to hear us, but God obviously *wants to be asked.* Again, we note the importance of the sign of raised up hands. *Even wordless signs* can be prayer. Finally, the reading brings out the *importance of help* in prayer. Moses could not have kept his hands outstretched without the help of Aaron and Hur. The more help we get from others in our prayer, the more effective it will be.

"This widow is wearing me out," declares the corrupt judge in Jesus' parable. Well, we never wear God out, but again the obvious conclusion is that persistance is prayer's most necessary ingredient. We must never lose heart and never have any doubt about our personal worth.

God is good: that is the good news of the gospel. He is a generous Father who gives meaning and purpose to our lives. In the Alternative Opening Prayer we beg:

Lord our God, Father of all,
you guard me under the shadow of your wings
and search into the depths of our hearts.
Remove the blindness that cannot know you
and relieve the fear that would hide us from your sight.

There is a certain mysteriousness about prayer of petition. It doesn't change God; it changes *us.* God may not answer our prayers as we would like right now; God may have other objectives that are better for us in the long run.

Again, there is something deeper here than prayer of petition as it is usually understood. What Jesus really wants us to do when we pray is to desire God, to yearn for God with all the power of our hungry hearts.

> See how the eyes of the Lord are on those who fear him, on those who hope in his love, that he may rescue them from death and feed them in time of famine (Communion Antiphon).

God wants to give himself to us, to fulfill the deepest desires of our hearts, to make us whole. But God's self-giving depends on the depth, even the *passion,* of our desire for him. I do not want to underestimate the importance of prayer for all the needs of our lives, the needs of those who are dear to us, the needs of our Church. For example, can anything be more necessary in our days than prayer for vocations to the priesthood and religious life, prayer for the missions?

But we must never forget that the greatest need in all our lives is the gratification of the deepest hunger in the human heart—for the fullness of truth, life and above all, love; in a word, for the very God who is the fullness of truth, life, love.

> Our help is from the Lord
> who made heaven and earth (Responsorial Psalm).

473 MONDAY OF THE TWENTY-NINTH WEEK IN ORDINARY TIME

YEAR I

READING I Rom 4:20-25
GOSPEL Luke 12:13-21

Today Paul sums up all that Abraham was and has meant not only for his own people, but for us as well. "Abraham never questioned or doubted God's promise; rather, he was strengthened in faith and gave glory to God, . . . Thus his faith was credited to him as justice." And that precisely is the way Paul wants us to believe in Jesus, our Savior. Is he asking too much?

The rich man in the gospel, on the other hand, is a living example of how *not* to act as a Christian. Security is not to be found in what one has but what one is. And what a person is, or should be, is a child with hands and heart outstretched to the Father, trusting in his loving care as Abraham did. Lord, enlarge the barns of our hearts and fill them with an overflowing desire for your love. "Happy the poor in spirit; the kingdom of heaven is theirs" (Alleluia Verse).

YEAR II

READING I Eph 2:1-10
GOSPEL Luke 12:13-21

Today Jesus tells us, "Avoid greed in all its forms. A man may be wealthy, but his possessions do not guarantee him life." What then provides security in life? Apparently, not great possessions, which Jesus ridicules in this incident. I suspect that the answer is that a person's life is made secure by what that person *is* in the sight of God, not by what that person has. What a person is or should be is a child with hands and heart outstretched to the Father, trusting solely in the Father's loving care. To make ourselves rich in the sight of God, all we have to do is to empty ourselves of everything but our hunger for God. By grace we have been saved through faith—not because of works, lest any person boast.

The Lord made us, we belong to him (Responsorial Psalm).

474 TUESDAY OF THE TWENTY-NINTH WEEK IN ORDINARY TIME

YEAR I

READING I **Rom 5:12, 15, 17-19, 20-21**
GOSPEL **Luke 12:35-38**

Paul tells us today that Jesus is the second Adam, the new head of the human race. Sin and death entered humanity through the disobedience of the first Adam. Holiness and a sharing in divine life come to us through the obedience of Jesus, whose words are the guide of all our lives:

> Here am I, Lord;
> I come to do your will (Responsorial Psalm).

Does Jesus want fear of hell to motivate our preparedness for death? Hardly. The best preparation is loving desire for him. And that loving desire can come only from a loving intimacy that Jesus himself grants to those who learn how to keep their eyes fixed on him and the ears of their hearts open to him as he speaks and shows himself to us in these daily gospels and in prayer.

> Be watchful, pray constantly,
> that you may be worthy to stand before the Son of Man
> (Alleluia Verse).

Hunger, thirst, desire for Jesus is its own reward.

YEAR II

READING I **Eph 2:12-22**
GOSPEL **Luke 12:35-38**

Besides providing an excellent overview of the theology of redemption, Paul today also provides us with a perfect statement of the purpose and effects of the sacrament of reconciliation. In this sacrament Jesus breaks down the barriers which keep us apart from him and one another. The primary thrust of the renewed rite of reconciliation is to emphasize the communal nature both of sin and of reconciliation and to create a new person in Jesus by restoring peace through his cross, to unite all in a single body and to reconcile them to God. Reconciliation is not a sudden accomplished fact. It is a process that takes place slowly, personally, painfully. The external act of confessing one's sins privately or participating in a public penance service is terribly important—essential in furthering the process of conversion and reconciliation. The Lord speaks peace to his people, but we have to want that peace.

475 WEDNESDAY OF THE TWENTY-NINTH WEEK IN ORDINARY TIME

YEAR I

READING I **Rom 6:12-18**
GOSPEL **Luke 12:39-48**

Today Paul draws a personal consequence for us from the fact of Christ's having died for us: "Do not . . . let sin rule your mortal body and make you obey its lusts; . . . Rather, offer yourselves to God as men who have come back from the dead to life. . . ." We have been redeemed; it is up to us to stay redeemed. The best place to stay redeemed and to "offer ourselves to God" is at this altar, at the daily or weekly celebration of our redemption we know of as the Mass. The Christian life is not static. It is day by day growth in intimacy with Jesus and our fellow members of this redeemed body of Christ, the Church. Flannery O'Connor put it well: "I suppose it (the Church) is like marriage, that when you get into it, you find it the beginning, not the end, of the struggle to make love work." Our best help in making love work is the Eucharist.

YEAR II

READING I **Eph 3:2-12**
GOSPEL **Luke 12:39-48**

Today's Reading I is a perfect corrective for those who are enthusiastic about Christ but want to do without the Church. Paul would say that you cannot have Christ without the body of Christ, the Church. It is through the Church that "God's manifold wisdom" is made known everywhere. The Church is Christ, Christ is the Church, as the old saying goes. Whenever we are tempted to criticize the Church, especially the hierarchy, we need to remind ourselves that the Church is the living body of Christ. Christ is the head, we are the members, and the Holy Spirit is the life principle uniting us all together. If one member suffers, the whole body suffers. The sins of a single member diminish the health of the whole body. But if one member is glorified, the whole body rejoices.

> Shout with exultation, O city of Zion,
> for great in your midst
> is the Holy One of Israel! (Responsorial Psalm)

476 THURSDAY OF THE TWENTY-NINTH WEEK IN ORDINARY TIME

YEAR I

READING I Rom 6:19-23
GOSPEL Luke 12:49-53

Paul is still drawing conclusions from the fact of our having been redeemed by Christ. He knows all too well that we are weak and sin-inclined, still free to indulge ourselves shamefully. He can only hope that the grateful awareness of Christ's having made us new creatures in baptism will cause us to want to live up to our dignity. He reminds us that "The wages of sin is death, but the gift of God is eternal life in Christ Jesus our Lord." Eternal life—not just in the world to come, but even now.

> Happy the man who follows not
> the counsel of the wicked . . . ,
> But delights in the law of the Lord
> and meditates on his law day and night (Responsorial Psalm).

That kind of meditation on the Lord's law can well make us all want to make Paul's words our own: I count all things worthless but to gain Jesus Christ and to be found in him.

YEAR II

READING I Eph 3:14-21
GOSPEL Luke 12:49-53

In the gospel Jesus is stating a fact of life, but is not approving of it. In his lifetime and ever since, he has occasioned hatred and division. Christ's intention and desire is peace, but his very presence in our lives often causes harshness and pain. He does not will that pain, but is he to abstain from inviting followers because of it? Jesus always will disturb people. The demands of Christianity are not light. Christianity is not a cult of peace of mind, at least not before a decision and a struggle. But if Christ dwells in our hearts through faith, if we are rooted and grounded in love, if we really know the love of Christ that surpasses all knowledge, then we will be filled with all the fullness of God, and nothing else will matter.

477 FRIDAY OF THE TWENTY-NINTH WEEK IN ORDINARY TIME

YEAR I

READING I Rom 7:18-25
GOSPEL Luke 12:54-59

Paul must have had a bad day when he wrote today's passage from Romans. He had been speaking with such joy and confidence in his having been redeemed by Christ and now this! "What happens is that I do, not the good I will to do, but the evil I do not intend." Well, welcome to the human race, Paul! Paul is simply experiencing what we all go through. Though we are redeemed by Christ, there are apparently unredeemed areas in our personalities that still have to be rescued and elevated. We are still free. Life remains a struggle. It becomes more and more apparent that we need Christ and his grace, not just for the beginnings of salvation, but for the entire, lifelong experience. "What a wretched man I am! Who can free me from this body under the power of death? All praise to God, through our

Lord Jesus Christ!" Paul not only has the right ideas but the right words. For both we thank him.

YEAR II

READING I Eph 4:1-6
GOSPEL Luke 12:54-59

How eager are we to maintain the unity of the Spirit in the bond of peace? We can hardly lead a life worthy of our calling unless we make that effort. Paul reminds us again of who we are as members of Christ's body. There is one body and one Spirit—one life principle uniting us all together—there is one Lord, one faith, one baptism, one God and Father of us all who is above all and through all and in all. But that ideal has not been universally achieved. It has always been endangered precisely because Christians have generally not been eager to maintain the unity of the Spirit in the bond of peace. Whoever contributes to the division in denominations, in parishes, in families, in religious communities, retards the work of Christ. If we really wish to see the face of the Lord, let us come together!

478 SATURDAY OF THE TWENTY-NINTH WEEK IN ORDINARY TIME

YEAR I

READING I Rom 8:1-11
GOSPEL Luke 13:1-9

Paul reminds us again today that life is a constant conflict between the flesh and the spirit, as if we didn't know. We too often narrow the meaning of "flesh" to the appetites of the body, but "flesh" covers the possibility of sins of mind and heart as well as bodily appetites. To indulge in gossiping, slander, uncharitable thoughts and judgments, any kind of self-serving, is to indulge the flesh. Paul indicates that there is only one lasting remedy—allowing the Holy Spirit to flood our being. "If anyone does not have the Spirit of Christ, he does not belong to Christ." That's a statement that ought to make all of us ask ourselves what part the Holy Spirit has in our lives. A good test would be our desire (or lack thereof) for God. "Lord, this is the people that longs to see your face" (Responsorial Psalm). Come, Holy Spirit!

YEAR II

READING I **Eph 4:7-16**
GOSPEL **Luke 13:1-9**

In the Church each member is gifted in different ways by God. It would be a pretty dull group if every one were the same. The ideal proposed by Paul is that each of us develop his or her talents "to build up the body of Christ, till we become one in faith and in the knowledge of God's Son." Paul's (and Christ's) desire is that we all grow into mature and responsible members who are able to give a reason for our faith, who are secure in it, who, speaking the truth in love, contribute to the upbuilding of the Church in love.

If up to now we have lived our lives with no reference to building up the body of Christ, Jesus tells us in the gospel that it is never too late to begin. The fruit he expects of us is wholeness. May we not disappoint him!

149 THIRTIETH SUNDAY IN ORDINARY TIME — Cycle A

READING I **Exod 22:20-26** **READING II** **1 Thess 1:5-10**
GOSPEL **Matt 22:34-40**

Reading I: Some directives from God for good behavior towards aliens, widows, orphans, and neighbors.

Reading II: Paul praises the Thessalonians, who imitate the Lord and spread the good news to every region of their land.

Gospel: Wholehearted love for God and neighbor is Jesus' answer to the lawyer who asks Jesus which is the greatest commandment.

In *The Man on a Donkey,* H.M.S. Prescott describes a crucifix on the wall of a home as the image of a tormented man, nailed to a cross; and she says that "the people there lived comfortably with it, because they knew it too well to see it for what it was." Sometimes I wonder if the same judgment might not be made of us—not only about the crucifixes we live with but about the familiar sayings of Jesus in the Gospels as well. We hear them so often that they lose all meaning for us. We live too comfortably with them to understand them for what they are. Today's gospel might well be a typical example.

Another problem we Christians have is that, when Jesus tells us that we have to love God with all our hearts and our neighbor as ourselves, we do not know how to carry out the command. And we do not know how to love, primarily because we do not know Scripture well enough. Scripture tells us *that* God loves us and *how much* God loves us by revealing what God has done for us, especially in giving us Christ Jesus. And we see that object lesson of love every time we look at a cross, really look at it, and remember how undeserving of that love we are.

> Unless we believe in his love for us and are buoyed up by that assurance, we haven't started to be Christians. It's the first question we'll be asked on judgment day: "Did you believe that God loves you as an individual, that he knew you, desired you and waited for you day after day?" (Louis Evely, *That Man Is You,* Westminster, Md.: The Newman Press, 1963, 121)

Love for God on our part is *our responsiveness to God's having loved us.* Our love must be wholehearted; it is more than mere words. To say to God, I love you means admitting our dependence on God, acknowledging our poverty, agreeing that we are empty and in need of enrichment from someone greater than ourselves. Our responsiveness to God's love for us means living for God and allowing God to share with us his compassion and tenderness for the poor and unloved of our world: it is practical concern for the needs of others. Without a practical concern and caring for the unloved, our love for God is a sham.

There are two things to be said about us as God's special creation. First, God has made us *free,* and that means that we are capable of loving. Without freedom, love is impossible. Love cannot be forced from anyone; it cannot be acquired or bought by gifts. And unless we exercise our freedom by choosing to love, it will disappear, and we will run the risk of becoming mechanical men and women. That God has made us free, has made us in his own image, means that he shares with us his capability to love.

The second truth about us is that we are born incomplete human beings, and the only way to become complete and whole is by loving *and* allowing ourselves to be loved. The human heart cries out for love, and if love is denied it, its possessor will develop into a wounded, stunted person. It is dangerous to generalize, but we can wonder about the difficult people we have met and possibly have to deal with: did they as children have the love they needed in order to develop normally? We might also wonder about ourselves if we are hard to live with.

Contrariwise, if any one of us amounts to anything, if we have friends who enjoy being with us, if we are respected and esteemed, we most often have to attribute the credit to those who have trusted us, believed in us, loved us. Among that number, the one who has loved and trusted in us most of all is Jesus. The crucifix tells us that. May we never allow ourselves to live comfortably with it! And may our hearts always be open to that love!

We know by experience that love is the most difficult task in the world because it makes such strong demands on us. We know, too, that we are afraid to love because, as Father Adrian van Kaam writes, it means opening oneself to being hurt. Therefore there are few prayers that we need more than today's Opening Prayer, with which we begin this Eucharist:

> Almighty and ever-living God,
> strengthen our faith, hope and love.
> May we do with loving hearts
> what you ask of us
> and come to share the life you promise.
>
> I love you, Lord, my strength (Responsorial Psalm).

THIRTIETH SUNDAY IN ORDINARY TIME

READING I **Jer 31:7-9** **READING II** **Heb 5:1-6**
GOSPEL **Mark 10:46-52**

Reading I: God promises to bring the people back from captivity; he will console, guide and lead them home.

Reading II: Jesus is the divine high priest, our representative before God who offers sacrifice for our sins.

Gospel: Jesus restores sight to a blind beggar who calls out to him with faith.

It would seem that there is more symbolism in the eyes than in any other bodily organ, except perhaps the heart. Eyes provide vision. We see people. We see the glory of God reflected in the glory of nature, in sunrises and sunsets, in rainbows and clouds. And when we see all the beauty in our world and in the universe, we are filled with the blessed grace of a sense of wonder, awe, gratitude, joy.

This natural vision is a sign of a deeper, more glorious vision—an insight into the glory of God, creator of all beauty, into the meaning of life and our relationship with Jesus, Son of God, Savior.

Correspondingly, there are several kinds of blindness. There is the blindness of those who are born without sight or those who lose their sight and who therefore need implants and glasses of varying strength. And then there is the spiritual blindness of those who do not wish to see any meaning in life, those who have no spiritual values, no spiritual vision, are self-centered and self-satisfied, blind to the needs of the poor, concerned only with self and self-advancement.

Recall the sons of Zebedee in last Sunday's gospel. They wanted the first places in Christ's kingdom. They had been with Jesus for almost three years, but they did not see him for what he really was; they did not know him.

Bartimaeus, the blind man of today's gospel, is a symbol of all the people in this world who want to see Jesus, of those who wish for a deeper vision of reality, of meaning for their lives. Blind people cannot see Jesus because the seeing Christians fail to show Jesus to them.

"What do you want me to do for you?" Jesus asks the blind man. "Rabboni," the blind man says, "I want to see." With that desire, the man opened his whole being to Jesus, and that is precisely what *faith* means; that is the heart of Christian spirituality.

"Be on your way," says Jesus. "Your faith has healed you." And immediately he received his sight and started to follow him up the road—up the road to Jerusalem, to Calvary, to resurrection.

Bartimaeus' sight is restored by Jesus. But there is something deeper here. It is that *God sought Bartimaeus first.* That is why God sent Jesus to him. Jesus is the everlasting sacrament, the sign, of God's seeking us and all who are in need of the vision of God, and that includes everyone everywhere. And once God finds us, or once we allow God to find us and we decide to follow Jesus up the road, we too become what Jesus was: missionaries, signs of God's seeking others through us.

The Thirtieth Sunday in Ordinary Time is usually "Mission Sunday" in our country. Special collections are taken up in our parishes with good reason, because missionaries are women and men *in need.* They preach the gospel and make converts, but they also help the natives of the particular country to live more humane lives. They teach them in schools, help them to cultivate their land, dig wells, build bridges. Missionaries abroad and in our own land *never* have sufficient finances to do full justice to their work of bringing Christ to people in need of him.

And there never are enough missionaries. You do not have to be a priest or a Sister to be a missionary. In our time more and more laypeople—couples, students, doctors, nurses, and other professional people are dedicating one or several years of their lives to work in the missions, either at home in our country or in the Third World. Without exception they find that time the most satisfying and joyous period of their lives.

The world is full of blind people of all ages crying out to Jesus, "I want to see!" Jesus now depends on men and women who are willing to become other Christs for these blind children of God. (If any of you are willing to answer Christ's call, see your pastor.)

The great majority of Catholics, however, cannot go to the missions because they are raising families, or they are members of religious orders engaged in different kinds of religious activity equally necessary for carrying on Christ's mission. Their missionary effort must be of a different nature: offering God their work, their sufferings, their old age, and eventually their dying for missionaries and their work. Every Christian must be mission minded. Concern for the missions is essential for anyone who wants to be known as a Christian.

The Lord has done great things for us;
we are filled with joy (Responsorial Psalm).

The Lord wants to do great things *through* us, and we will be filled with even more joy.

ALTERNATE FOR THIRTIETH SUNDAY IN ORDINARY TIME Cycle B

A SENSE OF WONDER

The sense of wonder in a person is essential to religious development and spirituality. The experience of wonder lifts a person out of her or his ordinariness and carries that person into the sphere of the Lord God, creator of all that is. Sacred Scripture is permeated with the human response of awe and wonder at the glorious works of God. The psalmist says: "The Lord has done great things for us" (Responsorial Psalm). "O Lord, our Lord, how glorious is your name over all the earth" (Ps 8).

"The wondrous voice of God was found in all things, great and small, in the resounding storm and the gentle breeze, in the pomp and ritual of the temple" (author unknown). In wonder at the deeds of Jesus, in the apostles' "amazement went beyond all bounds: 'He has done everything well! He makes the deaf hear and the mute speak' " (Mark 7:37).

Most children have this sense of wonder, which *may* be one of the reasons why Jesus told us that we have to become like little children. Unfortunately, many of them are on their way to losing it before they grow up, mainly because the potential wonder in them is deadened by too much TV, or it is not encouraged by insensitive parents or teachers, for whom facts are more important.

But what is wonder? It is a combination of amazement, delight, surprise, fantasy, and awe that makes a person want to cry out in praise and joy. Do you wonder if it is possible to be genuinely religious without wonder? You may recall the song that was popular some years ago:

> Take care to wonder at the world through which you wander;
> never hurry by an open door;
> for we live in a universe full of miracles galore.

Wonder arises only from those who see more deeply and have a clearer vision of scenes and all manifestations of beauty than what appears on the surface. They see behind and below and above external appearances. There is an old medieval tale about two men who were mixing mud that was to be used in building a cathedral. When asked what they were doing, one of them replied: "Can't you see? I'm mixing mud." The other said, "I'm building a great cathedral." Some people see mud. Others envision greatness. "Master, I want to see!"

There may be students who, if asked what they are doing in college, would reply, "I'm working for a degree so that I can get a good job." And we cannot fault him or her for that ambition. But I hope that more deeply in their minds there is a nobler ambition which will enable them to say, "I'm building the cathedral of my mind, my heart, my whole personality."

Here are some hints that might help us to foster a sense of wonder. We need, first of all, to develop a deep reverence and respect for all things, especially for all persons. For as Christians we believe that the God who made all things and all persons sees that they are good (see Gen 1:31), and he loves and respects them.

Then we can try to develop more and more our capacity for surprise at beauty and goodness wherever they are found. Surprise and delight—that's what wonder really is. We can also use more optimism than is customary with many Christians. It must be difficult, if not impossible, for a pessimist to have a sense of wonder. The person who can wonder is one who sees good in everything and is amazed at how much good and beauty there really is in our world. We take it for granted that the mountains are beautiful, but there is also beauty even in a desert or the vista of distance beyond distance, in rolling plains. But if we have difficulty finding it in these places, we can always wait till the stars appear in the night sky.

It is tragic not to develop the potential sense of wonder in all of us, but even more tragic to lose it; for then we become the prey to despair, dejection, loss of hope. In *The Man of La Mancha,* when Don Quixote looks into the mirror and sees only his aged self and consequently loses his noble vision, at once he starts to die.

Please God that will never happen to any of us here, no matter how old we may be in years. And it will not happen if we make up our minds to keep our eyes fixed on Jesus, who has done great things for us and continues to do great things. Jesus who always answers our prayer for vision with the assurance, "Go, your faith has saved you." I am sure that he will not mind if we also believe that our sense of wonder, permeated with grateful love, has helped along.

"Take care to wonder at the world through which you wander."

151 THIRTIETH SUNDAY IN ORDINARY TIME Cycle C

READING I Sir 35:12-14, 16-18 **READING II** 2 Tim 4:6-8, 16-18
GOSPEL Luke 18:9-14

Reading I: The Lord, a God of justice, hears the cry of the oppressed and the wail of the orphan.

Reading II: Paul writes to Timothy from prison; he reviews his life and awaits his reward. Though abandoned by friends, the Lord stands by him.

Gospel: "Everyone who exalts himself shall be humbled while he who humbles himself shall be exalted."

The lesson of today's gospel is needed by almost every follower of Christ; there may be a bit of the Pharisee in us all. The one in today's gospel placed his trust in himself and in the exact fulfillment of the six-hundred-odd demands of the Law (as interpreted by the scholars). The tax collector placed his trust exclusively in God's forgiving mercy. The Pharisee *thought* he was rich in God's sight; the tax collector *knew* he was poor and in need of divine mercy. He went home justified, reconciled with God, for

The Lord hears the cry of the poor (Responsorial Psalm).

But the world is full of another kind of poor in addition to those who live destitute lives with little or no means of sustaining their physical life. This kind of poor includes those who have never heard of Christ, who do not know him, whose lives have never in any way been influenced by him. Today is Mission Sunday, and we have to think about all those people today. Actually, the claim might be made that it is impossible to be a true follower of Christ and not be deeply concerned about contributing to his essential work—bringing the good news of God's love to all peoples.

Jesus himself was the first missionary. He was sent into the mission field of the world by his Father, who so loved the world that he gave his only Son to reconcile it to himself. The Son in turn so loved the world that he gave his life, he died and rose from the dead out of love for all peoples everywhere. And then he sent his apostles to carry on his work and ever since there have been more and more "sendings." The missionary movement had its origin in the very heart of God.

As Jesus was a missionary, so too is his Church. And as followers of Christ, members of his Church, it is our nature to have the mind of Christ. It is necessary to be mission minded not just on Mission Sunday but always.

What do missionaries do? They preach the gospel. They bring the Church with the sacraments and the Word of God to pagan peoples. They also strive, like the first apostles, to form worshiping communities, which in turn spread the gospel and attract new members by their mutual love.

But missionaries also see their work as including not only the care of souls but of the whole person, soul *and* body. This is not a new idea. It was Jesus' concern, too: recall the many miracles of bodily healing he worked. Missionaries are concerned not only with preparing people for the world to come but also with making it possible for them to live decent, human lives in *this* world. Missionaries maintain schools, they help people cultivate the land, they build roads and bridges and hospitals.

Another characteristic of modern missionary work is that it recognizes that the people of Third World countries need not give up their native cultures, languages, customs in order to be Catholic. Pope Paul VI was the first modern pope to recognize this fact. "You may, you must, have an African Christianity," he told the people in one of the nations of that continent some years ago.

All this means that the Church is being enriched by the native cultures of these countries. It is not only giving, it is also *receiving*—and thus is becoming more and more catholic, that is, universal.

What can we do for the missions? The main emphasis today, of course, is to contribute what we can to the financial upkeep of the missions, the missionaries, and the people they serve. *No* mission anywhere ever has enough. Thank God, American Catholics have always been generous. And it isn't only the foreign missions that need help. Almost every day pastors receive pleading letters from Indian, Black, and inner-city missionaries in our own country.

So we give what we can, but once we have given, we don't stop thinking in a missionary manner. I repeat: if we are a Christian, we must be a missionary at heart. And there may even be some who could consider giving a year or so of their lives to become missionaries themselves. Not even invalids or the aged are exempt from helping the missions. Their lives of suffering can be offered as a powerful prayer for the missions.

You may recall last Sunday's reading about Moses. As long as Aaron and Hur held up his arms, the people were victorious in battle. Anyone who suffers, especially invalids and the aged, can hold up the arms of our missionaries and so help them in carrying on Christ's mission.

> The Lord hears the cry of the poor (Responsorial Psalm).

Missionaries have heard the cry of the poor. Can we also hear it?

479 MONDAY OF THE THIRTIETH WEEK IN ORDINARY TIME

YEAR I

READING I **Rom 8:12-17**
GOSPEL **Luke 13:10-17**

Paul tells us today that we are adopted children of God. When a human parent adopts a child, he does not give the child its life, but only his name and a right to become his heir. But God's adoption is greater. The Father gives us his own life. Jesus is the only begotten Son of the Father, but we are baptized into his body and share in the very life that is in him. We also receive the Holy Spirit, and by reason of his presence we know we are truly loved by the Father. Our old life of sin is—or ought to be—past. "If we are children, we are heirs as well: heirs of God, heirs with Christ, if only we suffer with him so as to be glorified with him." Does the awareness of our divine adoption make any difference in our spiritual life? Or do we rather think and act like orphans who have never known a parent's love?

YEAR II

READING I **Eph 4:32–5:8**
GOSPEL **Luke 13:10-17**

The gospel shows the ridiculous limits to which Phariseeism can lead its adherents. The Pharisees object to Christ's healing of a woman who had been sick for eighteen years. Their essential mistake was in thinking you could legislate morality, set up a system of rules, and people will be religious if they obey them. They themselves observed all the rules, but were they religious?

Paul has a different system: tell people who and what they are as members of Christ's body: you are the beloved children of God, he says. Therefore, act out of the fullness of your being. Live and act according to what you are. God has loved you; respond to his love by loving one another. "Be kind to one another, compassionate, and mutually forgiving, just as God has forgiven you in Christ. . . . There was a time when you were in darkness, but now you are light in the Lord." Paul is telling us to walk as children of light. Is that expecting too much?

480 TUESDAY OF THE THIRTIETH WEEK IN ORDINARY TIME

YEAR I

READING I Rom 8:18-25
GOSPEL Luke 13:18-21

"The sufferings of the present [are] as nothing compared with the glory to be revealed in us." That's a comforting thought, but what follows is exciting and fascinating. Paul seems to say that all of creation in some way shared in the fall of our first parents and is in need of redemption. And even though Jesus has redeemed us and creation and reconciled us to the Father, redemption still has to become operative in us and in creation itself. "We know that all creation groans and is in agony even until now . . . we ourselves . . . groan inwardly while we await the redemption of our bodies. In hope we were saved." All this might well be what Jesus is hinting at when he says that the kingdom of God is like yeast kneaded into the flour "until the whole mass of dough begins to arise." Paul is right when he says, "I consider the sufferings of the present to be as nothing compared with the glory to be revealed in us" and in the world in which we live. Do you think you can wait?

YEAR II

READING I Eph 5:21-33
GOSPEL Luke 13:18-21

This passage from Ephesians 5 gets Paul into a lot of trouble with women, for many of whom he is a terrible chauvinist. In judging him, we must not forget that he was reflecting attitudes prevalent in his time. Actually, what Paul is doing here it trying to help the Ephesians (and us) understand more about the nature of the Church as Christ's body. He uses the most intimate of all human unions, that between a loving husband and a loving wife, to show the relationship between Christ and his Church. "This is a great foreshadowing; I mean that it refers to Christ and the church." Paul really places the greater burden on husbands: they are to love their wives "as Christ loved the church." Love like that equalizes persons so that they are no longer male and female, they are both equally one in the body of Christ, as he says in Galatians (3:28). "Defer to one another out of reverence for Christ" (Reading I). That's for us all!

481 WEDNESDAY OF THE THIRTIETH WEEK IN ORDINARY TIME

YEAR I

READING I Rom 8:26-30
GOSPEL Luke 13:22-30

Reading I speaks of "predestination," a scary word for many Christians who believe that God has already decided that some of us are going to be saved and some damned and there's nothing we can do about it. Not so. No one is damned except through that person's malicious free choice. God *wills* all people to be saved, and "the Spirit too helps us in our weakness . . . the Spirit himself makes intercession for us with groanings which cannot be expressed in speech." That's pretty powerful praying. Moreover, Paul reminds us, "We know that God makes all things work together for the good of those who have been called."

In the gospel Jesus is also concerned about salvation; his answer to the question about the number of the saved may sound harsh, even out of character for him. He is simply telling us to take advantage of the graces he won for us by his death and resurrection. He died for the salvation of all. But if we reject his salvation, that's our funeral.

YEAR II

READING I Eph 6:1-9
GOSPEL Luke 13:22-30

You would look in vain if you tried to find any justification in St. Paul for an authoritarian and harsh attitude toward children or servants. Paul accepts the fact of slavery that prevailed in the civilizations of those days; but his accepting slaves as persons and as equal members of the body of Christ, each one loved and redeemed by Christ, was an important step in the eventual liberation of slaves.

Then as now, mutual respect for the dignity of every person flows naturally from membership in Christ's body. There is no partiality with the Lord, who is Master both of the free and the enslaved.

Mutual respect for persons is the best way to come to know Christ and—best of all—to be known and recognized by him when the time for our judgment arrives. The Lord is faithful in all his words.

482 THURSDAY OF THE THIRTIETH WEEK IN ORDINARY TIME

YEAR I

READING I Rom 8:31-39
GOSPEL Luke 13:31-35

Paul gets carried away today, and we ought to let him take us with him in his flight of love. "Who will separate us from the love of Christ?" he cries, and he lists all the possibilities that cannot separate us. But there is one thing that *can* prevent Christ's love from entering our lives: it is our own perversity, our own deliberate, free decision. Selfishness, self-pity, vanity, and above all, indifference can turn us from him, make us sidestep his open arms and heart. We are all old enough to know that we are our own worst enemies. Such is the awesomeness and wonder of human freedom. But we reflect that were it not possible for us to resist love, we could never be capable of receiving and returning it. May we always give thanks to the Lord for everything: for the love he continues to hold out to us and also for the wonder of our being!

YEAR II

READING I Eph 6:10-20
GOSPEL Luke 13:31-35

Paul's final instruction to the Ephesians and to us is a warning against the attacks of the powers of darkness and the fatal attractions of worldliness. He uses the image of a Roman soldier's equipment to describe the Christian's best protection: armor, breastplate, boots, shield, and helmet refer to spiritual qualities like truth, the word of God, a living faith in one's being loved by God, and above all, a living spirit of prayer.

We all know from personal experience how crucial Paul's warning is. Without prayer and meditation on God's word as daily nourishment for a lively faith, we can easily slip away into the captivity and destruction that Paul warns about today. Christ has done everything for us, but we can throw it all away through carelessness. May we never forget:

> Blessed be the Lord, my Rock! (Responsorial Psalm)

483 FRIDAY OF THE THIRTIETH WEEK IN ORDINARY TIME

YEAR I

READING I **Rom 9:1-5**
GOSPEL **Luke 14:1-6**

> Praise the Lord, Jerusalem.
> He has proclaimed his word to Jacob,
> his statutes and his ordinances to Israel.
> He has not done this for any other nation (Responsorial Psalm).

Paul, this former Pharisee, adds other Jewish favors from the Lord: the covenants, the adoption, the glory, the worship, the promises, the patriarchs. From them came Jesus, the Messiah, Savior of the entire world. He is torn by two loves—for his people and for the Jesus whom they rejected. The degree of his love for the Jewish people is underscored by his admission that he would "even wish to be separated from Christ for the sake of . . . the Israelites." But it was not to be, at least in Paul's lifetime. Paul will be coming back to this problem tomorrow. I suspect he is still praying for his people and that some day his prayer will be answered.

YEAR II

READING I Phil 1:1-11
GOSPEL Luke 14:1-6

Today we begin Philippians, perhaps St. Paul's warmest, most loving epistle. Today's reading is mainly a greeting, but it contains deep theological insights. He says: "I am sure . . . that he who has begun the good work in you will carry it through to completion, right up to the day of Christ Jesus." This good work is that of God's grace in us—it is union with Christ and other members of the body of Christ. It implies growth, a flowering that should never end. He goes on to pray that our love for one another will more and more abound and improve our knowledge and deepen our discernment. This is striking—the idea that love can improve knowledge. Ordinarily we think of it the other way around. But there is no contradiction, since there is knowledge of the heart as well as of the head. We need both, but most of all we need to hold one another in our hearts as Paul did.

484 SATURDAY OF THE THIRTIETH WEEK IN ORDINARY TIME

YEAR I

READING I Rom 11:1-2, 11-12, 25-29
GOSPEL Luke 14:1, 7-11

"The Lord will not abandon his people" (Responsorial Psalm). True, many of the Jews rejected Christ, but their rejection does not mean that God has rejected them. Paul makes the point that the unbelief of Israel has brought salvation to the Gentiles. Paul foresees a time when in God's design Israel will ultimately accept the gospel and as the New American Bible says, their acceptance of Christ will benefit the world even more than their original unbelief. Israel remains dear to God; it is still the object of his special providence, the mystery of which will one day be revealed. God forgive Christians for the anti-Semitism of history and whatever prejudices we still retain against the people who gave us Jesus, Mary, and the apostles. May we never forget the words of Pope Pius XI: "We are all spiritually Semites."

YEAR II

READING I **Phil 1:18-26**
GOSPEL **Luke 14:1, 7-11**

Today's Reading I gives us some idea of how much Christ means to Paul, how very much he loves him. "To me, 'life' means Christ," he says, and the New American Bible comments: "Both life and death take their meaning from Christ." Paul is drawn by two loves: for Christ and for his people. He longs to be with Christ, but he realizes that his people need him; and if he remains with them and works for them, he can help them love Christ more; he can multiply and magnify human love for Jesus. Love has driven him throughout his apostolate: now at the end, that love is overpowering. If all Christians had that kind of love, the world would long ago have become Christ's. "My soul is thirsting for the living God," says the psalmist today. May the thirst for God in Paul's heart overpower us, too!

152 THIRTY-FIRST SUNDAY IN ORDINARY TIME — Cycle A

READING I **Mal 1:14–2:2, 8-10** **READING II** **1 Thess 2:7-9, 13**
GOSPEL **Matt 23:1-12**

Reading I: The Lord is displeased with the people who returned from Babylon for turning away from him and making void the covenant.

Reading II: Paul reviews his joyous life of service to the Thessalonians and thanks God for their openness to his preaching.

Gospel: Jesus again condemns the externalism of the Pharisees and Scribes: "All their works are performed to be seen."

Jesus' opposition to the scribes and Pharisees reaches its climax in the final week before they condemn him to death. He tells his disciples: "Observe everything they tell you. But do not follow their example. . . . All their works are performed to be seen." These religious leaders sought human prestige rather than the divine will. They talked a good game of religious observance but never showed it in their lives. Actually, they led a double life: they demanded from the people religious observance that they failed to fulfill themselves.

In the very religious ceremonies which had originally been intended to give glory to God, they assumed glory for themselves; they exalted themselves, not God. The heart of religion has to be in the human heart, not in fancy external observance. "True worship is an act of love," says Father Beck, "and to love is to know what the Loved One wants."

We have heard all this before, again and again. Why is it all that necessary? Do we think Jesus intended his words only for the Pharisees of his own time and that they have no relevance to our lives? Or that Christ intends his warnings only for the hierarchy and clergy of the Church and not for the laity and religious? It would be a serious mistake to draw any such conclusions. The Church officials may be the most in danger. But legalism and hypocrisy are human failings, and we are all human.

Jesus is so vehemently opposed to the Pharisaic way primarily because it contradicts all that he was in himself and all that he came to accomplish in the world, namely, to reestablish the creator as the Lord of life, as the one Supreme Being in the minds and hearts of all peoples. In a word, Jesus came to undo the evil of the first Adam, who chose self rather than God, who wanted to be like unto God, who by his sin he became the root cause of all subsequent evil in the world.

The purpose of worship at the time of Christ and now is to intensify our relationship as creatures with God our creator, to make us realize in our inmost being that God alone is the supreme and only Lord of our lives. To make that sublime action into an occasion for self-exaltation is idolatry.

So Jesus' harshness with the Pharisaic mind was not just resentment on his part. The truth is that they were destroying themselves, and by their example they were helping others in every age to destroy themselves. Jesus died for them as well as for the innocent; and on the cross he was to pray, "Father, forgive them; they do not know what they are doing" (Luke 23:34).

The liturgies of these last Sundays of the Church Year have been and will continue to be challenges to all of us to repentance, to conversion, to preparing ourselves for our encounter with Christ at life's end. Jesus' plea for repentance—to the Pharisees then and to us now—is not *primarily* to do good deeds and to pray more (no harm in that, of course), but to *re-center our lives on God,* to recognize in our heart of hearts our total *dependence on God.*

And from centering our life on God flows our attitude of loving care for others. That's precisely what Christ did. He gave his entire life over to the Father. He cared for all who were in need of any kind. "Only one is your teacher, the Messiah. The greatest among you will be the one who serves the rest. Whoever exalts himself shall be humbled, but whoever humbles himself shall be exalted." This is the gospel of the Lord!

153 THIRTY-FIRST SUNDAY IN ORDINARY TIME Cycle B

READING I **Deut 6:2-6** **READING II** **Heb 7:23-28**
GOSPEL **Mark 12:28-34**

Reading I: Moses gives the people the great Jewish prayer, the Shema: "Hear, O Israel! The Lord is our God, the Lord alone!"

Reading II: Jesus' priesthood does not pass away. He lives forever to make intercession for us.

Gospel: Asked which is the first of all the commandments, Jesus simply repeats the familiar Shema, first proclaimed by Moses.

Many years ago I read about a little girl who made up her own night prayer. She thanked God for all the people in her family and school, naming them one by one. She thanked God for all the nice things that happened that day: for her birthday, for spring and flowers. But when she was tired, she simply tumbled into bed and said, "Thank you, God, for God!"

Maybe she had the secret of all prayer, the secret for knowing how to fulfill the greatest commandment of the Law. Because God is God, we have to, want to, love him with our whole being. Because

God is God, we have to thank God for being God, we have to, want to, thank God for the being we have from God.

Why does God command us to love him? Not because he needs our love. We recall the words of Weekday Preface IV:

> You have no need of our praise,
> yet our desire to thank you is itself your gift.
> Our prayer of thanksgiving adds nothing to your greatness,
> but makes us grow in your grace.

We could also say, "You have no need of our *love.*"

Love makes us grow and mature. We cannot be complete human persons without it. We come into the world as incomplete beings. The only way to be fully grown up is in and through loving and allowing ourselves to be loved; loving God, neighbor, loved ones, self. Our hearts are stretchable: the more love expands them, the more human, indeed, the more like unto God we become. Without love given and accepted we are mental invalids. Without love, life has no meaning, no direction. Because God is God, our Creator, each of us is worthwhile, precious, deserving of being loved. Thank you, God, for making us the way you did!

We are deeply aware of our need to love and to be loved. The problem is: how do we do it? The Bible might have the answer. Moses gave the people this great commandment only after God had delivered them from years of desperate slavery in Egypt. Remembering God's great goodness and favors is one of the best ways for learning true love for God. The Old Testament, especially the Book of Psalms, is full of lovely expressions of God's love for us, and it would be hard to improve on those human expressions of love for God. In the Book of Jeremiah, God says to his people:

> With age-old love I have loved you;
> so I have kept my mercy toward you (31:3).

And we reply with the words of the psalmist:

> I love you, O Lord, my strength,
> O Lord, my rock, my fortress, my deliverer (Ps 18:1).

How do we love? Parents do not tell their children how to love them. A child's love is instinctive when she or he *experiences, feels* the joy of being loved and cared for. So, too, the love between spouses. One fact is certain: when you love, there is more to you than there was before you gave and received love.

Mother Teresa has said: "The world is suffering much, because of a terrible disease. But this is not hunger or leprosy; it is suffering from the lack of the feeling of being wanted, of being loved, of being someone to somebody." Do we have to look far in any family, any parish, any town, for persons in that kind of need?

There can be no thinking or speaking of love without some reflection on love of neighbor. Jesus tells us today, "This is the second (commandment), you shall love your neighbor as yourself." And St. John tells us: "If anyone says, 'My love is fixed on God,' yet hates his brother, he is a liar' " (1 John 4:20). Love of neighbor cannot exist without forgiveness. And forgiving love is the most difficult challenge in our lives. But it is impossible to love God without it. It is also impossible without God's help. That is why we pray in Eucharistic Prayer II: "Make us grow in love." Not "help us," but "make us." And God does precisely that, for, as St. Paul writes: "The love of God has been poured out in our hearts through the Holy Spirit who has been given to us" (Rom 5:5). So, if we have difficulty practicing forgiving love, why not let the Holy Spirit do it in and through us? Why not open our hearts to the Spirit?

Loving both God and neighbor is hard because it makes such difficult demands on us. Arriving at perfect love is a lifetime work. It is never easy to empty oneself, to give oneself away, and that is precisely what love requires of us. We are also afraid to love because, as Fr. Adrian van Kaam writes, opening oneself to love means opening oneself to being hurt.

We cannot live in this world—and certainly not in the world to come—without love. So we may as well accept the word of the scribe in today's gospel: "He (God) is the One, there is no other than he. Yes, to love him with all our heart, with all our thoughts and with all our strength, and to love our neighbor as ourselves, is worth more than any burnt offering or sacrifice."

Thank you, God, for God. Thank you for this most essential of all your teachings! Help us, make us, grow in love.

THIRTY-FIRST SUNDAY IN ORDINARY TIME

READING I Wis 11:22–12:1 **READING II** 2 Thess 1:11–2:2
GOSPEL Luke 19:1-10

Reading I: All things belong to God, the lover of souls, and God overlooks the sins of people that they may repent.

Reading II: The Thessalonians believed that Jesus would be returning soon and Paul begs them not to be agitated or terrified.

Gospel: Jesus invites himself to spend a day with Zacchaeus and defends himself when the people murmur that he is a guest at a sinner's house.

Jesus must surely have smiled, even laughed a little, when he looked up into that sycamore tree and saw that small, well-dressed man peering at him through the leaves. Zacchaeus is a hated tax collector for the Romans, a public sinner who has become rich in his position. And obviously despised by his fellow Jews. *But he wants to see Jesus.*

Why does he want to see Jesus? Well, he has heard that Jesus is a wonder worker, a most extraordinary man. So naturally, he is curious. But there is more in him than human curiosity. Zacchaeus is a type of every person who has ever lived. Of course, he has everything that most people desire and work for: wealth, security, a nice home, and all that he needs to sustain himself. But he is not satisfied. He wants, he needs more. So he climbs that tree and waits for Jesus. Jesus is the "more" that his hungry heart had desired.

And Jesus does not disappoint him. He looks up and sees the sinful tax collector. "Zacchaeus, hurry down," he says. "I mean to stay at your house today." Zacchaeus joyfully obeys. The hunger in his heart is already becoming satisfied. Full satisfaction will come when he eats with Jesus, listens to him, makes up his mind that in this man all his human desires and hopes are fulfilled.

The Pharisees, of course, are shocked. "He has gone to a sinner's house as a guest," they complain. They hardly realize that they could not have said anything more complimentary, more beautiful, more descriptive of Jesus, the God-man! Jesus defends himself: "Today salvation has come to this house, for this is what it means to be a son of Abraham. The Son of Man has come to search out and save what was lost."

The story of Zacchaeus is the drama of life. It illustrates and plumbs the depths of our existence. The human heart has an insatiable hunger for fulfillment, for joy and satisfaction that only the God who created the heart can gratify. And God is always trying to do just that. God seeks us more than we seek God. God seeks us even *before* we seek him. If Zacchaeus climbed that tree it was God's seeking that had driven the sinful tax collector up into the tree.

When the human person's search for God and God's search for that person coincide, or when the human person slows down and allows God to catch him or her—that is salvation, that is redemption. That's what Jesus Christ is all about. Jesus inviting himself to be a guest in the house of the tax collector was a redemptive act.

The Pharisees say: "He has gone to a sinner's house as a guest." I wonder if this might be the origin of the name "Sinners' Church," which is one of the glories of Catholicism. Dr. Eugene Kennedy writes that the Catholic Church is a family: "It makes room for everybody because in the end it is the home of sinners."

I hope that all of us will always feel at home in this old family. The Food and the Drink are the best: it is Christ himself in the Eucharist. And the company is good, too, and always fascinating, with its combination of sinners and saints, with Jesus as our permanent guest.

May the desire to see Jesus grow in all our hearts, for now we know where we can be sure to find him: in Zacchaeus' house, in this parish family, in this old Church, the home of sinners! "You spare all things, because they are yours, O Lord and lover of souls." (Reading I).

> Lord, you will show me the path of life and fill me with joy in your presence (Communion Antiphon).

485 MONDAY OF THE THIRTY-FIRST WEEK IN ORDINARY TIME

YEAR I

READING I Rom 11:29-36
GOSPEL Luke 14:12-14

In the gospel our Lord continues explaining true hospitality. It is easy and pleasant to give parties and dinners for close friends and loved ones. But the one who really wishes to be God-like has to open his or her heart and table to the others: the poor, the lame, the blind. True charity does not look for any rewards or return invitations.

It is difficult to follow Paul's reasoning when he tries to explain justification for the Roman Christians as being the result of the Jews' rejection of Jesus. Even the commentators have difficulty here. What is essential to remember is God's saving mercy for all. We can settle for Paul's magnificent cry of wonder at God's mysterious ways: "How deep are the riches and the wisdom and the knowledge of God! How inscrutable his judgments, how unsearchable his ways! . . . For from him and through him and for him all things are: To him be glory forever. Amen." That's a grand prayer for any occasion.

YEAR II

READING I Phil 2:1-4
GOSPEL Luke 14:12-14

Paul tells us today that if our grace relationship with Jesus gives us courage, fills us with the enthusiasm of the Holy Spirit, increases our affection and sympathy for others, then we ought to allow Christ's thinking to affect our daily living. More than once Paul counsels his people to put on the mind of Christ. The mind of Christ is healing, it is not self-seeking, it looks always to the needs of others.

Family, community, parish living involves relationships that are so easily wounded. When all insist on their own way, chaos results. There is only one solution: each must ask, what would Jesus think about this situation? What would he want? When we can answer that question then we can say, in you, Lord, I have found my peace.

486 TUESDAY OF THE THIRTY-FIRST WEEK IN ORDINARY TIME

YEAR I

READING I Rom 12:5-16
GOSPEL Luke 14:15-24

The gospel dramatizes the rejection of the prophets in ancient times and the rejection of Jesus himself by his contemporaries. What about our rejections? Jesus invites us: Come to me, all you who labor and are burdened, and I will give you rest. Often our excuses for staying out of his arms are as flimsy as those in Jesus' story today.

In Reading I, Paul draws conclusions from the doctrine of our oneness with Christ and with one another. In the Body of Christ there are many functions and vocations. There is also much advice; but it all comes down to one rule: "Your love must be sincere," because your love for and service of one another is love for and service of Christ. Love has invited you to this banquet. May we celebrate divine love with the collective love of all our hearts.

YEAR II

READING I Phil 2:5-11
GOSPEL Luke 14:15-24

Today Paul gives us the shortest, most beautiful biography of Christ ever written. Jesus who is God from all eternity gives up his divine position and takes upon himself the condition of a slave; he becomes one of us, like us in all things except sin. Even more, he becomes a criminal for our sakes and undergoes the most disgraceful of deaths in order to reconcile all people with the Father.

The Father raises him from the dead, restores him to his original status, and makes him Lord over all creatures in heaven and on earth. Paul tells us, "Your attitude must be Christ's." I have come to ask myself, how willing am I to empty myself of my own will, become the servant of others and become obedient to the Father's will even unto death? Can I call myself a Christian if I do not at least want to have that attitude?

487 WEDNESDAY OF THE THIRTY-FIRST WEEK IN ORDINARY TIME

YEAR I

READING I Rom 13:8-10
GOSPEL Luke 14:25-33

"Anyone who does not take up his cross and follow me cannot be my disciple." These are the key words in Jesus' teaching today. The cross is different for different people. For some it is simply becoming a Christian and trying to live according to gospel principles. For some it may be sickness, old age, loss of loved ones, family or personal disgrace. Crosses seem to be fashioned by the Lord according to the degree of a persons' courage or moral character. If you do not have a cross or if it is slow in coming, be patient, and do not go looking for it. It will find you. When it does, accept it graciously, cheerfully, and even gratefully as a sign of Christ's having chosen you to help him carry his. If you find youself rebelling a little, do not be discouraged. All that Jesus wants is your willingness—and your love. Love is not only the fulfillment of the law, it is the weight of the cross.

YEAR II

READING I Phil 2:12-18
GOSPEL Luke 14:25-33

Today's gospel is about the cost of discipleship. Jesus does not require that we hate our loved ones in order to follow him; it's a matter of preference, of choosing who is number one in our lives. He tells us that following him is a matter not only of taking up our particular cross, but of continuing to carry it throughout life. It is a matter also of renouncement—of detachment from all possessions for the sake of Christ.

Each of us has his or her own cross to carry; it varies according to our strength. It may be something as insignificant as the cheerful carrying out of daily duties. The life of the disciple of Jesus can be summed up in two words—attachment and detachment. Attachment to the will of Jesus, detachment from possessions. Such is the cost of discipleship. Is it too high? Not when we realize how very much Christ loves us and has done for us.

488 THURSDAY OF THE THIRTY-FIRST WEEK IN ORDINARY TIME

YEAR I

READING I Rom 14:7-12
GOSPEL Luke 15:1-10

"None of us lives as his own master and none of us dies as his own master. While we live we are responsible to the Lord" (Reading I). Refusal to admit that responsibility to the Lord is what sin is, whether it is original sin or the one any of us committed yesterday. The one element common to every sin is the refusal to admit that we are totally dependent on God our creator for everything we have and are. "Both in life and in death we are the Lord's." That is the basic fact of our human existence. St. Paul draws important conclusions: Since we *all* belong to the Lord, we must treat one another, judge one another, help one another as members of God's family—or accept the tragic consequences. "Every one of us will have to give an account of himself before God." The one thing we shall have to give an account of is our success or failure in loving one another.

YEAR II

READING I Phil 3:3-8
GOSPEL Luke 15:1-10

St. Paul tells us that for him nothing can outweigh the supreme advantage of knowing Jesus. The kind of knowledge that Paul has in mind is more than knowing *about* Jesus. It is *in-depth* knowing, knowing with our heart and our mind, knowing him in all his self-manifestations, above all that self-manifestation that he gives in today's gospel. For no other image describes Jesus better than "this man [who] welcomes sinners and eats with them." Jesus goes to absurd lengths to seek out sinners and bring them back to him. We have all felt that love in our own lives. Nothing in all the world can compare with the supreme advantage of knowing the wondrous, forgiving love of Jesus that we can experience as often as we go to confession and, above all, in the Mass where he continues to welcome us sinners and to eat with us. Let all hearts rejoice in that love.

489 FRIDAY OF THE THIRTY-FIRST WEEK IN ORDINARY TIME

YEAR I

READING I **Rom 15:14-21**
GOSPEL **Luke 16:1-8**

"Give me an account of your service, for it is about to come to an end," Jesus tells us in today's gospel parable. The best way to prepare to give that account is contained in the Alleluia Verse:

> He who keeps the word of Christ,
> grows perfect in the love of God.

Another way is loving fidelity to whatever vocation God has called us. Paul is one of the best examples of that kind of fidelity. Love for Christ drove him, and he had to preach; it was a point of honor for him to do it. He knows he is Christ's instrument, but he is aware of his own weaknesses. He could not have been an easy man to live and work with; he wore out several helpers. But who knows, if he had been easy to live with, the good news might never have reached the pagans. For all we know, we are Christians today because of the seed sown by Paul. "The Lord has revealed to the nations his saving power" (Responsorial Psalm) through St. Paul. He continues to want it made known through us. Would that some of Paul's zeal would rub off on us!

YEAR II

READING I **Phil 3:17–4:1**
GOSPEL **Luke 16:1-8**

In the gospel Jesus surely does not mean to praise dishonesty. Rather, he wants us to be as concerned and farsighted about our spiritual growth and eternal future as this crooked steward is about his present job.

The best way for us to do that is to imitate Christ, as St. Paul recommends. But how to imitate Christ? One way is to do what you think Christ would do in your particular situation. But that's not so easy to figure out. John Garvey says that imitating Christ is not aping his external appearance or manner of speech; it is rather the acceptance of the substance of his life and teaching and making that our own. It comes down to "a radical obedience to God's will." That's what Paul recommends in today's Reading I. "For these reasons, my brothers, you whom I so love and long for, you who are my joy and my crown, continue, my dear ones, to stand firm in the Lord."

490 SATURDAY OF THE THIRTY-FIRST WEEK IN ORDINARY TIME

YEAR I

READING I **Rom 16:3-9, 16, 22-27**
GOSPEL **Luke 16:9-15**

We learn interesting facts about Paul and about early Christianity in today's conclusion to Romans. It is obvious from Paul's final greeting that women played an important role in his apostolate. He calls Prisca and Aquila "my fellow workers in the service of Christ Jesus and even risked their lives for the sake of mine." We learn that Paul had a secretary named Tertius, who insists on getting into the act. And finally, we have the doxology, which in a few words sums up the content of the epistle. Paul has been preaching the good news of Jesus Christ—the revelation of a mystery hidden for many ages, manifested through the prophets and through him: "made known to the Gentiles that they may believe and obey." The mystery is justification and salvation from God himself made available to all who are willing and eager to receive it. Because of Paul we can all cry out, "I will praise your name for ever, Lord" (Responsorial Psalm).

YEAR II

READING I **Phil 4:10-19**
GOSPEL **Luke 16:9-15**

Jesus is emphatic in declaring, "No servant can serve two masters. . . . You cannot give yourself to God and money," because both require full service. We put our trust either in riches or in God. Who wants to make that choice?

Today Paul says goodbye to his beloved Philippians. He thanks them for their kindness to him and tells them that all they have done for him is an authentic sacrifice. An example to us in so many ways, Paul here shows us one of the finest of Christian virtues—knowing how to accept love and kindness graciously. He also invites us to imitate him in making the most of life as it is: "Whatever the situation I find myself in I have learned to be self-sufficient." It has been said that Christianity is the only religion that considers life itself to be worship. That's what it was for Paul and Jesus. Please God, that's what it is for us all.

155 THIRTY-SECOND WEEK IN ORDINARY TIME — Cycle A

READING I **Wis 6:12-16** **READING II** **1 Thess 4:13-18**
GOSPEL **Matt 25:1-13**

Reading I: Wisdom is God's gift and is easily perceived by those who love her, but she needs to be sought.

Reading II: Death does not end life. Those who die believing in Christ are forever with the Lord.

Gospel: We do not know when the Lord will come. If we are wise, we will always be prepared.

The last Sundays of the Church Year are characterized by Scripture texts about Christ's Second Coming at the end of the world and our own inevitable death and judgment. We are not going to live forever in this world, but we *are* going to live forever. Our deepest concern, if we are wise, has to be where we will spend our eternal future—with God and our departed loved ones or forever separated from God and loved ones.

We simply do not know when we will meet Christ, the divine Bridegroom face to face. Therefore, if we are wise, we will always be prepared. The chief concern of today's liturgy is to help us form a truly Christian mentality about how we ought to live in this world, so that we will be best prepared for life in the world to come. It is no accident that today's Reading I is from the Book of Wisdom.

What is wisdom? Who is a wise person? Educators believe that wisdom is the goal of all education rather than just a gathering of facts. Wisdom is that mysterious element of heart and mind that remains after facts are forgotten. In this sense, one never ceases wanting to become more and more educated. Parents need to grow in wisdom as much as children do. So wisdom is not mere intelligence. You can't take a test to find out your grade in wisdom. Wisdom is a disposition of *openness* and *attentiveness to meanings.* It has been said that to be wise is to put everything in its proper perspective. It is the ability to take the long view about life and its meaning and not to be held up or defeated by setbacks.

Wisdom involves planning, but not in the sense of trying to program one's life or even one's career. Our planning as Christians has to allow for a place for God in our life. What wisdom comes down to is hopeful alertness and attentiveness. This is the attitude that best disposes us for the future, including the confrontation with God our judge at our death. This kind of attentiveness and hope, permeated by loving desire for God, is what Jesus wishes to elicit from us today.

> O God, you are my God whom I seek; . . .
> My soul is thirsting for you, O Lord my God (Responsorial Psalm).

The wisdom we so desire and need involves, above all, attentiveness to the Jesus of the Gospels—to what he has done for us when he lived, suffered, died, and rose. Attentiveness to what he *is doing for us now* in the sacraments, especially in the Eucharist and in the sacrament of reconciliation. Attentiveness to the fact that every moment of our lives is shot through with the living presence of Jesus.

> The Lord is my shepherd; there is nothing I shall want (Communion Antiphon).

Wisdom is attentiveness to the immensity of God's personal love for each of us without exception *and* our loving, grateful response to that love.

> Be watchful and ready:
> you do not know when the Son of Man is coming (Alleluia Verse).

You do not know the moment of your death. When you go to sleep tonight, do you know if you will wake up in this world or the next? Many people do not even want to think about such warnings. They say that it is morbid even to consider them. But such an attitude is terribly unrealistic and above all, lacking in wisdom. It is also deficient in an awareness of the real nature of happiness: the complete gratification of the deepest desire of our hearts, the desire for love in all its fullness, the desire for God.

What we pray for is a share in God's own eternal vision of being, God's vision of life. This is the kind of wisdom that enables us to see that everything we do has a future significance. *There is a tomorrow.* There is a God, not only in our present, carrying us into that tomorrow, but there is a God *in* that tomorrow, calling to us, waiting to greet us. There can only be one answer to that call:

> O God, you are my God whom I seek;
> for you my flesh pines and my soul thirsts
> like the earth, parched, lifeless and without water.
> My soul is thirsting for you, O Lord my God (Responsorial Psalm).

156 THIRTY-SECOND SUNDAY IN ORDINARY TIME Cycle B

READING I **1 Kgs 17:10-16** **READING II** **Heb 9:24-28**
GOSPEL **Mark 12:38-44**

Reading I: A poor widow gives Elijah her last handful of flour and is rewarded with a limitless supply of flour and oil.

Reading II: Christ entered into heaven to appear before God on our behalf. He will appear again to bring salvation to all who await him.

Gospel: Jesus contrasts the spirit of giving by the wealthy with that of a poor widow who gives all that she has.

As we approach the end of another year of being taught or evangelized by Christ in these Sunday Mass readings, the Church likes to summarize and emphasize the great lessons in religion and life that we have heard during the year. You recall that last Sunday Jesus stressed the absolute need for love of God and neighbor if we are to be his followers. Today that lesson in loving is illustrated in the lives of two women, both widows.

What these widows have in common is their willingness to give all that they have without counting the cost or consequences. The first widow gives her entire supply of food to the prophet Elijah; the second gave only two small coins, but "she gave from her want," as Jesus observes. Both widows gave small gifts, but what they gave symbolized the giving of *themselves.* They gave without calculating the future, as the scribe in the gospel probably did.

What is significant about this incident in Mark's Gospel is that it comes near the end of Jesus' life—just a short time before Jesus gave all that he has and is, out of love for us all. It is also significant—especially in our time—that Scripture gives us two women, both widows, to demonstrate to Christians in every age how *they* ought to live, how *they* ought to respond to Jesus' love poured out for us all.

As Jesus will give himself at the Last Supper and on Calvary, as these two women give themselves and all that they possess without counting the cost or calculating what they will receive from their gift, so must Christ's disciples, women and men of all ages, desire to *give themselves* to the Lord and to those in any kind of need. The two widows exemplify the true value system that Jesus brings to the world.

This is not a lesson in how to provide for the upkeep of a parish or the missions or a college. Their needs are obvious to all: they cannot continue in existence without financial support. But what we contribute should be given with love, not with any hope of reward in this life or the next. Our Alternative Opening Prayer provides us with the ideal we need to keep in mind:

> Help us to become more aware of your loving design
> so that we may more willingly give our lives in service to all.

It is always good to remind ourselves that God does not need our gifts, whether they be great or small. God does not need our worship, our praise, our thanks; but God also knows that we cannot be ourselves, we cannot be whole and fulfilled Christians and human beings unless we give our hearts to him and respond to his love by the unselfish love of our hearts.

God knows, too, that we cannot be fully human unless we learn *to see Christ in one another,* especially in the poor.

So many Christians go through the motions of religious practice. They wouldn't dream of missing Sunday Mass or disobeying any of the Church's commandments. But it is always possible for us all to miss the point of what it is all about. And what is that? It is about becoming like the two impoverished widows of today's readings. It is about learning how to become human *and* religious by giving oneself away—to one another, to anyone in need, and through them to God.

Can we do it? It surely isn't easy. It wasn't easy for Jesus either. It takes great courage, but more than anything else, it takes a whole heartful of loving trust and faith. It means really believing Jesus when he tells us in the Alleluia Verse:

> Happy the poor in spirit;
> the kingdom of heaven is theirs!
>
> The Lord is my shepherd; there is nothing I shall want. In green pastures he gives me rest, he leads me beside the waters of peace (Communion Antiphon).

157 THIRTY-SECOND SUNDAY IN ORDINARY TIME Cycle C

READING I **2 Macc 7:1-2, 9-14** **READING II** **2 Thess 2:16–3:5**
GOSPEL **Luke 20:27-38**

Reading I: The seven Jewish brothers demonstrate their loyalty to God by suffering death rather than violate one of God's laws.

Reading II: Paul prays that Jesus will strengthen the Thessalonians, and he asks them to pray for his continuing missionary efforts.

Gospel: Jesus refutes the Sadducees' refusal to believe in the resurrection with his words: "God is not the God of the dead but of the living. All are alive for him."

One of the most painful agonies of the people who lose a loved one in death is the sense of loss. And the only possible consolation to offer the bereaved is that their departed loved one lives on with God and will rise again, a belief that is beautifully expressed in the Preface of Christian Death I:

> In him, who rose from the dead,
> our hope of resurrection dawned.

The sadness of death gives way
to the bright promise of immortality.
Lord, for your faithful people life is changed, not ended.

The Sadducees were worldly enemies of Jesus who refused to accept the growing belief in the resurrection of the body, which had become popular only a couple of centuries before Christ. Jesus accepted this belief, made it his own, and expanded it. In his answer to the Sadducees today, he affirms the resurrection along with the transformation of the body. He says: "Moses in the passage about the bush showed that the dead rise again when he called the Lord the God of Abraham, and the God of Isaac, and the God of Jacob. God is not the God of the dead but of the living. All are alive for him."

All this may not be very exciting for us. But Jesus' words, "All are alive for him," can be comforting for those who have lost loved ones. We are the living. God is our God. And we are alive for him, we are alive *with him now.* What is implied in the idea of living with God and for God? Living for God goes along with the different vocations to which we are called—marriage, the religious and/or priestly life, the single life "in the world," and all the other vocations that accompany these major ones, like being a doctor, a lawyer, a nurse, a teacher, a business man or woman, a farmer, and many others. Every vocation continues creation in its own way, and living our vocation to the fullest is to live for God.

Living for God implies discovering and developing whatever talents the creator has given us. We never cease perfecting ourselves in whatever vocation we have. We never give up learning. In a word, we strive always to grow and develop *as human beings,* for that is what we are. We are not angels. Along with our natural talents, we also strive to grow in the natural virtues of honesty, sincerity, concern, mercy, and understanding. Above all, we strive to grow in love. It is impossible to live for God without love at the core of our existence. No matter how old we become, we never cease growing into wholeness, never finish striving to know, to love, to understand.

When God became man in Christ Jesus, it was more than a human body that he assumed. He became one with *human life,* all of it—joys, sorrows, pain, work, sickness, growing old, dying. Life is not a punishment, it is a gift. It is not a sentence, it is living with Christ. In other words, we can encounter God *in our everyday life,* not just when we are praying at Mass. We can encounter God in our working, our playing, our serving, our recreating. God is with us and we are with God in every act of our daily living. We are not alone—ever! Jesus is waiting for us in the heart of the world. Life is therefore a divine adventure in which we cooperate with Christ in building the kind of world he died for.

This might very well be what St. Paul had in mind when he wrote in 2 Thessalonians: "May our Lord Jesus Christ himself, may God our Father who loved us and in his mercy gave us eternal consolation and hope, console your hearts and strengthen them for every good work and word. . . . May the Lord rule your hearts in the love of God and the constancy of Christ" (Reading II). For that good prayer there is only one response—Amen, So be it!

491 MONDAY OF THE THIRTY-SECOND WEEK IN ORDINARY TIME

YEAR I

READING I **Wis 1:1-7**
GOSPEL **Luke 17:1-6**

The Book of Wisdom is God's answer to the beautiful prayer, "Guide me, Lord, along the everlasting way" (Responsorial Psalm). Wisdom is definitely associated with the purpose God had in mind in creating us. Its main concern is to teach us how to live and attain our best potential as persons, made in God's image. Wisdom will define and describe itself in the course of the readings to come, and I predict that we will be pleasantly surprised. No human counselor has all the answers to all of life's problems. If we listen attentively, we will find that wisdom is indeed a kindly spirit and a true friend of the human heart.

If Jesus uses the strongest possible language to show his contempt for a person who would lead a little one into sin, it is simply because he loves his own that much. We can make our own the disciples' prayer: Increase our faith so that we may really believe in your love for us.

YEAR II

READING I Titus 1:1-9
GOSPEL Luke 17:1-6

The epistle to Titus is one of Paul's "Pastoral Epistles." These letters were written to the men he left in charge of his Christian communities, but they contain good advice for all Christians—bishops and pastors as well as the laity. The very vocation of a bishop as God's steward demands that he be upright in every way. But the very vocation of every Christian requires that we be upright in every way: the virtues listed by Paul are for us all.

Jesus adds a virtue that Paul takes for granted: priests, bishops, people must learn how to forgive—again and again. No parish, family, or community life is possible without the willingness to forgive on the part of all. Lord, we are the people who long to see your face. Increase our faith so that we may believe that to see your face, we have to learn to forgive.

492 TUESDAY OF THE THIRTY-SECOND WEEK IN ORDINARY TIME

YEAR I

READING I Wis 2:23–3:9
GOSPEL Luke 17:7-10

Wisdom acquired now is not only guaranteed to make life interesting, it is the best possible preparation for the life to come. "The souls of the just are in the hands of God, and no torment shall touch them" (Reading I). This verse and those that follow indicate why this reading is so popular at Catholic funerals. Death is not the end, and those who see it as such are called "foolish" by the author. No, the dead are at peace. During life they are indeed tried as gold is tried in a furnace, but by patient endurance of life's sufferings they are found worthy of life with God forever. But life with God is not pious inactivity. The verse "They shall judge nations and rule over peoples" indicates another Christian belief, popularized by St. Therese of

Lisieux, who said she would spend her heaven doing good on earth. It all begins with wisdom.

YEAR II

READING I Titus 2:1-8, 11-14
GOSPEL Luke 17:7-10

"The salvation of the just comes from the Lord." This Responsorial Psalm sums up Paul's theology of redemption, especially as stated in the last part of today's Reading I. God's grace has not only appeared to us in Christ Jesus, it trains and empowers us with the strength and courage to renounce irreligion and unworldly passions and to live sober, upright, and godly lives; it gives us the strength to practice all the virtues he recommends in the first part of the reading.

So being virtuous is not primarily an act of determination on our part. It is God's grace in us and our cooperation with that grace—cooperation that is likely to arise more readily in our hearts when we trust in the Lord, above all, take delight in him. He delights in us. Why not reciprocate?

493 WEDNESDAY OF THE THIRTY-SECOND WEEK IN ORDINARY TIME

YEAR I

READING I Wis 6:1-11
GOSPEL Luke 17:11-19

Authority is a frightening responsibility since it makes weak, vulnerable mortals stand-ins for God himself, the source of all authority. There can be only one guide for those in authority (parents would surely be included)—the will of God, which they must strive always to discern. They can never go wrong if they follow the psalmist's advice:

Defend the lowly and the fatherless;
render justice to the afflicted and the destitute.
Rescue the lowly and the poor (Responsorial Psalm).

Jesus is the one who best knows how to exercise authority. Notice how gently he works in today's gospel. He heals ten lepers and then makes use of the occasion to teach us the necessity of giving thanks to God (and others) who do good to us and for us. Not that God needs our thanks; we need to be thankful if we are to flourish as human persons, created in his own image and likness. Thank you for listening.

YEAR II

READING I Titus 3:1-7
GOSPEL Luke 17:11-19

Even though we are baptized Catholics, we all need conversion—a deeper commitment to Jesus, as the readings of Advent and Lent constantly remind us. Ignorance, misguidedness, ill-will, hatred for others and for ourselves—all this is typical preconversion behavior. It is unworthy of those to whom the kindness and love of God have been revealed in baptism and in personal conversion. Yet we know from experience that, when we forget what Jesus has done for us in baptism, when we forget that "The Lord is my shepherd" (Responsorial Psalm), we can easily slip back into preconversion attitudes and behavior.

One of the best ways of reminding ourselves of Jesus' goodness and kindness to us—and keeping our conversion alive—is by cultivating a constant attitude of thanksgiving. There is no better opportunity for that than at the table of the Eucharist, *the* thanksgiving that the Lord has prepared for us.

494 THURSDAY OF THE THIRTY-SECOND WEEK IN ORDINARY TIME

YEAR I

READING I **Wis 7:22–8:1**
GOSPEL **Luke 17:20-25**

The wisdom described so beautifully in Reading I is not the same as a vast store of knowledge. The list of adjectives the author uses to describe wisdom gives the impression of inexhaustible infinity. Wisdom "is an aura of the might of God, and a pure effusion of the glory of the Almighty . . . the image of his goodness." In a word, wisdom is a divine gift—a sharing in his very being—that God gives to holy souls, to those who truly love him. Jesus, the Word, the Son of God, is divine Wisdom incarnate. If we would possess and enjoy true wisdom, he gives us the way and the means: "I am the vine, you are the branches. He who lives in me and I in him, will produce abundantly" (John 15:5). To be wise you do not have to be learned. Just let Christ live in you, love in you, direct your life, and your wisdom will abound.

YEAR II

READING I **Phlm 7-20**
GOSPEL **Luke 17:20-25**

The kingdom of God Jesus speaks about so often is definitely not a political kingdom. It is God's lordship over minds and hearts and lives. "The reign of God is already in your midst." Do we recognize, do we realize God's loving lordship over our lives? Recognition does not just happen. It has to be prepared and cultivated, and Jesus is the one who does it best. He does it whenever the gospel is proclaimed.

But Christ's work in our hearts is fruitless unless on our part there is an inner readiness to give ourselves over to the lordship of God and to allow him to rule our lives. So each of us has to ask the cutting question: do I have this inner readiness to give myself over, or do I still want to rule my own life? Before answering, remember: The Lord opens the eyes of the blind. The Lord lifts up those who are bowed down.

495 FRIDAY OF THE THIRTY-SECOND WEEK IN ORDINARY TIME

YEAR I

READING I Wis 13:1-9
GOSPEL Luke 17:26-37

The created world, in all its beauty and wonder, is a sign, a sacrament that reveals the beauty, wonder, power, and mystery of its creator. This is the message of Reading I, which, in turn, is perfectly summed up in our Responsorial Psalm:

> The heavens declare the glory of God,
> and the firmament proclaims his handiwork.

"Remember Lot's wife," Jesus warns us in the gospel. God had saved Lot and his family from destruction and commanded them not to look back at the burning city of Sodom. God had called them to a new life. But Lot's wife remembered the pleasures and comforts of the good old days in Sodom; she disobeyed God's command and immediately became a column of salt. Conclusion: do we want to live in the past or are we willing and ready to respond to God's voice calling us ever onward into a new and unknown life?

YEAR II

READING I 2 John 4-9
GOSPEL Luke 17:26-37

The themes of 2 John are love and truth. John urges us to let our Christianity show forth in our lives in two ways: by adhering to the great commandment of love and by adhering to the truth about Jesus. This truth was threatened by deceivers who denied the reality of the incarnation. Can you imagine what life would be like without Jesus? Can you imagine what it would be like without love?

But loving is hard work. It is also an art, and according to Erich Fromm, the practice of any art requires discipline, concentration, patience. And, of course, there must be a supreme concern for acquiring the mastery of the art. Can we call ourselves genuine followers of Jesus if we do not have that supreme concern?

496 SATURDAY OF THE THIRTY-SECOND WEEK IN ORDINARY TIME

YEAR I

READING I **Wis 18:14-16; 19:6-9**
GOSPEL **Luke 18:1-8**

"Remember the marvels the Lord has done," says the psalmist. The marvel of marvels for the Jews was the Lord's freeing them from slavery in Egypt and leading them to the Promised Land. Details are in Reading I. Through the ages Jews have obeyed that divine command to remember. But their remembering had the mysterious and special power of bringing the original event into their midst, enabling them to share its reality. What the Lord did for his people then, Jesus has done for us. He delivered us from slavery to sin and has reconciled us to our God by his death and resurrection, which he anticipated at the Last Supper, the first Mass, when he said, "Do this in memory of me." At this Mass we obey Jesus: we do what he did, and in doing it, we remember the marvels the Lord has done for us. We sing to him, we proclaim all his wondrous deeds.

Rejoice, hearts that seek the Lord! (Responsorial Psalm)

YEAR II

READING I **3 John 5-8**
GOSPEL **Luke 18:1-8**

Is there anyone who does not need Christ's advice about praying always and not losing heart? The widow in the gospel refuses to take the corrupt judge's no for an answer to her pleading. Finally in sheer self-defense, he gives in. Christ's point is that if a judge who fears neither God nor man can be worn down, then surely a loving and merciful Father will care for the needs of his beloved children when they cry out to him day and night.

Christ's question, "When the Son of Man comes, will he find any faith on the earth?" sounds as though he does not have much faith in mankind. It may well be a warning to us that without persistent prayer—prayer of petition, prayer of constant awareness of God's presence to us—our faith will fade and eventually die. God forbid!

THIRTY-THIRD SUNDAY IN ORDINARY TIME

READING I **Prov 31:10-13, 19-20, 30-31** **READING II** **1 Thess 5:1-6**
GOSPEL **Matt 25:14-30**

Reading I: A portrait of the ideal wife who is faithful, creative, charitable, kind. "Her value is far beyond pearls."

Reading II: We do not know the day or hour of the Lord's coming; therefore it behooves us to be "awake and sober."

Gospel: The parable of the servants who receive varying amounts of silver pieces from their master and the way each servant invests the amount he has received.

The Church continues her deep concern for having her children ready, alert, and hopeful for their encounter with Christ at the end of their life in this world. Today's gospel uses different imagery than last Sunday's, but the message is the same: *be prepared,* be prepared by growing and maturing as a person—a goal best accomplished by developing and perfecting the special gifts and talents the Lord has given us.

We usually think of Christ's parables as warnings to us as individuals. Today's parable, however, could have a broader application, namely, to the entire Church. The ideal wife in Reading I stands for the Bride of Christ, the Church. She too must develop her talents and be prepared as a Church for Christ's Second Coming.

But we are the Church, and every moment and aspect of our lives, including our suffering, are essential in building the Church, helping her to grow to completion and fullness. We probably seldom think of this—if ever. Paul wrote his letters to the *Churches;* Jesus told his parables to the group of the disciples who were to become the Church.

Christ wants each of us and all of us together to grow into mature Christians—not from fear of damnation—but because his Bride the Church depends on us. What Christ insists upon is that what the Lord began when he brought us into being come to fulfillment. You may recall the somewhat overworked phrase of St. Irenaeus, "The glory of God is the human person fully alive, fully realized."

So the crucial problem for each of us is to discover our individual talents and gifts and bring them to perfection. There are some talents that are common to all of us: just about everyone is capable of sharing, caring, loving, and responding to love. But not everyone has the talent of creative achievement in playing an instrument, constructing a building, teaching a class, writing a poem, or preparing a meal.

It probably is safe to claim that there is no one without her or his special talent, but too often it lies dormant, waiting to be discovered. That is where parents and teachers come in. They are generally more capable of discovering talents than the child. But parents need to be warned that they cannot force a skill on a child if his or her heart is not in it. This is a dangerous effort that often does more harm than good.

Whatever our talents might be, what Erich Fromm says about the art of loving can be applied to whatever talents each of us has. The development of any talent requires *discipline, concentration, patience,* and a *supreme concern* for the mastery of the particular talent. Great musicians become great only after hours, days, years of work and practice.

The one talent we are all called to mature in is that of loving—loving God, loving one another. And growing in love is never easy. We make progress and then fall back. But we never give up because the end is so very worthwhile.

The art of loving may become less difficult if we learn how to accept love, learn how to allow ourselves to be loved and to respond to that freely given, often unmerited love. In Eugene O'Neill's play *Moon for the Misbegotten* the heroine says to the drunken, desperate man lying in her arms, "Maybe my love could still save you, if you would only let it." We might wonder if O'Neill realized that he was really writing about God and of the love that God has for each of us.

Allowing God to love us, giving in and responding to God's love, allowing God to hold us in his protective arms, may be the greatest talent of all. For our sake, for the sake of Mother Church, may we not bury this talent in the ground, but rather, may we let it grow and expand and envelop our entire being!

> Live in me and let me live in you, says the Lord;
> My branches bear much fruit (Alleluia Verse).

159 THIRTY-THIRD SUNDAY IN ORDINARY TIME Cycle B

READING I Dan 12:1-3 **READING II** Heb 10:11-14, 18
GOSPEL Mark 13:24-32

Reading I: Using strange, apocalyptic language, Daniel promises deliverance to the captive Jews.

Reading II: A contrast between the effectiveness of human sacrifices and the sacrifice of Jesus, which takes away all sin.

Gospel: Jesus describes the natural phenomena that will be visible at the end of the world.

As we come close to the end of the Church Year, our readings remind us of the end of the world and the Second Coming of Christ. Such readings are known as "apocalyptic literature," and it is important for us to know what this kind of literature *is* and what it is *not*.
—It is *not* biblical prophecy, it does not predict the future, as many fundamentalist Christians believe.
—It is *not* an invitation to withdraw from concern for our world.
—It *is* intended to encourage us to bring the good news of Christ to the world with greater intensity of effort, to bear witness to the gospel in our lives.
—It was originally, and still *is*, consoling literature. When it was first used in the centuries before the birth of Jesus, its primary aim was to bring comfort and consolation to Jews who were devastated by the attempts to paganize them by Antiochus Epiphanes, who actually set up a statue of the pagan god Zeus in the holy of holies of the Temple in Jerusalem. The moral of this literature is that people of faith can resist temptation and conquer adversity. The Lord God is in control of events, and the Lord will emerge victorious in the end.

> The Lord says: My plans for you are peace and not disaster; when you call to me, I will listen to you (Entrance Antiphon).

Time is running out for each of us without exception; and Jesus insists strongly that we have to be prepared to give an account of the way we have lived our lives.

> Be watchful, pray constantly,
> that you may be worthy to stand before the Son of Man (Alleluia Verse).

Being prepared involves realizing that God is present to us in creation—present to us in our daily life, work, suffering, and joy. "I am with you always, until the end of the world" (Matt 28:20), Jesus assured the apostles and us, but how real is his presence to us?

For us to live fully as God wants us to live, we must try to know why God chose us, and what God wants us to be and do. What meaning does life have for us? Either the world is without meaning and therefore life is not worth living or the drama of life is being directed by a great love, a great plan, whose source is God. Christianity is not to be reduced to a complex of rules and rituals. It must be the beacon that lights up every human path.

For many of us it is difficult to grasp the idea that we can meet and live with Jesus in our daily life and work. We seem to think that our only contact with him is when we are praying or reading Scripture or at Mass. We do not take Paul's words seriously: "The life I live now is not my own; Christ is living in me" (Gal 2:20).

Jesus tells us in today's gospel, "When you see these things happening, you will know that he is near, even at the door." So, stand erect, look around, discover Christ in your daily life, rejoice in his presence with and in you, take courage, never give up hope because the God of hope, the God of love, will never abandon those whom he loves, those who love God.

Death will come. Time will expire. But those who learn to live fully, who learn to share themselves with others, need have no fear. They simply pass into the fullness, the flowering of life and of love that will remain forever—that fullness for which they hungered all their lives.

Keep me safe, O God; you are my hope (Responsorial Psalm).

THIRTY-THIRD SUNDAY IN ORDINARY TIME

READING I **Mal 3:19-20** **READING II** **2 Thess 3:7-12**
GOSPEL **Luke 21:5-19**

Reading I: When the end comes, evildoers will be punished, but for the just the sun of justice will arise with its healing rays.

Reading II: Paul urges the Thessalonians to work hard, and he warns those who are unruly "to earn the food they eat."

Gospel: Jesus foretells the destruction of the Temple and the end of time. But those who are faithful to him should not fear.

The president of a large company decided to give a "better management award" to the best achiever in the company. At a meeting of the board of directors he announced that the first award would go posthumously to Christopher Columbus because (a) he started out not knowing where he was going; (b) on arriving he didn't know where he was, and (c) on returning to Spain he didn't know where he had been.

It would be tragic if at the end of our lives we were to receive such an award. Jesus surely wants us to know where we came from—that we existed before all ages in the mind of God, who gave us life and being at a special moment in history. Jesus wants us to know where we are now—that we are in the world God created, a world the creator wishes us to enjoy, to develop, and negatively, not pollute or destroy. And Jesus surely wants us to know where we are going—what our destiny is to be after we leave this world.

What Jesus is most concerned about is what we are doing now with the life that the Lord has given us: our physical life and above all our spiritual life, our relationship with him. He wants us to grow and become the fully developed persons we are capable of being. This means more than anything else growing in our capacity to love God and one another.

Actually Jesus is our teacher in the school of loving, and he uses every possible teaching aid, especially his own example, his works and his words, his life of service to all, especially to those in any kind of need or trouble. And he uses the ultimate teaching aid to show us how to love: he suffers, dies, and rises from the dead. Even more, he lives with us now, ready to come to our help in any situation or need.

Any kind of teaching, in any school, from grade school to the university, is or should be an act of love, because that's what teaching was for Jesus. And every one of us is a teacher in one way or another, parents more than anyone else.

Jesus also teaches us how to be good students: he teaches us how to see and how to listen. Sometimes he even shocks and startles us into listening with the full attention of mind and heart, as he does today in the gospel.

Listening to Jesus, following him, absorbing the lesson of his life, has obstacles, as we all know. Here are some of them: too much preoocupation with ourself and our personal problems; listening half-heartedly and carelessly, listening without eager love and desire; listening without hope and expectation. We cannot listen to Jesus unless we make ourselves available to him, vulnerable to his word, ready to say *yes* to him.

At the end of another liturgical year (how may do we have left?) we really ought to evaluate our progress in learning Christ. A favorite question of one of our modern politicians is, "Are you better off now than you were six years ago?" Maybe the question belongs more to Jesus. He asks it, but with a different intention and meaning than that of the politician. Jesus wants to know if we are better lovers. That's what matters most.

Are we better listeners? Have we grown in intimacy with him, do we know him with our hearts? Speaking of our hearts, intimacy with Christ is impossible if our hearts are divided by antagonisms, indifference, lack of concern for others, especially those who are in any kind of physical or emotional need.

Jesus assures us in today's Communion Antiphon:

> I tell you solemnly, whatever you ask for in prayer, believe that you have received it, and it will be yours, says the Lord.

So we take him at his word and beg:

> Father, may we grow in love
> by the eucharist we have celebrated
> in memory of the Lord Jesus,
> who is Lord for ever and ever. Amen (Prayer after Communion).

497 MONDAY OF THE THIRTY-THIRD WEEK IN ORDINARY TIME

YEAR I

READING I **Macc 1:10-15, 41-43, 54-57, 62-63**
GOSPEL **Luke 18:35-43**

The Book of Maccabees relates the exciting story of another crisis in Hebrew history—a period dominated by Antiochus Epiphanes, whose reign brought a serious temptation to the Jews to forget their covenant with God and worship pagan idols. Some Jews conformed to public laws, but many, at the risk of their lives, remained faithful to the one true God. Led by the Maccabee brothers, Israel will emerge intact from the ordeal.

The familiar "I am the light of the world" both illustrates and explains the miracle of the gospel. The blind man's plea—"I want to see"—is now a universal cry springing from the hearts of anyone who is afflicted in any way. Lord, I want to see and understand the meaning of life, the meaning of the suffering that weighs upon us. That plea will be answered for all those who trust in Jesus' words:

> The man who follows me will have the light of life (Alleluia Verse).

YEAR II

READING I **Rev 1:1-4; 2:1-5**
GOSPEL **Luke 18:35-43**

The plea of the blind man in the gospel is our prayer now and always. We need a new vision, eyes of faith, in order to understand something of the mystery of life. And we surely need eyes of faith in order to get some meaning out of the Book of Revelation, which we begin today.

Revelation is the last book of the Bible, and it is the most confusing and difficult—and the most exploited by people with vivid imaginations who can find backing in it for whatever weird predictions they want to discover. The New American Bible tells us that it is resistance literature, composed to meet a crisis—namely, the persecution of the early Christians by Rome. It is an exhortation and admonition to stand firm in the faith against the paganism that threatened them. We need the admonition as much today as they did then. Jesus, Son of David, have mercy on us all!

498 TUESDAY OF THE THIRTY-THIRD WEEK IN ORDINARY TIME

YEAR I

READING I **2 Macc 6:18-31**
GOSPEL **Luke 19:1-10**

There is considerable contrast between the two men who are the heroes of today's readings. Zacchaeus was a tax collector and therefore, in the eyes of the Jews, automatically a crook, a sinner. Eleazar was a scribe who comes off as one of the noblest and most honest of all biblical characters. He could have escaped death by dissimulation, but he could not have lived with himself if he had. Besides, there was the love for God and God's Law that ruled his life. So he went to his death, upheld and sustained by the God he had loved so fearlessly.

Zacchaeus did not have that kind of character. He did not confess that he was a sinner. If he was, he had some points in his favor: he gave half of his belongings to the poor, and if he defrauded anyone, he repaid him fourfold. Best of all, he wanted to see Jesus. That kind of desire brought Jesus to his house. It is a formula that can work for us, too, if we want it badly enough.

YEAR II

READING I **Rev 3:1-6, 14-22**
GOSPEL **Luke 19:1-10**

"Here I stand, knocking at the door. If anyone hears me calling and opens the door, I will enter his house and have supper with him, and he with me." This sentence from today's Reading I tells us a lot about how Jesus feels about us—how much he desires to be a part of our lives. The same truth is beautifully dramatized in the gospel. Jesus invites himself into Zacchaeus' house. The fact that Zacchaeus is a public sinner makes no difference to Jesus.

The hunger for God planted in every human heart is nothing compared to God's hunger for us, for our love. He knocks at the doors of all our hearts. All we have to do is to open the doors to him so that he can enter and commune with us. The failure to open the doors will leave us empty and lukewarm, and then he will spew us out of his mouth. And who wants that?

499 WEDNESDAY OF THE THIRTY-THIRD WEEK IN ORDINARY TIME

YEAR I

READING I **2 Macc 7:1, 20-31**
GOSPEL **Luke 19:11-28**

What Jesus is talking about today (and what Reading I also indicates) is that being a Christian and living according to God's law involve taking risks. The first two servants in the gospel parable "play the market" with their master's money, and they make a profit. The third servant plays it safe and gains nothing. Jesus, of course, is not talking about financial gains, but rather about God's will made flesh in the Law. Implicitly, he is being critical of the Pharisees who see the Law as a treasure to be buried, as a dead letter containing no more mystery than what they have already discovered rather than as a challenge to be exploited for the good of others. Being a Jew, really following the Law was worth dying for, as these seven brothers demonstrated. So too, our Christian faith. It is given to us to be shared, not concealed or hidden. I have chosen you from the world to go and bear fruit, says Jesus to us. He means every word.

YEAR II

READING I **Rev 4:1-11**
GOSPEL **Luke 19:11-28**

"Holy, holy, holy, is the Lord God Almighty, who was and is and is to come!" This is our God—who he is and what he is: infinite, boundless holiness, the totality of love and life. To live with him forever is our destiny if, like the responsible servants of the gospel, we build up the treasure of faith in our hearts and are willing to share it with others. All the deep hungers of our hearts for the fullness of truth, life, love, joy will find complete gratification in him who first created our love-, life-, truth-starved hearts.

The Mass contains within itself all that is needed to give us a foretaste of the heaven here described. Do we not cry out, "Holy, holy, holy, Lord God of hosts"? "Let everything that has breath praise the Lord!" May we not allow overfamiliarity with the Mass to bury its meaning for us.

500 THURSDAY OF THE THIRTY-THIRD WEEK IN ORDINARY TIME

YEAR I

READING I **1 Macc 2:15-29**
GOSPEL **Luke 19:41-44**

We may admire Mattathias' zeal for God's supremacy, but it would hardly be a good idea for us to follow his example and kill others who do not share our beliefs. We can regret religious freedom, but it may well be God's own idea. There is a considerable evolution of religious outlook between Mattathias and Jesus. Jesus foresees the coming destruction of Jerusalem and he weeps. He has been presenting himself to the people there as Love in person, and they have rejected him. God woos human hearts, he does not force himself on them.

> If today you hear his voice,
> harden not your hearts (Alleluia Verse).

But they do harden their hearts, they refuse to hear him, and they seal their own doom. Jerusalem is a symbol for the Church, for a nation, for a religious community, for each of us. May we all take to heart the warning of Jesus. It rises from his love.

YEAR II

READING I **Rev 5:1-10**
GOSPEL **Luke 19:41-44**

The Jews in Egypt were saved from death by the blood of the paschal lamb. We are saved, we have access to eternal joy and love by the blood of the spotless paschal Lamb, Jesus our Lord. Praise the Lord! With his blood he ransomed us for God out of every tribe and tongue and people and nation, and he has made us all into a kingdom of priests to serve our God. This is our true destiny in eternity.

The Mass is the place where we best exercise our priesthood, where we best serve our God, where we water the seed of eternal praise that the Lord has planted in our hearts—the seed that will blossom forever in eternity.

> Sing to the Lord a new song
> of praise in the assembly of the faithful. . . .

Let them praise his name in the festive dance, . . .
For the Lord loves his people (Responsorial Psalm).

The Lord delights in us. How marvelous this is.

501 FRIDAY OF THE THIRTY-THIRD WEEK IN ORDINARY TIME

YEAR I

READING I **1 Macc 4:36-37, 52-59**
GOSPEL **Luke 19:45-48**

We can all benefit by the striking contrast between the attitudes toward the Temple demonstrated by the Maccabees and some of the contemporaries of Jesus. "Yours, O Lord, are grandeur and power, majesty, splendor and glory. For all in heaven and earth is yours" (Responsorial Psalm). This great God has made the temple in Jerusalem his special dwelling place. Reading I tells of its purification and rededication by the Maccabees, and "there was great joy among the people." Less than two hundred years later Jesus has to throw merchants and traders out of that same Temple with the words, "Scripture has it, 'My house is meant for a house of prayer' but you have made it a den of thieves."

Holiness both of places and of people is its own language. But it can speak only to hearts that are open to love and goodness and beauty. May we always "praise your glorious name, O mighty God!" (Responsorial Psalm)

YEAR II

READING I **Rev 10:8-11**
GOSPEL **Luke 19:45-48**

The scroll is the word of God. The deeply symbolic act of eating it means that it becomes bone of one's bone and flesh of one's flesh. "Take it and eat," the angel commands John. "It will be sour in your stomach, but in your mouth it will taste as sweet as honey." It is sweet because it foretells the final victory of God's people, and sour because it announces the suffering they must endure (NAB).

The command to eat the scroll is addressed to us, too. We are called to consume God's word. It may announce some sufferings to us, but it will also assure us of final victory. It will bolster and encourage us to bear the sufferings. The people in the Temple hung on Christ's words, they couldn't get enough of him. That same Jesus speaks to us day after day at this Mass. Do we believe that? Really believe? Take and eat, and you will see how sweet that word is.

502 SATURDAY OF THE THIRTY-THIRD WEEK IN ORDINARY TIME

YEAR I

READING I **1 Macc 6:1-13**
GOSPEL **Luke 20:27-40**

"I will rejoice in your salvation, O Lord" (Responsorial Psalm). These words may express the sentiments both of the Jews victorious over the pagan king's armies *and* of the king himself who repents of his evil deeds and is converted on his deathbed. The old refrain keeps reappearing in human history: it is God and God alone who saves.

> I will give thanks to you, O Lord, with all my heart;
> I will declare all your wondrous deeds (Responsorial Psalm).

The question may be: what is this salvation? The Sadducees did not believe in the resurrection of bodies and probably not in life after death, so they try to get Jesus to commit himself on the matter and make himself ridiculous in the eyes of the people. Jesus destroys their absurd argument with words that still delight our hearts: "God is not the God of the dead, but of the living. All are alive for him." And that includes us.

READING I Rev 11:4-12
GOSPEL Luke 20:27-40

We need to remind ourselves that the Book of Revelation is resistance literature, composed to meet the crisis of the Roman persecution of the early Christians. Today we get some details on both the persecutor—the beast who comes out of the pit (which probably stands for Nero)—and the two witnesses who give powerful testimony for Christ but are killed by the beast. Their bodies become an occasion of joyful celebration for the people, and after three days God's life enters into them again and they are raised up to heaven.

We are now Christ's witnesses. We may not suffer persecution as these two did, but pain, suffering, the cross, and death are our lot. But we do not forget: God is still in charge of his world and Christ of his Church.

> Blessed be the Lord, my rock, . . .
> My refuge and my fortress,
> my stronghold, my deliverer (Responsorial Psalm).

161 CHRIST THE KING Cycle A

READING I Ezek 34:11-12, 15-17 **READING II** 1 Cor 15:20-26, 28
GOSPEL Matt 25:31-46

Reading I: The Lord promises to be a shepherd to his sheep. He will care for them, feed them, bring back the strays, and judge them.

Reading II: After destroying every sovereignty and power, Christ will hand over the kingdom to the Father so that God may be all in all.

Gospel: Jesus describes the last judgment. His criterion for heaven will be our success, or lack of it, in caring for the poor, the hungry, the ill.

The Lamb who was slain is worthy to receive strength and divinity, wisdom and power and honor: to him be glory and power for ever (Entrance Antiphon).

Christ is the beginning and the end, the alpha and the omega. We end this year of grace with the Feast of Christ the King, and next Sunday we begin a new one with the First Sunday of Advent.

Reading I and the Responsorial Psalm depict the Lord God as a shepherd who serves, watches over, loves, knows, and cares for his sheep. But the Lord is also one who judges, thus linking Reading I with the gospel. The term "shepherd" in the Old Testament always had overtones of kingship. David is called "the shepherd-king."

Jesus is King of Kings and Lord of Lords, and today we celebrate that kingship. Although the Feast of Christ the King goes back only to its institution by Pope Pius XI in 1925, the idea of Jesus' kingship goes back to the earliest days of Christianity. It had its origin in the works, the signs, Jesus performed and the authority with which he proclaimed the kingdom of God.

We need to remind ourselves that Christ's kingship does not imply domination or oppression. It is rather a kingship or lordship that is creative in those who acknowledge it; divine lordship brings a person into a new dimension of being and of life. He or she "is brought into the liberating sphere of the non-world, the divine" (Fr. Eugene Maly).

Father Maly goes on to say that if Jesus is Lord and king for a person, he has a claim on the person to listen to his words and respond to them: listen and respond, not with pious thoughts, but with deeds. Our happiness in this world and the next depends on our response.

It is the gospel that tells us how we are expected to respond to Christ's lordship over us. It is Jesus' final discourse before entering upon his passion. The key idea is that Jesus will never be king of our hearts unless *we serve our deprived sisters and brothers as he did.*

The gospel shows Jesus and the poor on the same side. Jesus not only converges with but is concealed in the leftovers of society. "As often as you neglected to do it to one of these least ones, you neglected to do it to me." The poor are actually the ones who judge whether or not we are deserving of salvation.

It is also interesting (and mysterious) that those who are judged did not recognize Jesus in the poor. Neither did those who are saved. Jesus is incognito in the poor. So it seems obvious that "practical service to the poor is the most crucial element of our Christian life" (Father Beck). The conclusion is obvious: it is impossible to be committed to Christ without being committed to Christ's unfortunate sisters and brothers. We have to ask ourselves: who are the hungry, the homeless, the naked, the thirsty, the prisoners, in our lives?

But this is not a feast for threats. Jesus wants us to emulate him and his compassion, not just to save our skins and get to heaven, but because we love him. He wants us to respond to the love that he has poured out for us by our personal works of mercy to all who are in need of any kind.

Reading I is God's own love song for his people: "I myself will pasture my sheep; I myself will give them rest, says the Lord God." And we respond with the most beloved and beautiful of all the psalms: "The Lord is my shepherd, there is nothing I shall want." It is also our response to Jesus' own declaration of his love for us in John 10:

> The good shepherd lays down his life for the sheep . . .
> I am the good shepherd.
> I know my sheep
> and my sheep know me.

Christ lived, suffered, and died out of love for us; he saw us as poor and needy and came to our aid. May our celebration of this feast bring us to rededicate our lives to him and to carry on the blessed work that he has given over to us!

Blessed is he who comes in the name of the Lord (Alleluia Verse).

162 CHRIST THE KING Cycle B

READING I **Dan 7:13-14** **READING II** **Rev 1:5-8**
GOSPEL **John 18:33-37**

Reading I: Daniel's vision of the Son of Man before God who gives him dominion, glory, and kingship over all creation.

Reading II: Jesus, the faithful witness, is coming amid the clouds, and every eye shall see him.

Gospel: Pilate asks Jesus if he is king of the Jews and Jesus replies: "My kingdom does not belong to this world."

Most of the feasts of the liturgical year celebrate *events* in the life of Christ. This feast celebrates an *idea:* Jesus is King of Kings and

Lord of Lords. "The Lord is king; he is robed in majesty" (Responsorial Psalm).

In the gospel we see Pilate, the representative of Roman imperialism, confronting Jesus, crowned with thorns, victim of a night of betrayal, insult, beating. Pilate is the one who is ill at ease, afraid and uncertain. He asks, "Are you the king of the Jews?"

Jesus is the one who is in control. Yes, he is a king, but his kingdom is not of this world. His is not a rule of power; he came not to dominate, to tyrannize over lives, but to serve. His will be a "kingdom of truth and life, a kingdom of holiness and grace, a kingdom of justice, love, and peace" (Preface).

It seems inevitable that we should want to contrast Christ's kingship with the world situation today. Who or what rules our world? Is it Christ or is it force of arms, engineering and computerized superiority? Pilate's question is still valid: "Are you a king?" Today he might ask, does your kingship have anything at all to do with the world situation today?

These are not easy questions to answer, but they have to be faced by us who call ourselves Christians, followers of Christ our king. Perhaps the beginning of an answer could be found if every Christian seriously and honestly answered the question, is Christ king in my life? Is there any attachment that I prefer to Christ? Anything I consider more important than Christ? As professed followers of Christ, we have to face up to our responsibilities without evasion.

Everything seems to point to the fact that we are at a turning point in human history and in the history of Christianity: a turning point that has its foundation in Christ's words, "My kingdom does not belong to this world."

"Christ's kingship does not depend on armies and bombs and missiles, but on the power of truth. It is not national, but rather transcends all boundaries of class, sex, color, religions. . . . It does not oppress human lives, but rather lifts and frees people. It does not reside in territories that have to be defended . . . , but rather in the hearts and minds of people, ordinary people, as those hearts and minds are open to his presence" (Alex Campbell).

"My kingdom does not belong to this world." Jesus had no intention or desire to be a political leader. His is a kingdom of hearts belonging to people who live in this world. Building and strengthening *this* kingdom is our concern, the concern of every Christian. We begin by making Christ our king in reality, not in any vain future hope. We determine to make our lives *Christ-centered* by deciding to serve him totally, intensely, in all that we do. He has to become king of our minds and hearts.

And he showed us by personal example how to make him our king: he served others. We recall how he washed the feet of his apostles at the Last Supper, how he spent his life caring for all who were in any kind of need, how he hung on the cross and died out of love for us all.

His is a kingdom of hearts, of *our* hearts. We make Christ our king by *serving those in need.* But even more necessary is that we open our hearts to the servant-king Jesus and welcome him into our lives, as Mary his mother welcomed him when she said, "Let it be done to me as you say." "Fill us . . . with your kindness, [O Lord], that we may shout for joy" (Psalm 90).

Christ's kingdom is in the making, and we are part of it. We will not see its universal and final fulfillment in our lifetime, at least not in our lifetime in this world. But there is another lifetime that will last forever, and in that lifetime, if we have made Christ the king of our hearts, if we have served others as he did, we will know that we had our own personal part in it. And we will rejoice.

> The Lord will reign for ever and will give his people the gift of peace (Communion Antiphon).

163 CHRIST THE KING Cycle C

READING I **2 Sam 5:1-3** **READING II** **Col 1:12-20**
GOSPEL **Luke 23:35-43**

Reading I: The people ask David to be their king. He agrees and is anointed king of Israel.

Reading II: Jesus is the image of the invisible God, the firstborn of all creation. He is the head of his body, the Church.

Gospel: THIS IS THE KING OF THE JEWS is the inscription over the head of Jesus hanging on the cross.

What a contrast between the Jesus of Reading II and the Jesus of the gospel! It is hard to believe that they are one and the same. But they are, and both of them speak to us today; both hope for our personal response.

Undoubtedly, the Jesus whom most people experience in their lives is the suffering Jesus of the gospel, the Jesus who continues to suffer in the lives of his people who are starving and homeless everywhere, those who are being persecuted in communist countries and those countries dominated by dictators, people in our prisons, asylums, nursing homes, and hospitals. As a matter of fact, people everywhere, especially parents of families.

It is men, women, and children who suffer and agonize everywhere, who cry out to their Jesus on the cross, "Jesus, remember me when you enter upon your reign." What did the good thief mean when he asked Jesus to remember him? He surely meant much more than don't forget that you saw me at your side up there on that hill. I believe he meant, remember who I am. Remember that I am *someone*, a human person who, despite everything I have done, despite my criminal past, I am still someone who wants to count as a human being created in the image and likeness of God.

And Jesus answers, "I assure you: this day you will be with me in paradise."

Without doubt the relationship between Jesus and the good thief has deep meaning for us. The thief sees Jesus as a fellow sufferer, but he also sees his personal salvation in this dying Jesus. When he begs Jesus to remember him, he is not asking for a miraculous deliverance from the cross. What he wants is some meaning for his wretched life, some kind of self-identity as a man. We are like the good thief. Life cannot make much sense until we find out who we are and accept ourselves for who we are.

The good news about the image of Jesus on the cross *and* Paul's description of him as Lord and king of all is that, whoever we are, whatever our failures, however much we are hurting, God comes to us in this Jesus and tells us that we are his beloved children and that he loves us totally and irrevocably. And God not only gave us the crucified Jesus as a sign of his love but also a sign that he is working in and through our daily suffering to bring us to fulfillment as mature Christians, as other Christs.

Jesus on the cross with that sign over his head has to give us a new or renewed sense of our being worthwhile. To be a Christian means to recognize who we are in the sight of God, to realize God's love for us, that divine love made flesh in God's Son Jesus hanging on the cross. The Jesus who continues to live with and in us, who guides us along the way, nourishes us daily with his Body and Blood and with his word.

To be a Christian is to be willing above all to allow Jesus to love us and to be everlastingly grateful for his love. "Jesus, remember me. . . ." He responds, this day you will be with me in paradise. I am here on this cross because I love you. That's who you are!

So, may we always "give thanks to the Father for having made [us] worthy to share the lot of the saints in light. He rescued us from the power of darkness and brought us into the kingdom of his beloved Son. Through him we have redemption, the forgiveness of our sins" (Reading II).

503 MONDAY OF THE THIRTY-FOURTH, OR LAST, WEEK IN ORDINARY TIME

YEAR I

READING I Dan 1:1-6, 8-20
GOSPEL Luke 21:1-4

The Book of Daniel relates a story of heroic adherence to God's Law on the part of his people, the noblest of whom are Daniel and his three companions. Their loyalty to the law is going to make us want to "glory and praise God for ever" (Responsorial Psalm). But even more noble is the poor widow whom Jesus presents to us as a true model for Christian living and giving. Jesus is not giving a lesson in parish financing: if parishioners gave only two copper coins, we could not even pay the light bills. But what Jesus is concerned about is the spirit in which we all contribute to any worthy cause. The poor widow contributed—not to fulfill a law or to put God in debt to her—but simply to make an act of love for God. With a little watching over our motives, the spirit in which she gave can probably be accomplished with a large gift as well as a small one. All we have to do is to see to our love.

YEAR II

READING I Rev 14:1-3, 4-5
GOSPEL Luke 21:1-4

"Lord, this is the people that longs to see your face (Responsorial Psalm). The martyrs so dearly longed to see the Lord's face that they counted persecution and death as gain. John's vision of heaven and of Jesus the Lamb is a little symbolic but full of deep meaning. There is great and joyful celebration to the accompaniment of the beautiful sounds of nature and musical instruments.

The martyrs sing a new song before the throne. These are the ones who, because they faithfully followed Jesus the Lamb on earth, now follow him joyfully in heaven, feasting on his love. Their earthly longing to see the face of the Lord is now satisfied forever and ever. That same way—faithfully following the Lamb and living by and on his gospel, above all, longing to see his face—is open to every one of us.

504 TUESDAY OF THE THIRTY-FOURTH, OR LAST, WEEK IN ORDINARY TIME

YEAR I

READING I Dan 2:31-45
GOSPEL Luke 21:5-11

In Reading I Daniel interprets the king's dream, predicting a succession of kingdoms, ending in one that "shall never be destroyed." It is the kind of prophecy that also characterized the times when the Gospels were composed, times when the end of the world was on everyone's mind. In the Gospels it is often difficult to know which event Jesus has in mind—the destruction of Jerusalem and the Temple or the end of the world. Such is the case in today's gospel. The coming of the end of the world is a popular subject in every age, including our own. Some modern writers have made millions on books predicting the approaching end—books that cannot endure the light of biblical scholarship. Such authors try to scare people into being good. That is not Jesus' way or intention. Rather:

Be faithful until death, says the Lord,
and I will give you the crown of life (Alleluia Verse).

The best way to be faithful is to be full of loving desire for God.

YEAR II

READING I **Rev 14:14-19**
GOSPEL **Luke 21:5-11**

This last week of the Church Year will be filled with prophecies and warnings of the end of the world. The readings will reflect the mentality of the latter part of the first century, out of which the Gospels emerged. There are at least two ways of considering the last days: with terror, anxiety, and dread or with eager longing and expectation. The latter is the Christian way.

Here we are 2000 years later, and the end has not come yet. But false prophets (Jesus warns against them in the gospel) continue to try to scare people into being good and joining their cults. As for us, we believe that the Lord is indeed going to come to judge the earth; but we need not fear if we are true to Christ and to ourselves—above all if we seek the Lord with longing desire and hope. We remember that he seeks us, too. With that kind of twofold seeking, we've got it made.

505 WEDNESDAY OF THE THIRTY-FOURTH, OR LAST, WEEK IN ORDINARY TIME

YEAR I

READING I **Dan 5:1-6, 13-14, 16-17, 23-28**
GOSPEL **Luke 21:12-19**

King Belshazzar commits a sacrilege in profaning the sacred vessels of the Temple. Daniel's words to him are a perfect definition of his sin—and every sin ever committed: "The God in whose hand is your life breath and the whole course of your life, you did not glorify." When any human refuses to remember his obligation to glorify God his creator, he sins, and he brings about his own doom. On that very night Belshazzar is slain.

The theme of end-times that characterizes this week's readings continues in the gospel. Jesus predicts the suffering of his disciples. They will be tried, falsely accused, and hated, and some will be put to death—all because Jesus was hated and despised himself. But this is the paschal law: suffering and death are a prelude to resurrection and glorification. We have the faith today because of the suffering and martyrdom of these disciples of Jesus.

YEAR II

READING I Rev 15:1-4
GOSPEL Luke 21:12-19

John's purpose in writing the Book of Revelation was to instill courage in Christians being persecuted for their faith. The beautiful imagery of today's Reading I reminds us of God's ultimate triumph over the enemies of his people. Standing on the shore of the sea of glass, the saints (including us) will sing Moses' triumphant Exodus song, realizing that they too have had their Exodus, their going-out, from the Egypt of oppression and sorrow. At long last we will understand the mystery of our life with all its pain and suffering, and we will join in the triumphant song:

> Mighty and wonderful are your works,
> Lord God Almighty!
> Righteous and true are your ways,
> O King of the nations!
> Who would dare refuse you honor,
> or the glory due your name, O Lord?
> Since you alone are holy,
> all nations shall come
> and worship in your presence.
> Your mighty deeds are clearly seen (Reading I).

506 THURSDAY OF THE THIRTY-FOURTH, OR LAST, WEEK IN ORDINARY TIME

YEAR I

READING I Dan 6:12-28
GOSPEL Luke 21:20-28

The story of Daniel in the lion's den is more than a charming fable. It is possible to enjoy seeing Daniel rescued and to miss the reason why. The reason is that Daniel believed in God's love for him and trusted in that love. His faith and trust not only rescued him but also converted the king to faith in the living God. Who can equal the king's tribute to the Lord: "He is the living God, enduring forever . . . his dominion shall be without end"?

Daniel is not only a model of faith and trust for the king, but for all of us who fear the end of the world or our own approaching death. May we all, like Daniel, truly believe in God's love for us, and may Daniel's trust be our trust. Then, as today's gospel tells us, "When these things begin to happen and signs of death approach, stand up straight and raise your heads, for your ransom is near at hand."

YEAR II

READING I Rev 18:1-2, 21-23; 19:1-3, 9
GOSPEL Luke 21:20-28

Commentators say that Babylon stands for the Rome that persecuted Christians. Today John sees it as already fallen and doomed to oblivion. The New American Bible tells us that the imagery is not to be taken literally but that it does point to the ultimate victory of God's justice.

In the gospel Jesus' prophecies of the destruction of Jerusalem and of the end of the world are intermingled. Some people are terrified at the thought of the end of the world or of their own death. Some refuse to think about death at all. The thoughtful Christian avoids both extremes and heeds Christ's advice. When things like old age or serious sickness come upon you:

> Lift up your heads and see;
> your redemption is near at hand (Alleluia Verse).

You have longed to see God's face. The time is near. "Blessed are those who are invited to the marriage supper of the Lamb (Responsorial Psalm).

507 FRIDAY OF THE THIRTY-FOURTH, OR LAST, WEEK IN ORDINARY TIME

YEAR I

READING I Dan 7:2-14
GOSPEL Luke 21:29-33

No one will deny that Daniel was a man of vision and of vivid imagination. There is not much point in trying to fathom the meaning of all those visions. What is essential is to zero in on the "one like a son of man coming, on the clouds of heaven; . . ." There is a right way and a wrong way to understand Daniel's sensational prophecies. The wrong way is exploited by those modern prophets of doom who try to scare the hell out of people and too often cause them to end up on psychiatrists' couches. The other way is that of Jesus himself and his earliest followers who eagerly looked forward to Christ's Second Coming. Dread of judgment is dangerous and destructive. Desire for Christ is healthy and life giving. Jesus gives us the right directive.

> Lift up your heads and see;
> your redemption is near at hand (Alleluia Verse).

YEAR II

READING I Rev 20:1-4, 11–21:2
GOSPEL Luke 21:29-33

It is dangerous to take the numbers mentioned in the Book of Revelation too literally; for example, seeing the thousand years as a precise prediction of the reign of the Messiah on earth. Whenever anyone sets a date for the end of the world, there is a possibility of any number of foolish and dangerous happenings for many innocent people.

At the end of the Book of Revelation, it is again good for us to be reminded that Satan has already been defeated and overcome by Christ's death and resurrection; and it is good to remember that the suffering we endure in this life is temporary. The new heaven and the new earth, the new Jerusalem, symbolize the blessed condition of those who are faithful and loving now. It will be a bridal condition, one of which love is the essence, and it will last forever. It is worth waiting—and suffering—for.

508 SATURDAY OF THE THIRTY-FOURTH, OR LAST, WEEK IN ORDINARY TIME

YEAR I

READING I Dan 7:15-27
GOSPEL Luke 21:34-36

God has never revealed what the world and life in it will be like after the Second Coming of Christ. It is a fascinating topic to speculate about, not to try to describe in infallible terms. In today's Reading I, our last reading from Daniel, we have a glimpse of that world, but without too many details: "Then the kingship and dominion and majesty of all the kingdoms under the heavens shall be given to the holy people of the Most High, whose kingdom shall be everlasting: all dominions shall serve and obey him."

We may safely say that all the deep desires for truth, love, life, joy, peace, that God our creator has planted in our hearts shall be finally and fully satisfied. There will be no more hatred, war, violence, no more fear. God will be our all. We will know for sure that our life was worth all the pain, sorrow, and anguish we have endured.

YEAR II

READING I Rev 22:1-7
GOSPEL Luke 21:34-36

"Happy the man who heeds the prophetic message of this book!" It is a message, not of annihilation and destruction, but of hope and longing. "Come, Lord Jesus!" (Responsorial Psalm) We look forward to a glorious fulfillment both of our own lives and of God's creation. Our faith is rooted in the past—on what God has done for us in Christ Jesus. But a faith that has only a past and no present and future is no faith at all.

Our God is One who has come, but he is also One who *is to come.* The redeeming work begun by Jesus must go on. Christ is the beginning but also the end of all things. May we each work and pray and hope—not for the destruction of the world, but for its gradual growth toward perfection according to the spirit of Christ Jesus!

> For he is our God,
> and we are the people he shepherds, the flock he guides.
> Marana tha! Come, Lord Jesus! (Responsorial Psalm)

MAJOR FEASTS IN ORDINARY TIME

524 PRESENTATION OF THE LORD February 2

READING I **Mal 3:1-4** **READING II** **Heb 2:14-18**
GOSPEL **Luke 2:22-40**

Reading I: The Lord, whom people seek, will come to the temple; he will purify and refine the people.

Reading II: Jesus had to become like his fellow humans that he might be a faithful high priest before God on their behalf.

Gospel: Luke's account of Jesus' presentation in the temple forty days after his birth.

Forty days ago we celebrated the birth of Jesus. Today we celebrate his presentation in the temple in Jerusalem in fulfillment of the ancient Jewish law. On this day Jesus, Son of God and Son of Mary, goes forth to meet his people for the first time. Mary carries him in her arms to present him to the Lord.

The just and pious man named Simeon takes the child in his arms and blesses God in these grateful words:

Now, Master, you can dismiss your servant in peace;
 you have fulfilled your word.
For my eyes have witnessed your saving deed
 displayed for all the peoples to see:
A revealing light to the Gentiles,
 the glory of your people Israel.

And Simeon's partner in hoping, the prophetess Anna, who had been spending all her time praying in the temple, sees the child and goes out to spread the good news "to all who looked foward to the deliverance of Jerusalem."

Simeon and Anna are two of the most symbolic people in all sacred history. They represent Israel, indeed, all humanity, waiting and longing for Jesus, the promised Messiah. They had longed to see the glory of God's face shining in human eyes. And here he is!

The Byzantine liturgy calls this presentation "Hypapante," "The Encounter." "With Simeon the old age of the world receives into his arms the eternal youth of God. But already the shadow of the cross is profiled and darkness will turn back the light" *(Missel Dominical de l'Assemblée,* p. 1355, Paris, Brepols, 1981).

The shadow of the cross . . . Simeon says to Mary: "This child is destined to be the downfall and the rise of many in Israel, a sign that will be opposed—and you yourself shall be pierced with a sword—so that the thoughts of many hearts may be laid bare." The fulfillment of that prophecy, when Mary looks up at this same Jesus hanging on the cross, is all too familiar to us all. Here Mary and Joseph offer two turtledoves, symbolic of the offering she will make of Jesus on Calvary—the offering that Jesus makes of himself.

Back of all the dramatic reality of this occasion and that which it prefigures is another truth that we may not forget, namely, God's own love for us all, God's own longing desire for all human hearts and the love they are capable of generating.

Today is the traditional day for the blessing of the candles that will be used in the coming year in our liturgies. Candles are symbols of Christ who is the light of the world. Candles are also symbols of human hearts afire with grateful love. May the burning hearts in us today continue to glow ever more brightly until Mary, mother of Jesus and our mother, will hold us in her arms and present us to the Lord.

587 BIRTH OF JOHN THE BAPTIST June 24

READING I Isa 49:1-6 **READING II** Acts 13:22-26
GOSPEL Luke 1:57-66, 80

Reading I: A prophecy of the origin of John, the work he will do and the kind of man he will be.

Reading II: Paul speaks of Jesus as the descendent of David and of John as his herald who prepared the way for Jesus by preaching penance and conversion of life.

Gospel: Luke's account of the birth, the circumcision, and the naming of John, son of Elizabeth and Zachary.

All through Jewish history God sends his prophets to preach repentance and conversion to his people. Finally God sends the greatest of the prophets, John, whose specific mission is to prepare the way for Jesus the Messiah by preaching a baptism of repentance for the forgiveness of their sins. Today we celebrate the birth of this great man.

> You, child, will be called the prophet of the Most High; You will go before the Lord to prepare his ways (Alleluia Verse).

The hand of God is evident in John's conception and birth more than in any other historical figure except Jesus himself. The gospel of this feast's Vigil (Luke 1:5-17) relates the account of the angel's appearance to Zachary to tell him that his barren wife, Elizabeth, will have a child who will be "great in the eyes of the Lord."

The gospel of the feast continues that of the Vigil and tells of John's birth and circumcision, at which the neighbors and relatives want to call the child after his father, Zachary. But Elizabeth and her husband insist on the name John, the name designated by the angel when Zachary first received the news that he would be a father. "What will this child be?" the neighbors ask. "Was not the hand of the Lord upon him?" Indeed it was.

When John grew up, the gospel tells us, he went to live a penitential life in the desert "until the day when he made his public appearance in Israel." The Gospels provide us with occasional glimpses of John in action, carrying out his appointed mission. He attracts many followers and disciples, a couple of whom become disciples of Jesus. Some of John's followers are so enthusiastic about him that they become disturbed at hearing that Jesus was also baptizing, and "everyone is flocking to him" (John 3:26). John responds: "I am not the Messiah; I am sent before him. It is the groom who has the bride. The groom's best man waits there listening for him and is overjoyed to hear his voice. That is my joy, and it is complete. He must increase, while I must decrease" (John 3:28-29). (I prefer the Revised Standard Version, in which John calls himself "the friend of the bridegroom.")

The Gospels do not tell us, but it is not difficult for us to imagine the degree of love and respect that Jesus had for this fearless and dedicated cousin of his.

John was killed "in line of duty," when he condemned King Herod for his adulterous marriage to Herodias. And how that must have pained Jesus! John died then, but his work lives on; in fact, it will never be ended, not as long as there are people in this world who wish to become followers of Jesus or who wish to intensify their union with him. Today's Alternative Opening Prayer articulates John's work now:

> God our Father,
> the voice of John the Baptist challenges us to repentance
> and points the way to Christ the Lord.
> Open our ears to his message, and free our hearts
> to turn from our sins and receive the life of the gospel.
> We ask this through Christ our Lord.

The way to Jesus then was through John the Baptist. It is still the way. For us, without John and his message, there is no Christ.

591 STS. PETER AND PAUL, APOSTLES June 29

READING I Acts 12:1-11 **READING II** 2 Tim 4:6-8, 17-18
GOSPEL Matt 16:13-19

Reading I: Peter in prison is miraculously freed by an angel of the Lord.

Reading II: Near the end of his life Paul in prison looks back with gratitude on his dedicated life in spreading the faith.

Gospel: Peter calls Jesus the Messiah and Jesus calls Peter the rock on which he will build his Church.

This feast takes us back to the beginnings of the Church, and it reminds us of the kind of persons on whom Jesus built his Church. It is good and important for Christians in any age to be reminded that these founding pillars of the Church were so terribly human and frail, but it is even better to be reminded of how, through cooperation with God's grace, they came through to a worthy and heroic end.

After all his protestations of loyalty, Peter denied three times that he even knew Christ (Luke 22:55-62). After the resurrection, when Jesus appears to the apostles at the Sea of Tiberias, he asks Peter three times, "Simon, son of John, do you love me more than these?" (gospel of the Vigil Mass)

Jesus is not trying to "rub it in" after Peter's threefold denial. That's not his way. But he undoubtedly does want to give Peter a chance to make up for his cowardly failure to stand up for his Master. More than all else, Jesus wants to solidify the promise he made in the neighborhood of Caesarea Philippi: to make Peter the rock foundation of his Church. When Jesus says to Peter: "Feed my lambs. . . . feed my sheep," he is surely not talking about animals. He is referring to Peter's future position in his Church. I am sure that Jesus loved (and enjoyed) Peter very much.

Then there is Paul. What would Christianity have been like without him? He is perhaps history's best example of human response to divine grace and its power. In Reading II of both the Vigil Mass and the Mass during the Day, Paul reviews his entire life, beginning with his preconversion hatred and persecution of Christians and ending with his imprisonment shortly before his martyrdom. "I have fought the good fight, I have finished the race, I have kept the faith."

He gives all the credit to Christ: "The Lord stood by my side and gave me strength, so that through me the preaching task might be completed and all the nations might hear the gospel."

It was love for Jesus that drove him to spend himself without any holding back in spreading the knowledge and love of Jesus. It was love for Jesus that buoyed him up to shed his blood for the faith. It was love that drove him to share Christ and his good news with all future generations of Christians by writing his epistles.

This is one of the most important and necessary feasts of the entire Church Year. It surely brings out the humanness of the founding pillars of the Church, and we always need that reminder. They were human beings, not angels. They were as frail and as capable of sinning as we are. This fact must be the source of much consolation and encouragement to us. We know enough about Peter and Paul to realize that if God could work in them and bring them to the fullness of their being, God can do the same in us—if we only choose to give in to his grace.

It is terribly important to realize that the work of becoming a whole person, a saint, is the work of a lifetime of receiving Jesus into our lives and allowing him full power over our hearts. Christ was everything for Peter and Paul. He must become everything for us.

It was only after his personal failures, his denials of Christ, that Peter was able to cry out: "Lord, you know everything. You know well that I love you!" (John 21:17) Peter has shown us the way. We, too, are human; we have sinned, as he did. God grant that the hour will soon come when we can make Peter's words our very own as we cry out: "Lord, you know everything. You know well that I love you!"

READING I Dan 7:9-10, 13-14 **READING II** 2 Pet 1:16-19
GOSPEL Cycle A Matt 17:1-9
Cycle B Mark 9:2-10
Cycle C Luke 9:28-36

Reading I: A vision of the Lord God and of the Son of Man who receives dominion, glory, and everlasting kingship.

Reading II: Years after the event Peter shares his memory of Jesus' transfiguration with his Christian flock.

Gospel: The account of the transfiguration of Jesus by each of the synoptic evangelists.

The Feast of the Transfiguration is full of meaning and beauty for all Christians. And God knows we need meaning and beauty in our lives.

Not long before his passion and death Jesus takes Peter, James, and John up a high mountain where he is transfigured before their eyes. His face became as dazzling as the sun, his clothes as radiant as light (Matt 17:2). Moses and Elijah appear, conversing with Jesus.

The apostles are so overjoyed they want to settle down there. Peter speaks to Jesus: "Rabbi, how good it is to be here. Let us erect three booths on this site, one for you, one for Moses, and one for Elijah" (Mark 9:5). Then they hear the voice of God speaking from a cloud: "This is my beloved Son on whom my favor rests. Listen to him" (Matt 17:5). Hearing that voice, they fall down, overcome with fear. In a moment Jesus comes to them, lays his hand on them and says, "Get up! Do not be afraid." They go back down the mountain with him, wondering to themselves what it all meant.

One thing the incident means to us is that it gives us an idea of the natural human reaction to the experience of the divine. First, the apostles are filled with joy. Then, aware of their sinfulness and unworthiness, they fall down, overcome with fear and awe. We need joy, fear, and awe if we are to grow and mature as followers of Jesus. We need the vivid awareness of being in God's presence and being filled with joy. But we also need the awesome fear of our unworthiness as sin-inclined creatures.

But back to the mountain of the transfiguration. We may notice that the Lord God's words here are almost the same as those Jesus heard at his baptism. In both instances the words echo one of the "Servant Songs" of the prophet Isaiah, "Here is my servant whom I uphold, my chosen one with whom I am pleased" (Isa 42:1).

Who is Jesus? He is God's Son, but he is a Son who is also a servant—a Suffering Servant who will obey the Father's will even to the extent of sweating blood and dying on a cross. The mount of the transfiguration will become Mount Calvary, which Jesus will climb after he carries his cross through the streets of Jerusalem.

Our task as Christians is to be open and ready to receive the full communication of all that Jesus is, says, and does. "Listen to him," the Father tells us. It isn't only words that Jesus wishes to give us but his very self. We respond to him not only with our words of praise, thanksgiving, and petition but with receptive hearts and lives. We follow him up the mountain of the transfiguration and down again into daily life, passing through the garden of Gethsemani where we sweat blood, through the streets carrying a cross, and up to Calvary. But that is not the end.

Transfiguration, transformation, is what life is all about. And the goal? That at the end of our gradually transforming life the Father can look upon each of us and say, this is my beloved child on whom my favor rests. Enter into the joy of the Lord!

> Lord,
> you revealed the true radiance of Christ
> in the glory of his transfiguration.
> May the food we receive from heaven
> change us into his image (Prayer after Communion).
> Amen, Amen!

READING I Rev 11:19, 12:1-6, 10 **READING II** 1 Cor 15:20-26
GOSPEL Luke 1:39-56

Reading I: The woman clothed with the sun and wearing a crown of twelve stars can be seen as a symbol of Mary.

Reading II: Paul's vision of the end of the world when Jesus, Son of Mary, will hand over the kingdom to the Father.

Gospel: Mary, carrying Christ in her womb, visits Elizabeth who addresses her as "mother of my Lord."

All honor to you, Mary! Today you were raised above the choirs of angels to lasting glory with Christ (Entrance Antiphon, Vigil Mass).

Mary is taken up to heaven, and the angels of God shout for joy. We would like to share in the shouting and joy of the angels today.

The Gospels do not provide us with an account either of the death or of the assumption of Mary into heaven. But belief in her assumption goes back to the earliest days of the Church. Her tomb was venerated, but there were no relics of her body, as was the case with the apostles and the earliest martyrs. The main meaning of the assumption is that the corruption of death and the grave did not touch her.

In the Creed, we profess our belief in the resurrection of the body. We believe that on the last day we will rise again. Mary's assumption is the first instance of Christ's resurrection becoming fully operative in redeemed humankind. As Reading II has it: "Christ has been raised from the dead, the first fruits of those who have fallen asleep." May we not claim, then, that Mary is the "second fruits"?

Mary is the first human person in whom the victory of Jesus is complete, the first member of his body to share in his own resurrection to glory, the first to enter heaven in the fullness of her personality. The assumption instructs us on "the need to restore a balanced outlook on the unity of the human personality" (Father Carr). We are not body alone, not soul alone, but *soul and body together*.

What does Mary's assumption mean for us now? For an answer we go back to Christ's resurrection and ascension. By virtue of his resurrection and ascension, Jesus lives now in a new existence in which he is present to and in our world, present to and in us. "Know that I am with you always," he said as he was about to ascend to the Father. And he meant it.

As Jesus is present to and in us by virtue of his resurrection, so is Mary. As *A New Catechism* states it so beautifully: "Mary is more in the world than any other woman. Other famous women in history are remembered; Mary is addressed. She is the most closely present of all women. . . . We can experience the presence of Jesus and Mary by speaking to them in prayer" (Herder and Herder, New York, 1970, 475).

Mary is the new Eve, the new mother of all the living. She is the new Israel. Throughout Jewish history God sought to fashion a people who might eventually say yes to the creator. Mary is Israel in its ultimate perfection. She is also the Church, the body of Christ, the new people of God, the one who followed her Son most perfectly, the one who best exemplifies the attitude of *total receptivity* to God's insistence on giving himself, sharing divine life with us. "I am the servant of the Lord. Let it be done to me as you say" (Luke 1:38).

Mary's opening of her life to God was an act of profound faith. She believed in her vocation and gave herself over to it with every fiber of her being. Without thinking of herself, she trusted in God and said yes; she consented to let God take over her life (Louis Evely).

What is so remarkable about Mary, then, is her faith. She lived a life of faith exactly as we do. We must not think of her as some unapproachable queen to be admired from afar, but rather as an available example to be imitated in our everyday lives. Of all the saints, Mary's greatness and glory is that she is the one who is most available for our imitation. We can't be the mother of God, as she was. But we can say yes to God as she did and so share her glory, her holiness.

"Blest are they who hear the word of God and keep it," Jesus says (gospel of the Vigil Mass). "I am the servant of the Lord. Let it be done to me as you say," says Mary.

> May we follow her example in reflecting your holiness
> and join in her hymn of endless life and praise (Alternative Opening Prayer).

READING I Num 21:4-9 **READING II** Phil 2:6-11
GOSPEL John 3:13-17

Reading I: When the complaining Jews were bitten by snakes in the desert, they were healed by gazing on a bronze serpent lifted on a pole.

Reading II: Jesus emptied himself of his divinity and took the form of a slave, obedient unto death. Therefore, God highly exalted him and gave him a name above every other name.

Gospel: As Moses lifted up the serpent in the desert, so must the Son of Man be lifted up.

We should glory in the cross of our Lord Jesus Christ, for he is our salvation, our life and our resurrection; through him we are saved and made free (Entrance Antiphon).

Today we try to be obedient to that exhortation as we celebrate the triumph (and also the mystery) of the cross on which hung the world's Savior. If we already glorified in the cross in the springtime of the year, on Good Friday, it is appropriate to do it again in the fall with this feast. We cannot do it too often. Recall how on Good Friday we had the dramatic unveiling of the cross and how we all kissed it. That was an act of love and of loving gratitude; it was also an act of *healing* of hearts.

So today is a day for all of us to again look on the cross with that same loving gratitude and once again be healed of our failure to help Jesus carry it, our failure to live up to our dignity as followers of Jesus. "The very sight of Jesus lifted up on the cross has power to bring men and women to faith and repentance" (Fuller). If the Israelites were healed of their snakebites by gazing on the bronze serpent lifted on a pole (Reading I), may we not expect the healing of wounded hearts by looking at the broken body of Jesus hanging on his cross?

The Cost of Discipleship was written by Dietrich Bonhoeffer, who was killed by the Nazis in the last days of World War II. That title describes an idea that is providential in any age. We have to pay a great price in order to be authentic and genuine followers of Jesus. It means giving up one's own will, removing any obstacle or attachment that prevents us from belonging wholly to him. Recall Jesus' words: "Whoever wishes to be my follower must deny his very self, take up his cross each day, and follow in my steps" (Luke 9:23).

Self-discipline, leaving selfish attachments behind, is the only way to find one's true self. To give ourselves away is to receive ourselves back, infinitely enriched, filled with the love of Christ's own heart. There can be no soft mattresses on the cross we carry in imitation of Jesus.

The personal cross that Jesus asks each of us to carry may not be the same for all. It may be personal illness or old age; but surely for most of us it is the anguish and pain of those we love, their (and our) loss of loved ones. And who of us can rest easily in the presence of all the suffering in our world, especially in Third World countries? We are closest to Christ when our hearts are filled with the world's pain.

> I—once I am lifted up from earth—will draw all men to myself (John 12:32).

Jesus belongs to every people on the earth. He identifies with them and they with him. I have seen a crucifix carved in Tanzania. The body and face of the Christ on the cross is a native of that country.

The passion of Christ will last as long as people suffer in our world, and it is this passion, this suffering, that he asks us to share with him. May we do it in the spirit of St. Paul, who understood something of the mystery of Christ's passion and actually experienced it. He writes: "Even now I find my joy in the suffering I endure for you. In my own flesh I fill up what is lacking in the suffering of Christ for the sake of his body, the church" (Col 1:24).

So, through suffering we become coredeemers with Christ. Through suffering and only through suffering we come to glory. Remember what this feast is called: The Triumph of the Cross. The cross led to Christ's triumph; it will lead to ours as well.

> We should all glory in the cross of our Lord Jesus Christ, for he is our salvation, our life and our resurrection; through him we are saved and made free (Entrance Antiphon).

ALL SAINTS

November 1

READING I Rev 7:2-4, 9-14 **READING II** 1 John 3:1-3
GOSPEL Matt 5:1-12

Reading I: A vision of heaven, with a great crowd before God's throne and the Lamb, crying out, "Salvation is from our God . . . and from the Lamb."

Reading II: We are God's children now, and some day we shall be like him and we shall see him as he is.

Gospel: Jesus teaches us the Beatitudes—the way to holiness.

> Let us all rejoice in the Lord and keep a festival in honor of all the saints. Let us join with the angels in joyful praise to the Son of God (Entrance Antiphon).

That antiphon surely sets the tone for this feast. "Let us all rejoice!" Rejoice, give praise and thanks! Why? Because of the triumph of God's love and grace in the numberless sisters and brothers of ours in the family of God. This is a family feast, with a tinge of nostalgia, and above all, happy memories of loved ones who are now forever with the God for whom they hungered during their life.

It is also a celebration of what we are, hopefully, in the process of becoming ourselves. It is a feast of potential saints, *our* feast.

Do we ever think of ourselves as potential saints? Probably not, mainly because of the inadequate idea most of us have of what saintliness is. All the publicity that accompanies canonization doesn't help much either. And then there are the miracles that are necessary if one is to be canonized. Who of us thinks of him or herself as a miracle worker?

This feast tells us that the saints were ordinary women and men like ourselves who opened their hearts and lives to the divine love and life that God wishes to share with all of us. They were totally receptive to God's self-giving; there was no holding back. They joyfully allowed themselves to be possessed by God. "See what love the Father has bestowed on us in letting us be called children of God!" (Reading II)

So holiness is the gift of God. "Salvation is from our God, who is seated on the throne, and from the Lamb!" (Reading I) But God cannot make us saints without our consent. What is required on our part? The answer is in our response to Reading I: "Lord, this is the people that longs to see your face." Longing for God, deep desire to possess and be possessed by the infinite source of all joy and blessedness—this is the attitude we need to cultivate if we wish to be holy. It is an attitude that is instinctive in our hearts. We need only become aware of it.

The gospel of the Beatitudes also contains some practical and necessary advice for us: "How blest are the poor in spirit. . . . Blest are they who show mercy. . . . Blest too are the peacemakers. . . ." As *A New Catechism* points out, the Beatitudes do not designate eight different classes. Taken together, they describe a *mentality* that characterizes persons "who have nothing to hope for from the world and look to God for everything . . . people whose lives resemble the way of submissiveness and loving service which Jesus himself adopted at his baptism" (Herder and Herder, New York, 1970, 99).

I have said that this is a family feast. The saints and we make up this family. They have reached their goal, but they will always be deeply concerned about us and our progress along the way they followed. They were and are great lovers.

> Father, . . .
> may their prayers bring us your forgiveness and love (Opening Prayer).

668 ALL SOULS November 2

(A priest may celebrate three Masses on All Souls Day, with different readings for each Mass. The following are the readings from Mass I.)

READING I **Job 19:1, 23-27** **READING II** **1 Cor 15:51-57**
GOSPEL **John 6:37-40**

Reading I: Job is convinced that his Vindicator lives, and in his inmost being he is consumed with longing for God.

Reading II: An expression of Paul's belief that Christ will come again soon; then death will be swallowed up in victory.

Gospel: It is the will of God that everyone who looks upon Jesus and believes in him shall have eternal life.

Like yesterday's feast, All Souls' Day is a family feast. We can be grateful that the expression "poor souls" is giving way to "holy souls." Those who have gone before us in the Lord are not poor. They have it made, although they may still languish in purgatory. What is purgatory? We do not know. How long does purgatory last for a soul? Again, we do not know. The only reference in the Old Testament is in 2 Maccabees 12:43-45 which tells of a collection that Judas Maccabeus took up for expiatory sacrifices for soldiers who had died defending their country. Our "separated brethren," the Protestants, do not believe in purgatory.

Reading I from the Book of Wisdom (Mass II) is consoling and enlightening: "The souls of the just are in the hand of God, and no torment shall touch them. They seemed, in the view of the foolish, to be dead; and their passing away was thought an affliction and their going forth from us, utter destruction. But they are in peace."

There is also food for thought in the opinion of a modern writer, Barry McGrory, who writes about the "continual conversion, now going on within us, which is heightened or manifested at death and which may continue after death, beyond time and place."

This is a feast for the faithful departed, but perhaps it is even more a feast for us who are still on our way. The Alleluia Verse for Mass I is intended for us as much as for those who are dying:

> Come, you whom my Father has blessed, says the Lord;
> inherit the kingdom prepared for you since the foundation of the world.

We can complement that saying of Jesus with another one recorded by Matthew: "Come to me, all you who are weary and find life burdensome, and I will refresh you. Take my yoke upon your shoulders and learn from me, for I am gentle and humble of heart" (11:28-29).

Come to me. Take my yoke upon your shoulders. If we obey him, something wonderful will happen: he is the one who will take our yoke on his shoulders. Climb on my back, he says, and I'll carry you. I won't promise to relieve you of the pain and anguish you so often suffer, but I can and I will help you to see it as a sharing in my own passion and death, and you will be a coredeemer with me.

There is an additional secret to our becoming holy souls, saints: and that is to take others on our backs, help them carry their burdens, their crosses. A newly married bride and groom might well pray: Now our joys are doubled, because the happiness of one is the happiness of the other. Now our burdens are halved since when we share them we divide the load. As Jesus shares his yoke with us, we must try to share the yoke of others, especially the yoke of those who do not know him.

> The Lord is my shepherd;
> there is nothing I shall want (Responsorial Psalm).

Pictures abound of Jesus carrying a lamb on his shoulders. Perhaps we never realized how true to reality they are.

May our inmost being be consumed with longing for him!

671 DEDICATION OF ST. JOHN LATERAN — November 9

(The readings for this feast are taken from the Common of the Dedication of a Church, and there is a great variety from which a celebrant may choose. The one idea they all have in common is that churches are special dwelling places of the most high God and are sacred. For our purposes we will concentrate on the following.)

READING I Ezek 43:1-2, 4-7 **READING II** 1 Cor 3:9-13, 16-17
GOSPEL John 2:13-22

Reading I: The prophet sees the glory of the Lord coming from the east; he falls prone as the glory of the Lord fills the Temple.

Reading II: Paul tells the Corinthians that they are God's temple and that the Spirit of God dwells in them.

Gospel: Jesus drives the merchants from the Temple and when challenged by his enemies, he says: "Destroy this temple and in three days I will raise it up."

Today we celebrate the Feast of the Dedication of St. John Lateran, the Pope's own cathedral, the mother church of all Catholics. The readings celebrate the dwelling place of the most high God. Ezekiel sees the glory of God coming from the east, "and the earth shone with his glory." This very world of ours is God's most elementary dwelling place. "The heavens declare the glory of God" (Psalm 19:1).

> Earth's crammed wtih heaven
> and every burning bush afire with God (Elizabeth Barrett Browning).

But in human history, including ancient primitive religions, the presence and glory of God began to be localized in specific places: in buildings, temples, shrines. In today's gospel Jesus calls the Temple in Jerusalem "My Father's house." The holy of holies in the Temple was preeminently the place where the divine Presence dwelled. These places were literally filled with an atmosphere that called forth from human hearts a reaction of reverence, awe, holy and loving fear, personal unworthiness.

In the gospel Jesus says to his enemies: "Destroy this temple and in three days I will raise it up." And John comments: "Actually he was talking of the temple of his body." So God's dwelling place is all creation; God's dwelling place is the Temple in Jerusalem; God's dwelling place is the body of Jesus; and St. Paul develops the idea still further.

He asks us in Reading II: "Are you not aware that you are the temple of God, and that the Spirit of God dwells in you?" Paul was not speaking only to individual Christians. To be sure, the individual human body is sacred and must not be violated by any unworthy act. But Paul was writing to the *entire Christian community* at Corinth, and today he is speaking to us, to the Christian community to which we belong. "Are you not aware that you are the temple of God, and that the Spirit of God dwells in you?" And he shocks us with his conclusion: "If anyone destroys God's temple, God will destroy him. For the temple of God is holy, and you are that temple."

There is a variety of ways by which this temple can be destroyed or its foundations undermined, the commonest ones being sins against charity, indifference to the poor, the lonely, the aged and ill, failure to forgive, or any kind of factionalism.

At Holy Mass the temple of God which we are gathers together to worship our God. Here to this altar we bring our gifts, the gift of our lives, our hearts, our whole beings. But there is one necessary condition that will make our gifts acceptable—mutual charity, mutual reconciliation. It is good to remember Jesus' words: "If you bring your gift to the altar and there recall that your brother has anything against you, leave your gift at the altar, go first to be reconciled with your brother, and then come and offer your gift" (Matt 5:23-24).

Jesus is telling us that the most noble of all human activities, the worship of God, the recognition of God's lordship over all beings, cannot take place without reconciliation with other members of our communities and families. As long as there is antagonism in our hearts toward anyone, our worship is a sham. And may we not forget the familiar quote that "the opposite of love is not hatred but indifference."

But lest we end on a negative note of admonition, we remind ourselves that this is a feast of celebration and gratitude for all the holy places where the Lord is at home for us. Its true flavor and meaning is best expressed in the Preface of today's Mass:

> Father, all-powerful and ever-living God,
> we do well always and everywhere to give you thanks.
> Your house is a house of prayer,
> and your presence makes it a place of blessing.
> You give us grace upon grace
> to build the temple of your Spirit,
> creating its beauty from the holiness of our lives.
> Your house of prayer
> is also the promise of the Church in heaven.
> Here your love is always at work,
> preparing the Church on earth
> for its heavenly glory
> as the sinless bride of Christ,
> the joyful mother of a great company of saints.
> Now, with the saints and all the angels
> we praise you for ever.

Holy, holy, holy Lord, God of power and might,
heaven and earth are full of your glory.